T0418730

Hitler's Deserters

Hitler's Deserters

Breaking Ranks with the Wehrmacht

DOUGLAS CARL PEIFER

OXFORD
UNIVERSITY PRESS

Oxford University Press is a department of the University of Oxford.
It furthers the University's objective of excellence in research, scholarship,
and education by publishing worldwide. Oxford is a registered trade mark of
Oxford University Press in the UK and in certain other countries.

Published in the United States of America by Oxford University Press
198 Madison Avenue, New York, NY 10016, United States of America.

Library of Congress Cataloging-in-Publication Data
Names: Peifer, Douglas Carl, author.
Title: Hitler's deserters : breaking ranks with the Wehrmacht / Douglas Carl Peifer.
Other titles: Breaking ranks with the Wehrmacht
Description: York, NY : Oxford University Press, 2025. | Includes
bibliographical references and index.
Identifiers: LCCN 2024037159 (print) | LCCN 2024037160 (ebook) |
ISBN 9780197539668 (hardback) | ISBN 9780197539682 (epub)
Subjects: LCSH: World War, 1939–1945—Desertions—Germany. | Military
deserters—Germany—Biography. | Desertion,
Military—Germany—History—20th century. | Germany
Wehrmacht—Biography. | Courts-martial and courts of
inquiry—Germany—History—20th century. | Collective
memory—Germany—History—20th century.
Classification: LCC D810.D57 P45 2025 (print) | LCC D810.D57 (ebook) |
DDC 940.54/8—dc23/eng/20240927
LC record available at https://lccn.loc.gov/2024037159
LC ebook record available at https://lccn.loc.gov/2024037160

DOI: 10.1093/oso/9780197539668.001.0001

Integrated Books International, United States of America

Contents

Preface

It took Germany more than sixty years to come to terms with how the Third Reich had treated Wehrmacht deserters. In the immediate postwar period, a few families and friends of those court-martialed by the Wehrmacht on the charges of desertion, undermining the military spirit, and treason pressed charges in occupation-era courts against the military prosecutors, judges, and commanders who had condemned their sons to death. They argued that German military justice in World War II had been incredibly harsh, that it had reflected Nazi worldviews, and that those in charge needed to be punished. Simultaneously, a handful of authors and playwrights on the intellectual left published stories, memoirs, and plays that challenged persisting images of the deserter as a coward, a scoundrel, and selfish egoist ready to leave his comrades in the lurch to save his own skin. Legal proceedings against military jurists and commanders stretched past the occupation period into the early years of the Federal Republic, when West German courts eventually decided that the Wehrmacht jurists and commanders had properly followed the law. Desertion, the defendants pointed out, was deemed a crime by militaries around the world, and they claimed that the Wehrmacht had not been any harsher in enforcing military law than had the Americans and British.

Former Wehrmacht jurists began to create a narrative that portrayed Germany's wartime military justice system as independent of and even resistant to Nazi influence and ideology, an account that was at odds with short stories, plays, and reminiscences of literary figures such as Heinrich Böll, Werner Richter, and particularly Alfred Andersch. By the late 1950s, efforts to rehabilitate deserters and punish former Wehrmacht jurists had stalled in West Germany. The critical views of the Wehrmacht painted by the literary left were pushed to the fringes by an outpouring of memoirs by former Wehrmacht commanders who pinned all blame for wartime crimes and excesses on Hitler, the Party, and the SS. The Wehrmacht, these former generals and admirals claimed, had fought for Germany bravely and honorably. Those who deserted, they asserted, had betrayed their comrades and the German nation and had been justly punished.

In East Germany, a different narrative emerged. East Germany's Socialist Unity Party rejected the sanitized memory of the Wehrmacht as an institution impermeable to Nazi penetration. Instead, East Germany's leaders insisted that the Wehrmacht had been a pillar of the Nazi state. They reminded the public that Wehrmacht leaders had planned wars of aggression and perpetrated war crimes on an unprecedented scale. Those who deserted its ranks or joined the Soviet-sponsored National Committee for a Free Germany, according to this narrative, were to be commended. East Germany's leadership instrumentalized Wehrmacht veterans willing to work with the state as part of its propaganda campaign against West Germany, using them to warn Germans on both sides of the Iron Curtain that the same old gang that had led Germany into a disastrous war against the Soviet Union under Hitler was now assisting the Americans in planning an even more catastrophic war using atomic weapons. The blatant use of the past as a propaganda tool to undermine West German remilitarization made it easy to dismiss East German versions of the past, even when they touched on the truth. The Wehrmacht's leadership had been closer to Hitler than veterans in Adenauer's West Germany cared to recall. As for its military justice system, East German historians were not far off the mark in characterizing it as an instrument of repression, sentencing between 25,000 and 30,000 German soldiers, sailors, and airmen to death for desertion, subversion of the military spirit, and treason.

By the 1970s, West and East Germany had situated the Wehrmacht deserter in very different places of remembrance. The dominant West German narrative found little to commend those who had abandoned their comrades in arms, while the state-controlled East German version lambasted those who had defended the Third Reich and its regime to the bitter end. Beginning in the 1970s, West Germany embarked on a new phase in its quest to come to terms with the Nazi past. Wehrmacht deserters and German military justice became a hotly contested topic in West Germany. Brought to the public's attention by peace activists who wanted to force West Germans to think about conscription, militarization, and war in general, the deserter debate soon narrowed to the question of Wehrmacht deserters. Launched by activists who questioned why West Germany should honor Stauffenberg and those associated with the 20th of July 1944 attempt on Hitler's life while continuing to stigmatize those who had deserted from the Wehrmacht, the public debate about deserters continued after German unification, finding a political resolution only in 2002. The debate about rehabilitating Wehrmacht deserters illustrates how a dormant historical issue can be activated and contested to create a new interpretation of the past.

During the 1990s and 2000s, prompted by activists, German politicians and judges began to question the judgments reached during the Adenauer era. They turned to historians for guidance, discovering that scholars had compiled numerous studies about deserters, the German military justice system, and the role of the Wehrmacht in the Nazi state in response to political scandals (the Filbinger Affair) and deceptive apologias on the part of former military jurists. Little of this scholarship has been translated into English, in part because some of the monographs delved pedantically into the minutia of military law and processes, in part because the German studies on desertion during the Third Reich fell between old-school Anglosphere military histories addressing campaigns, operations, and war, and international scholarship centered on the Holocaust, debates about the level of popular support for the Nazi regime, and literature about resistance in the Third Reich.

As courts and the Bundestag grappled with petitions and motions related to compensation and rehabilitation, they relied on historians to answer basic questions about desertion during the Third Reich. New scholarship shook the foundations of the narratives established in the 1950s, addressing questions that had been left unasked and unanswered. How many German military personnel had deserted, and how many deserters had been apprehended and executed? Was the Wehrmacht's military justice system fundamentally different from that of other militaries, and if so, how and why? If it was harsher, was this because Nazi worldviews and radicalism had penetrated the Wehrmacht and its justice system? Or was it because of the lessons that Germany's military had drawn from the trauma of mutiny and revolution in 1918, reflecting a refusal to admit that Germany had been defeated on the battlefield? How had the Wehrmacht defined desertion, why had conscientious objectors been tried as deserters, and what was the odd charge of *Wehrkraftzersetzung* (underming the military spirit) leveled against those who undermined or subverted the military spirit?

As historians addressed these questions, momentum built to overturn the court-martial verdicts pertaining to desertion, undermining the military spirit, and treason. Additional questions arose. Who were the soldiers, sailors, and airmen who had been condemned to death on these charges? Why had they deserted? Was there an archetypal deserter? Why had so few German military personnel deserted and so many fought to the bitter end? What was the balance between consent and coercion in maintaining military discipline? Had the Wehrmacht deserter been a coward, a resister, a victim, or all of the above?

This book addresses two dimensions of the debate about Wehrmacht deserters. The first dimension is the historical. It draws upon the scholarship on Wehrmacht deserters that began appearing in Germany in the 1980s and peaked during the 1990s. Almost none of this literature has been translated into English. I stand on the shoulders of giants and acknowledge an intellectual debt to Fritz Wüllner, Manfred Messerschmidt, Fritz Seidler, Norbert Haase, Paul Heider, Jörg Kammler, Wolfram Wette, and others. In addition, I drew on primary records to put a face to the numbers, consulting archival sources in

Germany, Switzerland, and the United Kingdom to reconstruct the stories of Wilhelm Hanow, Ludwig Metz, Hans Kanzenbach, Stefan Hampel, Jakob Bug, Karl-Heinz Leiterholdt, Helmut Gustav Gaebelein, and Willi Herold. These micro-studies show how the motives, methods, destinations, and outcomes of desertion varied widely. They support the contention that there was no typical deserter, but a conglomerate of individuals who deserted for different reasons, with the path and outcome of that decision following different trajectories based on when, where, and how the act of desertion unfolded. The author acknowledges and thanks Magnus Koch, Lothar Gruchmann, Kristina Brümmer-Pauly, Heinrich Walle, Eric Rust, and others for pointing the way to the primary sources that undergird these micro-studies. These micro-studies provide a sense of the process, the individual, and the personal experiences behind the statistics so laboriously compiled by Gruchmann, Messerschmidt, Wüllner, and Brümmer-Pauly.

The vast majority of German military personnel did not desert. They fought tenaciously long after hope for a German victory had disappeared. A combination of factors generated loyalty within the ranks, ranging from the inculcation of a culture of conformity to the role of ideology and camaraderie to conceptions of masculinity to notions of patriotism, nationalism, and German identity. Why then did some break ranks and desert? Motivations varied. According to their own accounts, they deserted because of fear of punishment, war weariness, poor treatment, ethnicity, homesickness, fear of injury, moral reservations, and the encouragement of girlfriends. Much as the modern reader might wish that moral reservations and political opposition were major causes for desertion, they lagged well behind fear of punishment and resentment over poor treatment.

The second dimension is interpretive. While all history is interpretive in its selection of what topics to study, how to remember the Wehrmacht deserter illustrates the interaction between present concerns and the past beautifully. The Germans have a word for "coming to grips with the past"—*Vergangenheitsbewältigung*. The process that led to an overturning of military court-martial verdicts relating to desertion was long and contentious, and the government's contention in 2002 that Wehrmacht deserters had acted honorably was not shared during the Adenauer years. Historians contributed to a public debate about the status of Wehrmacht deserters, but the debate was initiated by peace activists who wanted to use the Wehrmacht deserter as an icon to stir up a broader debate about civic responsibility, conscription, and militarization. Historians were part of the process of reframing the past, but they did not control the debate. Surviving deserters, the families and friends of executed deserters, the wartime military lawyers, judges, and commanders who tried and sentenced deserters, postwar authors, playwrights, intellectuals, and peace activists all had an interest in shaping how the public thought about Wehrmacht deserters. Germany's coming to terms with desertion and military justice during the Third Reich was a protracted, contested, and difficult process.

This book limits its analysis to Germans who deserted the Wehrmacht, that is, Germany's military. It does not include an examination of Germans who deserted the SS and the Waffen-SS, which were offsprings of the Nazi Party. There are two reasons for excluding these organizations, one analytical and the other practical. Analytically, this book grapples with the question of why some military personnel—largely conscripts but including career professionals—chose to desert while most did not. More than 18 million Germans served in the Wehrmacht, representing all layers of society and the nation itself. The makeup and ethos of the SS were quite different, in that the SS claimed to be an elite and drew on those most receptive to Nazi worldviews. Postwar debates about Wehrmacht deserters focused on "the little man," the ordinary German soldier, sailor, or airman, and whether or not desertion was justified. The Wehrmacht deserter became an icon around which Germans debated consent, coercion, and conformity in the Third Reich's military. Including deserters from the Waffen-SS or foreign auxiliaries in the book's analysis would skew its findings, clouding rather than contributing to postwar debates about the deserter as coward, victim, or role model. At a practical level, the SS had its own system of discipline and courts-martial. SS desertions and legal proceedings are not included in the Wehrmacht legal records. Extending the book's focus beyond Wehrmacht deserters to include deserters from the Waffen-SS, foreign auxiliary formations, and other Axis forces would necessitate consulting entirely different sets of primary sources, a feat I will leave to others.

The second comment relates to translating German legal terms and concepts into English. The Wehrmacht's system of military justice is replete with terms, positions, and titles that have no exact English equivalent. When no exact equivalent exists, I have used titles and terms most American and English readers understand, such as judge advocate corps, court-martial, and confirming authorities. The German terms and titles appear in parenthesis and in the endnotes.

Many thanks to Nancy Toff of Oxford University Press for her careful reading of the draft manuscript and her helpful editing recommendations. Last but not least, thanks to my mother, Doris, for her lively storytelling, her love of travel, and her belief that one never stops learning, and to my wife and fellow historian, Beth, for her support, encouragement, and insights throughout this whole project.

1

Putting a Face to the Numbers

The incident remained vivid in his memory. The sixty-three-year-old Berliner remembered how, as a nineteen-year-old German soldier, he had been forced to watch the execution of one of his fellow soldiers for desertion.[1] Following the Allied landings in North Africa in November 1942, the German Army had occupied Vichy France. His company had been stationed in Homps, a sleepy little country village about twenty-five miles from Carcassonne. Following the New Year's Eve celebration of 1942/1943, rifleman Schewe had disappeared. Military police found Schewe in a nearby village, staying with a girl he had befriended. They confined him in the local school and notified higher authorities of the incident. The gears of the German military justice system went into action, and the company soon heard that the military court in Carcassonne was trying Schewe for desertion. Someone probably told Schewe, who jumped out of the second-floor window and attempted to escape. Two officers were sent to find him, and they found him hiding with the same girlfriend.

The elderly Berliner recounted that news began to circulate in January or February 1943 that Schewe had been condemned to death. Rumor had it that the entire company would have to attend the execution. His platoon was ordered to provide the firing squad. The noncommissioned officers selected for the task were told that some of them would be firing blanks, presumably to relieve their consciences.

Early one morning before the sun had risen—the elderly Berliner could not remember the specific date—the entire company of around 140 men was ordered to assemble. Its four platoons marched down the chaussée leading to Lezignan, eventually swerving off the road and continuing down a country path. They arrived at an open field, the Berliner recalled, where everything had been prepared in advance. A wooden post stood in the middle of the empty field, with fresh dirt around it indicating that the post had been recently erected. The company's commandeered Bedford truck was already there, with a wooden coffin in the back. The company was put at attention. The culprit's platoon was placed closest to the post so that "they could see exactly what happened to those who abandoned the colors."[2] The Berliner recalled that he was in the first row of the platoon, about fifteen meters from the execution post.

The firing squad took position in front of the post, and rifleman Schewe was tied to it. The commanding officer read the verdict and then stood aside as a chaplain approached the condemned man. The Berliner remembered thinking it odd that the chaplain carried a sidearm. The chaplain announced, "May God judge you justly."[3] A soldier began to blindfold Schewe, but he declined, and the man stood back. The old man recalled that Schewe had blond hair and was a Berliner like him. A lieutenant ordered: "Ready. Aim. Fire" (Legt an! Feuer!). One of the noncommissioned officers later told the Berliner that Schewe had looked him straight in the eye. The men of the firing squad had been told to aim at the heart, and the old man remembered that Schewe's breast was a bloody mess when he crumpled at the post. Worst of all, he was still alive and groaning terribly. The company's first sergeant walked up to Schewe, still tied to the post, and delivered three pistol shots to the head. The groaning ceased.

The company began to march back to camp. Schewe's corpse was placed in the coffin in the back of the Bedford. The truck overtook the marching soldiers on the way back to Homps. The Berliner recalled that blood was dripping out of the tailgate. He said that it was the sort of thing one never forgot. Rifleman Schewe was buried in a pit dug in the local French cemetery, near a monument to the French dead from World War I. The Berliner remembered seeing the grave the next day. It was covered with flowers, placed there overnight by the local French population.

This account was given to the German historian Norbert Haase in the late 1980s by an elderly German man who wished to remain anonymous. Ernst Jünger, best known in the English-speaking world for his memoir of World War I (*Storm of Steel*), kept a journal during World War II as well. The entry for May 29, 1941, describes a similar episode. Jünger's account contains many of the same details as the Berliner's recollection but differs in tone and detail. Jünger was stationed in Paris at the time, serving as a staff officer. He recorded his impression of the execution he witnessed as follows:

> To add to the flood of repugnant things that oppress me comes the order to be present at the execution of a soldier sentenced to death for desertion.... The matter concerns a corporal who left his unit nine months ago

to disappear into the city where a French woman gave him shelter. He moved around, sometimes in civilian clothing and sometimes in the uniform of a naval officer as he went about his affairs. It seems that he felt a false sense of security and not only made his lover jealous but also beat her. She took her revenge by reporting him to the police, who turned him in to the German authorities. . . .

In the clearing we meet the detail. We form a sort of corridor of two rows in front of the ash tree. The sun is shining after the rain that fell on our way here; drops of water glisten on the green grass. We wait a while until shortly before five o'clock. Then a car pulls up the narrow forest road. We watch the condemned man get out, followed by two prison guards and the clergyman. Behind them a truck appears, driving the burial detail and military issue coffin: "cheapest model, standard size."

The man is led between the two rows; at that moment, I am overcome with a feeling of trepidation, as if it were suddenly difficult to breathe. He is placed before the military judge, who stands beside me: I note that his arms have been secured behind his back with handcuffs. He is wearing gray trousers made of good material, a gray silk shirt, and an open military tunic that has been draped over his shoulders. He stands erect and is well built, and his face bears pleasant features of the sort that attract women.

The sentence is read aloud. The condemned man follows the procedure with the highest degree of attention, and yet I still have the impression that he doesn't understand the text . . . A tiny fly plays about his left cheek and alights several times close to his ear. He shrugs his shoulders and shakes his head. The reading takes barely a minute, but time seems extraordinarily long to me. The pendulum becomes long and heavy. Then the guards lead the condemned man to the ash tree; the clergyman accompanies him. . . . The clergyman softly asks him a few questions; I hear him answer them with jawohl [yes sir]. Then he kisses a small silver cross while the doctor pins a piece of red cardboard the size of a playing card onto his shirt over his heart.

In the meantime, the firing squad has followed a signal from the first lieutenant and has taken their positions standing behind the clergyman, who still blocks the condemned man. He now steps back after running his hand down the prisoner's side once more. The commands follow, and with them I again awaken into consciousness. I want to look away, but I force myself to watch. I catch the moment when the salvo produces five little dark holes in the cardboard, as though drops of dew had landed

> upon it. Their target is still standing against the tree; his expression shows extraordinary surprise. I see his mouth opening and closing as if he wanted to form vowels and express something with great effort. This situation has something confusing about it, and again time seems attenuated. It also seems that the man is now becoming menacing. Finally his knees give out. The ropes are loosened and now at last the pallor of death quickly comes over his face, as if a bucket of whitewash had been poured over it. The doctor rushes up and reports, "The man is dead." One of the two guards unlocks the handcuffs and wipes the glistening metal clean of blood with a cloth. The corpse is placed in the coffin. It looks as if the little fly were playing around him in a beam of sunlight.[4]

The Wehrmacht sentenced between 25,000 and 30,000 German soldiers to death.[5] Some of these cases involved crimes ranging from theft to murder, but the vast majority of death sentences pertained to the crime of desertion. Most experts put the number of German soldiers executed as a result of Wehrmacht courts-martial somewhere between 18,000 and 22,000.[6] The sight of German soldiers hanging from trees and lampposts with signs noting that these were cowards who had refused to fight became commonplace during the chaotic final months of World War II in Europe. The Wehrmacht's role in waging a brutal war of racial extermination on the Eastern Front is now well known, and the linkage among genocide, war, and ideology has been established. Less well known is how the Wehrmacht acted brutally toward its own soldiers, seeking to stifle dissent within its own ranks by sentencing tens of thousands of its own soldiers to death, penal battalions, and labor camps. The intent was to send a clear message: shirkers, deserters, and those who criticized the regime too loudly were to be punished so severely that others would be deterred from similar actions.

As the Federal Republic of Germany debated invalidating military convictions from World War II in the 1990s and 2000s, heated discussions arose about whether these deserters were cowards and criminals who had abandoned their comrades in the midst of danger, or whether they were resisters who acted like sand in the gears of the well-oiled German war machine. Some insisted that German soldiers who deserted because they were appalled by the mass killings they had witnessed in the East, or because they disagreed with the policies and ideology of the Third Reich, should be rehabilitated, while those who deserted because they wanted to save their own skin or because they had committed some minor infraction and wanted to evade punishment should not. It soon became apparent that the records simply did not exist to review each case individually. Allied air raids started a fire in the Wehrmacht's main record repository in 1945, destroying many of the records related to the German military justice system. In addition, ascertaining the motivation behind desertion from court records is problematic. During the war, German soldiers brought before military tribunals would have been foolish to claim they had deserted because of political reasons, war weariness, or ethical concerns. After the war, deserters who survived had every reason to claim in their memoirs that their motivations had been noble, and that cowardice, self-preservation, and criminality had nothing to do with their decision to desert.

The reasons for desertion ranged from the admirable to the ignoble, and categorizing all deserters as resisters, cowards, or asocials is problematic. The decision to desert, moreover, was in some cases carefully considered and planned in advance, and in other cases it was an impulsive act, with geography, the military situation, unit dynamics, ethnic background, and personality playing important roles. There was no "typical" deserter, though Hitler and the Wehrmacht vowed that all deserters should know that while they might die at the front, if they deserted and were caught, they would most certainly die through execution.

Facts, figures, and frameworks provide much of the evidence for understanding military desertion in the Third Reich. Yet equally important is understanding that desertion was a highly personal, individual decision. The following four accounts make no claim to be representative, but they put faces and context to the often faceless statistics.

Wilhelm Hanow

In the late afternoon of July 22, 1942, one of Frau Gustave Hanow's neighbors called the police. The neighbor had seen someone moving in the house Frau Hanow rented from the widow Müller. The neighbor had seen Hanow leave the house and suspected the person she saw through the windows might be Hanow's husband, Wilhelm, whom the German military had been looking for since 1939. It was hard to keep secrets in the little country town of Gnoien in Mecklenburg. Its population was only around 3,000, and everyone knew everyone. The town's name harkened back to its Wendish origins a thousand years earlier, and one could see the spire of the red-brick Protestant Marienkirche from Hanow's home at Jungfernstrasse 36.[7]

The chief of police and an assistant arrived soon after receiving the neighbor's report and found Frau Hanow in the house. They had searched the residence before and had asked Frau Hanow each time if she knew where her husband was or corresponded with him. She had always denied having any idea as to his whereabouts. The two policemen began to comb through the house room by room. During the search, Sergeant Major Gehrke heard a sound in the pantry. When he tried to enter, he found that the door was locked. The policemen sent for a locksmith, who soon managed to open the door. When they entered the pantry, it was empty; a window to the backyard was ajar. They continued their search in the shed behind the house. Glancing up, they noticed a trapdoor to the loft being held shut from above. The trapdoor could only be secured from below, and someone in the loft was holding it closed. One could see fingers protruding along the trapdoor's edge. One of the policemen went to get a stepladder. Realizing that he could not escape, rifleman Wilhelm Hugo Karl Hanow reluctantly surrendered to authorities at 6:30 p.m. on June 22, 1942. He had been missing from his unit for more than two and a half years. That evening, the local police turned him over to the reserve army battalion located in Gnoien, who in turn delivered Hanow to a military prison located in Güstrow on the 24th of July.[8]

Wilhelm Hanow was transferred to the military's main detention facility for cases under investigation in Berlin, and the military began to assemble evidence that a court assigned to the Hanow case would consider. The investigating officer contacted civilian authorities about Hanow's behavior prior to his call-up in 1939, examined his service record from World War I, and ordered a forensic report that included physical and psychiatric evaluations of the defendant. These materials painted a very negative picture of Wilhelm, focusing on his problematic relationship with his father, his employers, and the law. As for his relationship with his wife, no letters or statements provided insights into why she chose to shelter her husband for more than two years, risking severe punishment for doing so. The court verdict and its accompanying justification reflect the assessments of a military judicial system that internalized the values and norms of the Third Reich. Hanow's defending lawyer provided a rare example of humanity in the midst of an inhumane system. He twice asked for a revision of the military court's sentence. General Friedrich Fromm, as commander in charge of the Replacement Army, rejected these pleas for leniency. He confirmed the court's verdict and the death sentence it had recommended.

Wilhelm Hugo Karl Hanow was already forty-four years old when Germany invaded Poland in 1939. He was born in Posen (then part of the German Empire) in 1895, the son of railway clerk Wilhelm Hanow and his wife, Amalie. Hanow had served on the Eastern Front in World War I and was awarded an Iron Cross Second Class. He was among the hundreds of thousands of German soldiers transferred from the Eastern to the Western Front in the fall of 1917, but he fell off a moving train while answering the call of nature. The fall knocked him unconscious, and he suffered a cut to his head that was sufficiently serious to send him to a military hospital. He was deemed as fit for garrison duty but was mustered out of the German military before the end of the war as lightly disabled.[9]

Hanow spent the next decade drifting between various jobs, living with girlfriends, and moving about Berlin, Silesia, and Posen. His relationship to his father and two sisters came to an end after a series of run-ins with the law. He was convicted nine times for either embezzlement, theft, or fraud during the Weimar era, and he served seven stints in prison between 1918 and 1930.[10] Hanow is alleged to have drunk considerably, blowing through any money he received through work or swindle.

In 1932, Wilhelm Hanow married Gustave Kumpf, who apparently had a stabilizing effect on his life. He took up the trade of chimney sweep, living a crime-free life for almost a decade. Town authorities had no complaints regarding the chimney sweep. In 1939, Wilhelm was called back to arms, reporting to Infantry Reserve Battalion 202 in Güstrow as ordered on August 26, 1939.

Hanow's battalion saw no combat in the Polish campaign and was stationed near Toruń (German: Thorn), Poland, at the close of the campaign. The area was in the so-called Polish Corridor between Prussia and East Prussia, and it was annexed into the Third Reich as part of the newly created Reichsgau Danzig-Westpreussen. Its Gauleiter, Albert Forster, targeted the Polish and Jewish populations of the ethnically mixed area for expulsion or extermination from the outset, reprimanding his subordinates for "not spilling enough Polish blood."[11] Whether Hanow, who spoke Polish, was directly involved in any of the mass executions, round-ups, or forced expulsions is unknown. No mention of the massacres is made in any of the court investigations, nor did Hanow's defense attorney ever bring up the topic. What we do know is that the end of combat operations in Poland did not mean the end of violence. The SS, sometimes supported by ethnic Germans and Wehrmacht units, unleashed an orgy of violence in the region. Hanow's unit did not see combat in the short Polish campaign, it but may well have been drawn into or heard of the violence and terror involved in ethnically cleansing the area around Toruń.[12]

Hanow's company commander recalled that Hanow had been a well-behaved soldier. Some in the company thought him a hard man without scruples who fraternized with Polish women. On Thursday, November 16, his company commander sent Hanow to the nearby town of Leslau (Polish: Włocławek) to buy tobacco products and other supplies. He was entrusted with sixty Reichsmarks.

On his way to the tobacco shop, Hanow stopped at the *Soldatenheim* (enlisted club) in Leslau to drink some beer. There he met some other soldiers who had been demobilized and were on their way home. Hanow decided to demobilize himself, returning home to Gnoien some 300 miles to the west. Arriving in Gnoien, he initially told his wife he was just visiting. After spending a night at home, he confessed to her that he had deserted. She pleaded with him to turn himself into the authorities, but Hanow replied that he would be shot as he had been absent from his unit for longer than five days.

Gustave Hanow decided to hide her husband, Wilhelm. For two years and eight months, she shared her rations with him, scrounged the area for extra potatoes, emptied the chamber pot kept in the attic where he slept, and was Wilhelm's only social connection. She put herself at risk, as the police made explicit each time they questioned her about her husband's whereabouts.[13] Shortly after her husband's arrest, the chief prosecutor for the Rostock district initiated proceedings against Gustave for aiding and abetting desertion. The prosecutor asked that the military court inform him of the outcome of its case against Wilhelm Hanow, explaining that his office could not proceed with its case against Gustave Hanow until her husband's status had been resolved.[14]

In the justification portion that accompanied the military court's verdict, the members of the court-martial stated that determining whether Wilhelm Hanow had been guilty was straightforward. He had confessed to desertion, and the circumstances of his arrest made it clear that he had no intention of returning to the Wehrmacht. The focus of its deliberations revolved around determining the appropriate sentence. The recommended sentence rested on the tribunal's assessment of the accused man's mental competence, his "overall asocial personality," and the tribunal's interpretation of the Führer's intentions. Adolf Hitler had issued guidance (*Führer Richtlinien*) in April 1940 concerning the appropriate punishment for desertion. The death penalty was to be imposed if a deserter had acted out of cowardice, intended to flee to another country, had been charged with desertion before, had a substantial criminal record, and in cases where desertion was a group endeavor. A prison sentence was permissible if the desertion was due to military mistreatment or abuse, reflected youthful rashness, or was motivated by serious difficulties at home.[15]

The military court drew heavily on a forensic evaluation it had commissioned from Berlin's University Institute for Forensic Medicine and Criminology. The evaluation acknowledged that Hanow had stayed out of trouble ever since his marriage in the early 1930s but gave him little credit for this. Instead, it dwelt on his criminal record and the shady life he lived in the 1920s. The forensic report concluded that Hanow was physically healthy, mentally sound of mind, but a "weak-willed, aimless psychopath who lacked the energy to overcome life's difficulties."

The military court drew on the forensic report and Hanow's civilian criminal record in reaching a verdict and making a sentence recommendation. It seemed clear to all that Hanow had intended to avoid further military service, and that he had been mentally competent when he made that decision. The phrasing of the court's recommendation illustrates how Nazi reasoning resonated in military sentences: "There is no reason to let such a worthless individual live.... The court is convinced that the accused never made and never will make a positive contribution [to society]."[16] It had no reservations recommending the death penalty, noting that the ultimate punishment was necessary to deter others.

Hanow's defense attorney, Walter Henkel, made a brave effort to save his charge from the death penalty. In a first plea for clemency to the commanding officer who decided whether to accept the court's verdict and sentence, he reminded the *Gerichtsherr* that Hanow had lived a crime-free, responsible life ever since he got married a decade earlier. This proved he was not "asocial" and that he had the potential to become a productive member of society. Henkel indicated that Hanow was ready to make amends for his crime by volunteering for the most hazardous military duties. The plea was rejected.

Henkel tried once again. In a letter dated March 19, 1943, he made several arguments. He noted that Hanow had served bravely in World War I, earning an Iron Cross Second Class. He again pointed out that Hanow had lived a blameless life for ten years. He connected Hanow's troubles in the 1920s to a sad, troubled childhood. He claimed that Hanow's experience hiding in an attic for years without proper nourishment must have been motivated by some sort of psychiatric trauma.

Both pleas for clemency were rejected. On Friday, May 14, 1943, Wilhlem Hanow was transported to the Brandenburg-Görden prison. The officer in charge verified Hanow's identity, read the verdict, and turned him over to the executioner. Hanow was escorted to the guillotine, rendering no resistance. At precisely three minutes past six in the evening, his head was separated from his body.[17]

Gustave Hanow undoubtedly suffered consequences for her role in sheltering Wilhelm. The Landgericht Rostock would have been informed, and the proceedings for aiding and abetting desertion would have restarted. She, too, could have been executed, but more likely than not she was sent to a concentration camp. We simply do not know what happened to munition worker Gustave Hanow. We only know that she risked her life hiding her chimney sweep husband, and that her neighbor turned them in.

Ludwig Metz

In the early morning hours of May 16, 1942, a German Army officer seeking to desert crept across the border separating the Third Reich from neutral Switzerland. He had reconnoitered the area several weeks earlier while visiting an aunt who lived in Weil am Rhein, a German town directly on the Swiss border near Basel. He had found that the border was tightly guarded, with barbed wire fencing, armed border guards manning observation posts, and patrols sweeping back and forth. Discouraged by his private reconnaissance, Lt. Ludwig Metz had failed to muster the nerve to cross the border at that time. Metz chose to do what many other German deserters did, attempting to submerge himself among the civilian populace while considering what to do. Metz took a train to Munich, a city he knew well, living with an old girlfriend while claiming to be on leave.[18] Metz knew the clock was ticking. He had deserted from his unit, the 132nd Infantry Regiment, two months earlier. Two military policemen had visited his family in Frankfurt in April, asking whether they had seen the twenty-nine-year-old artillery officer. His father in Frankfurt was about to receive a letter from his commander, informing him that the unit, engaged in the siege of Sevastopol, had first suspected that Ludwig had been abducted by the partisans, but now had reason to believe that Ludwig was somewhere in Germany. Metz's father was instructed to contact authorities if he had any information about his son's whereabouts and warned that any attempt to withhold information or hide his son would result in severe punishment.[19]

Ludwig Metz knew that the net was tightening, and he took a train to Lörrach, near the Swiss border, on May 15. He spent the afternoon in a pub, anxiously waiting for night to fall. Once it grew dark, Metz moved in the direction of a wooded area near the border. He was wearing civilian clothes but had packed his uniform into a suitcase. He changed into the uniform once in the woods. He carried a loaded sidearm. Metz had heard that Swiss authorities were turning back refugees and hoped that his chances of internment would be higher if he was wearing his uniform and carrying a weapon.

All sorts of thoughts jostled in Metz's mind as he waited in the woods for the night to grow darker. As an officer, Metz agonized over his decision to desert. He remembered how proud he had been to wear the German Army uniform, and how hard he had fought for his fatherland over the last three years. How had it come to pass that Germany had tied its fate to a leader who reveled in violence and knew no moral bounds? Metz questioned his decision to leave his unit and ruminated over his relationship with his superiors. Had he been a difficult subordinate? Was his decision to desert justified? How would his decision affect his parents, his young sister, and his brother, still fighting for Germany on the Eastern Front?[20]

In the distance, Metz heard a church bell strike one in the morning. He moved toward the edge of the woods in which he was sheltering, toward the fields and vineyards that cascaded down from the Tüllinger heights. Sprinting across a field, he ran into a barbed wire fence, pulled the wires apart, and slipped through. He felt the barbs tear at his uniform, but he continued on, moving down the incline toward a small river in the valley below. To his dismay, Metz found that the Wiese River was flowing swiftly, filled with spring rains. Metz wandered around the vineyards and fields looking for some way to cross the river. Shortly before 5 a.m., he heard a voice call out, "You there, do you realize that you are on Swiss territory?"[21] It was a Swiss border guard. Metz had made it over the border. The border guard relieved Metz of his loaded sidearm, and Metz was escorted to Basel's Lohnhof prison. The Swiss border police notified the military that they had apprehended a Wehrmacht deserter, and within days Metz was transferred to Lucerne, where Swiss military intelligence officers interrogated him. The Swiss Federal Department of Justice and Police informed Metz that it would make a decision about his internment application after the Swiss military intelligence service had concluded its interrogation and submitted a report.

The Swiss Military Intelligence Service interrogated Lt. Metz for seven weeks, questioning him about his unit, German and Russian weapons, tactics, orders of battle, and his experience in the campaign of 1940 and on the Eastern Front. They questioned why he had deserted and asked about morale in the German military. The focus of the final report issued by Rigi, the codename of the section of the Swiss military intelligence service responsible for gathering and evaluating information about the Axis powers, was on practical information that would benefit the Swiss military. Why and how Metz had deserted was less important than what he could tell them about the Wehrmacht.

Although much of the interrogation focused on the tactics, techniques, and equipment that underpin military operations, the Swiss started their questioning by asking Metz what had driven him to seek refuge in Switzerland. They wanted to understand who he was and why he had deserted. Metz gave four reasons during the interrogation, later writing a much longer account of his experience on the Eastern Front and his flight from Crimea to the Swiss border. Metz explained that there had been serious disagreements between himself and his new unit commander, whom Metz viewed as an amateur with a weakness for food and drink. He claimed that the extermination policies being implemented against the Russian and Jewish civilian population weighed on his conscience. He doubted Hitler's assertion that the war had been one of necessity. Lastly, Metz was repelled by National Socialism's increasingly hostile attitude toward religion.[22]

The transcript of the Swiss military intelligence service's interrogation of Metz, a 600-page manuscript he wrote during his internment in Switzerland, German military records preserved in Freiburg, and two studies of his background, military experience, and flight provide an unusually rich set of sources for assessing one individual's path to desertion. Ludwig Metz was born on April 20, 1913, in Frankfurt am Main. His father, August, was a mechanic, and his mother was a housewife. Metz completed vocational schooling and a three-year apprenticeship at a perfume manufacturer, but he lost his job in 1932 as the Great Depression sent unemployment soaring. He had a younger brother and sister, and family ties were close and loving.

In April 1933, Metz joined the German Army as a private. He was assigned to artillery regiments in Wurzburg, Amberg, and Munich, steadily rising through the ranks to become a sergeant in 1936. His unit participated in the March 1938 occupation of Austria, and Metz was subsequently assigned to the 8th Mountain Artillery Regiment stationed in Innsbruck. After training in Hall, Metz joined the 8th Artillery Regiment of the 268th Infantry Division, seeing action against the Maginot line facing the Saar, and participating in the German attack against the Rhine-Marne canal during Western campaign of 1940. He was awarded the Iron Cross Second Class at the close of the campaign and was one of the select group of noncommissioned officers to be recommended for elevation into the officer corps.

Assigned to the 132nd Infantry Division as an officer candidate, he was unanimously recommended for promotion to second lieutenant after a period of observation. His closeout evaluation in December 1940 described Metz as sinewy, slim, and of middling height with a tough and resilient attitude. As for personal and leadership traits, the evaluation described Metz as "honest, with an open and lively personality, has a special sense of duty, exemplary leadership on and off duty, very good knowledge of artillery, good rider, open and confident impression in front of superiors, liked by peers and subordinates."[23]

Metz was promoted on January 1, 1941. The 132nd Infantry Division participated in the Axis occupation and dismemberment of Yugoslavia in April 1941, and it was subsequently assigned to security duties in the region. Two infantry battalions of the 132nd Infantry Division helped Ustasha militia suppress a Serbian uprising in villages of Kijevo and Tramošnja in May, hanging twenty-seven Serbs in the town square of Sanski Most. Whether Metz, assigned to the division's artillery regiment, had any knowledge of the reprisals is unknown. In June, the 132nd Division was sent to Carinthia for training. Metz's commanding officer evaluated him as a passionate, brave, and energetic officer whose character was upright and honest.[24]

The division was alerted on June 22 that the invasion of the Soviet Union had commenced, and within days it was moving to assembly areas in eastern Poland.[25] During the initial push into the Soviet Union, the division encountered almost no enemy resistance, advancing an average of forty kilometers a day. Resistance stiffened as the Germans pushed deeper into the Ukraine, and the Russians launched heavy counterattacks on the division's bridgehead across the Dnieper River in August. The 132nd Infantry

Division was one of the twenty-five German infantry divisions that cemented the Panzer armies' encirclement of Kiev in August and September, an operation that resulted in the death or capture of more than 600,000 Red Army troops. By the end of September, the division was marching into Crimea, where it participated in an enormously costly attempt to take the key stronghold, Sevastopol, in November and December 1941. Sevastopol, headquarters of the Black Sea Fleet, was ringed with fortifications, gun positions, and interlocking fields of fire. The German attempt to overwhelm these through direct assault, supported by intense artillery fire and air attacks, proved so costly that the Germans shifted focus in early 1942, besieging the fortress while clearing the Red Army out of the rest of Crimea. Erich von Manstein, commanding the German 11th Army, would order a second, successful assault on Sevastopol in June 1942 (Operation Sturgeon Catch). By then, Lt. Metz was in Switzerland. His unit, the 132nd Infantry Division, suffered grievous losses in the Crimea and would be transferred to the Leningrad front in August 1942.

Something happened that caused Lt. Metz, described at the outset of the Russian campaign as a passionate, brave, and energetic officer, to reassess his loyalty to comrades, duty, and the Führer. His unpublished memoir provides a glimpse into his changing mindset.[26] He describes his unit's assembly area before the assault on Sevastopol as "the gates of hell." "What was France, what was Yugoslavia, yes, what even were the bloodiest actions of the current campaign compared to the war of annihilation and the dance of death before Sevastopol?"[27] Assigned the duty of a forward observer accompanying an infantry attack on the heights outside Sevastopol, Metz recalled the monstrous sounds, the splinters and earth flying everywhere, and the craters with men seeking shelter converted to gruesome slaughter pits. The infantry company he accompanied, already depleted, suffered forty-six casualties as it assaulted the heights and was in the midst of preparing a final attack when it received orders to retreat. Casualties throughout the division were so high that its commander instructed regimental commanders to dissolve one battalion per regiment to fill out the remaining battalions.[28]

Metz did not list fear and exhaustion as reasons for his flight when he was interrogated in Switzerland, but surely they played a role. If nothing else, the deterrent effect of the death penalty for desertion must have lessened when one stared death in the face every day. The German Army, once it found out that Metz was beyond its reach, closed its search for him with the unperceptive explanation that he had deserted because of cowardice. For the German military, there were only two reasons why a German officer would give up the fight: he was either a traitor or a coward. Since none of Metz's associates believed he had any sympathies for the Reds or had connections to foreign/internationalist groups, the German military could explain his decision only in terms of cowardice.[29]

Fear, exhaustion, and a mounting sense of his mortality may have contributed to Metz's decision to desert, but their significance is impossible to assess. One can, however, gain some insight into Metz's motivation for desertion from the explanations he gave his Swiss interrogator when asked why he had come to Switzerland. Metz's military files confirm that there was increasing tension between him and his superiors following the December attack on Sevastopol. In January 1942, Metz told his commander that his heart was giving him trouble, and after inspection by the unit doctor, Metz was instructed to report to a field hospital in Simferopol. In Simferopol, he hitched a flight on a Ju-52 to Odessa, and then took the train to a better military hospital in Krakow, where he was given an electrocardiogram, various medicines, and three days of bed rest. He did so without authorization, merely informing his commander of his whereabouts when he was already in Krakow. When Metz returned to the unit, his commanding officer initiated an inquiry. Metz refused to sign the inquiry's conclusion, apparently ripping it up and submitting a different report. As a result, he was reprimanded, relieved of his duty as a battery commander, and told to report as an instructor to a training course on "the care and use of horses."[30] In addition, Metz's commanding officer wrote an interim evaluation that stood in stark contrast to the stellar evaluations Metz had received throughout his career. Metz was judged to have only "average abilities," his leadership abilities were criticized, and he was scolded about smoking excessively.[31]

This sequence of events must have been extremely humiliating to an enlisted man who had risen to the officer corps by dint of excellence. That he had gone to Krakow without authorization is beyond dispute. Whether there was any substance to the charge that he had failed to act with "drive and initiative" during an attack on Russian positions on February 22 is unknowable. Metz paints an entirely different picture in his memoir, one of a new commanding officer who didn't know his job and constantly nitpicked while failing to lead. The autobiographical account reveals that Metz was proud of his military skills and reputation, and perceived himself as more experienced and competent than his commander, a reserve officer who had been a bank director. The personal dislike is clear. Metz described his relationship with his commander as being "as bad as it possibly could be."[32]

Amplifying Metz's unhappiness with his commander was a growing disenchantment with the cause for which he was fighting. Metz told his Swiss interrogators that he was repelled by the extermination policies he could no longer dismiss as mere rumors. Two incidents clearly weighed on his mind. The first was a dinner with the military commandant of Simferopol, whom Metz knew from his days in Innsbruck. Metz had been invited along with seven other officers for a *gemütliches* supper of bread, sardines, sausage, cheese, eggs, honey, and sugar, followed up by bottles of Crimean wine. The conversation revolved around past campaigns, when the commandant abruptly asked Metz if he knew that Simferopol was now "*judenfrei*" (Jew-free)? When pressed what that meant, the commandant explained that several days after German forces had occupied the city, SS security forces had entered the town, registered all Jews, and told them to assemble in designated areas. After a couple of days, the Jews were instructed to report to assembly points, bringing a suitcase with travel clothes along with their jewelry, currency, and other valuables. The "poor people," explained the commandant, were then loaded onto trucks, taken out to an anti-tank trench outside the city, stripped to their undergarments, and executed by a shot to the head. The town commandant said the executions had lasted several days, and that 17,000 people had been slaughtered.[33]

Metz had asked if the commandant, as the responsible military commander for the city, could have done something to prevent the massacre. The commandant replied that he had been powerless, and that "his hands and his conscience were free of their [the Jews'] blood." He had explained that the incident was not an isolated one, and that the security services had perfected the process in such a way that twenty men could kill 3,000 civilians in a matter of hours. Metz remembered that the atmosphere in the room had been subdued, with those in attendance avoiding eye contact and saying nothing. Metz left the gathering deeply disturbed.

The second incident that stuck in Metz's mind was a conversation he had with a chief veterinary officer on a train after his medical convalescence in Krakow. Crossing the Dnieper River, they watched as starving Soviet prisoners working in wretched circumstances scrambled over food scraps being thrown out. His fellow traveler, who had seemed like a good-natured

Bavarian country veterinarian, told Metz not to worry; the prisoners were nothing more than subhuman Reds.[34] The veterinarian elaborated:

> The more of them that starve, the fewer we have to feed. [...] I personally participated in a mass execution of Jews, shooting them in their louse-infested skulls with real delight. You should join in sometime. You wouldn't lose a word over these miserable prisoners anymore. "What did I do to deserve to be killed," yelled one Jewish whore, pulling her hair. Bang! "And you claim to be a *Kulturnation*" said a white-haired Rabbi, raising his eyes to the heavens. Bang, and he's gone too! Let me tell you how much fun it was![35]

Metz told Swiss authorities that one of the main reasons he deserted was because of the mass execution of Jews. These measures had weighed on his conscience, causing him to question his faith in the German regime. He claimed that he had not personally witnessed the mass shootings, but he had heard about them from comrades, superiors, and Protestant pastors in the East. He told his Swiss interlocutor that Jews were killed regardless of their age or sex, and that suspicious non-Jewish civilians were likewise shot. The German executioners wore gray SS uniforms, with the letters SD stitched on the black rhombus badge they wore on their left sleeves.[36]

As an artillery officer assigned to an infantry division, Metz may well have learned of the mass killings only secondhand. The 132nd Infantry Division was involved in fighting around Kiev in September 1941, and rumors of the killing of more than 30,000 Jews at the ravines at Babi Yar outside that city at the end of the month probably began to circulate as the division was marching south into the Crimea. The mass execution of Simferolpol's Jews by Sonderkommando 11b of Einsatzgruppen D occurred December 9 through 13, as the 132nd Infantry Division was preparing for its assault on Sevastopol.[37] Simferolpol, located less than fifty miles from the German positions outside Sevastopol, was a major supply and transit hub for frontline German units. Metz certainly was not the only one to hear of the massacre there. He was twice confronted with accounts that verified that rumors of mass executions of civilians were true and that these massacres had been deliberate, organized, and authorized from above. Unlike others, he was unable to brush off or justify what was happening. He understood that the German regime was engaged in mass murder, and he found it increasingly difficult to reconcile his sense of what was right with his duty to serve.

The third reason Metz gave Swiss authorities for his desertion was a realization that the war Germany was fighting in the East was one of choice rather than necessity. Hitler, Goebbels, and the military hierarchy claimed that the war in the East had been forced on them, and that Germany had launched a preventive war against the Soviet Union because the Bolsheviks had been about to attack Germany. What Metz had seen firsthand was very different. For weeks, the 132nd Infantry Division had marched into the Soviet Union with scarcely a trace of resistance. Only as it pressed deeper into the USSR did the resistance stiffen, escalating into a merciless fight for survival that was grinding down both sides. He wondered how anyone could claim that the German attack had been anything other than the use of force to seize land and resources it coveted. Germany had tied its fate to a regime that glorified in violence and wrongdoing.[38]

As for the Russians being subhuman brutes unworthy of compassion, Metz's account of the war in the East reveals both a sense of superiority and sympathy for the civilian population in the East. Intermingled with descriptions of dirty peasants living in flea-infested hovels unfit for civilized habitation are accounts of a toddler he befriended and of a farm woman desperately trying to feed her family.[39] Metz reflected the Nationalist, anti-Bolshevik worldview of his peers, but while he described his opponents as ruthless and fanatical, he conceded that they were capable and courageous. If Germany was in a struggle for survival, it was because Germany had invaded other countries in its lust for power, territory, and dominance.

The fourth reason that Metz gave his Swiss interrogator for his desertion was his concern about National Socialism's increasingly hostile attitude toward Christianity. The manuscript he wrote in Switzerland after desertion is peppered with concerns about Nazism's promotion of paganism, its violation of Christian ethics, its euthanasia program, and its elevation of the Fuhrer into a pseudo-religious leader. Metz had participated in the Catholic Boy Scouts as a youth, and he saw no contradiction between Christian faith and military duty when he joined the Reichswehr in 1933.[40] By 1942, Metz had grave doubts that the two could be reconciled. One of his colleagues had heard that young German girls in the Bund Deutscher Mädel were being encouraged to couple with SS men outside the bonds of Christian marriage, and he told him that elementary students in Bavaria were now praying "Fold your hands and bow your heads, and think of Adolf Hitler, who gives us our daily bread and helps us in our time of need."[41] Metz worried that a German victory presaged dark times for Christian churches, given the regime's worldview.

Metz gave an array of reasons for deserting, and it is impossible to disentangle or prioritize them. A cynic might conjecture that the main reasons for his desertion was cowardice and a wounded sense of self-esteem, and that the other reasons he gave only served to make his case for internment in Switzerland more persuasive. But Metz had a stellar military record through 1941, had written about religious faith in the military back in 1934, and compiled his autobiographical manuscript *after* Swiss authorities had informed him that his request to be interned had been approved. Whether ethical concerns alone would have led him to desert if his relationship with his superior was better is unknowable, as is the question whether he would have deserted absent his ethical concerns.

Metz completed his duties as an instructor for the course on March 6, 1942. On March 17, his artillery regiment filed a report that Metz had failed to return from the course.[42] His commander suspected that Metz had been abducted or killed by partisans. That was not the case. Instead, Metz was in Munich. He had seized the opportunity several weeks earlier to steal various blank, yet properly stamped, military forms, including orders and travel passes. Traveling by truck and train, Metz proceeded from the Crimea to Munich via Melilopol, Dnipropetrovsk, Krakow, and Breslau. He arrived in Munich on March 15, 1942, and would spend the next two months moving about Germany before crossing the Swiss border in May.

Metz's two-month-long stopover in Germany reveals mounting desperation and a growing realization that he was placing family and friends in danger. He spent his first night in Munich with an old girlfriend; he then visited an aunt who lived nearby and subsequently rented a room at a boardinghouse. He told people he was in Munich for training and wandered around the city during the day, buying his meals at places that still did not demand ration cards. Within weeks, he began to run out of money. Metz sent a telegram to his mother in Frankfurt telling her to go to the local café on a designated afternoon in order to accept a telephone call from a relative. She did so, and he asked her over the phone to meet him in Munich, bringing some civilian clothes and 300 Reichsmarks from his savings account as he was slated to attend a military course in Salzburg. She sensed that something was wrong and asked if she could share the news with his father and younger sister. Metz replied that it was probably better not to do so.[43]

Metz's mother met him in Munich, bringing the requested civilian clothes and money. He subsequently went to Weil am Rhein, visiting a different aunt while using the same cover story about being on leave en route to a military course. His fifteen-year-old niece was disappointed that he was not wearing his uniform, as she had been looking forward to parading her officer uncle before her schoolmates and BdM (Bund Deutscher Mädel) troop. Metz used the opportunity while "on leave" to take a number of walks along the border, only to find it tightly patrolled. Dejected, he traveled around southern Germany, using his forged leave and travel papers and spending time in Augsburg, Ulm, Freiburg i.Br., and Munich. Against his better judgment, he visited his family in Frankfurt on April 8, climbing through an open kitchen window so that he did not have to ring the apartment bell in the middle of the night. His father was delighted to find Metz on the sofa the next morning, waking the mother and sister with the good news that their boy was visiting for a couple days en route to the front. Metz's mother kept her earlier meeting with Ludwig to herself.

Metz realized that he was endangering the family and bade them farewell after three days. The 132nd Infantry Division's military court had already issued a formal arrest warrant and was in the process of contacting the Kriminalpolizei in Frankfurt.[44] Days after Metz's departure, two military police (*Feldjäger*) visited the house, asking whether they had seen the lieutenant. His mother told them Ludwig had recently been home and was on his way back to the front. The military police informed the family that they should report any contact with Metz immediately.

Metz met his mother one last time at his aunt's house in Weil am Rhine. She asked him anxiously if he had deserted, and when he said yes, she burst into tears. She told him that authorities were already looking for him in Frankfurt, and she worried what would happen if he was caught. She asked whether it would not be best to turn himself in, to which Metz replied, "No mother, I would then be shot.... It is what it is. I'm going to Switzerland, and will tell you all about it tomorrow. But be careful with *Tante* (the aunt)—she doesn't know anything."[45] Metz's mother confided about this last meeting with his younger sister, and they agreed to keep his father in the dark. On May 16, 1942, Ludwig Metz crossed the German-Swiss border. He survived the war and would return to Germany after its defeat.

Hans Kanzenbach

On Thursday, May 28, 1942, Mademoiselle Guillochon noticed a stranger moving about the loft of her barn in the region of Maine, France. Noticing that he had been observed, the stranger fled across a field. He appeared to be about twenty years old and was wearing gray clothes and a hat. The next morning, she and her husband discovered that the stranger had spent the night at their farm. He apparently had helped himself to some eggs and milk, because they discovered eggshells and an empty six-liter milk can in the hayloft along with a German matchbox and torn-up German papers. Monsieur Guillochon noticed that someone had milked one of the cows dry. The couple reported the incident to the nearest police station, the French gendarmerie in Laval, a town in the district of Mayenne. The French police, investigating the incident, discovered boot prints in the mud that revealed the horseshoe-shaped metal heel plate that gave German military boots their distinctive sound when marching. They concluded that the impostor was very likely a German deserter.[46]

Over the course of the next week, the mysterious stranger was sighted at the farms La Passière, La Trochère, and Le Chataigniere situated to the west of Laval. Arriving at Le Chataigniere around 9 p.m. on the third of June, the deserter waved a red flag, fired his pistol into the air, and used sign language to indicate he had thirteen more rounds in his possession. The farmer gave the man some cider and allowed him to spend the night in his barn. The next day, local police received a call that a stranger appeared to be breaking into the farmhouse called Verger, whose owner was at work in the town of Port-Brillet. When the police arrived, the man was gone, as were a bicycle and some clothes. The deserter had attempted to gain entry to the empty farmhouse by shooting at its lock, and when that had failed to open the door, he used a lever to pry it ajar. Farmer Beucher gave a detailed list of the missing clothing to the French police but seemed particularly upset by the theft of the bicycle. The bike had been practically new, was chestnut brown with red stripes, and had gears, a headlight, and a rack behind the seat for carrying things. It belonged to his son.

The French chief of police in Loiron immediately informed the local German military detachment, the *Feldgendarmerie* in Laval, of the incident. Three German military police along with two French gendarmes on motorcycles searched the area for the deserter. Local authorities were alerted to look out for a German deserter who was armed and was last seen wearing civilian clothes. The German military police found the deserter's abandoned military boots in a field and determined that the torn bits of paper in Madame Guillochon's hayloft came from a German military pass authorizing a visit to the dentist. Putting two and two together, German authorities identified the deserter as Hans Kanzenbach of the 668th Infantry

Regiment of the 370th Infantry Division stationed nearby. He was described as being 1.66 meters tall, with blue eyes, a longish face, and a slouched comportment.[47]

The 8th Machine Gun Company of the 668th Infantry Regiment had reported the unauthorized absence/desertion of rifleman Hans Kanzenbach on May 28. Kanzenbach had complained of a toothache the previous day at muster and had been sent along with another dental sufferer to the German military dental clinic in nearby Laval. They had arrived there around eleven in the morning, and seeing the waiting line, Kanzenbach had told his buddy that he was going to do some shopping in town and would be back in half an hour. He never returned to the clinic and failed to show up for the evening muster back at the company. His commander reported his absence at 10 p.m.

The next morning, an investigating officer took sworn statements from various members of Kanzenbach's company. They paint a picture of someone who had not made much of an impression. His squad leader indicated that Kanzenbach had joined the unit only three weeks earlier and had followed orders without complaint. His personal appearance, however, left something to be desired in terms of dress and cleanliness. Another soldier commented that Kanzenbach enjoyed drinking, had told him that his girlfriend was pregnant, and had confided that he intended to marry the girl. Two members of his squad reported that they had given Kanzenbach some money to buy strawberries and other items in Laval but had not suspected that he planned to abscond. One bunkmate recalled that Kanzenbach complained about the long duty days and scanty chow. He remembered that Kanzenbach had commented several times that he was "sick and tired of it" ("*das ihm alles zum Halse heraushinge*") and suspected that Kanzenbach may have stolen a package of tobacco. Another recalled that Kanzenbach had ended a conversation about bad weather the day before by sighing, "My life is over." One colleague had an even more negative impression of Kanzenbach stemming from prewar interactions back home. Both came from the same village in Pomerania, and rifleman Laube claimed that the Kanzenbach brothers were known troublemakers and criminals. He stated that he thought Kanzenbach was capable of anything and was "not a good comrade."[48]

By nightfall on May 28, the company commander had sufficient information to file a formal report concerning Kanzenbach's unauthorized absence/desertion. Kanzenbach had prepared for his desertion by stealing his sergeant's pistol and eighteen rounds of ammunition. He had packed the pistol and some belongings into a laundry bag, which he had carried with him when he left to see the dentist in Laval. Kanzenbach had at least 140 French francs in his possession, which had been entrusted to him by two fellow soldiers so that he could buy some supplies for them in Laval. His commander did not think he had planned to commit suicide and suspected that he had left his unit for the purpose of evading military service.[49] This information was passed to German military police. When they received reports of a German soldier breaking into a farm west of Laval, they surmised that the soldier was Hans Kanzenbach. The search for Kanzenbach commenced, but for six weeks he evaded authorities. The German military suspected he was heading to his home in Pyritz, Pomerania, and alerted authorities there to be on the lookout for the man. As for the 668th Infantry Regiment, on June 5, 1942, it received orders to load up and commence movement to the Eastern Front the next day. Locating rifleman Kanzenbach was not a high priority for the unit.

Kanzenbach later explained that he had intended to check up on his girl in Pyritz and then turn himself in to military authorities.[50] His girlfriend had written him that she was feeling poorly and was about to give birth. Couldn't Kanzenbach visit her? Kanzenbach claimed that he did not bother asking for leave because the company had been told all requests for leave would be denied except in special circumstances such as a death in the immediate family. He assumed his supervisor would not grant him leave since he was unmarried. Traveling along field ways and side roads and subsisting on cherries and carrots, Kanzenbach evaded capture. He traveled westward for days until he realized he was traveling in the wrong direction. Kanzenbach claimed that he never stole anything but had worked for a farmer in Brittany for two weeks and had been given a bicycle in lieu of payment. He passed through Laval in mid-June and heard that his unit had been transferred to the Eastern Front. Continuing toward Germany, Kanzenbach cycled eastward via Paris, Verdun, and Metz. On July 17, the military police detachment in Walldürn in the Odenwald area of Baden received a call from the owner of a sawmill that an unknown soldier was lurking around the area. A military policeman was detached to investigate, and he arrested Kanzenbach early that morning. Kanzenbach was carrying a loaded pistol but made no attempt to resist. He told the arresting policeman that he was on his way to Pomerania and was carrying a pistol so that he could protect himself while traveling in France. He claimed he had not stolen anything during his flight and had not harmed anyone.[51]

Kanzenbach would be tried twice by military courts before being sentenced to death for desertion as a result of a third trial. The proceedings reveal one of the peculiarities of the German military justice system: reviewing authorities recommended overturning initial sentences, not because the rights of the defendant had been ignored or because the verdict had been too severe, but because the conviction and verdict had been insufficiently harsh.

Since Kanzenbach was captured in Germany, his case was transferred to replacement battalion 444 in Thionville, Lorraine (German: Diedenhofen, Wehrkreis XII), which provided the trained manpower for the 668th Infantry Regiment.[52] The German military court in Metz took up the case, meeting on September 16 to consider the evidence it had gathered from Kanzenbach's unit, French and German authorities, and statements made by Kanzenbach after his capture.[53]

The Metz military court found Kanzenbach guilty of the military charges of unauthorized absence, misappropriation of funds, reoccurring theft, and one count of burglary.[54] It sentenced him to seven years of imprisonment with heavy labor, deemed him unworthy of military service (*Verlust der Wehrwürdigkeit*), and withdrew all civil rights for a period of seven years.[55]

The court noted that Kanzenbach had a criminal record predating his conscription into the military, with six prior convictions for unintentional arson, embezzlement, and larceny. Given that the latter two had involved small amounts of money and that Kanzenbach had served his time, the military court refrained from characterizing him as a career criminal. It noted that his military record was clean of any disciplinary or legal charges and accepted with some hesitation Kanzenbach's contention that he intended to rejoin the German Army after visiting his pregnant girlfriend. The court explained that while Kanzenbach's six-week unauthorized absence came perilously close to desertion, the members of the court were not certain that Kanzenbach intended to evade military service permanently. This distinction was crucial, differentiating unauthorized absence from desertion, a capital crime. In the findings which accompanied the verdict, the Metz court explained that Kanzenbach was not particularly bright and had blundered around France and southern Germany because he was directionally challenged. It noted that he had not resisted arrest, had been wearing his uniform when arrested, and had been cooperative in detention. The court thought it improbable that Kanzenbach would have headed to Germany, where the "the probability of apprehension is highest," if his intention had been to permanently evade military service.[56] Seven years of imprisonment with heavy labor for unauthorized absence and petty theft was not a light sentence, but it was not a death sentence.

The verdict and sentence of the Metz military court had to be confirmed by the commander in chief of the Replacement Army, General Friedrich Fromm, before they took effect. Fromm could order a new trial if he disagreed with the verdict, the sentence, or the reasoning behind the two. He relied on his judge advocate for legal advice, and one of the legal department's senior military jurists was tasked with preparing a commentary to accompany the court's decision. The judge advocate's commentary on the Metz military tribunal's decision was devastating. It rejected Kanzenbach's story that he was only trying to reach his expectant girlfriend in Pomerania, claiming this was unbelievable. It waved aside the court's explanation that Kanzenbach had limited mental capacities and poor geographical knowledge, asserting that neither of these could explain why it had taken him seven weeks to get to Germany and why he was apprehended near Würzburg when he claimed he was heading to Pomerania. The judge advocate postulated a simpler explanation: Kanzenbach had deserted when he heard his unit was heading to the Eastern Front and had no intention of rejoining the Wehrmacht. The legal review recommended that Fromm reject the verdict of the Metz military court, and that several matters be investigated before proceeding with a new trial. On October 9, 1942, General Fromm overturned the verdict reached at Metz.

Kanzenbach's case was transferred to a different investigating officer, who sought to clarify a number of issues. He contacted town authorities in Pomerania and asked if Kanzenbach's story about a pregnant girlfriend was true. They confirmed that Kanzenbach had indeed been in a relationship with a Luise Böttcher, that their relationship had resulted in pregnancy, and that Böttcher had written Kanzenbach in May pleading that he visit her. The investigating officer also wrote to Kanzenbach's unit, the 668th Infantry Regiment, and asked when it had been notified that it was being sent to the Eastern Front. The investigator noted that this was of great importance, as Kanzenbach claimed he had not known that the unit had orders to go to the Eastern Front when he deserted on May 27. The unit replied that it had been notified of the transfer on June 5, a week after Kanzenbach had absconded.

Lastly, the investigating officer followed up on the allegation that Kanzenbach had been called up for duty earlier in 1939 but had failed to report as ordered. Local authorities informed him that Kanzenbach had been in jail at that time, and that his call-up had therefore been deferred. As these matters were being clarified, Kanzenbach was transferred to a different detention facility located at Kattowitz in Silesia. On January 22, 1943, a second military tribunal tried the milker from Pomerania. The second military tribunal noted that Kanzenbach's explanations had generally stood up to examination, and that the court did not believe that the "rather slow" defendant was a "cunning liar."[57] On January 22, 1943, a second military court found Kanzenbach guilty of unauthorized absence, two counts of embezzlement, one count of theft, and one count of burglary. It sentenced him to eight years of imprisonment with heavy labor, deemed him unworthy of military service, and withdrew all civil rights for a period of ten years.[58]

Once again, the judge advocate at the Replacement Army recommended that General Fromm reject the court's verdict and sentence. The judge advocate commented that he found the court's interpretation of the evidence faulty, and he noted that new evidence confirming the fact that Kanzenbach had a pregnant girlfriend did not rule out that he was motivated by his desire to evade service on the Eastern Front. The unit may only have received orders after Kanzenbach deserted, but surely he had heard rumors that it was going to be transferred. General Fromm duly overturned the second court's verdict and sentence and ordered yet another trial. Kanzenbach was transferred to Berlin and held at the military prison at Lehrter Street 61.

The Berlin garrison's legal department commissioned a mental evaluation of Kanzenbach prior to retrying his case. Professor Dr. Müller-Heß of Berlin's University Institute for Forensic Medicine and Criminology (*Universitätsinstitut für gerichtliche Medizin und Kriminalistik*) consulted documents from the overturned military trials, court records from Pomerania, and a growing file of statements, reports, and assessments related to Kanzenbach. The professor conducted his own evaluation of Kanzenbach, carefully examining his body and questioning him in order to generate physical and psychological assessments. Müller-Heß found no physical defects. As to Kanzenbach's mental health and mindset, Müller-Heß assessed him as having below-normal intelligence though possessing a "primitive cleverness." The professor found no history of mental illness in the family and described Kanzenbach's relationship with his parents and siblings as distant. The doctor portrayed Kanzenbach as a "primitive human," claiming that he was too egocentric to have any sense of community. He lacked ethical and moral feelings. The medical assessment was rife with Nazi-era language about "primitiveness," subpar intelligence, and inherent criminality. The professor painted a picture of an asocial personality, brushing aside Kanzenbach's claim that he deserted because he was concerned about his pregnant girlfriend.[59]

On May 25, 1943, the Berlin Garrison's military court sat to consider the Kanzenbach case. This was the third time a military court passed judgment on the case. It drew on the expert opinion of Müller-Heß to brush away Kanzenbach's explanation that he deserted in order to visit his pregnant girlfriend. It echoed the opinion of the judge advocate that Kanzenbach must have heard rumors that his unit was being transferred to the Eastern Front even if the official orders arrived after his desertion.[60] The court noted that Kanzenbach had two stepbrothers who had served time, and it concluded that he was an "asocial" with criminal tendencies. The fact that he had flunked out of school four times did not mitigate his crime, but rather substantiated his shiftlessness and subpar intelligence. The court ruled that rifleman Hans Kanzenbach had deserted his unit and condemned him to death.[61]

The Reserve Army's judge advocate raised no objections to the verdict and sentence, and recommended that they be confirmed. On June 18, General Fromm as commander of the Replacement Army did so. At 2 p.m. on June 25, Kanzenbach was informed of the court's ruling. He was transported to the Brandenburg-Görden prison that afternoon. At 5:09 p.m., he was escorted to the execution chamber. The officer in charge verified Kanzenbach's identity, read the verdict, and turned him over to the executioner. Kanzenbach was escorted to the guillotine, rendering no resistance, and within twenty-eight seconds he was decapitated. On June 25, 1943—more than a year after he left his unit in France—the Pomeranian milker Hans Kanzenbach was executed for deserting the German Army.[62]

Stefan Hampel

Füsilier Stefan Hampel was a *Mischling*, the offspring of a German father and Polish mother. His decision to desert in June 1942 from an infantry replacement battalion stationed in East Prussia reflected a conflicted relationship to the Third Reich. As a youth, he had earned the Hitler Youth's highest award, the Golden Honor badge, and he had volunteered for the

Reich Labor Service in 1934, a year before this donation of time and labor became obligatory.[63] Yet he also had an attachment to the Polish people and had spent part of his childhood in Poland. After he was apprehended for desertion, Hampel tried to explain his inner turmoil to his interrogators in these terms: he was "a German and a national socialist by conviction and upbringing" but one "who had certain feelings for the Polish people that a real German shouldn't have." Elaborating, he explained that he could not "despise the people to whom my mother belonged and whose language I spoke as a child without hating myself."[64] Hampel saw some terrible things in White Russia, and he decided he could no longer fight for a regime he had grown to detest.

The German term *Mischling* was pejorative, suggesting that one could not truly be German and Jewish, German and Polish, or German and non-German.[65] Hampel's parents did not have a happy marriage. His father had wed his mother while stationed in the East during World War I, abandoning her after the war. The mother came from a landed Polish family that owned property near Vilnius, an area that both Poland and Lithuania claimed during the chaotic postwar period. Hampel was born there, but his mother moved to Berlin after she tracked down his father. The marriage soon foundered, the parents separated, and for the first decade of his life, young Hampel was shuttled between his parents as they wrangled over whom should have custody of the boy. Hampel's father, a policeman, had a fierce temper and apparently took it out on his wife and child. When Stefan was nine, a German court awarded custody to his father, and his mother moved back to her family's estate in what was then eastern Poland. Hampel's father remarried, but the second marriage was likewise unhappy. He and his second wife fought constantly, taking out their frustrations on the boy. One suspects that the Hitler Youth was a welcome escape for young Hampel, giving him an outlet where he could engage in physical activities, make friends, and participate in the endless cavalcade of marches, bonfires, and inspirational speeches designed to mold young Germans into members of the NS *Volksgemeinschaft*. Hampel's Golden Hitler Youth badge shows that he was accepted as a comrade and as a leader. Missing his mother and at odds with his father, he volunteered to join the Reich Labor Service at the extraordinarily young age of fifteen.[66] He was the youngest boy at the Labor Service work site.

Young Hampel never forgot his mother. Following completion of his stint in the Reich Labor Service, he made his living as an agricultural worker.

He reconnected with his mother in Poland, visiting her several times. On one of these trips, Polish authorities arrested him, as he did not have a passport and travel authorization. The Polish intelligence service tried to recruit him as an agent, but Hampel declined and duly reported the incident to German authorities. His mother proved kind and supportive, sending her son some money so he could prepare for a college entrance exam. He passed the exam and was accepted into a program in political science in the fall of 1938.

Hitler had always expressed contempt for the Polish people but had muted some of his anti-Polish rhetoric for political expediency as he moved to reoccupy the Rhineland, annex Austria, and dismember Czechoslovakia in the second half of the 1930s. Once he consolidated his position, the German propaganda machine turned its focus on Poland in the spring of 1939. Young Stefan Hampel was bold enough to question various German claims as the manufactured Polish crisis heated up. On semester break in East Prussia, he was detained by the Gestapo for making "treacherous comments" insulting the regime (*Heimtückerei*). The police had been informed that Hampel was criticizing the German press; they noted that he had publicly remarked that "Roosevelt was not a servant of American Jewry but a smart and clever man," "Fascism, National Socialism, and Communism are all the same," and "The Führer violated the Munich agreement, and Germany bears responsibility for the war."[67] A Decree for the Protection of People and State, passed in February 1933, allowed the German police to detain indefinitely anyone they believed endangered public law and order. Arrested in June 1939, Hampel was detained without legal proceedings while Germany conquered Poland and Europe plunged into war. He was released without charge in June 1940, but the experience put an end to his ambition to study political science at the university. He emerged from detention physically weaker, psychologically traumatized, and disillusioned.

Hampel was able to find work as a switch operator with the Reichsbahn, but within months he received a conscription notice. He reported for duty on September 4, 1940. The German Army taught him to use the standard infantry rifle and trained him to be a radioman. He was posted to various communication and replacement units stationed in East Prussia, but he was not sent to the front after Germany launched its massive invasion of Russia in June 1941. The German Army may have suspected that he was not reliable because he had been born in Vilnius, had been detained by the Gestapo for making comments critical of the regime, and was a *Mischling*.[68]

For his part, Stefan Hampel had no desire to be a soldier. He was clearly intelligent, but he found Morse coding unrewarding and monotonous. His comrades found him to be an oddball who spent more time reading books than socializing. Hampel developed no close friendships with his comrades. He received no letters or packages from home and spent Christmas alone in the barracks. He was a loner.

In May 1942, Hampel was granted leave to go to Grodno to find out what had happened to his mother. He had not heard from her since before his detention, and he was worried. Hampel traveled to the family home and discovered that his mother, an uncle, and an aunt had all disappeared. Locals told him that the Red Army had evicted them from their homes when it occupied eastern Poland in 1939, and they had either been killed or sent to Siberia along with other Polish landowners, gentry, and intellectuals. He recovered a fur coat and some other items from the house, now occupied by German bureaucrats.

On his way back to his unit, Hampel witnessed one of the many mass executions taking place in the area. He later recounted the episode to the German military police in detail, citing it as a prime reason for his desertion. His handwritten biographical statement captures the searing encounter:

> In order to convey the enormous impression that this experience had on me, I want to briefly describe what happened. The [execution] detachment arrived in Wassiliski [sic. Wasiliszki, Poland; now Vasilishki, Belarus] that morning in trucks and on motorcycles. They came from another town, where they had shot all the Jews earlier in the morning. In Wassiliski, the ghetto had been hermetically sealed, and a giant pit had been dug in an open area. All the Jews from the ghetto were then driven out to the main street, where they had to kneel down in columns by family. A dense cordon of police proceeded to drive them toward the mass grave. Those who didn't move quickly enough, in particular old women and children, were shot on the spot. Afterwards, the street was covered with corpses. Arriving at the pit, the 2000 Jews were told to lay down on their stomachs. Family groups were instructed to stand up by turn, and examined by a commission of men in civilian clothing who took their money, jewelry and so forth. Men using leather whips drove them forward to the pit. The Jews had to strip down to their shirts and climb into the grave. I was shaken by the utter silence that prevailed as all this was happening. The Jews were in a state of shock as they climbed into the

> grave holding on to one another. Some of the children thought it was a game and were laughing, not understanding what was happening until they were kicked into the pit. Many women had babies at their breast. One of the policemen in the murder squad suffered a nervous breakdown, though he ought to have been used to such sights. He was hauled away screaming.[69]

Hampel was deeply shaken by the episode. He agonized over his mother's fate, wondering if she had been executed in a like manner by the Russians. Upon his return to his unit, he was transferred to a replacement battalion in Stablack, East Prussia. He requested leave to visit Grodno several weeks later, indicating that he still had family matters to settle. The request was denied because Grodno lay outside the one-hundred-kilometer radius established for weekend passes. Hampel resubmitted for a two-day pass to the nearby town of Rastenburg. The town lay on the same rail line as Grodno, but it is better remembered as the closest town to Hitler's secret Führer headquarters, the *Wolfsschanze* or Wolf's Lair. Hampel's leave request was approved, and he departed for the weekend in early June 1942. He never returned.

For almost a year, the Wehrmacht had no idea what had happened to Hampel or where he was. His unit issued the standard report regarding Hampel's unauthorized absence/desertion (courts would determine which charge applied), and the search was on. Hampel's policeman father, from whom he was estranged, had joined the SS and was fighting on the Eastern Front. His Polish mother was either dead or in Siberia. He had no brothers or sisters, and he had not kept in touch with acquaintances from his Hitler Jugend troop or his Labor Service formation. Yet despite this, the odds were high that the army would eventually apprehend him. Passes, identification papers, and ration cards were required for rail travel, for employment, for housing, and for food. The police and the military could count on much of the population to inform them of people who looked suspicious or out of place, and the law allowed them to arrest, interrogate, and detain anyone deemed dangerous to the state.

Eleven months after his disappearance, the German *Kriminalpolizei* got a lucky break. A man wearing a Reichsbahn uniform had checked into the Hotel Turner in Freiburg im Breisgau, about an hour's train ride from Switzerland. He had signed the register using the name Stephan Hampel. The hotel, as required, had given a copy of its guest list to the local police, who had crosschecked the guest registry with their wanted persons list. The police detained the man and discovered that he carried two different identity passes. He carried a Lithuanian *Personalausweis* issued by the city government of Vilna indicating that he was Steponas Paškevičius. He also carried a Reichsbahn *Personenausweis* issued to Stefan Hampel. Both passes had pictures of the same man.[70]

The German police used some "rough methods" to extract a confession from the detained man admitting that he was Stefan Hampel, missing from the German military for eleven months.[71] Hampel realized that anything he said could be used in his court-martial proceedings, and he was careful to protect anyone who might have helped him. He claimed he had returned to his mother's house, sold some of the belongings he had inherited, and had survived by living off the proceeds and working at various farms in the Vilnius-Grodno-Kaunas region. He confessed to acquiring a fake Lithuanian identification paper for one hundred Reichsmarks, but claimed he had done so solely to protect himself from partisans operating in the area. Lastly, he claimed that he was en route to Bavaria in the search for a job and had no plans to flee to Switzerland.

The real story may have been far more interesting. Hampel had indeed gone to his mother's estate near Grodno and had spent several months underground, continuously moving from place to place. Decades later, Hampel provided a different account than he had provided to the German police in 1943, for understandable reasons. He recalled that he had been able to establish contact with a Polish-Lithuanian resistance group, who had helped hide him along with some escaped Soviet POWs and five Jews. Hampel recalled that the members of his group were increasingly distressed by the mass shootings, ethnic cleansing, and disappearances in the region, and wondered if the rest of the world knew what was happening. He recalled thinking, "What is the Church saying? What is the Pope saying? He is silent, as is the International Red Cross."[72] In spring 1943, the group instructed Hampel to go to Switzerland and seek out the International Committee of the Red Cross in order to share his eyewitness account of what had happened in Wassiliski. He had almost made it to the border when he slipped up in Freiburg, signing the hotel register with his real name since he worried the clerk would wonder why a Lithuanian was wearing a Reichsbahn uniform. That slip-up led to his arrest, interrogation, and subsequent court-martial.

Hampel was tried for desertion and sentenced to death by the same court that tried Hans Kanzenbach.[73] The reviewing legal authority recommended confirming both the verdict and sentence, but General Fromm of the Replacement Army chose to convert the sentence to fifteen years of hard labor. Hampel never knew why Fromm did so. The Führer had specifically instructed that deserters who intended to flee to another country should be sentenced to death, and the police had found two maps in Hampel's room, one of the Basel region and the other of Konstanz on the Bodensee.

Four factors may have contributed to Fromm's decision. First, Hampel's defense lawyer argued that Hampel was not fully responsible for his actions because he was mentally incapacitated. His detention by the Gestapo had traumatized him, the mass killing he had witnessed had unhinged him, and mental illness ran in the family. Second, the psychiatric examination the defense requested helped Hampel. The psychiatrist concluded that Hampel was a decent man who could be reformed, though prone to letting his feelings overcome his reason. His difficult childhood had blurred his judgment. Third, an uncle wrote a letter pleading for a reduced sentence. The uncle noted that Hampel's father had volunteered for duty in August 1914, served four years at the front in World War I, and was again serving on the Eastern Front in this war as an SS-Obersturmführer. Hampel's father would be crushed if his only son was executed for desertion. The boy had acted out of youthful recklessness, thoughtlessness, and insufficient fatherly supervision. Lastly, Hampel's own plea for clemency was articulate, hitting all the right notes. Hampel acknowledged his guilt, explained that he had not acted out of cowardice, and asked that he be given the opportunity to redeem himself with his fellow soldiers and the German *Volk*. Hampel volunteered to participate in any "*Himmelsfahrtkommando*" (suicide mission) the army might have in mind, noting that his death might thereby save the life of someone more worthy.

Fromm's act of mercy in changing Hampel's sentence from execution to fifteen years of heavy labor was little more than an extended death sentence. The conditions at the Börgermoor camp in Emsland to which Hampel was transferred in July 1944 were appalling. The likelihood that Hampel would survive fifteen years of hard labor was exceedingly low. Hampel recalled how he was savagely beaten and forced to wear a symbol on his prison uniform designating him as *Fluchtverdächtigt* (high flight risk). The prisoners were fed such meager rations that they soon developed signs of severe malnutrition. Knowing that he would not be able to survive the winter of 1944/1945 under such conditions, Hampel volunteered for duty when the German Army started combing its military detention facilities and camps for manpower. He was assigned to Bewährungsbattalion 500, a special battalion composed of military convicts on probation, and sent into action in Silesia in the last months of the war. The battalion, one of several set up by the Germans as manpower became scarce late in the war, was very much a *Himmelsfahrtkommando.* Hampel again deserted and was eventually taken prisoner by the Russians. He barely survived the war.[74]

2
Overall Contours

The German military became an instrument of the Third Reich increasingly, incorporating Nazi values, worldviews, and extremism over the course of the 1930s. Hitler and the National Socialist movement in turn reflected certain perspectives, sentiments, and prejudices present in German nationalist circles since the nineteenth century and accentuated after Germany's defeat in World War I. The German military and the Nazi movement anticipated that Germany would at some point wage another war, and that this next war would be a ruthless enterprise.[1] And so it was: the German Army, when preparing for Operation Barbarossa, accepted that requisitioning in the East would starve to death tens of millions of Russians.[2] It aided and assisted Himmler's mobile death squads—the notorious *Einsatzgruppen*—as they massacred more than 2 million Eastern European civilians, including an estimated 1.3 million Jews, behind the front lines.[3] German military authorities shot tens of thousands of Greeks, Poles, Serbs, and others in areas occupied by the Wehrmacht, and they intentionally subjected millions of Soviet POWs to conditions that led to their death. The myth of a clean Wehrmacht, fighting honorably at the front and unaware of massacres perpetuated to its rear areas, has been thoroughly debunked.[4] Less well known is how nationalism, militarism, and Nazism resulted in a pitiless German military justice system that condemned between 25,000 and 30,000 German soldiers, sailors, and airmen to death for desertion, subversion, and other offenses. The German military carried out these sentences 70 percent of the time, shooting, hanging, or beheading between 18,000 and 22,000 of its own.[5]

These numbers pale in comparison to millions killed by war, genocide, and starvation, yet they tell a tale. The German military emphasized leadership, promoted camaraderie, and fostered the notion of a shared German identity and destiny. Around 17 million Germans served in the Wehrmacht, implementing, cooperating, and therefore consenting to the regime's agenda and war aims.[6] A great deal of attention has been paid in the English language literature to the small group of military officers who sought to depose

Hitler by detonating a bomb at his headquarters on July 20, 1944. Far less attention has been paid to the much larger group of Germans who decided at some point that they did not want to fight for the Third Reich.[7] In Germany, debate raged throughout the 1980s and 1990s over the figure of the Wehrmacht deserter. Progressives postulated that desertion was the resistance of the common man, while conservatives countered that most deserters had been motivated by personal rather than political reasons. Regardless of motivation, the German military viewed deserters and critics as a threat to the Third Reich's war effort. Understanding how the German military dealt with deserters reveals the interaction among consent, compliance, and coercion. It illustrates the interaction among German nationalism, Prussian military values, and National Socialism. It shows how difficult it is to break away from group conformity and how strong the forces were for promoting acquiescence and obedience within the ranks.[8]

The precise number of German military personnel who were charged with desertion, unauthorized absence, or with "undermining military morale" (*Wehrkraftzersetzung*) is impossible to determine, as is the number executed for these derelictions. We do know that it was extraordinarily high when compared to German military justice in World War I or British and American military justice during World War II. The most frequently cited figures are those compiled in the late 1980s by Manfred Messerschmidt, who served as chief historian at the German Military History Research Office for over two decades, and Fritz Wüllner, a retired business manager who made it his life's work to lay bare the nature of the Third Reich's military justice system. According to their initial calculations, German military judges sentenced around 35,000 members of the Wehrmacht to death, chiefly for desertion and undermining the military spirit.[9] Those fortunate enough to escape the executioner's noose or the firing squad were usually sent to military penal camps or special military penal battalions. Starvation, disease, and the extremely high casualty rates in these penal battalions meant that many granted a judicial reprieve merely had their deaths postponed.

There are three reasons why historians can make only rough estimates of how many German military personnel were executed by the German military. The most important reason is that many records were destroyed during the war. On April 14, 1945, the Heeresarchiv in Potsdam burned to the ground as a result of an Allied air raid. The German Army was by far the largest of the military services, and records related to army courts-martial went up in smoke. Historians have to work with those court-martial records that had not yet been sent to the archive, were stored elsewhere, or pertain to the navy (the German Navy stored its records elsewhere, and a higher proportion of its records survived the war). The surviving records are fragmentary at best, with one expert estimating that only 6 to 7 percent of Wehrmacht court-martial files survived.[10] Second, one can assume that a significant number of front-line courts-martial records never made it back to Berlin, particularly during the desperate fighting of 1943–1945 when entire German armies ceased to exist. These lost files are not reflected in the quarterly statistics. Third, during the last months of the war, flying tribunals sentenced German deserters and "shirkers" to death without keeping any records at all. One must estimate how many were killed by German military police, SS patrols, and ad hoc flying tribunals, which kept no records.

Historians therefore have had to estimate the number of German soldiers, sailors, and airmen executed by the German military, using the Wehrmacht High Command's quarterly statistical overview (*Kriegs-Kriminalstatistik für die Wehrmacht*) of military charges, convictions, and sentences as a starting point. These reports have survived for the period August 1939 until December 1944, with the last quarterly report incomplete.[11] Figure 1 provides a tabulation of these reports.[12]

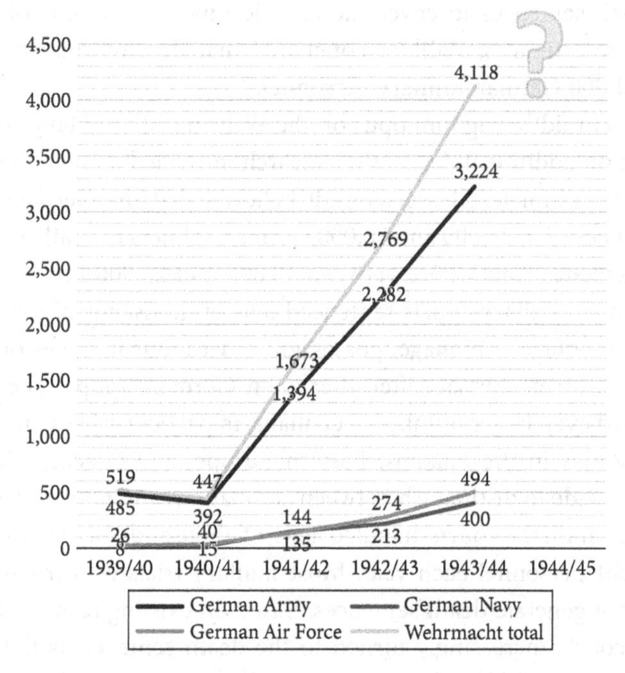

Figure 1. Death sentences carried out against members of the Wehrmacht, 1939–1944

The quarterly reports provide information about what charges were prosecuted, the accused member's military branch (the report only pertain to Wehrmacht members and did not cover the Waffen-SS, the *Sicherheitsdienst* [SD], or police), verdicts, and sentences imposed. They provide information about whether the accused was an officer, a noncommissioned officer, enlisted, or civilian, and their duty status. These quarterly reports break off in the fall of 1944. Given that German casualties, both civilian and military, skyrocketed during the last year of the war, one can assume that the military justice system's death toll for the entire war was much higher.

One frequently cited expert, Fritz Wüllner, laid out the reasoning behind his estimate of 21,000 German soldiers executed by the German military as follows. The quarterly statistical reports compiled by the High Command's legal office for the period August 1939 to December 1944 indicate that 9,732 military personnel were executed. Wüllner noted that the report for the last quarter was incomplete and added another 1,430 executions to the total. He concluded that another 3,000 delayed reports were not reflected in quarterly statistics for 1939–1944, that 1,000 for Wehrmacht civilian executions did not make it into the record, and that perhaps 2,000 death sentence records were destroyed or lost en route to Berlin. He added an estimated 4,000 death sentences to cover the chaotic final five months of the war. Using these estimates, Wüllner concluded that the Wehrmacht executed around 21,000 German military personnel.[13]

Messerschmidt's magnum opus on the Wehrmacht's military justice system, built on additional decades of research, provided a range in line with the Wüllner estimate. Messerschmidt believed that the German military sentenced between 25,000 and 30,000 German soldiers to death and carried out the sentence somewhere between 18,000 and 22,000 times.[14] In addition, German military courts sentenced tens of thousands of foreigners to death for sabotage, espionage, possession of weapons in zones of military occupation, or in reprisals after attacks on German troops. The German Army killed even larger number of civilians, in particular Jews, in antipartisan operations in the Balkans, Eastern Europe, and Greece, where little effort was made to distinguish between combatants and noncombatants.

German military courts handled tens of thousands of cases related to Wehrmacht personnel each year. Most military trials concerned offenses that did not generate death sentences. Based on existing records, it is clear that the courts increasingly turned to the death sentence as the military situation deteriorated. As Figure 1 shows, during the first year of the war,

German military courts sentenced 519 members of the Wehrmacht to death. By the fourth year, the number had risen to 2,769, increasing by another 150 percent the following year. The first three months of 1942 provide a snapshot into the military justice system at a time when the German offensive in the East had stalled and German forces were fending off powerful Soviet counterattacks. Military courts handled 34,399 cases during this time. Most cases pertained to enlisted personnel (27,615 cases), a significant number involved noncommissioned and senior noncommissioned officers (2,662 and 1,214 cases, respectively), and 471 cases involved officers (335 junior officers, 111 captains, 24 field grade officers, and 1 general).[15] Ninety percent of the proceedings ended in guilty verdicts, with penalties ranging from monetary fines to the death sentence. Figure 2 lists the top three derelictions punished by death in the first quarter of 1942, with theft, murder, misappropriation of Winter Help donations, and unauthorized absence coming in distantly at fourth through seventh place.[16] The upward trend in charges related to desertion and subversion of the military spirit is apparent in Figure 3, which takes data from the second and fourth quarters of 1943 and the second quarter of 1944.[17]

After World War II, former Wehrmacht judges and lawyers tried to brush away charges that the German military justice system had been particularly harsh and reflected Nazi worldviews. They countered that historically all militaries have viewed desertion as a capital crime, reminding interlocutors that the French had shot hundreds in World War I and claiming that the US

Charge	Charged	Convicted	Sentenced to Death	Execution carried out
Desertion	711	678	291 (12 sentences reduced to imprisonment w heavy labor)	279
Undermining the military spirit	943	673	56 (9 sentences reduced to long prison sentences)	47
Cowardice	155	104	23 (3 sentences reduced to imprisonment w heavy labor)	20

Figure 2. Snapshot of top-three charges resulting in military court death sentences, January 1–March 31, 1942

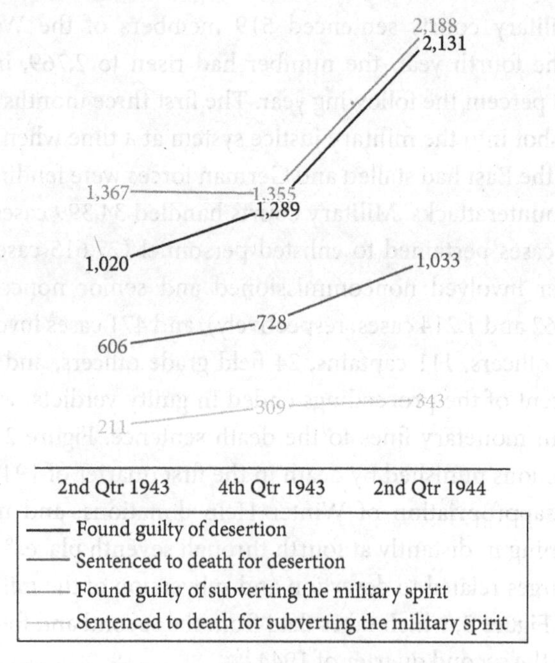

Figure 3. Trend in convictions and death sentences for desertion and subversion, German military courts, 1943–1944

military justice system had sentenced more Americans to "severe punishment" than had the Germans.[18] This reference to traditional military values is a smokescreen that obscures how different the Wehrmacht military justice was from its predecessor and from Western systems. As Figure 4 makes clear, the German Imperial Army was mild compared to Western militaries in the application of death sentence in World War I, ranking far behind Italy, Great Britain, and France in the number of soldiers sentenced to death and the number executed. Compared to its Imperial predecessor, the Wehrmacht was far harsher in its application of military justice.[19]

Postwar apologists also claimed that the US military courts had sentenced thousands of American service personnel to "prison terms which often exceeded all reasonable standards in their length" and had executed 146 members of the American armed forces. This intentional effort to relativize the Wehrmacht military justice system enraged those who knew better. In a forceful critique of one of these apologetic works, Fritz Wüllner pointed out that former Wehrmacht judge advocates were intentionally obscuring the

Nation	Sentenced to Death	Executed	Executed for Desertion
Italy	4,000	750	n.d.
Great Britain	3,080	346	266
France	2,000	300–400	n.d.
German Empire	150	48	18

Figure 4. Comparison to military justice in World War I

record. The United States executed precisely one soldier for desertion in World War II, the unfortunate Private Eddie Slovik.[20] Slovik deserted in October 1944, convinced that the US military would sentence him to imprisonment rather than shoot him. US forces were engaged in bloody conflict with the Germans in the Hurtgen Forest at the time of his desertion, and he was sentenced to death. His appeal for clemency reached General Eisenhower at the height of the Battle of the Bulge in December 1944, and Eisenhower rejected the appeal. On January 31, 1945, a US Army firing squad executed Slovik. Other US death penalties relate to murder, rape, and aggravated assault convictions. Australian historian Steven Welch delved further into the matter. His study used hundreds of case studies comparing the two military justice systems. Welch found that German military courts had sentenced deserters to death in 73 percent of the cases he analyzed, whereas US military courts in the European Theater had done so in only 4 percent of the cases. Eighty percent of the German death sentences were carried out.

The contrast to British military justice is even starker: the British Empire was fighting for survival in 1940–1942, and over 50,000 service members deserted during this period. None of those apprehended was executed, as Britain had abolished the death sentence for cowardice and desertion in 1930.[21] Comparisons between the systems point to stark differences, and efforts to claim that the Germans were only doing what the Anglo-Americans were doing are false. The German military executed at least 15,000 German deserters over the course of World War II.[22] This exceeds the entire number of judicial executions in Imperial and Weimar Germany from 1907 to 1932 (393 executions). During the short, three-month Poland campaign, the Wehrmacht executed two times the number of German soldiers executed by the Imperial German Army over the course of World War I.[23] Japan and the Soviet Union may have matched Nazi Germany in their zeal to punish soldiers suspected of inadequate motivation. Ideology, military culture, and totalitarian structures interacted in all three militaries to create policies and processes that set their military justice systems apart from those in the West.[24] What is striking in the German case is how Wehrmacht military justice drew on the same military penal code its Imperial predecessor had used in World War I, but interpreted and enforced that code in a merciless manner that swept aside liberal, Western protections introduced over the course of the last hundred years.

The Military Penal Code and the Special Wartime Criminal Law

The Wehrmacht's military justice system rested on Imperial Germany's Military Penal Code (the *Militärstrafgesetzbuch* [MStGB]) of 1872 and the Military Courts-Martial Regulations (the *Militärstrafgerichtsordnung* [MStGO]) of 1898.[25] The Imperial Military Penal Code and the Courts-Martial Regulations were the compromise product of efforts made during the nineteenth century and after German unification to update, reform, and humanize the Prussian military codes of 1808 and 1845. Nineteenth-century German reformers had pressed to add other protections and to limit the scope of military punishments during peacetime, but they had failed to weaken the central role of military commanders in supervising judicial proceeding. They nonetheless succeeded in doing away with Frederickian-era punishments such as running the gauntlet, lashing enlisted men, and shackling soldiers to prison walls or iron balls. The Social Democrats had opposed the existence of a separate military legal system during the Imperial era, and the military court-martial regulations of 1898 ameliorated some concerns by formalizing military courts of appeal and strengthening the role of judge advocates in the process. German military justice in World War I was generally no harsher than that of the Entente Powers, and when measured in terms of death sentences, it was considerably less harsh.

In August 1920, the Weimar coalition abolished the military judicial system, with the exception of shipboard tribunals on vessels operating overseas. Soldiers would be treated like other citizens when it came to criminal, versus mere disciplinary matters, during peacetime. Civil courts would adjudicate criminal matters involving military personnel, much to the outrage of nationalist groups horrified at the prospect of civilian judges—especially women—ruling on military matters.[26] Former military jurists, tacitly supported by the Reichswehr command, argued that the military as an institution operated by different rules even in peacetime, and that civilian courts were too slow and legalistic to replace the courts-martial system. One of the first priorities of Minister of War Werner von Blomberg after Hitler's accession to power was to reinstitute the military justice system uprooted by the Weimar Republic. In April 1933, von Blomberg let his colleagues in the cabinet know that "Since the political conditions have changed fundamentally as a result of the national awakening, the time has arrived to restore the military justice system, not only to counter the dangers that arise in times of war, but to prepare the necessary judicial preconditions for the creation of a new, significantly different German military."[27] He was pushing on an open door, as both nationalists and Nazis had been attacking Weimar-era restrictions on the military for the previous decade. In May 1933, the Reichstag passed a law that reestablished a military justice system distinct from the civilian judiciary effective January 1, 1934. The restored judge advocate corps drew heavily on military jurists who had cut their teeth in the Imperial era, recruiting younger lawyers trained in the Weimar and Nazi era as the decade progressed.

Already in 1934, a working group within the military took up the project of writing an entirely new code of military justice to replace the Imperial code of 1872 and the courts-martial regulations of 1898. The draft proposal stalled as party ideologues such as Hans Frank, head of the National Socialist Jurists Association and president of the Academy of German Law, objected that its language did not sufficiently incorporate National Socialist language and viewpoints.[28] Many Wehrmacht jurists saw little need to replace the old military code, as revisions in 1934, 1935, and 1940 did away with various reforms introduced before and after World War I. Even the head of the working group charged with creating a new military code conceded that there was nothing objectionable to the old Imperial code. It incorporated, he wrote, "markedly anti-liberal tendencies and reflected a perspective that then and now is compatible with National Socialism."[29] A draft of a new, Nazi-era military code was considered at the cabinet level but stalled there due to bureaucratic infighting. As war clouds loomed in 1938, Hitler signed an Order Imposing Extraordinary Wartime Laws and Penalties (the *Verordnung über das Sonderstrafrecht im Kriege und bei besonderem Einsatz*, usually shortened to the *Kriegssonderstrafrechtsverordnung* [KSSVO]) and an expansive Order Imposing Wartime Criminal Procedures (the

Kriegsstrafverfahrensordnung [KStVO]). The two orders, signed on August 17, 1938, took effect when Germany mobilized for war on August 26, 1939.

Military courts dealt with both civil and military crimes. During the first year of the war, for example, German military courts handled 31,863 cases associated with civil offenses and 46,070 cases related to military offenses.[30] Civil cases related to offenses defined in the Civil Law Book (*Bürgerliches Gesetzbuch*), which could range from murder, rape, and assault to theft, embezzlement, and forgery. Military offenses related to crimes particular to a military organization, such as desertion, cowardice, and failure to obey an order. The Military Penal Code (*Militärstrafgesetzbuch*) listed eleven types of military violations and offenses, with specifications and elaboration provided for each. Types of military violations included treason, plotting treason, and nonreporting of treason; endangering military effectiveness in the field, which included surrendering to the enemy and dereliction of duty; unauthorized absence and desertion; self-mutilation and avoidance of duty through deception; cowardice and duty derelictions caused by fear; criminal offenses directed against military order and discipline, which included fourteen specific charges ranging from threatening a superior to unauthorized assembly to mutiny to undermining military discipline (the German term *Untergraben der Manneszucht* has a gendered flavor); abuse of authority, which included the charge of insulting a subordinate; unlawful actions in the field against people and property, which included the charges of plundering, robbing the dead, and unauthorized requisitioning; unlawful property crimes, which included damaging military property, theft of military property, and embezzlement of military funds; violation of duties, which pertained to watch violations, freeing prisoners, and bribery; and other violations of military order and discipline, ranging from not reporting the crimes of subordinates to marrying without permission.[31]

The Order Imposing Extraordinary Wartime Laws and Penalties (KSSVO) expanded the legal framework further by increasing penalties for various offenses already in the civil and military penal codes. The KSSVO specified that those gathering and providing intelligence to the enemy would be sentenced to death; that francs-tireurs and partisans would be punished by execution; that individuals violating occupation orders were subject to hard labor, imprisonment, and fines; and that those "undermining the military spirit" faced the death sentence. This last paragraph served as a catchall to punish anyone openly refusing to serve in the military or encouraging others to do so; undermining the military effort and public support of that effort; persuading soldiers on leave and those liable to conscription to desert, becoming absent without leave, or failing to report for muster; mutilating oneself or others in order to evade service; and evading service through deception.[32]

The array of charges that could be levied against members of the military was vast, encompassing civil code violations, military offenses, and the special wartime laws encapsulated in the KSSVO. The military justice system enforced these laws upon a significant portion of the German population. In times of peace, military authorities and courts levied charges, tried, and enforced verdicts on active-duty personnel, reservists in duty status, and the civilian bureaucrats (*Beamten*) of the Wehrmacht and its services. During times of war, the scope of those liable to military charges and trials ballooned, encompassing POWs, civilians in combat zones and areas of occupation, foreign officers assigned to German commands, and the broad category of support personnel (*Gefolge*).[33] The latter ranged from nurses to munition workers to translators.[34]

Legality and Reality

The Military Penal Code in effect when Germany launched World War II appears incompatible with the "barbarization of warfare" that ensued.[35] Section Eight of the Military Penal Code, for example, pertained to illegal conduct toward civilians and their possessions during war, specifically forbidding plundering, corpse robbing, and devastating property. The section, however, forbade only unauthorized and individual resort to murder, requisitioning, and arson. It did not rule out the sanctioned use of violence against enemy civilians, the requisitioning of their property, or the ordered, intentional devastation of occupied territories. Imperial German forces had driven the Herero and Nama into the desert during the colonial subjugation of Namibia in 1904–1908, intentionally killing combatants and noncombatants without distinction. German units had burned Louvain in 1914, its High Command had initiated air and naval attacks that violated existing international law in World War I, and the German Army had thoroughly devastated Northern France as it was pushed back toward the Reich's frontiers in 1918.[36] None of those actions was punishable by military law.

Indeed, several scholars have argued that the German military had a predilection for escalation and that the concept of total war predated the Nazi movement. Carl von Clausewitz theorized about absolute and real war in his influential but unfinished study *On War* in the nineteenth century. Its opening chapter brushed aside international law as a self-imposed restriction hardly worth mentioning. Although the study as a whole grappled with the tension among political purpose, control, and escalating violence, by the turn of the nineteenth century most German officers interpreted the work as one advocating unrestrained violence.[37] Erich Ludendorff, the driving force behind German military decision-making during the second half of World War I, argued even after his estrangement from Hitler in the 1920s that Germany needed to embrace the concept of total war.[38] The consensus within the German military was that the military penal code had one purpose, that of maintaining discipline, order, and obedience. Section Eight's prohibition against plundering, robbing the dead, and wanton killing of civilians was intended to prevent soldiers from taking matters into their own hands. It was not conceived to protect noncombatants, but rather to prevent any unsanctioned, individual resort to theft, violence, and murder.

Hitler made it quite clear to the Wehrmacht's leaders as they prepared for war against Poland in 1939 that he envisioned the campaign as one directed against the Polish people as a whole. Speaking to his top generals on August 22, he declared:

> Our strength lies in our speed and our brutality. Genghis Khan hunted millions of women and children to their deaths, consciously and with a joyous heart.... I have issued a command—and I will have everyone who utters even a single word of criticism shot—that the aim of the war lies not in reaching particular lines but in the physical annihilation of the enemy. Thus, so far only in the east, I have put my Death's Head formations at the ready with the command to send man, woman, and child of Polish descent and language to their deaths, pitilessly and remorselessly... Poland will be depopulated and settled with Germans.[39]

The Polish campaign resulted in an estimated 70,000 Polish military deaths, an additional 133,000 military casualties, and the surrender of 700,000 Polish troops to the Wehrmacht. An additional 50,000 Poles died fighting the Russians, with perhaps 300,000 captured.[40] Poland's travails had only begun. In the area occupied by the Germans, German militias under the authority of the SS slaughtered an estimated 65,000 Poles and Jews in the first months of occupation following Poland's surrender.[41]

Hitler also sent five task groups, later increased to seven, to implement his vision of transforming parts of conquered Poland into settlement areas incorporated into the Reich, while leaving a portion of the former state as a dumping ground for undesirables. These *Einsatzgruppen*, formally charged with suppressing resistance, engaged in an unprecedented campaign of mass killings, ethnic cleansing, and theft targeting Jews and the Polish intelligentsia. While operationally independent of the German military, the Wehrmacht was charged with supporting them logistically and in some instances participated in executions, expulsions, and the seizure of property. The commander of the German Army was sufficiently alarmed by reports of unauthorized measures by army units that he condemned the disturbing number of cases of "illegal expulsion, forbidden confiscation, self-enrichment, misappropriation and theft... [and] rape of married women."[42] A few German commanders threatened to court-martial SS men who were conducting what they assumed were unauthorized mass shootings, only to discover that Hitler interceded to protect his killers.

General Johannes Blaskowitz, appointed as commander in chief of the East, wrote a number of memoranda protesting the mass killings of Jews and warning that these executions were undermining army morale and creating tension between the military and the SS. His protest reached Hitler personally, who raged that Blaskowitz should be relieved of command for his childish notion that one should wage war using "Salvation Army techniques."[43] Blaskowitz's superior failed to support his protests, and Hitler, irritated by his objections, signed an order in October 1939 specifying that SS and police personnel, even when operating in areas under military command, should be tried by their own courts rather than military tribunals. Blaskowitz was not punished for protesting the "crimes being committed in Poland by members of the Reich and representatives of its state authority," which made soldiers "disgusted and repelled."[44] But he was transferred to another command in May 1940 and was one of the few German generals among his peers who was not promoted subsequently.[45] General Georg von Küchler, who had earlier expressed reservations about mass executions in northeastern Poland, came around to the desired position by July 1940. He instructed his men to refrain from criticizing measures directed against the Jews, the Poles, and the Church in the General Government area of Poland.

He noted that Germany was in the midst of a racial struggle that had been going on for centuries, and he told his men that this struggle required "tough measures."[46]

If any German commanders retained lingering ideas about using the penal code to insulate the Wehrmacht from the murderous actions of *Einsatzgruppen* operating behind the front, or to punish members of the military who directly engaged in mass killings, theft, and war crimes, three orders in the spring of 1941 made it crystal clear that these measures had the regime's full backing as it prepared to attack the Soviet Union. On May 13, 1941, the Führer signed a decree that explicitly protected soldiers from being prosecuted in military courts for crimes against enemy civilians. "Punishable offenses committed against enemy civilians do not, until further notice, come any more under the jurisdiction of the courts-martial and the summary courts-martial."[47]

Six days later, the Führer signed a more expansive order pertaining to the conduct of troops during the coming war in Russia. The guidelines, distributed down to the company level on the eve of attack, asserted that "this war demands ruthless and aggressive action against Bolshevik agitators, snipers, saboteurs, and Jews, and the complete elimination of both active and passive resistance."[48] As one of the best studies of the Wehrmacht's role in the Holocaust lays bare, the Wehrmacht had become deeply complicit in murdering unarmed Jews—men, women, and children—using the mental construct that all Jews were Bolshevik, all Bolshevik were partisans, and therefore all Jews were partisans.[49] The infamous *Einsatzgruppen*, under direction of Heinrich Himmler and Reinhard Heydrich's Reich Main Security Office, killed more than 1.3 million Jews and 700,000 other enemy civilians between 1941 and 1945. The Wehrmacht killed untold numbers of civilians during antipartisan sweeps in Belarus, Russia, and the Ukraine.

A third order, usually referred to as the Commissar Order, provided additional instructions that ran counter to international law. The Guidelines for the Treatment of Political Commissars directed that all captured political commissars were to be shot immediately by front-line units, or if captured in the rear, turned over to the security services for execution. German officers and soldiers continued to talk of honor, comradeship, and loyalty even as the Wehrmacht prepared to launch a massive attack that anticipated killing prisoners, slaughtering Jews, and creating *Lebensraum* by starving millions.

The Wehrmacht's Military Penal Code included provisions that made the murder of civilians, the seizure of property, and other crimes punishable by court-martial. But step by step, new special regulations removed punishments for murder, theft, and the humiliation of enemy noncombatants while simultaneously increasing the penalties for opposing the regime openly. The Führer directives of May 1941 made clear that war crimes and mass murder were guiding principles for how the army would fight its war in the East, rather than aberrations or the consequence of bitter fighting. An individual soldier might opt out of shooting civilians and a few officers might write memos objecting to German policies related to the treatment of Jews and Poles without punishment. But order and discipline were to be maintained at all costs, and those who refused to conform were crushed by a military justice system designed to stifle dissent and ensure that the military supported Hitler, the Nazi regime, and its ideological agenda to the bitter end.

The Military Justice Apparatus

The Weimar Republic had dissolved the entire military justice apparatus, and it was only in 1933/1934 that the German military began to reassemble a core group of trained jurists. The total number of judge advocates (military jurists) in the Army, Navy, and Reich Ministry of War consequently consisted of no more than a few dozen jurists in 1934, ballooning in number as Germany rushed to expand its military (renamed the *Wehrmacht* in 1935), which now included an air force (Germany had been prohibited an air force by the terms of the Versailles Treaty). Hitler formally reestablished a German air force in February 1935, announcing its existence the following month.[50] Each service established a legal division within its general administrative department, the Army under the General Army Office (*Allgemeines Heeres-Amt*), the Navy under the General Navy Department (*Allgemeines Marineamt*), and the Air Force under its Central Office (*Zentralamt*).[51] The service departments recruited, trained, and provided judge advocates to their respective service commands, with the Armed Forces Judge Advocate General (the *Wehrmachtrechtabteilung* [WR]) initially focused on drafting revisions to the military code and providing overall guidance on how to interpret the code and court-martial regulations.

The majority of judge advocates were assigned to standing military courts established at various levels. Judge advocates performed duties ranging from investigating officer to defense attorney to prosecutor to court-martial judge. In 1938, the German Army had eighty-two military courts: two for border troops, seven for headquarters units, one at the brigade level, fifty-four divisional courts, and eighteen appeal courts established at the corps level. By November 1942, the number of army courts had risen to 742. This was in part due to increase in the size of the German Army which by then had three times as many divisions as it had in 1938 but also due to the establishment of military courts in occupied Greece, France, Eastern Europe, and elsewhere. If one adds to this an estimated 200–300 naval and air force courts, the number of German military courts exceeded 1,000 by 1943/1944.[52] Between 2,500 and 2,800 military jurists manned the machinery of military law. If one includes other jurists who served stints in the military legal apparatus at some point and jurists who retired, the number of jurists who cycled through the military justice system was considerably higher. They were all male.[53]

At the height of World War II, the German Army was more than three times as large as the German Air Force and six times as large as the German Navy.[54] The German Army consisted of the *Feldheer* (the operational Army) and the *Ersatzheer* (the replacement Army), along with personnel assigned to training commands, schools, or recovering from injuries. The *Feldheer* represented the German Army's fighting force, with the Replacement Army tasked with conscripting, training, and replenishing the fighting forces. Soldiers who deserted at the front were typically tried by courts-martial appointed by the division to which they were assigned, but if the suspect could not be apprehended or had deserted while in Germany on leave, in training, or for medical treatment and recuperation, he was tried by a court-martial convened by the commander of the designated military district (*Wehrkreis*) associated with the unit's reserve unit. The head of the replacement army was the sentencing authority (*Gerichtsherr*), confirming or rejecting the recommendations of military courts operating under his command. The German Air Force's Air Districts (*Luftgaue*) paralleled the Army's military districts geographically and served roughly the same functions. The German Navy had a distinctly different organizational structure, but those who deserted could likewise be certain that regional commands and naval district commanders were ready to try those who deserted while

Military District	Main Court	Secondary Courts
I (East Prussia, Memel, Bialystok)	Königsberg	Insterburg, Allenstein, Elbing
II (Mecklenburg, Pomerania)	Stettin	Schwerin, Köslin
III (Brandenburg, part of Neumark)	Potsdam	Frankfurt (Oder), Cottbus
IV (Saxony, Thuringia, northern Bohemia)	Dresden	Leipzig, Chemnitz
V (Württemberg, part of Baden, Alsace)	Stuttgart	Ulm, Ludwigsburg
VI (Westphalia, Rhineland, Eupen-Malmedy)	Münster	Bielefeld, Cologne, Wuppertal
VII (southern Bavaria)	Munich	Augsburg, Garmisch-Partenkirchen
VIII (Silesia, Sudentenland, part of Poland)	Neuhammer am Queis	Breslau, Oppeln, Liegnitz, Neiße
IX (parts of Thuringia, Hesse)	Kassel	Frankfurt a.M., Erfurt, Gießen, Gera, Jena, Weimar
X (Hamburg, Schleswig-Holstein, parts of Hanover & southern Denmark)	Hamburg	Bremen, Lübeck
XI (Braunschweig, Anhalt, Magdeburg)	Hannover	Magdeburg, Braunschweig
XII (Palatinate, Saar, Lorraine, Luxembourg)	Wiesbaden/Mainz	Koblenz, Mannheim
XIII (northern Bavaria, western Bohemia)	Nürnberg	Regensburg, Würzburg
XVII (parts of Austria, southern Bohemia, Moravia)	Vienna	Karlsbad, Linz
XVIII (Styria, Tyrol, Carinthia, northern Slovenia)	Salzburg, Berlin	Innsbruck, Graz

Figure 5. Military courts of the Reserve Army, August 1939

on leave, convalescing, or assigned to training programs in the Reich. Figure 5 lists the main and secondary army courts located in the Reich.[55] If one adds the hundreds of courts located at the divisional level at the front and in occupied territories, and the navy and air force's many courts, one gets a sense of the density of the judicial network designed to uphold discipline, punish offenders, and deter those who might contemplate desertion or engage in subversion.

The Military Court System

The Imperial German Army and Navy had vehemently resisted the idea of a military judiciary operating independently of the military chain of command, claiming that disciplinary matters fell under the purview of the commanding officer. The Prussian and Imperial German system was structured so that commanding officers controlled the process. Military jurists were primarily there to advise and assist the commander in enforcing military and civil law. Commanding generals did not intervene directly in court-martial proceedings, but their influence was tremendous in that they appointed the military judges, investigating officers, and prosecutors. In capital cases, the defendant had the right to a defense counsel. These defense attorneys usually came from the same pool of military jurists as the investigators, prosecutors, and legal advisers assigned to the command. In certain cases, defendants could draw on the service of a civilian defense attorney, but this was at the discretion of the court and limited to cases tried in Germany.[56]

The notion that the commanding general controlled and steered the military justice system was not peculiar to the German military. Under the Articles of War that guided the American military until the introduction of the Unified Code of Military Justice after World War II, the commanding officer likewise controlled the administration of justice within his command. William Tecumseh Sherman, commanding general of the Army, was skeptical of efforts to civilianize military justice. Speaking to a congressional committee in 1879, he cautioned that

> it will be a grave error if by negligence we permit the military law to become emasculated by allowing lawyers to inject into it the principles derived from their practice in the civil courts, which belong to a totally different system of jurisprudence. The object of the civil law is to secure to every human being in a community all the liberty, security, and happiness possible, consistent with the safety of all. The object of military law is to govern armies composed of strong men, so as to be capable of exercising the largest measure of force at the will of the nation. These objects are as wide apart as the poles, and each requires its own separate system of laws, statute and common. An army is a collection of armed men obliged to obey one man. Every enactment, every change of rules which impairs the principle weakens the army, impairs its values, and defeats the very object

> of its existence. All the traditions of civil lawyers are antagonistic to this vital principle, and military men must meet them on the threshold of discussion, else armies will become demoralized by engrafting on our code their deductions from civil practice.[57]

This sentiment endured in the US military well into the twentieth century, with command influence part of the system. Only after World War II, which exposed more than 13 million US citizens to military service, was the system reformed to provide substantial protection for those who serve. Under the Uniform Code of Military Justice, passed in 1950, US military commanders still retain important prerogatives, including the right to convene courts-martial, to decide what charges to pursue, and to select the jury. They do not appoint the military judge, however, and in contrast to the Wehrmacht, US commanders do not have the right to reject findings of innocence or order new trials in order to increase sentences.[58] During World War II, both American and German officers believed that the commander was ultimately responsible for maintaining order and discipline, and asserted that military law served a different purpose than civil law. But the number of death sentences underlines how radically different the systems were in their interpretation of disciplinary codes. Under the Articles of War, the US military conducted over 2 million courts-martial during World War II and executed 146 US servicemen. The German military conducted fewer courts-martial but executed somewhere between 18,000 and 22,000 of its own.[59]

In the Wehrmacht, the commanding general or admiral played a more important role than did military lawyers and judges. The commanding general (the *Gerichtsherr*) initiated formal investigations, convened the courts-martial, appointed its members, and gave overall guidance. Prosecuting attorneys were bound to follow the commanding general's guidance as related to the charges and punishment they pursued, as the commander of U-boats sharply reminded his subordinates in 1944.[60] Most importantly, the court's verdict and sentence took effect only after the commanding general approved them.[61] If a commander had doubts about the verdict or disagreed with the recommended sentence, he could reject them and order a new trial. The court's verdict and sentence, in short, were only advisory. The commanding general transformed the court's advice into a judgment.

Field courts-martial consisted of three military justices, the prosecutor, and in the case of death penalties, a defendant's counsel. The panel of three justices was headed by a military jurist and included two military members without legal training. Both were appointed by the commanding general who convened the court-martial, with one required to be an officer and the other either an officer or enlisted depending on the defendant's status. Since most cases involved enlisted men, this meant that field courts-martial usually included an enlisted man among the justices, though regulations later specified that the enlisted court member should be a noncommissioned officer—that is, a sergeant or petty officer and above. The *Reichskriegsgericht*, the highest military tribunal, initially had two sitting chambers, which increased to four over the course of time. Each chamber (*Senate*) consisted of five justices, two from the judge advocates corps and three from the officer ranks. The judge advocates needed to be experienced jurists, and the three military justices had to be colonels and above. Adolf Hitler, as commander of the German military, appointed the members of the *Reichskriegsgericht*.[62] A German admiral, Max Bastian, served as its president for most of World War II.

Judge advocates had civilian titles and were officials (*Beamten*) rather than military officers throughout the 1930s and up to the last year of World War II. In May 1944, they were awarded military rank and titles, with an *Oberstkriegsgerichtsrat* (Senior Court Martial Counsel), for example, becoming an *Oberstrichter* (Colonel Judge).[63] The panel of judges made its recommendation based on majority opinion. The accused's rights were limited to being heard and entering a final word at the end of the proceedings.

In capital cases, the courts-martial verdict and sentence were reviewed by a staff judge advocate, with the reviewer providing his own recommendation to the commanding general as to whether to approve or reject the court's verdict and sentence. These outside reviews played a critical role, as the Hampel, Hanow, and Kanzenbach cases showed. Before August 1939, Adolf Hitler, as commander of the armed forces, was responsible for reviewing and confirming death sentences levied against German officers and officer-grade Wehrmacht civilians. As the ultimate *Gerichtsherr*, he could reject recommended verdicts and sentences, order retrials, or could accept verdicts and reduce sentences. The Order Imposing Wartime Criminal Procedures (the KStVO) did away with the right to appeal. Commanding generals were delegated authority to confirm capital verdicts. The defendant had no right of appeal, though he or she could submit a plea for mercy and reduction of the sentence. The German Navy, noting that deterrent effect of the death penalty diminished if there was lengthy time lapse between sentencing and execution, specified no more than three weeks should elapse between the two. In "normal cases," the Naval High Command directed that once the commanding general had confirmed a capital verdict, the condemned should be executed within three days.[64]

Neither the German military code, court procedures, nor the intrusive role of commander (the *Gerichtsherr*) explains why Wehrmacht jurists acted so much more harshly than they and their predecessors had in World War I. To understand why the Wehrmacht treated deserters and subverters as threats, one must turn to how it explained Germany's defeat in 1918. Rather than admit that Germany had been defeated militarily in 1918, Wehrmacht leaders, veteran associations, nationalist politicians, völkisch groups, and the Nazi Party claimed that Germany had been stabbed in the back by Jews, Bolsheviks, democrats, and others who had encouraged desertion in the military and revolution at home.

3
Deadly Blend
Lessons Learned and Nazi Ideology

The Treaty of Versailles that ended World War I allowed Germany to retain a 100,000-strong army and a small navy, though it prohibited Germany from having an air force. Conscription was abolished, as was the German General Staff. Both officers and enlisted men were obliged to serve long term in order to prevent schemes designed to create a reserve cadre by cycling short-term volunteers through military schools and training courses. The leaders of the post–World War I German Army (the *Reichswehr*) and Navy (the *Reichsmarine*), forced to drastically reduce their personnel rolls, carefully evaluated the military skills and records of those who wanted to stay in the military as Germany demobilized. They sought to retain a spectrum of expertise but also used the imposed reduction to screen out officers and enlisted personnel whose social and political viewpoints appeared suspect to them. As a result, the Weimar Republic's military, far from incorporating the democratic and progressive values of the republic, reflected nationalist sentiments hostile to the parliamentary system. Its officers and noncommissioned officers deplored the November revolution that had brought down the monarchy, and embraced the notion that Germany had lost the war because it had been stabbed in the back by Bolsheviks, democrats, Jews, and military deserters.

The Stab-in-the-Back Narrative

The fiction that Germany had not lost the war at the front, but that its fighting forces had been stabbed in the back, emerged even as German armies were being pushed back toward the Reich's borders in October/November 1918. The reality was quite different. General Erich Ludendorff, more than anyone else, had been responsible for the disastrous decision to stake everything on a series of major German offensives on the Western Front.

Launched on March 21, 1918, the initial offensive (Operation Michael) broke through British lines, inflicted major losses on the British 5th Army, and pushed the front in the Somme region some sixty kilometers to the West. Follow-up offensives in April, May, and June succeeded in pushing the front farther to the West, but at tremendous cost. The German offensives of spring 1918 cost the Germans nearly 1 million men, including 125,000 dead and 100,000 missing, with elite formations suffering the highest losses.[1] Entente casualties were even higher, but they could be replaced. By mid-June, over 200,000 American troops were landing in France each month. In July, the French launched a major counteroffensive. In August, the British 4th Army, spearheaded by the Australian and Canadian Corps, attacked German positions in the Amiens sector. Ludendorff would later recall that August 8 was a "black day" for the German Army, acknowledging at the time that six or seven divisions had been completely broken. Inquiring what had happened, he received reports that whole units had surrendered to individual enemy soldiers and that fresh units going up to the line had been berated by those retreated. Even more worrying to the general, he recalled, was that German officers "in many places had lost their influence and allowed themselves to be swept along with the rest."[2]

German military morale had been high at the start of 1918's spring offensive, when Germany had been able to muster a numerical superiority on the Western Front for the first time since 1914. But once it became clear that Germany was able to push back Western forces at great cost but unable to force them to the peace table, German morale began to plummet. By April, Colonel von Lenz of the 6th Army was reporting that "The troops are not attacking, in spite of orders."[3] As Allied offensives drove German forces backward in the summer and fall, it became increasingly clear that German troops were tired of sacrificing themselves to regain lost positions. Ludwig Beck, then a major in Crown Prince Wilhelm's Army Group, wrote home that German troops "did not hold anymore" because they simply did not want to. Ludendorff later asserted that

> loss by desertion was uncommonly high. The number that got into neutral countries, e.g., Holland—ran into tens of thousands, and a far greater number lived happily at home, tacitly tolerated by their fellow-citizens and completely unmolested by the authorities. They and the skrimshankers at the front, of whom there were thousands more, reduced the battle strength of the fighting troops, especially of the infantry, to which

most of them belonged, to a vital degree. If these men had been got hold of, the recruiting difficulty would not have been so great.[4]

By fall 1918, units heading to the Western Front could expect that 20 percent of their men would not arrive at their forward positions. The influenza epidemic hit the German Army full force in the summer of 1918, so a number of those missing had fallen ill. If one counts those who overstayed home leave, stretched out convalescence, misplaced necessary paperwork or equipment, and deserted in addition to those genuinely sick, between 200,000 and 1.5 million soldiers may have been avoiding duty at the front, leading German military historian Wilhelm Deist to characterize this development as a covert military "strike" aimed at forcing an end to the war.[5] A more recent study by British military historian Alexander Watson takes issue with this assessment, claiming that the number of "shirkers" and deserters milling about in the rear has been greatly overinflated, and that most of the German missing were soldiers captured by Allied forces. Watson concedes that between 130,000 and 180,000 German troops deserted from troop trains in the last months of the war. He correctly points out that far more Germans surrendered to the Allies (~385,000 German soldiers) than deserted to the rear, contending that they did so because of exhaustion, disillusionment, and the recognition that Allied military superiority made defeat inevitable. Whole units began to surrender by October 1918, with officers tolerating and even facilitating these surrenders.[6]

Rather than admit that Germany had blundered in opting for war in 1914, miscalculated the costs and benefits of resuming unrestricted submarine warfare in 1917, and gambled on a military solution that was beyond Germany's capabilities in spring 1918, German nationalists preferred to blame domestic enemies for Germany's defeat. Ludendorff, who on September 29 had demanded that the government seek an immediate armistice, would later claim that the German military could have fought on for months, forcing the Allies to grant Germany more generous terms. He took no responsibility for creating the crisis that beset the German military after his spring offensives had failed, and instead claimed that the Army had been the victim of a "secret, planned, demagogic campaign" by Bolsheviks, Socialists, democrats, Jews, and assorted November criminals who had stabbed it in the back.[7] William II, writing from his refuge in the Netherlands after the war, echoed the sentiment: "after four and a half brilliant years of war with unprecedented victories, it [the German Army] was forced to collapse by the stab-in-the-back from the dagger of the revolutionist, at the very moment when peace was within reach!"[8]

Ludendorff was dismissed by the Kaiser in September 1918, absconded to Sweden, and upon his return to Germany engaged in efforts to overthrow the Weimar Republic. In 1920, he supported a coup attempt orchestrated by Berlin's military commander Walther von Lüttwitz, monarchist Wolfgang Kapp, and the leader of a Freikorps unit located outside Berlin. It failed spectacularly, though General Hans von Seeckt, head of the renamed General Staff, refused to confront the putschists, claiming that "German troops do not fire on German troops."[9] Immersing himself in anti-republican and völkisch circles, Lüdendorff again sought to overthrow the republic in 1923, marching side by side with Adolf Hitler and assorted SA men, party members, and anti-republicans as they headed toward the Bavarian Defense Ministry during the so-called Beer Hall Putsch that November. Ludendorff's vocal denunciations of the Weimar Republic, his active support for the coup attempts of 1920 and 1923, and his close associations with völkisch and paramilitary organizations created a growing rift between him and the Reichswehr. But his claims that the German Army of World War I had been stabbed in the back resonated within the Weimar military establishment and were repeated by the German National People's Party (DNVP), Freikorp formations, völkisch groups, and the 500,000 strong Stahlhelm.[10] The *Dolchstoßlegende* became a stable of the so-called national opposition, a spectrum much broader than the Nazi Party in the early 1920s.

Ludendorff's comments about the German military justice system in World War I bear repeating because they were written in 1919, well before his association with Hitler. That many other nationalist officers shared his conviction that the German military justice system in World War I had let them down is apparent in letters, journal articles, and the manipulation of postwar histories.[11] In *My War Memories*, written in Sweden between November 1918 and February 1919, Ludendorff recalled that discipline became an issue during Germany's final offensives, when many soldiers diverted their attention from driving onward to search houses and farms for food and alcohol.

> This impaired our chances of success and showed poor discipline. But it was equally serious that both our young company commanders and our senior officers did not feel strong enough to take disciplinary action, and exercise enough authority to enable them to lead their men forward

> without delay. The absence of our old peace-trained corps of officers was most severely felt. They had been the repository of the moral strength of the Army. In addition, during the first half of the war the Reichstag had made the penal laws more lenient. The commanders responsible for maintaining discipline were deprived of their most effective punishment, in that a sentence of "close arrest" no longer involved being tied up to a fixed object. No doubt this punishment was extraordinarily severe, and its execution should not be left to the juvenile and inexperienced company commanders, but to abolish it altogether was fatal. The mitigation may have been justifiable at the time, but now it proved disastrous. The frequent declarations of amnesty also had a bad influence on the men. The Entente no doubt achieved more than we did with their considerably more severe punishments. This historic fact is well established.
>
> Other evils in connection with the administration of justice were also due to the long war. The judges had come to regard military offenses with a leniency which was often incomprehensible. A contributory cause of this was that the cases which had occurred at the front were not dealt with immediately by the unit, but further in rear [sic] in quite different circumstances and after a certain time had elapsed. It should always have been remembered that there were many men in the Army who deserved no mercy whatever; of this the numerous deserters and skrimshankers are a melancholy proof. These people required severe punishment; that was demanded by the distress of our country, but also by consideration for those who were well conducted and brave.[12]

The Weimar Republic dissolved the entire military justice apparatus in the early 1920s, and it was only after Hitler's ascent to power that the German military began to reassemble a core group of trained jurists. They drew from a judiciary staffed by nationalists deeply hostile to the left and favorably disposed to the right. Both veteran jurists from World War I and younger lawyers trained in the Weimar era internalized nationalist claims that Germany had been stabbed in the back in 1918, and they concluded that Imperial Germany's military judicial system had been too lenient in its treatment of deserters, malcontents, and "shirkers." They were determined to learn from the mistakes of World War I, stifle unrest in its embryonic stage, and prioritize discipline and support for the war over individual rights and justice. Heinrich Dietz, the editor of the *Zeitschrift für Wehrrecht*, hammered home these supposed lessons in the leading journal of the judge advocate community.[13] Erich Schwinge, a professor of law at Marburg University who wrote the definitive commentary on Germany's Military Penal Code, made the same point, reminding his readers that "It is now established that that during the World War the German lawgivers did not counter the forces of disintegration with the energy and ruthlessness required by the seriousness of the hour."[14] Hans Bockelberg, a senior military judge, reminded his subordinates at the outbreak of World War II that

> We should not forget that the army was stabbed in the back in the last war, leading to the war's unfortunate outcome. This fact clearly underlines the importance of our assignment, and gives direction to our work [...] The required goal we seek can only be achieved by swift and sharp justice. Secondary concerns and legalistic quibbling need to be avoided at all costs. Don't be distracted by minutia.[15]

References to the experience of World War I continually crop up in court-martial records and psychological evaluations pertaining to Wehrmacht deserters, employing the same terms Hitler and the party used—such as "November criminals," "community parasites," and weaklings. To interpret this sort of rhetoric as incursions of Nazi coarseness into a conservative and legalistic enclave is incorrect. The Wehrmacht's military justice system was not radicalized because of National Socialism. Rather, it came to embrace National Socialist terms because the lessons military jurists learned from World War I were congruent with the lessons party stalwarts propagated. They reflected attitudes and conclusions they had formed independently.[16]

The Navy and the Trauma of Mutiny

The leaders of the Weimar Republic's Navy, renamed the *Kriegsmarine* in 1935, were particularly sensitive to charges that they had been lax in dealing with protests and mutiny in World War I. They were determined that the Third Reich's *Kriegsmarine* would nip dissent and desertion in the bud, and that Germany's Navy would be loyal to the Führer to the bitter end. The German naval officer corps had been deeply traumatized by the mutiny of the High Seas Fleet on November 3, 1918, and the subsequent popular revolt that swept aside the German monarchy on November 9. Discontent in the High Seas Fleet had been mounting since early 1917, as highly motivated younger officers and men volunteered for service in the U-boat service while frustration over rations, inactivity, and drill grew in the fleet. In August 1917, frustration had boiled over on the battleship *Prinzregent Luitpold* as 350 members left the ship and staged a demonstration in Wilhelmshaven. The incident had been contained, and two of the ringleaders were executed to set an example.[17] The Chief of the High Sea Fleet assured Berlin that order had been restored, warned his naval commander to look out for socialist agitators, and transferred enlisted sailors suspected of "unreliable political convictions" to the naval infantry units in Flanders.[18] The Imperial Navy embraced "patriotic instruction" on board ships and naval bases that ran counter to the sentiments of the Reichstag's July 1917 peace resolution. It asserted that the left wing of the Socialist Party, the Independent Socialists (USPD), had instigated the August mutiny, and downplayed its own responsibility for discontent on board its idle battleships. The Imperial Navy's open support of Heinrich Claß's Pan-German and anti-Semitic Fatherland Party, its efforts to have USPD parliamentarians expelled from the Reichstag, and its successful effort to create a naval equivalent to Hindenburg and Ludendorff's Supreme Army Command demonstrated an intensifying hostility toward parliament. The November 1918 naval mutiny and the revolution that ensued magnified an already pervasive antipathy among its officers toward the left, parliamentarianism, and pacifism.

The imperial naval command had only itself to blame for the November 1918 mutiny. On October 24, 1918, while a new German government was in the midst of negotiating armistice terms and after the U-boat campaign had been suspended, the naval command hatched a plan to launch the High Seas Fleet into the North Sea to attack the British fleet.[19] It was a desperate gamble, as the British Grand Fleet had been reinforced by five American battleships, had remedied various weaknesses made apparent during the Battle of Jutland, had a 2-1 advantage over the Germans in terms of firepower, and was eager for action. When German sailors in Wilhelmshaven received word to prepare their ships for a sortie on October 29, they simply refused to do so.[20] They feared that their naval commanders intended to send them on a glorious death ride that placed more value on the reputation of the navy than on their lives. Many doubted that the government had authorized the sortie, an apprehension that proved well-founded. When the admiral in charge of the III. Battle Squadron rounded up forty-seven ringleaders as the squadron returned to Kiel following cancellation of the sortie, the situation spun out of the navy's control. Arriving back in Kiel, hundreds of sailors mutinied and refused to follow orders. Mutinous sailors raised the red flag on the battleships *Thüringen*, *Helgoland*, and *Friedrich der Grosse*.[21] By November 3, the mutiny had become a revolution as sailors joined workers in protesting for peace. Worker, sailor, and soldier councils proliferated. The independent and mainstream socialist parties (USPD and SPD), along with Germany's communist party (KPD), vied for leadership of what had now become a revolution. The Reichsmarine and Kriegsmarine had an institutional imperative to embrace the notion that Bolsheviks, Jews, socialists, and democrats had unleashed the revolution. Its officer veterans bent over backwards to blame leftists in the Imperial Navy's enlisted ranks for the mutiny that sparked the revolution. They glossed over the fact that the Imperial Navy's High Command had planned a reckless fleet sortie behind the back of the German government.[22] As an outsider observed in 1925, the mutiny in Wilhelmshaven on October 30

> was preceded by scattered instances of insubordination to some of which political intent was ascribed. Yet the situation was peculiar. Peace negotiations were under way; the abdication of the Kaiser had been demanded; and still the men were ordered to get ready for a sudden sortie which was virtual suicide. Therefore they had a certain right to assume that their own commanders were guilty of insubordination, and could justify their conduct accordingly.[23]

This outside observer happened to be Adolf Hitler, and this recollection was published in *Mein Kampf*. Describing his own experience during the revolution, Hitler recalled that he had been convalescing in the military hospital in Pasewalk when one day, "suddenly and without warning.... Sailors arrived on trucks and called out for the Revolution." The German Navy could take comfort that Hitler ended his personal narrative of Imperial Germany's final days with a grudging admission that "the navy had done its duty for four years" and that the sailors' resistance to a "romantic and desperate maneuver" did not cause the November revolution.[24] Hitler, like Ludendorff, attributed Germany's defeat to Bolsheviks, Jews, and democrats who had stabbed it in the back. German naval commanders, whether traditional nationalists like Grand Admiral Erich Raeder or fervid admirers of the Führer like Grand Admiral Karl Dönitz, were all too eager to latch on to this explanation as well, as it absolved their former commanders of responsibility for reckless orders that contributed to mutiny and then revolution. In response to the Reichstag's Committee of Inquiry examining the causes of the German collapse in 1918, the Navy's representative Lieutenant Commander Wilhelm Canaris—later to become chief of the Wehrmacht's intelligence branch—fended off charges that the naval officer corps bore responsibility for the mutiny. He claimed that the fleet had been inwardly sound and that outside forces had stoked mutiny and revolution.[25]

Martin Niemöller, best known as one of the founders of the Confessing Church opposed to the Nazification of the mainstream Protestant church, had been a U-boat commander in World War I. Like so many other veterans and nationalists, he characterized the discord leading to overthrow of the Hohenzollern monarchy in 1918 as a crime.[26] With few exceptions, the German naval officer corps, both retired and active duty, greeted Hitler's appointment to the chancellorship with enthusiasm. Raeder heaped praise on the new "government of the national revolution" at the launching to the pocket battleship (Panzerschiff) *Admiral Scheer* in April 1933.[27] Raeder and the naval officer corps were determined to demonstrate loyalty to the new regime and to ensure discipline in the ranks. German naval courts would be harsher in their sentences and convictions in World War II than their army and air force equivalents.[28] Dissent, insubordination, and desertion would be squelched from the outset to avoid any repeat of October-November 1918. One navy judge made the connection explicit, explaining that "In determining the punishment I take into account whether the defendant could be considered a revolutionary type or not. I make sure that 1918 will not be repeated. I exterminate revolutionary types."[29]

After World War II, most Kriegsmarine veterans would bend over backward to depict the Third Reich's navy as an enclave averse to National Socialist worldviews. They would claim that the navy's ethos centered on seamanship, maritime expertise, and comradeship, and that it was more worldly and tolerant than Germany's other military services. The former may have been true; the latter was not.[30] The incidents in which the navy and the party came into conflict were rare and isolated. Grand Admiral Erich Raeder, who led the navy from 1928 through 1942, emphasized professional competence and discouraged political activity. This approach led to minimal friction with the party. This "nonpolitical" attitude within the Kriegsmarine, however, did not represent alienation from or disagreement with the regime, but was a holdover from the republican and imperial eras when the "nonpolitical" nature of service in the military had thwarted democratic, socialist, and communist penetration.

Raeder's successor, Karl Dönitz, abandoned the pretense that service in the navy precluded open support of the Nazi Party. At a conference for Kriegsmarine commanders in Weimar on December 17, 1943, Dönitz clarified his position, explaining that "It is nonsense to claim that a soldier or officer should be non-political. The soldier represents the state in which he lives; he is its most pronounced exponent. Therefore he must support it with heart and soul."[31] Dönitz hammered home his approval of Hitler and the regime in numerous speeches and comments throughout his tenure as Chief of the German Navy. His lecture to cadets at the Marineschule in Flensburg-Mürwik in January 1944, for example, included the admonition that "The German people owe everything, simply everything, to the Führer. Germany would be completely depopulated today if he had not been bestowed upon us."[32]

Grand Admiral Karl Dönitz was not alone in his high esteem of Hitler and his adoption of Nazi rhetoric. Postwar memoirs and naval histories have generally portrayed Dönitz as an aberration, stressing that most Kriegsmarine officers were apolitical and that few were members of the Nazi Party. Party membership, however, is a poor measure for ascertaining the penetration of National Socialist ideology within the navy, for German law forbade active-duty military personnel from joining the party or its affiliates. The Wehrgesetz [military law] of 1935 specified in paragraph 26 that "Soldiers may not be politically active. Membership in the NSDAP, its branches, and affiliated organizations becomes inactive for the period of active military service." This law was changed only in the aftermath of the failed assassination attempt on Hitler in July 1944, and the subsequent politicization and radicalization of German society and the Wehrmacht.

The navy proceeded quite ruthlessly against those who "undermined the military spirit" by criticizing the Führer and National Socialism. Kriegsmarine personnel initiated naval judicial proceedings through denunciations and investigations, and subsequent transactions lay exclusively in the hands of naval officers and naval jurists. More than 14,000 naval personnel, the great majority of whom were enlisted personnel, were charged with this offense during the course of the war.[33] While wise officers tolerated a certain amount of grumbling and dealt with most morale problems through nonjudicial channels, the numerous examples in which the death penalty was exacted for this charge show that criticizing the regime could cost a man his life. The following are examples of Kriegsmarine proceedings against those who criticized the regime or the party:

- U-boat commander Oskar Kusch, on patrol in the summer of 1943, made disparaging remarks about Hitler, claimed that the International Jewish conspiracy was a figment of German propaganda, and expressed doubt whether Germany could still win the war. Among the offenses later reported was a joke Kusch posted that asked, "What do the German people have in common with a tape worm? Both are surrounded by brown masses and are in danger of being eliminated." A fellow officer reported these comments upon return to port, resulting in Kusch's court-martial and execution.[34]
- Machinist-mate Artur W., in the presence of several anti-aircraft gunners, saw a picture of Hitler behind a fence and exclaimed, "Thank God that they've finally put that madman behind bars! We can thank him for this war. He wanted it." Artur W. was court-martialed for the comment and sentenced to ten years of imprisonment. The reviewing officer, Adm. Warzecha, felt that the death sentence was appropriate since Artur W. had a previous disciplinary record. A second court-martial sentenced Artur W. to death. Dönitz confirmed the order on May 4, 1945, and the Naval High Command requested verification that it had been carried out on May 9, two days after Germany's unconditional surrender.[35]
- Naval corpsman Norbert Engel privately commented to a nurse that he wished that the July 20, 1944, assassination attempt against Hitler had succeeded. She reported his comments to her husband, a naval lieutenant, who recommended pressing charges for the remark. Despite his youth and exemplary behavior, the naval court-martial authority (Commanding Officer, Netherlands) ruled that he should be sentenced to death for his opinion. Engel managed to escape from prison and find refuge among the Dutch resistance.[36]
- Lieutenant (junior grade) Forstmeier, an outspoken Bavarian, was a battery officer in Hammerfest, Norway, in the fall of 1944. One evening he and two chief petty officers were discussing the war and politics in private. Forstmeier became excited and exclaimed that Hitler was "the greatest criminal of all times," Göring "a charlatan," and

Goebbels a "liar." He pointed out that the war was lost and that "Ivan" was advancing to the West. Both chief petty officers reported the comments of their company commander, and the navy initiated court-martial proceedings. Forstmeier almost certainly would have been sentenced to death but for the quick thinking of a sympathetic naval lawyer who claimed that Forstmeier had merely been testing the political dependability of his chief petty officers. Forstmeier was lucky to get away with a prison sentence.[37]

The German Navy drew upon the lessons of the Great War as they applied to desertion. In February 1942, Vice Admiral Walter Warzecha, chief of the General Navy Department, delivered a long lecture to senior naval jurists. Reminding them that World War I had made it apparent that leadership and military law were mutually supportive, he emphasized to his audience that military proceedings were not about the individual and his motivation. They were about discipline and deterrence, and the outcome affected the organization as a whole. Warzecha instructed the assembled jurists that they were functionaries both of the state, charged with supporting its political directive across the board, and of the military, entrusted with supporting the military struggle. Warzecha cautioned them against ignoring general guidelines and treating specific cases as special. When it came to desertion, Warzecha was firm: every soldier and sailor must know that deserters would be shot, whether they deserted in Norway, the Balkans, or on the Channel coast. Personal factors and family consideration did not mitigate the crime.[38]

Dönitz, who replaced Erich Raeder as commander of the German Navy in January 1943, issued a directive to the troops that sought to ensure that all sailors understood the consequences of desertion. The directive explained:

> Desertion is one of the most disgraceful military crimes, a breach of trust against the Führer, one's comrades, and the homeland. Whoever abandons the flag weakens Germany's military strength and helps the enemy. Desertion by necessity entails other criminal acts. The deserter cannot sustain himself by honest means. Harsh punishment therefore is justified. Based on the sentences I have reviewed, it is apparent that desertion—and its serious consequences—most often springs from the following: homesickness,

> lovesickness, insufficient willingness to subordinate oneself, heavy-handed treatment, and fear of disciplinary or judicial punishment. None of these or similar factors justify leaving one's unit. Desertion does not make one's situation better but rather makes it worse. Apparently this is not clear to everyone.
>
> I therefore order that:
>
> All members of the German Navy, including support personnel, will be instructed on a quarterly basis about what desertion means and what its consequences are. Every individual must clearly understand: desertion will cost you your life. Only an immediate and voluntary return to one's unit within a week allows a milder sentence. Whosoever nonetheless deserts can expect to be pursued relentlessly. I expect military courts to weigh the failure of such untrustworthy weaklings against the willingness of decent soldiers to loyally risk their own lives. I will personally deny any appeals from deserters for clemency.
>
> Berlin, the 27th of April 1943 The Supreme Commander of the Navy
>
> Dönitz[39]

Naval veterans later downplayed the harshness of the Kriegsmarine judicial system and excused Nazi enthusiasts within the ranks of the Germany Navy as naive and ignorant of the nature of the regime they praised. The Kriegsmarine was not an isolated naval community immune to Nazi ideology, unaware of Nazi crimes, and unaffected by the Holocaust, but rather an organization subject to the same influences as other institutions in the Third Reich. In reaction to the experience of 1918, it was particularly vigilant against dissent, desertion, and mutiny. Hitler's selection of Grand Admiral Karl Dönitz as his successor may seem odd given the greater prominence of other contenders, but it reflects his recognition that the navy remained loyal until the bitter end.

A Shared Mindset about Desertion

Historians have offered a number of explanations for the Nazification of the German state and its institutions during the 1930s. While the forceful dissolution of alternative centers of power, ranging from political parties to independent trade unions to municipal governments, played a critical role in the Nazi consolidation of power, Hitler was careful not to challenge the German military directly after becoming chancellor in January 1933. The German military, for its part, welcomed the regime's round-up of communists, the banning of the Communist Party, and dissolution of parliamentary government. It stood by as an estimated 500 to 600 political opponents were killed and over 25,000 detained without trial during the new regime's first year in power.[40] Military leaders eyed the party's paramilitary organization, the *Sturmabteilung* (SA), apprehensively, but the June 1934 execution of its top leaders reassured them that Hitler recognized their exclusive claim to be the nation's only military force.[41] The murder of General Kurt von Schleicher and his close associate Major General Ferdinand von Bredow provoked scattered expressions of outrage, but most senior military leaders rationalized the murder of their former colleagues as the unfortunate consequence of Schleicher's political machinations in the final years of the Weimar Republic. Former colleagues made a point of drinking a toast to their memory, enrolling their names in their regiment's honor roll, and the army's top leaders pressured Hitler to rescind his accusation that Schleicher had been working to overthrow the German government. But the military was generally pleased with decapitation of the SA, interpreting the so-called Night of the Long Knives as an affirmation of the Wehrmacht's primacy.

In August 1934, Defense Minister General Werner von Blomberg suggested revising the oath that German military personnel had previously taken to the constitution (1919–1933 oath) and to the country (December 1933–August 1934 oath).[42] The changed oath would show that the military embraced Hitler's leadership, the *Gleichschaltung* (Nazi takeover) of German institutions, and Hitler's consolidation of the offices of the president and chancellor following President Erich von Hindenburg's death. The new oath, enunciated in the Law on the Allegiance of Civil Servants and Soldiers of the Armed Forces, was not an outside imposition on the military domain but rather an effort on the part of the military to reassure Germany's supreme leader that it no longer viewed itself as an institution separate and above the state as during the Weimar era. Instead, the military was embedded within the Third Reich and supportive of the *Führerprinzip* (leader principle). The changed wording of the oaths taken by those entering the military reflected not a reluctant adjustment to the new regime, but an enthusiastic embrace of its leader and his vision.

Wording of Oath, Weimar Republic, 1919–1933

I swear loyalty to the Reich's constitution and pledge, that I as a courageous soldier will always protect the German Reich and its legal institutions, [and] will be obedient to the Reich President and to my superiors.[43]

Wording of Oath following Enabling Act and suspension of Weimar Constitution, as reworded December 2, 1933[44]

I swear by God this sacred oath, that I will always loyally and honestly serve my people and fatherland, and will be prepared as a brave and obedient soldier to risk my life at any time as pledged.

Wording of Oath following Hindenburg's death and the consolidation of the offices of president and chancellor, August 20, 1934[45]

I swear by God this sacred oath, that I will render unconditional obedience to Adolf Hitler, the Führer of the German Reich and people, supreme commander of the armed forces, and will be ready as a brave soldier to risk my life at any time for this oath.

Blomberg may have embraced the regime more fully than some his subordinates, but studies of the Wehrmacht leadership during the 1930s indicate that most of its officers were favorably disposed to the regime's efforts to create a *Volksgemeinschaft*, to remilitarize, and to cast off Versailles Treaty restrictions. They welcomed efforts to invigorate a martial spirit throughout Germany, and they were far more often in step with Nazi policies than in opposition. Some senior officers later claimed that their sworn oath to Hitler had prevented them from taking action against him, but these very same men had sworn oaths to the Weimar Republic's constitution and its legal institutions. They had been less punctilious about observing their sworn oaths when it came to supporting parliamentary democracy and the rule of law than when it came to supporting Hitler and his new order.[46]

One of the leading authorities on the Nazi era has emphasized how many initiatives originated from below as part of a bureaucratic and institutional competition for power. Party chiefs, ministry officials, and officeholders worked toward the Führer rather than awaiting directives and specific guidance from above.[47] But working toward the Führer obscures another dynamic at work. Many found Hitler an attractive figure not because he mesmerized, misled, and persuaded them of his vision, but because he expressed certain worldviews, perspectives, and prejudices they had formed independently.[48]

Hitler left no doubt where he stood in regard to deserters and military justice. In countless campaign speeches and in his unpublished second book assembled in June–July 1928, Hitler hammered home the ideas he had formed in the early 1920s and expressed in *Mein Kampf*, which he wrote while imprisoned in Landshut in 1924.[49] Hitler's main idea was that world history revolved around a struggle for survival, a racial struggle pitting the Aryan peoples against a world Jewry bent on their destruction. Only by gaining *Lebensraum* (living space) could the Aryan people survive, and *Lebensraum* could be found only in the East. Germany's need for living space meant that it needed to prepare for a future war, where it would forcibly take lands in the East from peoples Hitler viewed as racial inferiors led by Bolsheviks and Jews.

Hitler advocated punishing deserters, shirkers, and revolutionaries in a way that would set an example for all. Expounding on the experience of 1918 in *Mein Kampf*, Hitler asserted:

> If, nevertheless, one wants to make weak, hesitating, or even cowardly fellows do their duty, then there is always only one possibility: the deserter must know that his desertion entails the very thing he tries to escape. At the front, one may die, as a deserter, one must die. Only by such a draconic threat against every attempt at fleeing the colors can a deterrent effect be achieved, not only for the individuals, but also for all.

He continued:

> For the voluntary war hero...no Articles of War were necessary, but for the cowardly egoist who in the hour of his people's distress evaluates his life higher than that of the community. Such a spineless weakling, however, can be deterred from giving in to his cowardice only by applications of the harshest penalty. If men continuously wrestle with death, and if for weeks they have to endure in mud-filled shell craters, without rest, sometimes with the worst kind of food, then the unreliable man, becoming uncertain, cannot be held by threatening him with prison or even penal servitude, but only by the ruthless application of the death penalty.[50]

Hitler connected desertion and war weariness with revolution and the stab in the back:

> An army of deserters, especially in the year 1918, flooded the military base and the home country and helped towards forming that great and criminal organization which, as the maker of the Revolution, we then saw suddenly before us after November 7, 1918...if in those days only one single division commander had come to the decision to pull down, with the help

of the division loyally devoted to him, the red rags and to have the "Councils" stood up against the wall, the Revolution could have been stopped in its tracks.[51]

The 1924 ramblings of an imprisoned putschist who never rose above the grade of corporal had no bearing on policy during the Weimar era. But once Hitler became chancellor, sales of *Mein Kampf* shot up. In this area at least, Hitler and the military leadership agreed: if there was a next war—as Hitler fully intended there would be—German military justice would be pitiless in dealing with malcontents, deserters, and those too weak to bear the strain of combat.

4

Ideology, Mindsets, and Military Law

Even before Hitler became chancellor in January 1933, German military officers, conservative nationalists, and supporters of the Nazi movement agreed on certain matters. They agreed that the Versailles Treaty was a monstrous imposition, placing intolerable restrictions on Germany, cutting off East Prussia from the rest of Germany, and burdening future generations of Germans with massive reparations payments. They agreed that German communists posed a threat to the nation. They agreed that someday Germany would need to throw off the restrictions of Versailles and revise its borders. And they agreed that the German government and military would have to stifle dissent and desertion within the ranks should Germany ever go to war again.

These areas of agreement did not constitute a full embrace of Nazi worldviews on the part of the Weimar-era military. Many military officers found Nazi brawling and lawbreaking repugnant, and its radicalism and embrace of violence alarmed some. Others thought its rabid anti-Semitism disturbing, and its populism unsettling. By 1928, many had come to terms with the Republic. The German military did not bring Hitler to power in the crisis years of 1930–1933, but after his appointment as chancellor in January 1933, Nazi worldviews and ideology penetrated into an institution that had prided itself as being above party ideologies during the Imperial and Weimar eras.

German military law operated in support of the state, and by July 1933 that state was firmly under the control of one party, the Nazi Party. The mindset of the Wehrmacht's senior leaders, the perspectives of the military jurists who interpreted the law, and the military code itself explain why the Wehrmacht punished dissent in World War II much more harshly than Imperial Germany's Army and Navy had in World War I.

A Politicized Military Leadership

After World War II, many German veterans sought to portray the leaders of the Wehrmacht as military professionals who had only followed orders.

They compared themselves to military professionals elsewhere, making a distinction between the deeply ideological officers of the SS and the nationalist professionals of the Wehrmacht. Dönitz and other German officers at Nuremberg pointed out that that the Defense Law (*Wehrgesetz*) of May 21, 1935, had prohibited active-duty officers from joining the party, and he insinuated that the officer corps had kept its distance from Nazi ideology. The Defense Law, passed six weeks after Hitler publicly announced his intention to introduce conscription, did indeed forbid soldiers from political activity. Apologists for the Wehrmacht and those attempting to portray it as a purely military instrument free of party penetration made much of paragraph 26, which laid out guidance pertaining to political activity in the German military. Membership in the party, its branches, and associated organizations was suspended while soldiers and officers were on active duty, and soldiers were forbidden from voting or participating in Reich plebiscites.[1]

This did not mean, however, that the military was apolitical in the sense that it had been during the Weimar era or during the Wilhelmine period, standing above party politics and distrustful of the political establishment. Instead, it reflected the relationship established in 1934 when Hitler made it clear that the party would brutally rein in the *Sturmabteilung* (SA)'s dreams of displacing the Wehrmacht in exchange for the Wehrmacht's pledge of unconditional loyalty to him and the new order he was creating. The Defense Law made this arrangement explicit.

In courting the Wehrmacht during his first days in power, Hitler focused on areas he knew would appeal to the service chiefs. In a dinner meeting with them four days after he was sworn in as chancellor, he explained to them that he would take a hard line against pacifists, would exterminate Marxism "root and branch," would battle against Versailles Treaty restrictions on German military forces, and would reintroduce national service in the future. The armed forces, he continued, would be strengthened so that Germany could eventually conquer living space in the East, but they should know that he had no intention of fusing the military and the party's paramilitary organization, the SA. He acknowledged that the military was Germany's most important institution, and he asked only that that it stay above the domestic struggle against the nation's enemies.[2]

As Hitler consolidated power in 1933–1934, imprisoning communists, socialists, and union leaders, abolishing parties, and banning Jews from the civil service, Germany's armed forces stood by. Many of its officers shared the same antipathy toward leftists, democrats, and Jews as party stalwarts did, and they greeted these developments without objection. Even a cursory look at statements made by the Wehrmacht's senior leaders indicates that being apolitical did not mean maintaining a critical distance from the party. Germany's Minister of War, General Werner von Blomberg, after initially cautioning his subordinates to stay above party politics, had come around by March 1933 and advised them to support the national revolution "without reservation."[3] Von Blomberg became an unabashed admirer of Hitler, advocating that German officers embrace National Socialist thinking and demonstrate absolute loyalty to the Führer even before Hitler moved against Röhm and the SA in the summer of 1934.[4] Once reassured that Hitler had no intention of replacing his generals with party activists and storm-trooper amateurs, Germany's military leaders became even more effusive in their embrace of the leader and his ideas. Blomberg's April 1935 directive on Wehrmacht training and education described the relationship between the party, the military, and Hitler in the following terms: "The armed forces owe their rebirth foremost to the leader and Reich chancellor and his political instrument, the National Socialist Workers Party (NSDAP). The Wehrmacht, SA, SS, Hitler Youth, Labor Front, police, and political organization are all part of a whole, and all strive for the same goals in their separate working spheres. Common purpose and comradeship bind all these organizations together."[5]

Blomberg was certainly not alone. General Werner von Fritsch, commander in chief of the German Army until his fall from grace in 1938, ensured that the army's first conscripts received instruction on the history of the Nazi Party, the struggle of the German race, and the organization of the Nazi state as part of their basic training.[6] He instructed his officers that only Aryan females were suitable for marriage, and he reminded officers that even within the confines of the officer's mess, they were to squelch "any criticism of the Führer and of the national socialist form of government."[7] His successor, Walther von Brauchitsch, likewise insisted that training establishments nurture a "securely founded National Socialist attitude" in addition to imparting military instruction.[8] From the outset, Hermann Göring told the group of officers he was assembling for a future Luftwaffe that it was not enough for them to be nationalist in outlook; they needed to adopt a National Socialist worldview.[9] Grand Admiral Erich Raeder, who jealously guarded the navy from external interference, proclaimed in the spring of 1939 that the party and armed forces stood shoulder to shoulder in the fight against Bolshevism and international Jewry. They were of one spirit and attitude, according to Raeder.[10] The high command was likewise supportive of the new government and its agenda. Wilhelm Keitel, head of the Armed Forces Office in the Reich's Ministry of War from 1935 to 1938 (he was appointed Chief of the Armed Forces Command after Blomberg's forced resignation as Minister of War in 1938) stood out in his obsequiousness, lecturing his subordinates that they should unconditionally affirm National Socialism and the Führer's leadership.[11] This certainly extended to anti-Semitism. Rudolf Schmundt, head of the army's personnel division, sent out a special directive to commanders when he heard that a German officer had been seen socializing with a Jewish veteran with whom he had served in World War I. Schmundt wanted to make clear that

> Every officer must be fully aware first that the Jewish lobby has challenged the German people's claim to *Lebensraum* and standing in the eyes of the world, and second has forced our nation to prevail against a world of enemies by spilling the blood of our best young men. Officers must therefore adopt a clear and totally uncompromising stance on the Jewish question. There is no difference between supposedly "decent" Jews and the rest. Nor may any consideration be given to relationships of whatever nature existed before the threat posed by Jews was common knowledge among the German people. Hence no connection, even of the most casual sort, may exist between an officer and a member of the Jewish race. The present struggle against the international enemy Jewish Bolshevism has clearly revealed the true face of Jewry. Every officer must therefore oppose it on the basis of firm inner conviction and refuse all association with it. Any infraction against this uncompromising stance will make him unviable and result in expulsion from the army. All officers are to be instructed accordingly.[12]

The perspective of Hermann Foertsch, a major in the home affairs department of the Wehrmacht, indicates a similar attitude from the mid-ranks. Writing in 1935, Foertsch advocated an ever-closer relationship between the party and the military. In *The Armed Forces in the National-Socialist State*, Foertsch insisted that the Wehrmacht should be as National Socialist in its sentiment as the Imperial German Army had been monarchist in its spirit. His well-received book would go through twelve editions, and Foertsch moved on to command troops at the divisional, corps, and army levels in World War II.[13]

In statements and in action, Germany's military leadership expressed support of Adolf Hitler and National Socialism. One of the leading historians of the Wehrmacht, Manfred Messerschmidt, goes so far as to assert that the model soldier was not apolitical, but rather deeply political.[14] The Wehrmacht's top leaders internalized Nazi worldviews and affirmed the political structure of the state, enthusiastically supporting Hitler's leadership. They insisted that the military stood apart from the party, but the relationship was that of two pillars supporting the same platform.[15] The military hierarchy insisted that as one of the state's two pillars, it was independent from the party. But both supported the leader's vision within their separate spheres of competence. That vision centered on the idea of a Germanic people's community (*Volksgemeinschaft*); the struggle for geopolitical and racial dominance; an implacable hatred of Jewry, Marxism, and democracy; and the quest to conquer and provide living space for the Germanic peoples in the East.

Not all German military leaders were as enthusiastic in their embrace of National Socialism and Hitler's agenda as were Blomberg, Keitel, and Dönitz. The major points of friction among the military, the party, and Hitler, however, tended to center on professional competencies and bureaucratic/institutional competition rather than disagreements about long-term goals, ideology, or worldviews. The military fended off attempts by the party's Office of Military Policy (the *Wehrpolitisches Amt der NSDAP* [WPA]) under Franz Ritter von Epp and Anton Haselmayer to gain a role in military education and training development. It jealously guarded its leading role in military matters, squabbling with Goebbels's propaganda ministry about the boundaries between instilling martial values among the people and within the military. The relationship between the military's intelligence branch—the Abwehr—and Himmler's Security Service (the *Sicherheitsdienst des Reichsführers-SS*) was deeply distrustful throughout the 1930s, plummeting into bitter rivalry during the war. While Hitler's decapitation of the SA put to rest military concerns about a brown-shirt takeover after Hitler became chancellor, the intrusion of the SS into the military domain became unmistakable as the SS's military wing increased from three regiments in the mid-1930s to more than thirty divisions at the height of World War II.

As Hitler steered Germany into war in the late 1930s, a number of senior Wehrmacht leaders grew uneasy. Minister of War General von Blomberg, elevated to the rank of Field Marshal in 1936, and Werner von Fritsch, commander in chief of the German Army, were concerned when Hitler informed them in November 1937 that he planned to incorporate Austria and Czechoslovakia into the Reich in the near future using military means if necessary. Both thought that the German military was unready and wanted more time to build German power before taking actions that might result in war with France and Britain. They were removed from office in 1938 because of their involvement in scandal, and they had neither time nor inclination to oppose Hitler openly.[16] Ludwig Beck, chief of the Army General Staff, grew increasingly alarmed over the course of German foreign policy in the spring of 1938, going so far as to urge the collective resignation of the army's leadership because he feared Hitler was about to plunge Germany into a wider war it could not win. Beck's call for collective action was based on his calculus of risk and the relative military power of Germany and the West.[17] Beck's reasoning sheds light on the same tension that would bedevil common soldiers and company-grade officers torn between their duty, conscience, and reason. Explaining why senior military commanders needed to intervene in a memorandum submitted to the Chief of the Army, Beck asserted:

> Vital decisions for the future of the nation are at stake. History will indict these commanders of blood guilt if, in the light of their professional and political knowledge, they do not obey the dictates of their conscience. The soldier's duty to obey ends when his knowledge, his conscience and his sense of responsibility forbid him to carry out a certain order.... Exceptional times demand exceptional measures.[18]

Beck's superior, General Walther von Brauchitsch, shared his concerns about the military balance of power but refused to confront Hitler over what he believed was a political decision. A meeting of the army's top generals in early August revealed that many shared Beck's worry that Germany's military was not ready for a major war, though some criticized Beck for being overly pessimistic and others questioned whether it was the "business of soldiers to intervene in political affairs."[19] Beck resigned on August 18, 1938. His opposition to Hitler in 1938 was based on his assessment of the geopolitical environment and Germany's military might. Beck was not entirely alone. The head of Germany's military intelligence branch, Admiral Wilhelm Canaris, his deputy Major General Hans Oster, and a handful of others grew increasingly alarmed, and they worked hard to convince Beck's successor to stage a coup. The conspirators went so far as to assemble a raiding party tasked with arresting or killing Hitler in September 1938. The plot collapsed when Britain and France coerced the Czechoslovakian government into ceding the Sudetenland to Germany, propelling Hitler's popularity in Germany to new heights.[20]

The flood of literature on the German military resistance to Hitler, and its importance to the Federal Republic's understanding of the role of the soldier in the state, may leave a misleading impression of its extent and influence as Germany went to war in 1939.[21] A number of generals did oppose the regime, but they were few, isolated, and ineffectual. The plots and plans they developed rested on highly questionable assumptions ranging from the army's ability to prevail over the Nazi Party and the SS to the assumption that the German public would accept the results of a military coup. While most of the military hierarchy stood aligned behind Hitler, influential figures such as Ludwig Beck and Wilhelm Canaris, chief of military intelligence, opposed the regime even before it put its appalling plans for aggressive war and genocide into action.[22] Beck and Canaris were initially attracted by Hitler's vision. They welcomed National Socialism's dismantling of parliamentarian democracy, its suppression of Marxists and socialists, Hitler's buildup of the German military, and his overturning the Versailles order. But Hitler's adventurism, his readiness to risk war, his treatment of Blomberg and Fritsch, and the brutality of the regime alienated the two conservative nationalists. The choices they made, unavailable to the common soldier, give a sense of the options available to officers who were repelled by the regime. Beck tendered his resignation before the outbreak of war when it became apparent that his superiors and peers were unwilling to confront Hitler, let alone seize control of the government.[23] In retirement, he became a central player in various conspiracies to overthrow the government, ranging from another attempt to organize a military coup in 1939 to aborted bomb plots in 1943 to the failed July 20, 1944, attempt to kill Hitler.

Canaris, however, decided to operate within the system. The Nazi Party's nationalism, its concept of a German community, and its anti-Semitism resonated with Canaris until Hitler's foreign policy made it clear that the Führer was bent on war. Canaris's aversion to the regime increased when he learned how German authorities were engaged in mass shootings of Poles and Jews during and following the Polish campaign. Canaris would protect military conspirators within the Abwehr, intervene to save small groups and individual Jews, and put out feelers to British and American intelligence services at various points in the war. But he simultaneously provided critical military intelligence to the regime and masked his opposition so carefully that historians are uncertain whether to label him as a resister. He ordered intelligence and sabotage operations that weakened the very powers that stood in Hitler's way.[24]

Beck's and Canaris's opposition would cost them their lives following the failure of the July 1944 conspiracy. Beck attempted suicide following the collapse of the coup, failed, and was shot. Canaris, already under a cloud of suspicion, had been removed as head of military intelligence in February 1944 when Hitler consolidated German intelligence and placed it under control of the Heinrich Himmler. Within days of the Stauffenberg assassination attempt, Canaris was arrested. He was interrogated by the SS security service for months, beaten, starved, and then hanged on April 9, 1945.[25] To point out that Beck, Canaris, Oster, and other military opponents were isolated and ineffectual at the start of the war does not diminish their efforts. Instead, it underlines out how difficult and dangerous military resistance was, and it conveys the reality that the vast majority of generals, commanders, and military leaders stood by the regime until the end.[26]

The tone and tenor of an organization are set by the public statements of its senior leaders, by its training and educational program, and by the field-grade officers and noncommissioned officers who translate orders into action. Henning von Tresckow and a number of other field-grade officers recognized the nature of the Nazi regime in the 1930s, and other officers would do so over the course of time. But as Germany headed into war, few military leaders questioned the necessity, the prospects, or the annihilationist agenda of the war.[27] A systematic analysis of the worldview and political leanings of the hundreds of commanding generals/admirals designated as *Gerichtsherrn* is impossible, given the destruction of many records, but it is undeniable that these commanders confirmed thousands of death penalties and ordered the execution of 18,000 to 22,000 their own soldiers, sailors, and air personnel.

The Mindset of the Military Jurists

The Wehrmacht's military jurists played a critical role in interpreting military law, in organizing and guiding court-martial proceedings, and in reviewing the outcome of military trials for the commanding generals who would affirm or reject verdicts and sentences. One of the first studies of the Wehrmacht's military justice system, written by two veterans of it, sought to portray German military judges and lawyers as impartial interpreters of military law who did what they could to mitigate Nazi extremism.[28] Otto Schweling, a former Luftwaffe judge, and Erich Schwinge, a professor of law who had served as an army judge during the war, claimed that many of the jurists who joined military law community did so because they were concerned about the Nazification of Germany's civil law system. They became military jurists, they said, because they perceived the military legal establishment as a safe zone relatively free of National Socialist thinking. Schwinge and Schweling argued that for many, joining the military legal community was a form of inner migration.[29] This may have been the case for a few individuals who had run afoul of Nazi bureaucrats, but to portray the community as a whole as resistant to Nazi worldviews is deliberately misleading. Even a cursory examination of commentaries and speeches from the period provides a very different picture. The military legal community reflected the same tendencies prevalent in German civil law, exhibiting a tendency to harshness, a disinterest in individual rights and guilt, and an emphasis on the military community as embodiment and defender of a racially defined German people's community.

Hans Frank, Reichsminister and head of the National Socialist Jurists Association, asserted in the mid-1930s that "Everything that serves the *Volk* is just, anything that hurts it is unjust."[30] The concept rejected both positive law, with its built-in protections for the individual, and natural law, which derived from God, nature, or reason. The Third Reich's senior jurists proclaimed that law sprang from the people's community (*Volksgemeinschaft*). Rudolf Lehman, the Wehrmacht's senior jurist at the start of World War II, explained to his subordinates that the ultimate font of German law was the people's leader, Adolf Hitler. His orders, whether written or verbal, trumped written military codes. Lehmann cautioned military jurists that the mission of military courts was not to search for truth—"if there was such a thing"—but to focus on using the law to preserve the community.[31]

The Military Penal Code

Hitler's written and oral outbursts about deserters, cowards, traitors, and the like were insufficient to serve as a replacement for a written penal code and written instructions for the conduct of military trials. Efforts to replace Germany's Military Penal Code with a new National Socialist military code stalled in the 1930s. Imperial Germany's Military Penal Code, updated and revised in 1934, 1935, and 1940, along with the Order Imposing Extraordinary Wartime Laws and Penalties, defined the military and wartime crimes that the court-martial system enforced. During the 1930s, two schools of thoughts developed as to how to interpret military law. The Marburg school continued to stress that those on trial needed to be charged with specific violations as defined by the code, and maintained that prosecutors needed to present evidence supporting the charge. The more radical Kiel school criticized this approach as liberal and formalistic, reflecting the poisonous influence of the Enlightenment.

The University of Kiel's law department had experienced a more dramatic turnover in faculty than had Marburg as the Nazis purged Jewish and liberal professors from the school, replacing them with younger National Socialist jurists. The Kiel school maintained that judges should focus on the character of the delinquent and his relationship to the state rather than on specific charges and evidence. Erich Schwinge, whose commentary on the military penal code would go through four editions, taught at Marburg. His commentary continued to emphasize deeds, derelictions, and procedures. Yet by 1936, he was urging his colleagues that they needed to adapt their interpretation of military law to meet the requirements of the time.[32]

The Marburg school generally prevailed in the Wehrmacht's treatment of deserters until the institution of flying tribunals during the last months of the war. Specific charges remained important, certain procedures were usually followed, and some effort was made to provide evidence that the person on trial had committed the crime. Nonetheless, protections for the defense were minimal, and judges who were too insistent about evidence found themselves replaced by hardliners.[33]

Ernst Fraenkel, a German-Jewish lawyer and political scientist who left Germany for the United Kingdom in 1938, captured the dynamics of the Third Reich state and its legal system perceptively in his 1941 study *The Dual State*. Fraenkel had come to recognized that the Reich operated at two levels. On the one hand, Germany continued to have laws, institutions, and procedures that supposedly channeled and guided the power of the state. Fraenkel termed this the "normative state." On the other hand, Germany's leaders and those working toward the Führer's intent were not bound by norms, rules, and procedures. They rejected the idea of natural law and resorted to naked displays of power when it suited them. This "prerogative state" rested on the notion that the Führer's will was the ultimate source of authority, and they could overrule law and norms when they stood in the way of Hitler's agenda. The military judicial system reflected the dynamic Fraenkel described at the national level. Military laws, institutions, and procedures continued in force but had to reflect, adapt, or be ignored if they diverged too openly from the Führer's intent.[34] There was, however, little divergence between the military and the party when it came to dissent and desertion in the armed forces.

The military's legal community embraced the concept of offender typologies (*Tätertypus*), an idea developed earlier by Erik Wolf at the University of Freiburg. Wolf postulated that certain types of people were prone to committing criminal acts.[35] Court-martial juries, military judges, and legal reviews considered not only the charge and evidence supporting it, but the upbringing, reputation, and criminal record of the accused. Judges considered the accused's juvenile record, whether he came from a stable family, whether he or his parents were heavy drinkers, whether the accused had completed school, and what sort of reputation the accused had at home and in the unit. Those characterized as asocial or criminally disposed were punished more severely than those from "good stock."[36] One study concludes that almost half of those charged with desertion had dropped out of school, that between 50 and 75 percent were unskilled workers, and half of those tried had civil misdemeanor records.[37] Schwinge, teaching at Marburg, had no compunction about characterizing Germany's deserters in the Great War as psychopathic inferiors.[38]

The concept of criminal types existed outside of Germany as well, but it proved particularly virulent when coupled with Nazi racial stereotypes, its concept of biological criminality, and anti-Semitism. The vocabulary used in court findings, reviews, and commentaries reveals how National Socialist thinking and offender typologies intermingled, with frequent use of terms such as shirkers, slackers, asocials, failures, inferiors, and pests.

The very nature of desertion made it easy to categorize the accused as asocial. To survive, the deserter might steal food and supplies before absconding, might pilfer from farmers during his flight, and might buy or forge documents authorizing leave, transportation, or accommodation. The court considered these other infractions as reflections of the character of the accused.

In addition to considering the background and character of the accused, court-martial juries had to consider the intent of the accused. The difference between unauthorized absence and desertion could be the difference between confinement and the death penalty. Conscientious defense attorneys pointed out that the distinction between the two charges rested not only on the length of absence but on the intent of the soldier. The two infractions were defined in Part II, Section 3 of the Military Penal Code:

Unauthorized Absence (Paragraphs 64 and 65)

64. Anyone who leaves his unit or duty station without authorization or stays away from them and is intentionally or negligently absent for longer than three days—in the field for longer than a day—will be punished with imprisonment or military confinement for up to ten years. In less serious cases, the sentence can be reduced to a fortnight of enhanced arrest.[39]

65. Those who intentionally or negligently fail to rejoin their unit or another unit within three days if separated in the field; or who fail to report back to duty when released from prisoner of war detention are likewise to be charged with unauthorized absence.[40]

Desertion (Paragraph 69)

(1) Anyone who intends to permanently evade their obligation to serve in the armed forces, and leaves or stays away from his unit or duty station will be punished for desertion.[41]

(2) It is immaterial to the charge of desertion whether the deserter, in leaving or staying away from his unit or duty station, does so for the length of the war, for a particular military operations, or because of internal unrest; or seeks to evade military service in general or to evade duty in those parts of the armed service subject to deployment and movement.

These clauses make it clear that what distinguished the deserter from the soldier who was absent without leave was the soldier's intention. If the accused intended to permanently evade their obligation to serve, then they were considered deserters, but if they overstayed their leave, or left their unit without permission and intended to return, they were considered absent without leave. Both charges had serious consequences, with desertion in time of war punishable by death or lifelong imprisonment. Since only the most foolhardy or stupid apprehended deserter would admit that he had intended to permanently evade his military obligation, members of the court-martial had to carefully weigh circumstantial evidence. If the accused no longer wore a uniform, had thrown away his rifle, resisted arrest, attempted to escape from confinement, or was caught trying to cross the border into a neutral country, court-martial juries considered this indicative of intent. Long absences with no effort to report to nearby military units, the use of forged documents, and prior planning likewise were assessed in determining the intent of the accused. The line separating the deserter from the soldier who had unintentionally become separated from his unit, or claimed that he planned to return to service at a later date, was blurry and open to interpretation. Though one can find cases where the charging authority, court, and commanding officer chose to use the less serious charge of unauthorized absence rather than desertion, the frequency and consequences of the more serious charge provide insight into the mindset that prevailed in the military judicial system.

To give a sense of the frequency of the two derelictions at the start of the war, consider the following statistics covering the period of the Polish campaign. Between August 26 and December 31, 1939, 9,710 German military personnel were charged with various and multiple violations of the military penal code. The most common military infraction was unauthorized absence, which constituted about one out of four military violations (2,225 of 9,017 proceedings). Only one case resulted in the death penalty, most probably because there were additional charges involved. Desertion was a far less common infraction, with only 357 cases prosecuted during this time period. Seventy-five of these cases, or about 1 out of 5 cases, resulted in the execution of the accused.[42] An additional eighty-five German military personnel were shot for desertion in the first three months of 1940, following the end of the Polish campaign (see Figure 6).[43]

Time Period	Wehrmacht Personnel Executed as result of court martial
August 26–December 31, 1939 (Polish Campaign)	109
January 1–March 31, 1940 (Sitzkrieg or Phony War)	147
April 1–June 30, 1940 (Denmark, Norway, Western Campaign)	140
July 1–September 30, 1940 (Battle of Britain, Battle of Atlantic)	121
First Year of War	517

Figure 6. Wehrmacht personnel executed as a result of court-martial

The uneven application of the death penalty for desertion, and an awareness that some of those executed did not fit the profile of cowards or unredeemable social outcasts, led Hitler as commander in chief to issue a clarification of how deserters should be punished. The Führer directive of April 14, 1940, provided the following guidance:

> The death sentence is required if the offender acted out of fear of personal danger, or if the special situation of the specific case makes it indispensable for the maintenance of discipline.
>
> The death penalty is generally appropriate in the case of repeated or collective desertions and in the event of flight or attempted flight abroad. The same applies if the perpetrator had significant previous convictions or committed crimes while deserting.
>
> In all other cases of desertion, it is necessary to consider whether the death penalty or a prison sentence is appropriate, taking into account all the circumstances. A prison sentence is generally to be regarded as sufficient if desertion stems from juvenile imprudence, inappropriate official treatment, difficult domestic circumstances or when the perpetrator's motives were not dishonorable.[44]

The Führer's directive of April 14, 1940, signifies a certain backtracking of interwar rhetoric advocating the summary execution of deserters and malcontents. Yet following the assault on the Soviet Union and the escalating barbarization of World War II, German military commanders and judges turned ever more frequently to the death sentence. Grand Admiral Erich Dönitz made clear to naval personnel that neither "homesickness, lovesickness, insufficient willingness to subordinate oneself, heavy-handed treatment, and fear of disciplinary or judicial punishment" justified leaving one's unit. He directed all commands to provide quarterly instruction that emphasized that "desertion will cost you your life." Dönitz informed naval courts to act appropriately and told his commanders that he would personally deny any appeals from deserters for clemency.[45]

When one of the naval commands asked for elaboration from the Naval High Command on the apparent discrepancy between the Führer guidance on April 1940 and Dönitz directive of January 1943, they were informed that the former had been issued after only one year of war, whereas the latter reflected the lessons of four years of war.[46] A memorandum from the head of the Luftwaffe's legal division to Air Force judges in December 1944 made the same point: the Führer's directive had been issued at a time when the military situation had been entirely different. One could not expect the Führer to constantly update every directive. Military judges should show initiative and act as necessary without seeking further guidance, recognizing that the highest priority in the current environment was upholding military discipline. The Führer's instructions were not to be used as excuses from acting "with the necessary hardness to meet the challenge of the times."[47] Ian Kershaw, a leading scholar on the Third Reich, described this sort of anticipatory interpretation of Hitler's intent as "working toward the Führer."[48] While the Führer never formally rescinded his guidance of April 1940, after the German invasion of the Soviet Union, everyone in the German military chain of command understood that the war had entered a new, merciless phase.

The number of German military personnel executed for desertion rose dramatically as the military situation deteriorated. Military commanders sought to use the death penalty associated with the charge of desertion as a deterrent, executing 519 Wehrmacht personnel in the first year of the war, 1,673 in the third, and over 4,000 in the fifth year.[49] The overall number of German deserters shot by the Wehrmacht can only be estimated at between 18,000 and 22,000, given incomplete records, but the surviving records show that the two military charges most likely to result in execution were desertion and undermining the military spirit.[50] The number of Wehrmacht personnel executed for these charges skyrocketed in the final year of the war, particularly after flying tribunals were empowered to try and execute suspected deserters and subverters on the spot in February 1945. The legal distinction between unauthorized absence and desertion, so important at the start of the war, faded in significance as did the need to present evidence of intent.

Alongside desertion, those who absconded from the military, helped others to desert, or refused to serve in it could be charged with the very elastic crime of "undermining the military spirit." Hitler signed an Order Imposing Extraordinary Wartime Laws and Penalties (the *Kriegssonderstrafrechtsverordnung* [KSSVO]) in August 1938 and put it into effect on August 26, 1939. The KSSVO applied to German civilians, Wehrmacht personnel, and foreigners in areas occupied by Germany. The special wartime law covered espionage (paragraph 2), irregular combatants (paragraph 3), violations of orders issued by military commanders in the occupied foreign territory (paragraph 4), and undermining the war effort/subverting military morale (paragraph 5). German military occupation authorities formally tried, imprisoned, and executed well over 100,000 foreign civilians for violating the KSSVO, and Wehrmacht partisan hunts and mobile killing groups killed at least 1.5 million Jews in the East without any legal proceedings whatsoever. The number of Germans executed by German military courts pales in comparison to the number of Jews, Poles, Russian, Greek, and other non-Germans executed by Germans. Nonetheless, that thousands of Germans were executed by German military and civilian courts for undermining the war effort shows that some dared criticize the regime or desert from its ranks.[51] The overwhelming majority did not.

Paragraph 5 of the KSSVO went beyond the military penal code, including desertion as one of several acts that "undermined the war effort" and merited the death penalty. In addition to deserters, those who helped or encouraged deserters, those who refused to serve, those who undermined discipline in the force, and those who publicly undermined the military spirit were subject to the ultimate punishment: death. This section of the KSSVO specified that

(1) For undermining the war effort, the death sentence will be applied to:
   1. Those who publicly call on or encourage a refusal to serve in the German military or in the militaries of its allies, or who otherwise publicly seek to cripple or undermine the military spirit of the German people or of its allies;
   2. Those who undertake to induce a soldier or conscript on leave to disobey, to oppose, or to act violently against a superior; or to desert or become absent without leave; or to otherwise undermine discipline in the German or allied armed forces;
   3. Those who undertake to evade military service themselves or enable others to do so—in whole, in part or temporarily—through self-mutilation, by deceptive means, or otherwise.

(2) In less serious cases, detention and imprisonment are permissible.

(3) In addition to capital punishment and imprisonment, confiscation of assets and personal property is authorized.[52]

The Third Reich provided no conscientious exemption from military duty, but since conscription had been prohibited by the Versailles Treaty, Germans who had no desire to serve in the military were not compelled to do so during the first years of the new regime. The introduction of mandatory military service in March 1935 put Germans opposed to military service in a conundrum: stay true to one's conviction and suffer punishment, or comply.

Although a few mainstream Protestants and Catholics refused to serve in the military because of moral reservations, neither church opposed military service per se.[53] The Jehovah's Witnesses, numbering only around 25,000 members in the Reich—less than 0.05 percent of the Reich's population in 1933—stood out for their stubborn refusal to render the Hitler salute, take loyalty oaths, participate in plebiscites, or serve in the military.[54] The Nazis tapped into existing hostility to the sect, which nationalist papers, the mainstream churches, and conservatives had perceived as unpatriotic, internationalist, and Bolshevik. Raids on Jehovah's Witnesses' offices began shortly after the Nazi takeover of the German state, as the Gestapo sought to intimidate its members and terrorize the movement out of existence.[55] By 1937, around 6,000 Witnesses had been consigned to Germany's concentration camp system, where they were forced to wear a purple triangle.

The Nazi attitude toward Jehovah's Witnesses differed from its perception of Jews, Roma and Sinti, and Slavs. Jehovah's Witnesses were deemed Aryan Germans who might be reintegrated into the *Volksgemeinschaft* (the German community) if they gave up their stubborn refusal to recognize the state's authority. Nazis believed that Jews, Roma and Sinti, and Slavs, however, could never become German, and needed to be removed, exterminated, and subjugated. Deemed ethnically Germans, the Jehovah's Witnesses' refusal to render military service infuriated authorities bent on forging a unified, compliant German community subordinate to the Führer's will. The Gestapo used threats, torture, and camp imprisonment to drive home the costs of noncompliance, while offering relief to those Witnesses who backed away from their opposition to military service. At the local level, police authorities drafted an array of statements designed to give those detained relief if they submitted to the state. Few did. Due to discrepancies between statements used in various cities and states, in December 1938 the Reichsführer SS issued a standardized statement that offered detainees and those eligible for release from the camps a way out. To be released, one simply needed to denounce the sect, disassociate oneself from its teaching, and "obey the laws of the State and... become a completely integrated part of the people's community."[56]

As would be the case in later courts-martial of deserters, German psychologists set the tone in categorizing conscientious objectors as asocials.

Professor Johannes Lange, director of the psychiatric and neurological institute at Breslau University, assessed that based on his examination of Jehovah's Witnesses, they were not mentally deranged and should therefore be held responsible for their actions. But he dismissed religious conviction as a primary motivation for refusing military service, asserting that most Witnesses used religion as a cover for their cowardice and a justification for the public attention they craved. Lange conceded that a few Witnesses may have been principled in their opposition to service, but callously remarked that they should be happy to suffer punishment as martyrs to their God.[57]

In November 1937, Hitler had shared his intention to forcibly acquire living space in the East with his top military commanders, and his diplomacy over the course of 1938 and the first half of 1939 underlined his bellicose intentions. Given the small number of conscientious objectors resisting conscription, the Third Reich and its Wehrmacht might have quietly accommodated the few holdouts to military service. In January 1939, jurists on the *Reichskriegsgericht*, the military's highest court, cautioned against making any sort of exceptions. They advised that allowing anyone, including conscientious objectors, to evade military service would undermine German military preparedness because "The undisturbed process of mobilization requires that every person liable for military service follows orders without opposition.... This means that even one person's refusal to perform military service can impede the military strength and security of the Reich."[58]

The Order Imposing Extraordinary Wartime Laws and Penalties, put into effect three days before the invasion of Poland, made desertion a capital crime. Given that there was no avenue for conscientious objection, those who failed to report for duty after conscription were regarded as deserters; the penalty for desertion during wartime was death. Already in September, military jurists were asking for further guidance about how to handle conscientious objectors, specifically Jehovah's Witnesses. They were informed that Hitler had refused to make any accommodation. That a considerable number of military jurists and commanders were uneasy about sentencing conscientious objectors to death is apparent in that Wilhelm Keitel, chief of the High Command, felt compelled to twice take up the issue with the Führer in the fall of 1939. In November, thirteen Jehovah's Witnesses were sentenced to death and twelve were executed. This monthly figure was almost equal to the total number of Witnesses executed the previous year, showing how the transition from peace to war worsened their situation.[59] Keitel shared the Führer's thoughts with his staff in December 1939:

> Based on the Special Penal Regulations during War, article 5, clause 3, the Reich Military Court has imposed death penalties on a considerable number of so-called Earnest Bible Students who refused to perform military service. The executions have been carried out. Several recent court decisions prompted me to present this urgent problem of handling the Earnest Bible Students again to the Führer.
>
> The Führer has made the following decision:
>
> In Poland alone, more than ten thousand decent soldiers have been killed. Thousands of soldiers have been seriously wounded. If he requires such sacrifices from every German man fit for military service, he is unable to grant a pardon to people who persistently refuse military service. In this regard, the reason a person refuses military service is irrelevant. Even mitigating circumstances, or circumstances that would have a bearing on an act of pardon, cannot be taken into consideration in this case. Therefore, if it is not possible to destroy the will of a man who refuses military service, the sentence has to be carried out.
>
> The judicial convening authorities and the various courts should be informed about this Führer decision.[60]

Hitler's brutality was captured in one of his after-dinner monologues at his military headquarters in East Prussia, the Wolfschanze. Reflecting on conscientious objectors and the Jehovah's Witnesses in the summer of 1942, the Führer explained that those elements

> who refuse to go to war because of their religious convictions should be reminded of the fact that they obviously have no problem taking the food others have fought for. For the sake of justice, this is not acceptable. Let them starve to death. The fact that they—the so-called Bible Students, 130 in number—were not left to die, but instead were shot to death, should be considered a special act of mercy on his part. Incidentally, these 130 executions had quite a sobering effect. On hearing of these executions, thousands of like-minded individuals lost courage and no longer tried to evade military service by quoting some Bible texts. If someone wants to be successful in warfare and, particularly, if he wants to lead a people through difficult periods of time, he should make sure of one fact: during these periods, anybody who excludes himself from the people's community, actively or passively, will be eliminated by the people's community.[61]

It is all too easy to become ensnared in the overlapping and reinforcing legalese of the Military Penal Code and the Order Imposing Extraordinary

Wartime Laws. Once at war, the Third Reich in effect treated conscientious objectors as deserters.[62] Those who aided and abetted desertion could be brought up on the KSSVO's catch-all charge of undermining the military spirit (*Wehrkraftzersetzung*), a charge that could also be applied to those who publicly criticized the war. Explaining why people refused to comply or be silent—whether objecting to military service, deserting from it, assisting others, or publicly undermining the war spirit—tends toward generalizations. Analyzing why an individual acted as they did paints a more nuanced, complex picture that encompasses overlapping motives, the individual's background, social status, and history, and the interaction between the person, the military, war, and the state.

5

Putting More Faces to the Numbers

Quantitative studies that parse human beings into categories and numbers tend to lose the sense of personality that allows humans to empathize and understand one another. It is precisely because people identify and empathize with individual stories rather than statistics that aid organizations provide narratives of a particular case when making appeals for donations and support. Likewise, breaking down deserters in terms of their age, ranks, service, and ethnicity provides a broad sense of the demography of desertion, but it obscures the individuality of a particular deserter. The vast majority of German military personnel did not desert, and one cannot speak of the "typical deserter." Each case was different.

The most ambitious quantitative study of German deserters, compiled by Kristina Brümmer-Pauly in 2006, combed through tens of thousands of German military justice files that had survived the war. The files dated from the start of the war to its end, and they included records from the German Army, Navy, and Air Force.[1] Her study excluded the SS and its subordinate organizations for the same reasons this study does: SS personnel, including Waffen-SS personnel and SS divisions recruited from outside Germany, were not judged by German military tribunals, but rather by their own tribunals. In addition, the SS did not rely on conscripts as did the military services, and it was less representative of the German population as a whole and more representative of the most ideologically oriented element of that population.

Quantitatively, most deserters were Army personnel (90.5 percent), with Air Force (7 percent) and Navy personnel (2.5 percent) making up a smaller portion of the cases studied. Given the relative sizes of the services—in 1943, some 6.55 million Germans served in the Army, 1.7 million in the Air Force, and 780,000 in the Navy—this makes sense.[2] The vast majority came from the enlisted ranks, though noncommissioned officers and officers made up a small proportion of the total. Seventeen percent were identified as *Volksdeutsche*—that is, either ethnic Germans from outside the Reich's 1937 boundaries or ethnic Germans from areas annexed into the Reich following the outbreak of war. Most were between twenty-one and thirty years of age (64 percent), almost one out of five was younger than twenty (18 percent), around one out of ten was between thirty-one and thirty-five (12 percent), and those over thirty-six years of age constituted the smallest segment (6 percent).

One out of three (30 percent) had been punished for some sort of military infraction prior to desertion, with another 27 percent having both military and civil penalties on their record. Most files did not list whether the individual was a member of the Nazi Party, leading one to infer that military courts did not take party membership into account when trying desertion cases.[3] The legal department of the Wehrmacht High Command compiled quarterly statistical overviews (*Kriegs-Kriminalstatistik für die Wehrmacht*) from August 1939 through December 1944 which list military charges, convictions, and sentences for each quarter. These reports show that desertion was relatively rare in 1940/1941, with fewer than 500 death sentences carried out, increasing tenfold for the same period in 1943/1944.[4] The number of Germans who deserted in the last year of the war was certainly even higher, but it is impossible to determine because at least a portion of those who made it to the other side were listed as missing in action.

Statistics tell a story, but the human dimension is equally instructive.

Jakob Bug

Around noon on Saturday, August 26, 1939, the forty-one-year-old German farmer Jakob Bug received his draft notice in the mail. Bug had served with a Bavarian field artillery regiment on the Western Front in World War I, had earned the Iron Cross Second Class, and was in a military hospital when the war ended. Like many others, he had been adrift in the post-World War I world. Bug had found comfort in the teachings of the Jehovah's Witnesses, then known in Germany as *Ernste Bibelforscher.* He married in 1923, and the childless couple centered their life on their faith. Bug settled in Iggelheim, less than five miles from his birthplace outside Mannheim, and worked at the I. G. Farben factory in Ludwigshafen as an insulation installer. In 1938, his father gave him some land, enabling Bug to become a small-time farmer.[5]

Bug's notice of conscription instructed him to report to assembly area #12103—Mannheim's Rheinau school—no later than 8:00 a.m. on Monday.

The conscription notice warned him that he would be considered a soldier as of midnight Sunday. Bug's neighbor, aware that he had received the conscription order, advised him that he better show up as ordered. Instead, Bug went about his daily business Monday morning. A policeman showed up at the Bug home around 11 a.m., but no one answered his knock. A neighbor told the policeman that that he had seen Bug bicycle off to work earlier that morning, and that Bug usually returned to the house in the evening. The policeman came back at 7 p.m., demanding to know why Bug had not shown up to the assembly area as ordered. Jakob Bug said nothing and was detained. In his report, the police captain noted that Bug's behavior had provoked considerable negative commentary among his neighbors.

The local police, the district police, and the military cooperated with each other seamlessly. Local police visited Bug's home less than four hours after he failed to report for military service in Mannheim on Monday morning. Within days, the Gestapo, the provincial police station in Neustadt, and the military district commander in Ludwigshafen had coordinated Bug's arrest and confinement and had initiated legal proceedings. On September 2, farmer Jakob Bug II from Iggelheim stood before a military lawyer who notified him that legal proceedings were beginning and asked him for a statement. The next day, Bug was charged with violating paragraph 69 of the military penal code, desertion. His own statement, those of his neighbors, and the local police captain's report were filed as evidence along with his conscription notice and military pass.

In his statement to the military investigator, Bug stated his position unequivocally. He had not complied with his conscription notice because "my faith forbids me from becoming involved in such worldly matters.... My God is Jehovah. Jehovah said in the Bible, 'love thy neighbor as thyself.' If I had followed the conscription order, then I would have been obligated under circumstances to shed blood. My God has forbidden shedding blood."[6] Bug acknowledged that the conscription notice had explicitly informed him that as of midnight Sunday, he would be regarded as a soldier and would be subject to military law. But Bug countered that he believed that he was not a deserter since he had never joined the military, nor had he sworn an oath to the flag.

The investigating officer speedily located Bug's military record from World War I. His prior service did not impress the lawyer. While acknowledging that Bug had served at the front and received the Iron Cross, the investigator insinuated that by 1918 he had become a shirker or slacker.

The report noted that Bug had reported to sickbay in March 1918 for chafed feet, and that the following month he had accidentally shot himself in the foot while cleaning his pistol. He had spent the rest of the war in a military hospital convalescing.

The military court-martial convened on September 6. Bug defended himself by explaining that he had read the conscription note only superficially and had not understood that Germany was at war. The court rejected these excuses, noting that his neighbor had told him to follow the conscription order just like everyone else. As for the explanation that he was a Jehovah's Witness and that his faith forbade him from shedding blood, the court sharply rejected this as justification. Instead, its members noted that the ideas of the Jehovah's Witnesses were dangerous to state security, and that Bug's crazy ideas ("*Wahnideen*") did not relieve him from rendering required military service to the Fatherland. He was found guilty of desertion. The court ruled that Bug's stubborn refusal to serve in the military required an exemplary, deterrent punishment because "this sort of behavior endangers the state and the military."

The court felt compelled to explain why it recommended fifteen years of confinement instead of the death sentence. In the justification that accompanied the sentence recommendation, the court stated that it believed Bug had been on the verge of changing his mind when his wife, Katherina ("Kätchen"), managed to smuggle a note in his laundry that reassured her husband that "the peace of Jehovah is with you. Be calm and strong." In addition, the court recognized that Bug had earned the Iron Cross as a runner for his regiment in World War I, and that he vehemently rejected insinuations that his injury had been self-inflicted. No evidence contradicted that statement. The court concluded that Bug had indeed deserted, in that he intended to permanently evade military service. But this decision had occurred before reporting for duty, and therefore had not damaged unit morale. The court believed that fifteen years of confinement would send a sufficiently strong message.

The court-martial recommendations needed to be confirmed by a commanding general with judicial authority before they went into effect. In this case, the confirming authority was the Commander of the Replacement Army. The legal department at the High Command attached a review of the court's verdict and sentence to the package forwarded to the confirming commanding general. Its commentary is notable both for its bureaucratic meticulousness and the mindset it reflected:

Legal Commentary on the Criminal Proceedings against Conscript Jakob Bug II on the charge of desertion

The recommended sentence seems too mild. Bible Students present a major threat to the People's Community at the present time. The recommended sentence of imprisonment enables them to achieve their objective of avoiding military service. It will encourage others to behave the same. Therefore in principle, the death sentence is the only appropriate tool for dealing with Ernest Bible Students. Whoever is not willing to fight for the Fatherland at this time commits a crime of such severity that it merits the death sentence.

...the accused should be sentenced to death, lose all civil rights, and lose the right to serve in the military. I recommend confirming the guilty verdict but not the sentence.

Berlin, 22 September 1939
Stegmann
Legal Adviser
High Command of the Army
(Commander of the Replacement Army)[7]

The commanding general followed the legal adviser's advice, and a new court-martial was convened on October 10, 1939, with a different judge and panel. The court-martial deliberated for a little over two hours. No additional evidence was presented. Bug was given the opportunity to make a new statement. He reiterated his beliefs but seemed to backtrack on his refusal to conform. He stated that he was willing to serve and had overcome his reservations about shedding blood.[8]

Katherina Bug desperately tried to get in contact with her husband, writing letters to various authorities. She had no success. Bug's defense attorney from the first trial refused to talk with her after she failed to greet him with the Hitler salute.[9] Prior to the second court-martial, Bug again was asked about his past. Someone raised the question about why he had been dismissed from I. G. Farben after years of service. Bug explained that the firm had given its workers time off to listen to one of the Führer's radio speeches at a local tavern, but that he had not done so. He explained that he had not attended because he did not drink, the room was overflowing, and he planned to read the speech in the paper the next day. But his absence had been noted by his supervisors at I. G. Farben, and he had been dismissed.[10]

The second court-martial found Bug guilty and recommended a long prison sentence. The legal officer reviewing the court decision—a different jurist from the first reviewer—took issue with the sentence recommendation, claiming that it was too mild. Preparatory to trying Bug for a third time, the military transferred him from the military detention center in Mannheim to the psychiatric division of the military hospital in Heidelberg. Dr. Fuchs, the division's head, was instructed to conduct a thorough physical and psychological examination of the conscientious objector. His examination would help inform members of the third court-martial who would take up the Bug case once the examination was completed.

The psychiatrist's report runs thirteen typed, single-space pages. The psychiatrist asked Bug questions ranging from his relations with his parents to what dreams he was having, supplementing his psychiatric assessment with a physical examination listing everything from the tattooed bird on Bug's forearm to a small scar on the sole of his foot. Bug's wife was allowed to visit on the condition that she answer some questions. Perhaps to the disappointment of the psychiatrist, she described her husband as hard-working, temperate, and loyal.

Bug openly acknowledged that he had never enjoyed confrontation and fighting. As a child, he felt badly about killing the rabbits his family raised, and one of his major regrets from World War I was that he had gotten in a fight with a fellow soldier over a trifling matter the day before his comrade died in combat. Bug explained that after the war, he had made the decision to avoid all physical confrontations. When pressed by the psychiatrist about what he would do if someone attacked a helpless individual or attempted to rape a young girl, Bug retorted that he had never been in such a situation. But he was committed to following God's admonition: "Thou shalt not kill."[11]

The Heidelberg psychiatrist concluded that Bug showed no indications of mental illness, though he could not rule out mental disturbance and hallucinations. He concluded that Bug was intelligent and competent, though a "soft and sensitive type." The psychiatrist seemed to search for words that might offer an avenue that would not lead to the death sentence, concluding that Bug's mental capacities at the time he committed his infraction might have been significantly impaired due to the after-effects of an earlier inflammation of the brain.

The third military court-martial found Bug guilty of desertion on February 2, 1940. It sentenced him to fifteen years of imprisonment, revoked his civil liberties for ten years, and revoked his right to military service.

The reviewing attorney at the High Command of the Army recommended that the verdict and sentence be rejected. He acidly commented that the notion that a bout of influenza in 1936 had reduced Bug's mental capacities three years later was absurd. Much more likely, to the reviewing lawyer, was that Bug was acting on his religious convictions. And his stubborn insistence on avoiding military service was a danger to the Fatherland. The reviewer recommended transferring the case to Berlin and instructing the Berlin Garrison Commander to seek the death sentence.[12]

In March 1940, Jakob Bug was transferred to the Wehrmacht Detention Facility in Tegel, Berlin. Another psychiatric evaluation was ordered, this time from the Institute for Forensic and Social Medicine at Berlin's Charité. The psychiatry department at the institute was deeply involved in Action T4, the involuntary euthanasia of handicapped patients. The psychiatric report did not, however, conclude that Bug suffered from any mental deficiencies that might have excused his "crime against the German people." Instead, it painted the picture of someone who had slowly come to the conviction that killing others was wrong. "His refusal to perform his patriotic duty springs from a one-sided, obstinate, and false religious worldview that has intensified over the years."[13] The Charité psychiatrist noted that while in detention, Bug had again amended his stance against military service, indicating that if given another opportunity, he would serve. The psychiatrist deemed this as insincere. When pressed whether he would be willing to shed blood for his country, Jakob Bug had remained silent. The Charité psychologist believed that Bug was thickheaded, fanatical, and unyielding. But he evaluated Bug as fit for trial, neither mentally incompetent nor suffering from mental illnesses.

On April 22, 1940, a fourth court-martial convened. It found Bug guilty of desertion, sentenced him to lifelong confinement, and permanently deprived him of civil and military rights. This again fell short of expectations, exasperating the jurist reviewing the recommendations. The reviewer tartly noted that the death penalty should have been applied, but since the court chose to believe that Bug's recantation was sincere, the reviewing jurist recommended that the Commander of the Replacement Army approve both the court's verdict and its sentence.

The military files related to Jakob Bug end here. Presumably, he was transferred to one of the military's penal camps. Whether he eventually was released from camp in exchange for service in one of the Wehrmacht's punishment battalions is unknown. The probability of surviving a military penal camp until the end of the war was low, as was the probability of surviving extended service in one of the Wehrmacht's punishment battalions, nicknamed *Himmelsfahrt Kommandos* (low survival assignments/commands) for good reason. Jakob Bug's narrative and that of his wife, Kätchen, fade into the blur of probabilities and statistics.

The Third Reich and its military refused to make any exceptions for conscientious objectors, regarding them as deserters from the Wehrmacht and betrayers of the People's Community. Jehovah's Witnesses made up a substantial portion of conscientious objectors condemned to death by the Wehrmacht; an estimated 250 Witnesses were executed as a result of military proceedings. Ten thousand Witnesses were arrested, interrogated, and detained at some point during the Third Reich.[14] Kätchen was one of these, but whether she was among the estimated 2,000 Witnesses sent to concentration camps is unknown. While the Jehovah's Witnesses stood out as a group in their stubborn refusal to join the military, one can find other cases where individuals did the same for deeply personal reasons. For some it was because they never felt German, and considered themselves Austrian, Alsatian, or Poles. For others, it was because they interpreted the scriptures differently than did the mainstream churches which had long abandoned pacifism.[15] But for most, the decision to desert was distinct from the decision to serve in the military. It came after months of perceived abuse from fellow soldiers or superiors, after the sense of not fitting in became unbearable, as combat fatigue overwhelmed unit loyalty, as individuals struggled with their conscience and sense of morality, or as the hope for a German victory faded away.

Karl-Heinz Leiterholdt

Around 8:30 a.m. on May 29, 1944, military convict rifleman Karl-Heinz Leiterholdt saw his chance to escape from the Wehrmacht Punishment Detachment to which he was assigned. Leiterholdt and the other members of the 1st Company, Wehrmacht Punishment Detachment 11, were shoring up a dirt road in Army Group Center's rear area near Vitebsk in what is now Belarus. The noncommissioned officer who was supervising the detachment of seventeen Wehrmacht convicts had stepped away to provide instructions to another group, and Leiterholdt slipped into the nearby woods under the guise of gathering firewood. The supervising sergeant, returning to the main body, noticed that Leiterholdt was gone and launched an immediate search for the missing man. The search party failed to find Leiterholdt, and his absence was duly reported to the military police.[16] His name was added without delay to the wanted list circulated within the Reich and in areas occupied by the German military.

Four weeks later, a German military police patrol (MPs) conducting a routine check of papers stopped a young officer candidate on the streets of Berlin and asked for identification and papers. The officer candidate was wearing the Iron Cross First and Second Class, four combat ribbons, and the equivalent of a Purple Heart. His arm was in a sling, his head was bandaged, and he claimed to be on convalescent leave. The MPs immediately suspected that something was amiss with the officer candidate's paperwork. The young man had presented identification papers that had been reported as stolen several weeks earlier, and the travel pass looked like it had been altered. As military police questioned the suspect, they discovered that the sling and bandage were ruses. Under pressure, Leiterholdt confessed that he had presented someone else's identification and had altered the leave and travel documents he had shown. He claimed he had disguised himself as a decorated officer candidate so that MPs would not check his papers, and he insisted that he was not a deserter. Leiterholdt elaborated that he had heard that the Western Allies had landed in Normandy, and he claimed that he had left his work battalion in Belarus in order to make his way to the fighting front in Normandy. When pressed as to how he could have known that the Allies had landed in Normandy a week before D-Day, Leiterholdt corrected himself to say that he had heard rumors that the Western Allies were about to land.

Leiterholdt was a doomed man. In the spring of 1944, however, the German military still went through the formalities of trying deserters by court-martial before executing them. Three factors sealed his fate. First, Leiterholdt had deserted from a punishment battalion. The soldiers serving in these units had already been convicted by military tribunals, and they were serving their time in these units in lieu of incarceration in a military prison camp. In February 1944, a military tribunal had sentenced Leiterholdt to five years of imprisonment for unauthorized absence, and his prison term would not be completed until July 1950. Deserting from a punishment detachment was viewed by the Wehrmacht as the equivalent to a prison break, and guards used deadly force to enforce discipline.

Second, Leiterholdt's record of civil infractions, military convictions, and performance evaluations reinforced Nazi-era typologies of the criminal asocial at odds with the German community and its military arm, the Wehrmacht. Members of the court were not only informed of Leiterholdt's military disciplinary record but also of his failures and transgressions before he was conscripted into the military. Leiterholdt had dropped out of primary school (*Volksschule*), and had worked in a mine and on a farm as a youngster only to be sent to a reformatory after stints in the working world. The reform school failed to check the young man's wayward tendencies; in April 1940, a juvenile court sentenced Leiterholdt to two weeks of imprisonment for petty theft. He apparently never joined the Hitler Youth or other Nazi clubs or trade groups, though his military files provide no explanation. In the spring of 1940, he was conscripted into the Reich Labor Service (*Reichsarbeitsdienst* [RAD]), serving his mandatory year of labor service to the Reich working on various construction projects behind the Eastern Front. In March 1941, shortly after completing his time in the RAD, Leiterholdt was conscripted into the German Army.

The young soldier completed eight weeks of basic training in Belgium and was then posted to the Calais region for the rest of 1941. His unit was transferred to the Eastern Front in the spring of 1942, and Leiterholdt was wounded in combat operations in the Donets Basin. He had already been disciplined for a number of minor infractions prior to his injury, with incidents ranging from stealing beer to forgetting to bring his helmet with him to an eleven-hour unauthorized absence. Following treatment at a field hospital, he was posted back to Germany for convalescence. There he made a number of choices that culminated in the five-year prison sentence that landed him in a punishment detachment, ranging from wearing medals he had not earned to petty theft to talking to another prisoner while in confinement.[17] As for his performance, the only evaluation solicited by the court was from the detachment from which he had deserted. Predictably, it was not positive. The captain in charge of the 1st company, Wehrmacht Punishment Detachment 11, assessed Leiterholdt as slack and unsoldierly, adding that his work ethic had been below average and that the man needed to be frequently reminded about the importance of cleanliness and order.

The justification for sentencing Leiterholdt to death demonstrates that Wehrmacht military courts were influenced by factors beyond the charge itself. In addition to examining whether Leiterholdt had deserted—the court found his story of leaving his unit in order to make his way to Normandy preposterous—court members examined Leiterholdt's prior criminal and disciplinary record, his performance, and his party affiliation.

On each of these counts, they found him wanting. The court asserted that Leiterholdt's actions were those of someone who had deliberately set himself apart from the people's community. The wording of the verdict conveys how intertwined military and Nazi worldviews had become by the fourth year of the war:

> The accused gives the impression of a human who is primitive and mentally limited. He is not, however, mentally incompetent. Indeed, the manner of his crime suggests a certain farmer's slyness, cunning, and cleverness incompatible with mental incapacity.... Even if the accused was mentally deficient as specified in para 51, subparagraph 2 of the Reich Criminal Code, this would not preclude imposing the ultimate penalty, death. It is a recognized prerogative of military justice to condemn even mentally challenged persons to death when the severity of the crime and the personality of the accused demands this punishment. The accused has been an asocial person since his early youth; almost one year in a reform school and previous punishments have not dissuaded him from continuing his criminal lifestyle. He has gone too far. He must be expelled from the German people's community, whose best sons are falling at the front. He must be exterminated in order to avoid debasing the community's lifeblood.[18]

A third factor made it extremely unlikely that Leiterholdt would escape the death penalty. On July 20, 1944, Colonel Claus von Stauffenberg attempted to kill Hitler by planting a bomb in a room where the Führer was receiving a briefing. The explosion killed four attendees but only lightly wounded Hitler. The Gestapo and SS correctly suspected that General Friedrich Fromm, commander in chief of the Reserve Army, had been aware that Stauffenberg and others in his command had been planning to assassinate Hitler and take control of the German government. Fromm had convened a hasty court-martial when it became apparent the coup was failing, and he ensured that Stauffenberg and associates were executed before they could be interrogated.

Hitler, Himmler, and those charged with investigating the conspiracy believed Fromm had been covering his tracks. As commander in chief of the Reserve Army, Fromm had been the commander who confirmed or rejected the verdicts and sentence recommendation of military courts-martial conducted in Germany. Fromm was swiftly relieved of duty in the aftermath of the failed coup—he would be expelled from the German Army in September 1944 and executed in March 1945. Heinrich Himmler, Reichsführer SS, was entrusted with command of the Reserve Army. Immediately after Leiterholdt's trial, his defense attorney entered an appeal for clemency, requesting that the death sentence be commuted to a prison sentence. His attorney argued that Leiterholdt was mentally challenged and had indeed intended to make his way to Normandy in order to fight at the front. The appeal noted that the defendant was young, had been wounded in combat, and had not acted out of cowardice. The attorney requested that the verdict be rejected, and if that was not possible, that the death sentence be commuted into imprisonment.

The likelihood that Heinrich Himmler, now the *Gerichtsherr* presiding over Leiterholdt's court-martial, would reject the court's verdict and sentence recommendation was nil. On October 12, 1944, Himmler confirmed the death sentence, indicating that he would not entertain any pleas for mercy.[19]

Karl-Heinz Leiterholdt was executed by firing squad on October 19, 1944. The execution was meticulously planned and documented, taking place at the Murellenschlucht shooting range in Spandau. Arrayed alongside Leiterholdt were five other condemned German soldiers ranging in age from twenty to thirty. The condemned men, detained at the military prison Spandau, were notified that their appeals for clemency had been rejected and that they were to be executed at 1400. The firing squad of ten enlisted men, commanded by a major, reported to the execution site at 1530. The condemned men arrived soon afterward. The execution squad was ordered into place five paces in front of the condemned men. The verdict was read. At 1605, the order was given to fire. A medical officer confirmed the deaths of the six men at 1618.

The Leiterholdt case illustrates the problematic nature of the source material on Wehrmacht deserters. The military and court records pertaining to Leiterholdt give a very good picture of where, when, and how he deserted, when he was apprehended, what sort of family he came from, how he had performed in school, whether he had joined the party, his civil and military disciplinary record, and so forth. What they do not impart is his inner mind, his motivation, and his intent. As far as the court was concerned, Leiterholdt was an asocial with a criminal past who deserved no mercy. Leiterholdt certainly did not conform to the expectations of the German military, of the party, and of German society during the Third Reich. Whether there was more to his story than that of a dropout, a petty thief, and breaker of rules is unknown. There is a German folk song that has the refrain "Die Gedanken sind frei" (one's thoughts are free). But expressing thoughts critical of the military or of the party would greatly increase the likelihood of a death sentence when on trial for desertion. Leiterholdt's internal thoughts, motivation, or attitude toward the war, the German Army, and the Reich went with him to the grave.

Helmut Gustav Gaebelein

In July 1942, the commander of the 8th Panzer Division, Major General Erich Brandenberger, received two letters from the director of a prominent Berlin bank. The director's son, radioman Helmut Gustav Gaebelein, was assigned to the headquarters communications group. Helmut had been missing since June 25 and several searches had failed to find him. On the June 29, his commander had listed him as absent without leave. Subsequently, the 8th Panzer Division's judge advocate dispatched a letter to Berlin asking police to contact Gaebelein's father and inquire whether he had any information about his son's whereabouts or intentions.

The father, a devoted National Socialist and veteran of World War I, was indignant at the insinuation that Private Gaebelein might have deserted. In a four-page letter to Major General Brandenberger, Director Gaebelein informed the general that it was inconceivable that his son would have left his unit of his own volition; the young man must have disappeared because of an accident or criminal assault. The father explained to the general that he personally had served as a reserve officer in the Great War, had been awarded the Iron Cross, and that both Helmut and his seventeen-year-old brother had volunteered for military service rather than wait to be conscripted. The father assured the general that while he understood that war calls for sacrifices, he needed to defend the honor of his son and the Gaebelein family against insinuations of dishonorable behavior. A week later, the bank director wrote a second, more pointed letter to Major General Erich Brandenberger. This one informed the general that the information that he (the father) had received from his son's company commander was "entirely unsatisfactory." The father demanded to know "when my son was last seen, with whom he last spoke, and what circumstances justify" the assumptions that he had absconded.[20]

The 8th Panzer Division was recovering and refitting, and it was assigned to a quiet sector of Army Group North's front near Lake Ilmen. General

Brandenberger found time to reply, reassuring the Berlin bank director that "no one is claiming or assuming that your son Helmut acted dishonorably." He explained that everything possible was being done to find the missing soldier, and that search groups had been dispatched to comb the area and interrogate Russian civilians. Without elaborating, the general noted that circumstances suggested that that the young man may have suffered from some sort of mental breakdown, and this was why the division's judge advocate had reached out to Berlin for information.

Director Gaebelein followed up his correspondence with the general by contacting the division's judge advocate directly. He told the lawyer that his son had never left home or school without permission and had earned good grades at Berlin's well-regarded Schiller Gymnasium, a humanistic high school. He attached a copy of the last letter he had received from his son, along with the boy's high school grades. The list of subjects—Greek, French, Music—clearly communicated that the family was upper middle class; the father made sure that authorities knew he was a National Socialist, a veteran of World War I, and the recipient of the Iron Cross.[21]

In early October, some three months after his son disappeared, the Gaebelein family received a postcard from Bern, Switzerland. The card was signed by Josef Gloor, but Gaebelein's father and mother recognized the handwriting as that of their eldest son.[22] Their world was shaken to the core. Director Gaebelein, who must have anguished over the decision, decided to contact the responsible military and civilian authorities forthwith. On October 22, noting that the situation had changed, the German Army removed Gaebelein from the rolls of the 8th Panzer Division, transferred him to the German Replacement Army, and instructed the Berlin Garrison Command to take up the legal proceedings against Gaebelein. Evidence continued to be gathered, but the court-martial was put on hold, pending Gaebelein's apprehension. Gaebelein, however, was in Switzerland, and the Swiss would not turn him over.

The Gaebelein case, in contrast to that of Leiterholdt, is richly documented and provides insights from multiple perspectives.[23] The Berlin Garrison Command assembled the normal sorts of documents associated with court-martial cases, ranging from statements from fellow enlisted soldiers to commander evaluations to Gaebelein's military, medical, and school records. In addition, his file is filled with the letters his father sent to the 8th Panzer Division, to German diplomats in Switzerland, and to the Berlin military court. His father provided a multipage account of his son's life experience to the German embassy in Switzerland, emphasizing his son's psychological vulnerability and alleged mental confusion as factors that needed to be taken into consideration by German authorities. In addition, the file contains reports of German police interviews with relatives and acquaintances, of letters turned over by the family, and of files the Germans acquired from the Swiss.[24]

The Swiss assembled a trove of documents that provide a different perspective and more depth to the Gaebelein case. Swiss military authorities questioned Gaebelein about how and why he deserted, pressing him for details about the composition, training, and procedures in his communications company.[25] The Swiss police also commissioned a Bernese psychologist to conduct a nine-month-long assessment of Gaebelein's mental health while the detainee's status was being determined. Lastly, Gaebelein wrote his own account for Swiss authorities that explained how he managed to travel from the Leningrad front across the Swiss frontier to Lucerne in June 1942. Gaebelein's essay provides his own version of his upbringing, experience in the Hitler Youth, and attitude toward National Socialism.

In German court-martial records, the voice of the deserter is absent or warped by an awareness that the court will consider his guilt or innocence and may well condemn him to death. Defendants had to choose their words carefully, and defense attorneys had to frame motives appropriately. Those deserters who made it to the other side, such as Gaebelein and Metz, could speak more freely, though they, too, knew that authorities—in this case the Swiss—were considering whether to return them to Germany, where they would face the death penalty. Nonetheless, the tone, dating, and details that Gaebelein provides in his account, supplemented by the long report by Dr. Klaesi of Bern, allow us to reconstruct not only how he deserted but why.

According to Helmut Gaebelin's account, on the morning of June 25, he wrote a letter home, giving no indication that he was in mental anguish. He had lunch with his fellow signalers in the 8th Panzer Division's radio room, and lay down on a bench afterward. Around 1:30 p.m., his sergeant noticed that Gaebelein had stepped out of the room but assumed the radio operator was going out to answer nature's call, as the private had left his cap, belt, and weapon by the bench. Duty recommenced, but Gaebelein failed to return. The sergeant and another radioman made a quick attempt to find him, and when they could not find him in the bunkroom, notified the captain in charge of the communications group that he was missing for the shift. When Gaebelein failed to show up for supper, the radio group sent out two men to search surrounding villages. When the evening radio watch (shift) turned over at 3 a.m., the entire watch was ordered to search nearby swamps and riverbanks. His unit continued to search for Gaebelein throughout June 26, inquiring in nearby villages and among neighboring German units if anyone had seen their missing radioman. On June 29, the communications group launched an additional search that went further afield, visiting four other villages and the two closest Russian towns. The residents of one of the towns reported they had seen someone who matched Gaebelein's description but that the German soldier had declined offers of food and simply continued walking in a westward direction. That evening, the division generated a formal wanted-persons report that provided German military and civilian police with a description of Gaebelein. The post listed the following information about the missing private:

Height: 172 cm
Build: slim
Hair color: dark blond
Eye color: brown
Distinguishing marks: small scar above upper lip
Last seen wearing military working clothes (green tunic, gray trousers) but without hat or belt.

Gaebelein recalled that he had carefully chosen his clothes so that he could blend into the population, leaving behind his jacket, belt, and cap with military markings. He set off in a southwesterly direction from the divisional headquarters, taking a circuitous route to the nearest train station at Loknja. The weather was warm and dry, but the hike was more difficult than he had anticipated, since his route took him through swamps and dense woods. He spent a night in a German-occupied village, sleeping in a sauna. The next day, he made it to a road and hitched a ride on a truck heading to Loknja. No one questioned him when he joined the chow line at a Wehrmacht field kitchen that night. On June 27, he hopped a freight train headed to Dno, hiding in the caboose. Arriving in Dno around midnight, he was fortunate enough to find that a German troop transport train filled with soldiers on leave was scheduled to depart for the Reich that day. This train took him to Virballen (Virbalis) on the border between Lithuania and East Prussia, where he got on another military troop transport train headed to Cologne. Four days after he had deserted from his unit on the Leningrad front, Private Gaebelein was in Cologne, where he purchased a train ticket to Lucerne, Switzerland. He selected scenic Lucerne, on the *Vierwaldstättersee*, as his destination because he had vacationed there with his family before the war and was familiar with the city.

Gaebelein's four-page, single-spaced account of his flight conveys a sense of satisfaction that he had outsmarted military police and train inspectors during his journey. In his account, he is cool, collected, and calculating. Gaebelein describes how he hid in the lavatory for one segment of his trip and in the caboose for another; how he got off a train car at one end as inspectors checked papers and then got back on at the other end as they moved down the aisle; and of how he evaded two passport controls when the Cologne-Lucerne train stopped in Basel, Switzerland. In early July, less than two weeks after he deserted, Gaebelein disembarked from a passenger train at the Lucerne railway station. It was late at night, and he wandered over to the nearby lake where he planned to sleep on a bench for the night. A stranger approached him and struck up a conversation. According to Gaebelein, the man offered him something to eat and Gaebelein went to the stranger's house because he was hungry. The next day, Swiss police noticed the young man wandering around the lakefront early in the morning and asked who he was and where he resided. He gave them the address of the man who had fed him the night before. When Gaebelein visited his benefactor later that morning, two Swiss detectives arrived shortly thereafter and detained him. Swiss authorities, after questioning him closely, decided against forcibly returning Gaebelein to Germany. He would survive the war, emigrating to Argentina in 1948 and then to the United States in the early 1950s.[26]

Private Gaebelein had been with his unit—the 2nd company, Panzer Signals Detachment 84 attached to 8th Panzer Division headquarters—for only a little over four weeks when he deserted. He explained that he had entertained notions of deserting well before his last assignment. Gaebelein volunteered for military service during the fall semester of his final year at Schillergymnasium, and like other volunteers, was awarded his graduation certificate early. He reported for duty to the Ludendorff caserne in Berlin on December 3, 1940, where he received basic training as a signalman (radio operator). Most of his fellow trainees were fellow gymnasium graduates, largely from the Berlin region. In January, he and ten other trainees were transferred to a communications detachment stationed in Lublin, Poland. He found military life unbearable and threatened to commit suicide. His commanding officer arranged for Gaebelein to receive rest and psychiatric care at a German military hospital in the Carpathian Mountains. In August, he was transferred to a convalescent unit in Berlin and granted fourteen days of leave at his parents' home. That December, he was posted back to the Ludendorff caserne to refresh his skills as a radioman. In April 1942, he and other graduates of the communications course loaded aboard trains headed eastward. He and ten other enlisted communication specialists were assigned to Panzer Signals Detachment 84, a sub-element of the 8th Panzer Division. On April 30, 1942, Gaebelein reported for duty to the division staff located some twenty-five kilometers behind the front line. The sector was quiet except for occasional German artillery salvos intended to suppress Russian antiaircraft guns.

Gaebelein explicitly ruled out politics as a reason for his desertion when explaining his motivations to his Swiss interlocutors. "I want to be upfront from the start and state that political reasons had nothing to do with my reason for leaving my unit. I was never politically active and have no intention of becoming so in the future. While I do not support National Socialism unconditionally, I must admit a certain admiration for its intense drive and energy."[27] The Swiss official evaluating his case concluded that Gaebelein had deserted because he could not endure the pressure of military life, but that he had internalized Nazi worldviews and talked about the Russian people as if they were animals. As for the Jews, Gaebelein's own report reveals that he found them repugnant. He recorded that when he discovered that the stranger who took him home to feed him his first night in Geneva was a Jew, he had suppressed his aversion because he was hungry and needed help. The Swiss officer interviewing him noted that Gaebelein had nonetheless accepted money from the man.

If distress over politics or more precisely Nazi ideology did not contribute to Gaebelein's desertion, what were his motivations? One can rule out combat stress or fear since Gaebelein had just joined the unit, the sector was quiet, and his communications detachment operated well behind the front. Three other factors caused him to desert: weak nerves, schizoid personality traits, and depression; unease with *Kameradschaft* and hypermasculinity; and an unwillingness to subordinate his individuality to the group identity of the so-called German people's community.

Helmut Gaebelein explained to Swiss authorities that the primary reason for his desertion was his nervous disposition. Already as a child, Gaebelein claimed to have suffered from weak nerves. He explained that "I am from nature extraordinarily sensitive and susceptible to disturbances in my environment.... I overreact to things and take everything very seriously."[28] He had reacted to a hazing incident at his first duty station in Lublin by attempting suicide, he said, leading his unit commander to send him to a psychiatrist in Krakow who assigned Gaebelein to eight weeks of convalescence care in the Carpathian Mountains, followed by home leave. Posted to a different unit the next year, Gaebelein recalled that he never managed to get a good night's rest because the radio was always making noise in the background and because he had to stand night watch every other day. When he complained to his supervising sergeant that his condition was deteriorating because of lack of sleep, the sergeant reacted with astonishment, laughing at the private. Gaebelein elaborated that sleep deprivation caused him to make minor mistakes as a radio operator, and these errors nagged at his mind. He recalled, "I became embittered by the incomprehension others exhibited towards my condition, and my despair increased day by day." Gaebelein again contemplated suicide, but he was unwilling to give up on life. He saw desertion as his only way out of a downward spiral caused by nervous anxiety, lack of sleep, and worry about his deteriorating work performance.

Gaebelein's father, writing to the German consulate in Switzerland, explained that his son had always been a sensitive boy. As a baby, he had cried more frequently than his sister and brothers; as a teenager, he had been drawn to the Confessing Church and had spent an inordinate amount of time praying and fasting in his room before losing interest in religion; and as a military trainee, his son had responded poorly to the brusque instructional methods used by the military. Director Gaebelein suspected that Private Gaebelein had deserted because of some sort of nervous breakdown. Writing to the military court in Berlin, the father—who still loved his son and wanted to find a way for him to return safely to the Reich—argued that "in my opinion, it makes no sense to charge someone whose character and behavior have always been beyond reproach with a military crime [desertion] because he has put himself and his family in a problematic situation because of a nervous breakdown."[29] He recommended that his son be categorized as militarily unfit and be allowed the opportunity to serve the Reich in some other capacity once he had recovered.

Director Gaebelein was advocating for a solution utterly at odds with Third Reich policy regarding desertion. German military law and the Führer himself had been explicit: German deserters who fled abroad could expect the death penalty, and had Gaebelein's son returned, it was highly probable that he would have been shot. For two years, the father sought to persuade his son to return to Germany while prodding military authorities to drop criminal charges against his son. He failed on both counts.

The Swiss psychiatric evaluation provides a third prism on Gaebelein's explanation that he deserted because of his poor nerves. Responding to an inquiry from the German embassy about Gaebelein's mental health, the Swiss psychiatrist explained that "Gaebelein was in the midst of a mental emergency when he deserted and remains unwell." The final psychiatric report, submitted in September 1943 to the Swiss Department of Justice, concluded that Gaebelein had severe schizoid personality disorder manifesting itself through dangerous internal conflicts and rash decision-making. The supervising psychiatrist advised that Swiss authorities should retain Gaebelein for additional psychiatric care and treatment.[30]

Gaebelein may well have suffered from depression as well, though the Swiss evaluation did not identify him as clinically depressed. Yet in his letters from Switzerland to his parents, carefully preserved in the judicial file that German Army authorities were assembling, Gaebelein talks less of weak nerves than of melancholy and *Weltschmerz*. Gaebelein, trying to explain to his Nazi parents why he deserted, shared his anguish in a letter from Switzerland written in late 1942: "When will there be sunshine in my life again? Will the sun ever shine for me again? Up to now, my entire life has been darkness even if you never knew or sensed it. This is the first time that I can really share my inner thoughts. I live like a puppet without purpose, goal, or reason."[31] The letter was clearly a cry from the heart, as were his various half-hearted suicide attempts.

Schizoid personality disorder is characterized by an inability or disinterest in social relationships, a sense of detachment, and a tendency toward self-isolation. Gaebelein was certainly unwilling or unable to immerse himself into the Wehrmacht's small group dynamic centering on the concept of *Kameradschaft*. Gaebelein explained in his report for the Swiss that he was never comfortable with the group dynamics he first encountered in the Hitler Youth and rediscovered in the Germany Army. Gaebelein recalled how the film *Hitlerjunge Quex* had filled him with enthusiasm about the Nazi movement in September 1933, and how he had been an eager, early volunteer for the *Pimpfe* (the youngest, entry tier into the Hitler Youth). Yet over time, his enthusiasm had waned. He graduated from the *Pimpfe* into one of the Hitler Youth groups that focused on nautical activities and skills, the Maritime Hitler Youth. Meetings were three times a week, every weekend was taken with sailing and rowing, and his summer vacation had been replaced with Hitler Youth camps, long hikes, and boating. He found the Hitler Youth experience overly regimented, complaining that he had little in common with other members of the group, and confiding to his Swiss interrogator that the Hitler Youth had come to have only one purpose: the militarization of German boys. He personally had never been interested in such things, and he missed the opportunity to develop his own interests and private identity. While acknowledging that participation in the Maritime Hitler Youth group served to make boys more physically fit and imparted skills such as navigation and ship recognition, group cohesion had rested on involuntary *Kameradschaft* and discipline rather than friendship and mutual interests. "One is forced to constantly be with other people one personally finds vexing."[32]

Gaebelein found the military even more disagreeable than the Hitler Youth. His bunkmates and fellow radio operators described him as constantly reading, rarely engaging, and maintaining a distanced, somewhat condescending attitude. Gaebelein took any slights from a comrade or criticism from a supervisor personally, commenting that the noncommissioned officers were usually "not at my intellectual level." Gaebelein was not a joiner and found the hypermasculine physicality and tenor of the Hitler Youth and the German Army repellent rather than attractive. Gaebelein explained to the Swiss that "the military milieu is just too coarse for me." He added:

> The sole reason for my desertion was that I could not abide military service, whether at the front or at home. I did not get along with my comrades. I was always a lone wolf who was unable to become part of the group because my comrades either avoided me or teased me. I got along fine with my superiors. I cannot deal with military regimentation. My nature longs for freedom.[33]

Whether this sense of isolation and alienation, confirmed by members of Gaebelein's company, rises to a psychological disorder is uncertain. The Swiss psychiatrist may well have framed his conclusion along these lines in order to prevent Gaebelein's extradition to the Reich. What we can conclude is that Gaebelein did not adjust or fit into the culture he encountered in the Hitler Youth and the Wehrmacht. In his own words and those of his peers, he was sensitive rather than assertive, soft rather than hard, an introvert rather than an extrovert, and one who cherished individualism rather than group camaraderie.

Gaebelein and his fellow soldiers do not mention another factor that may explain why Gaebelein had trouble fitting into the hypermasculine culture of the Hitler Youth group or the Wehrmacht small unit: homosexuality. The evidence that Gaebelein was homosexual is limited and conjectural, but worth mentioning because it would have introduced another dynamic to his alienation from the military small group. The Swiss psychiatrist who examined Gaebelein describes the stranger he encountered his first night in Lucerne by the lake as a known homosexual. Swiss police apparently intercepted a letter from Gaebelein to that man and assumed that Gaebelein was gay as well.[34] However, none of his unit comrades made mention of this possibility, and neither Gaebelein nor his psychiatrist provided elaboration about his sexual orientation in his otherwise extensive file. Gaebelein may simply have encountered a sympathetic stranger who listened to his story, offered him some food, and happened to be homosexual. But if Gaebelein had any tendencies in that direction, they would have contributed to his alienation from a group culture that celebrated aggressive heterosexual masculinity and insisted that deviations from that norm were unacceptable if not repugnant. Ernst Röhm and SA leaders discovered in 1934 that Hitler's toleration of their homosexuality disappeared when he found their radicalism inconvenient. General Werner von Fritsch was ousted from his job in 1938 as commander in chief of the German Army over unsubstantiated allegations that he was a homosexual. And although the Wehrmacht did not pry into soldiers' sexual inclinations, it did charge and prosecute soldiers for homosexual acts, sending them to military prisons in the Reich.[35] Gaebelein may simply have been an introvert with a sensitive nature. Sensitivity and softness, however, were not characteristics the Wehrmacht and the Hitler Youth valued. They were deemed as unmanly, feminine traits that German boys and men needed to overcome.

Gaebelein made it clear that politics had nothing to do with his desertion. His Swiss interrogators noted that he talked about the Russians as subhumans and made little effort to hide his anti-Semitism. Nowhere in his long, self-absorbed account is there any mention of the treatment he must have seen of Jews and Poles when he was stationed outside Lublin in the Generalgouvernement. Nor does he dwell much on Nazi suppression of the Confessing Church, even though his father notes that Gaebelein had gone through a religious phase that caused tension within the family. What troubled Gaebelein was how National Socialism was extinguishing the personal realm. As he put it,

> I recognize without hesitation its [National Socialism's] achievements. One only has to think of the millions of unemployed who found jobs, of how the economy was revitalized, and of the push for technological progress. But the National Socialist system is at odds with my character.... Hitler's system is militaristic through and through, and this contradicts my nature. There is no longer any room for personal freedom in Germany today. Freedom of expression in Germany is also a thing of the past. In addition, National Socialism preaches holy egoism. German interests take precedence over the interests of all other countries without any consideration. That runs against my sense of justice. Of course, if one were to express such a view in Germany today, one would immediately end up in a concentration camp. Summing up my attitude toward National Socialism, I would say that I admire it but cannot connect to it personally.[36]

6

Molding Military Loyalty

Historians continue to the debate the relative importance of coercion and consent in the Third Reich. Public demonstrations, street fighting, and intimidation were hallmarks of Nazi electioneering during the final years of the Weimar Republic, and coercion and violence were essential to the Nazi consolidation of power in 1933 and 1934. Once in power, the Nazis wasted no time in arresting, beating, and detaining without trial political opponents on the left. Even before the Reichstag fire, Hermann Goering instructed police in Germany's largest state to work closely with the SA, instructing them to employ deadly force against communists without hesitation. SA, SS, and Stahlhelm members were deputized as auxiliary policemen, patrolling the streets alongside the police. Following the Reichstag fire, Hitler persuaded Reich President von Hindenberg to pass a decree "for the protection of the people and state" (the Reichstag Fire Decree), which allowed the state to arrest and incarcerate political opponents without charging them with a particular crime. The police and the SA detained tens of thousands of communists, social democrats, and union members, often brutally beating and torturing them. Hundreds died as a result of violence, and within months, an estimated 45,000 left-leaning Germans had been sent to camps hastily erected throughout Germany.[1]

Conservative and Catholic politicians would discover that they were not immune to violence if they objected to Nazi policies and the consolidation of German political, social, and cultural life under Nazi leadership. Seizing upon an arson attack on the Reichstag in February 1933, Hitler persuaded Germany's elderly president Paul von Hindenberg to sign a decree that suspended civil liberties and permitted the government to imprison Germans without charges. Soon afterward, the Nazis pushed the Enabling Act through the Reichstag. This act empowered the government to pass any laws it deemed appropriate without parliamentary approval. Communist parliamentarians were either in detention or in hiding, and only members of the Social Democratic Party voted against the law that eviscerated the Reichstag as an independent body. Nationalist and bourgeois parties voted for the Enabling Act, believing it was a step toward the restoration of law and order. But law meant little in the prerogative state, where the Führer's decisions trumped rules and procedures. By 1934, some conservatives sensed that Hitler's Third Reich was not merely authoritarian but an unbounded dictatorship. In June 1934, Hitler's Vice-Chancellor Franz von Papen gave a speech at the University of Marburg criticizing the Nazis for ignoring the rule of law. Hitler had been concerned that the SA was becoming a power unto itself for some time, and the Marburg speech alerted him to unease among the nationalist/conservative circles that had hitherto supported him.

Hitler moved ruthlessly against suspect storm troopers, recalcitrant conservatives, and others with whom he had a score to settle. In addition to eliminating the SA's top leadership, the SS murdered two army generals (General Kurt von Schleicher and his closest associate, Major General Ferdinand von Bredow) as well as two of Papen's closest advisers and the former leader of Catholic Action, a social-political movement. Edgar Jung, who had written Papen's Marburg speech, was murdered in the basement of a Gestapo office and his body dumped in a ditch. Erich Klausener, who led Catholic Action during the last years of the Weimar Republic, was gunned down as a warning to Catholic politicians.[2] The regime executed at least ninety Germans without trial in the Night of the Long Knives, and it detained more than a thousand others without filing charges.

Hitler justified his actions to the Reichstag on July 13, 1934. He claimed that Ernst Röhm, head of the SA, had been about to stage a coup, a suspicion fanned by Himmler, Heydrich, and others who would benefit from his fall. He brusquely asserted that "Mutinies are broken according to eternal, iron laws. If I am reproached with not turning to the law-courts for sentence, I can only say: in this hour, I was responsible for the fate of the German nation and thereby the supreme judge (*oberster Gerichtsherr*) of the German people....I gave the order to shoot those most guilty of treason."[3] The Reichstag broke into applause, and it subsequently passed legislation retroactively legalizing Hitler's extrajudicial murder of the SA leadership, Schleicher, and others. The Führer's judgment determined the rules and procedures, rather than rules and procedures setting limits to what Hitler could do.

The reaction of the German middle class, the military, civil servants, and much of state bureaucracy to the Nazi suppression of the left and the decapitation of SA suggests that they were willing to tolerate and embrace coercion against groups they distrusted.[4] In the last free election, in November 1932, around 1 out of 3 German voters (33.09 percent) had cast their ballots for the Nazi Party, but more Germans had voted for parties of the left (20.43 percent for Social Democratic Party, 16.86 percent for the Communist Party). Yet few Germans outside of the targeted groups raised objections as first the Communist Party and then the Social Democrats and independent labor movement were brutally suppressed and dismantled. During this initial phase, the state established more than seventy detention camps throughout Germany to cope with the thousands of communists, socialists, and union activists detained without charge. The regime was candid that work camps were intended to crush the spirit of regime opponents, reeducating the pliable and punishing and isolating the intransigent. Having demonstrated its willingness to use force against political opponents, the regime began to release rank-and-file leftists willing to adjust to the New Order in late 1933 and early 1934. By May 1934, the camp inmate population had dropped to a quarter of the number imprisoned in mid-1933.[5]

A good portion of the German population embraced the dismantling of the political left, believing that the benefits of "order" outweighed the costs imposed on people and parties they viewed as unpatriotic and threatening. The reaction of nationalists, conservatives, and the churches to the June 1934 extrajudicial killing of Röhm, other SA leaders, and others from across the political spectrum is telling. The churches remained silent, the legal profession endorsed the killings, and the German Army's leadership considered the lives of Schleicher and von Bredow a tolerable price to pay for the decapitation of their main rival, Röhm's paramilitary SA organization. In addition to sending Hitler congratulations on his "soldierly decision" to deal with "traitors and murderers," Minister of Defense Werner von Blomberg instructed his fellow generals to avoid Schleicher's funeral.[6] Only one general, Kurt von Hammerstein-Equord, chose to disregard the order, and his attendance was quietly overlooked as he had already resigned his post as army commander the previous year.[7]

In July 1933, Hitler signed a law designating the National Socialist German Workers Party as the only political party in Germany. Over the next two years, the Nazis consolidated their grip over Germany, taking over or dissolving competing organizations and institutions ranging from unions to professional organizations to cultural enterprises to the civil service.

By early 1935, outright coercion took a backseat in efforts to convince, convert, and transform those who had not voted for Hitler. Hitler understood that his government needed popular support and could not rule by force alone. Writing in *Mein Kampf* more than a decade earlier, he had expounded that governing authority rested in popularity, coercion, and tradition.[8] Once in power, he used all three as tools to generate compliance.

Several historians have argued that the targeted, selective use of terror by the Nazis during the regime's consolidation phase suggests a broader support for its actions and policies than many later cared to recall. The Nazi ideal of a Germanic people's community proved alluring even to those who had voted for the left, with programs such as "Strength through Joy" (*Kraft durch Freude* [*KdF*]) appealing to workers who hitherto had never been able to enjoy a holiday on the beach or in the mountains—let alone a cruise. The KdF and other Nazi programs and organizations—along with its leaders' anti-intellectualism—seemed to substantiate that the Nazi revolution was creating a classless, racially defined society.[9]

Significant portions of the public not only consented but endorsed the redirection of terror, intimidation, and separation as the Nazi state shifted the focus of its repression from political opponents on the left to those it defined as racial aliens and threats to the Germanic community. The chief threat, according to Hitler and his true believers, was the Jew, but Roma and Sinti, "asocials," and the handicapped were all targeted as incompatible with the new Germanic people's community. In September 1935, the Nazi regime announced two new laws. The first, the Reich Citizenship Law, declared that only those of German blood could be citizens, insisting that Jews could not be German.[10] The second, the Law for the Protection of German Blood and German Honor, banned intermarriage between Germans and Jews. It defined who was a Jew and who was of mixed race, and it began the process of classification, dehumanization, and persecution that culminated in extermination during the war.

How successful was the Third Reich at converting the roughly one out of three Germans who had voted either for the Socialist or Communist Party in 1932 to the racial worldview and expansionary agenda of the Nazis? One prominent historian, Robert Gellately, argues that the Nazis were surprisingly successful in convincing large parts of the working class to abandon Marxist conceptions of class for Hitler's vision of a classless, racially defined German community. As for the middle class and elites, many had already adapted themselves to the new order in exchange for nationalist rhetoric, rearmament, and a foreign policy that promised to overthrow the "shackles of Versailles" and restore German greatness. According to Gellately, consent was as important a pillar of the Third Reich as was coercion.[11]

The Gestapo, far from being a vast, pervasive instrument of surveillance and control, was relatively small. More people worked for the East German Ministry of State security in the 1980s than were employed by the Gestapo during the 1930s despite the fact that East Germany had less than a fourth of the population of the Third Reich.[12] The Gestapo depended on denunciations from the public to ferret out political opponents, and their files brim with examples of neighbors deciding to turn in neighbors over behavior deemed critical toward the regime and of pub patrons and work colleagues turning casual acquaintances in for cracking a joke that portrayed Germany's leader unfavorably.[13] Gellately notes that by 1939, some two-thirds of the "Aryan" German population belonged to one of the Nazi Party's branches or suborganizations, and while he acknowledges that the level of political commitment varied among these organizations and among their members, he asserts that many Germans had become "true believers" in the Nazi cause by the start of World War II.[14] An equally prominent historian, Richard J. Evans, argues that coercion should not be underestimated as an essential component of Nazi rule. He contends that the Gestapo, the camp system, and a Nazified judicial system created a pervasive fear that inhibited resistance and squelched nonconformity.[15] Fellow citizens may have denounced those who criticized the regime, but it was the Gestapo, the camps, and force that sapped the will of all but the bravest to resist the authority of Germany's leader.

An estimated 17 million Germans from four different generations served the German Army, Air Force, or Navy at some point in the war.[16] The overwhelming majority of Germans serving in the Third Reich's armed forces fought until killed, captured, or incapacitated by wounds or sickness. Even before he became chancellor, Hitler asserted that the state's authority rested on "popularity, coercion and tradition."[17] Once in power, he used all three of these to consolidate his position. Coercion played a role in his consolidation of power and in the Wehrmacht. But the threat of punishment does not adequately explain why German soldiers fought so doggedly, particularly after the tide of war shifted. Coercion surely played a role, but ideology, camaraderie, conceptions of masculinity, and ingrained nationalism explain why so many fought so long for a regime so repellent.

Ideology, Schooling, and the Hitler Youth

In 1942, more than a third of the soldiers in a typical German infantry division fighting on the Eastern Front were younger than twenty-six years of age and had grown up in the Third Reich. By 1945, over half the soldiers in the same division were younger than twenty-six.[18] The German school system and the Hitler Youth played a major role in influencing the mindset and worldview of this age group, with the education and training they received as boys and young men stressing obedience to the Reich and Führer well before the Wehrmacht hammered home the military conceptions of discipline, duty, and loyalty. Older men who had grown up in the Weimar Republic were more heavily represented in support and technical branches, among the noncommissioned officer corps, and in officer ranks above captain, but many troopers and junior officers were shaped by ideas they first encountered in the Reich's schools and youth programs.

Bernhard Rust, the Reich Minister of Science, Education and Culture, sought to Nazify the German educational system in multiple ways. An "old fighter" Nazi who had joined the party in 1921, he set about ousting leftists, Jews, and democrats from teaching positions once the Nazis gained power in 1933. As Reich Minister, he pushed to thoroughly Nazify the curriculum. German schools were instructed to emphasize history, but a National Socialist version of history focusing on the eternal struggle between the world's races for dominance. Germany's military past became a staple of the curriculum, with textbooks instructing students how German heroes from Arminius to Frederick the Great to Blücher had defeated Rome, France, Russia, and other powers in battle. Teachers regaled young minds about the First Reich and Frederick I (nicknamed "Barbarossa"), of Bismarck's Second Reich and Sedan, and of the new Third Reich which was casting off the shackles of Versailles. They told their charges that this new Reich embodied a new synthesis among the people, the state, and its leader (*Ein Volk, ein Reich, ein Führer*). Science instructors incorporated Nazi themes, with biology classes teaching about racial hierarchies, hereditary traits, and of the alleged danger that Jews posed to the Germanic community. Nazi pedagogues even managed to inject anti-Semitism and "racial science" into mathematics and physics classes, using word problems to drive home racial fabrications.

Many in the teaching profession had been conservative/nationalist even before the Nazi consolidation, and a significant number had voted for the National Socialists during the last months of the Weimar Republic.[19]

By 1937, all German teachers were required to be members of the National Socialist Teachers' League and subjected to workshops and summer refreshers emphasizing that the goal of all instruction was inculcating Nazi worldviews and attitudes. Not every teacher who survived the political and racial purges of the first years internalized this mindset, but one could be certain that there were die-hard Nazis in the administration or among the faculty.[20] These ideologues controlled the agenda and curriculum, carefully watching that others did not stray from it.

Instruction began with a mandatory greeting of "Heil Hitler," and teachers and students were required to listen to broadcasts of the Führer. Conformity and groupthink were enforced on students and teachers alike. A former pedagogue, commenting on the stifling of teacher initiative and of the constant flow of directives to the Reich's schools, complained that "Instead of freedom of learning, we have the most narrow-minded school supervision and spying on teachers and pupils. No free speech is permitted for teachers and pupils, no inner, personal empathy. The whole thing has been taken over by the military spirit, and by drill."[21]

Even more than the school system, the Hitler Youth cultivated the ethos of conformity and obedience, organized around the principle of hierarchical leadership and subordination. The Nazi youth group traced its origin to the mid-1920s, but it grew into a mass organization only after Hitler's consolidation of power. More boys had been members of nationalist Bündische Jugend groups, socialist or communist youth organizations, or religiously affiliated youth associations than had belonged to the NSDAP's youth organization when Hitler was appointed chancellor in 1933. But once in power, the Nazis began the process of merging and consolidating competing groups into their youth organization. Membership in the Hitler Youth had been a paltry 35,000 in 1931, rising to 100,000 by early 1933, 5.4 million by 1937, and 8.7 million by the beginning of 1939.[22] In December 1936, the Reichstag passed a law making the organization the only legally permitted youth organization, culminating a process that began in 1933 with the seizure of property, the dissolution of competing youth organizations, and the assimilation of their members.

The Hitler Youth used various means to elicit voluntary enrollment, ranging from peer pressure to the lure of athletic competition to special days off for Hitler Youth activities. For vocational students, apprenticeships hung in the balance, and university-bound students were not permitted to take entrance examinations if they failed to join the organization.[23] Theoretically, membership remained voluntary until March 1939, after which parents could be fined if they failed to enroll their children in the organization.[24]

The Hitler Youth and its female equivalent, the League of German Girls (*Bund Deutscher Mädel*), drew on boys and girls between the ages of fourteen and eighteen. At age ten, boys and girls could join the *Jungvolk*, a Cub-Scout-like entry organization to the Hitler Youth and League of German Girls. In the *Jungvolk*, young boys (*Pimpfe*) and girls (*Jungmädel*) were readied for the activities and organization of the youth organization they would join at the age of fourteen.[25]

Many were enthusiastic about joining these organizations because they offered the same sort of sense of belonging, adventure, and leadership training that scouting organizations and youth groups have always embodied. The Hitler Youth organized hikes, athletic competitions, camp activities, and trips. But layered over these and infusing the whole organization were two purposes of equal importance. First, athletic fitness and sports were promoted with the objective of making boys ready for military service. Boys were taught how to march in unison, how to listen to commands, and how to read maps and use compasses. Running and boxing made bodies fit for military service and nurtured the "toughness" of mind and body that the soldier should have. The hierarchical structure, the chain of command, the hazing of new members, the marches and inspections, and the camp life and songs all had a strongly military flavor. In addition, the organization sought to indoctrinate its members in Nazi leadership principles, racial viewpoints, and conceptions of government. Hitler's birthday became a major event, and Hitler Youth formations turned out for the endless stream of rallies, speeches, and events organized by the party. In a 1938 speech, Hitler was explicit about the military and political purposes of the Hitler Youth:

> After these youths have entered our organizations at age ten and there experienced, for the first time, some fresh air...we shall under no circumstances return them into the hands of our old champions of class and social standing, but instead place them immediately in the Party or the Labor Front, the SA or SS...And then the Wehrmacht will take them over for further treatment...And thus they will never be free again, for the rest of their lives.[26]

Helmut Gaebelein was not alone in remembering how he pestered his parents to allow him to join the *Pimpfe* after watching the film *Hitler Youth Quex* in 1933. The film, based on a propaganda novel lionizing Herbert "Quex" Norkus, tells the story of a working-class boy from Berlin's Moabit district who decided to join the Hitler Youth rather than the communist *Rote Jungfront* that dominated his neighborhood. "Quex," according to the propaganda book and film, joined the Hitler Youth rather than its leftist counterpart because the Nazi youth group embodied true comradeship reflective of the "people's community," whereas its rivals sought to attract candidates through alcohol, tobacco, and sex. Contrasting the nationalist, disciplined character of the Hitler Youth to the crass indiscipline and self-indulgence of its rivals, the film culminated in a confrontation between the youth groups that cost Norkus his life. Goebbels's propaganda ministry made sure the film had widest distribution, and Baldur von Schirach, the Reich Youth leader, transformed Norkus into a hero and role model for all German boys. Herbert "Quex" Norkus and Hitler Youth more broadly were supposed to embody a new Germany based on race, discipline, and followership as contrasted to Marxist class warfare or the democratic politics the Nazis decried. One scene from the film illustrates how boys were trained to obey and follow: when the new recruit is given his first uniform by his group leader, the troop leader earnestly tells him that the uniform symbolizes a Germany free of class structures and prejudice. The uniform "makes us all equal.... He who wears such a uniform does not have desires of his own anymore, he has only to obey."[27]

This sense of inclusion rested on a bedrock of exclusion. No Jews were allowed in the youth organization, nor were they allowed to use the athletic facilities, swimming pools, parks, and recreational facilities at its disposal. Nazi propaganda about Jews, gypsies, Slavs, and the handicapped was embedded in the program via films, scout papers, lectures, and songs. Boys were reminded that Germany was engaged in a struggle for survival, and survival went to the fittest, most disciplined, and most committed.

Baldur von Schirach realized that the Hitler Youth needed to offer more than ideology and propaganda. It needed to include the same panoply of scouting activities that had drawn boys to join the nationalist Bündische Jugend. Hiking, camping, sailing, archery, and the like were emphasized along with sports ranging from soccer to boxing to gymnastics. Special maritime, aviation, motorcar, equestrian, and mountaineer groups were created, focusing on sailing, flying, driving, riding, and climbing. Shooting ranges and obstacle courses were mainstays of various weekend and summer camps, underlining the connection between youth activities and premilitary training.

Hitler Youth groups typically met on Wednesday evenings for social interaction, instruction, and activities and again on Saturday for hikes, excursions, sport events, and rallies. Special events such as attendance at the Führer's speeches, local excursions, and summer camps created a constant churn of activity and excitement. For some, these activities were a welcome change from academic studies, religious instruction, and parental control. The plethora of leadership opportunities at multiple levels provided a sense of youth empowerment, structured and directed from above following party and military leadership principles. Others found the endless demands tiring, and the call for toughening boys a cover for bullying and humiliating weaker boys or those who did not fit in. One former Hitler Youth member recalled his summer experience in less than fond terms:

> We hardly had any free time. Everything was done in a totally military way, from reveille, first parade, raising the flag, morning sport and ablutions through breakfast to the "scouting games," lunch and so on to the evening. Several participants left the camp because the whole slog was too stupid for them. There was no kind of fellow-feeling between the camp inmates. Comradeship was very poor, and everything was done in terms of command and obedience... The camp leader was an older Hitler Youth functionary of the drill sergeant type. His entire educational effort amounted to barking orders, holding scouting exercises, and general slogging... The whole camp was more hyperactivity and an exaggerated cult of the muscular than a spiritual experience or even an active and co-operatively shaped leisure time.[28]

Not every boy or girl was an enthusiastic member of the Hitler Youth or the League of German Maidens. But most participated, and nearly one in ten rose to a leadership position at the local, regional, or national level in the vast, sprawling organization.[29] These young believers enforced discipline and conformity in the Hitler Youth, bringing the values they had learned in the Hitler Youth into the military once they became soldiers. The Hitler Youth was designed to ingrain patterns of obedience, toughness, and subordination to the group. Sensitivity, softness, and individualism were pushed aside in order to create the German boy of the future who would be as "tough as leather and hard as Krupp steel."[30] The organization served to militarize and Nazify German youth well before they became soldiers, sailors, or airmen to the Reich. It bred conformity, obedience, and loyalty to the group.

Kameradschaft

The Hitler Youth and the follow-on mandatory Reich Labor Service nurtured conformity and willing obedience to the group, party, and nation. Both sought to turn boys into men, specifically German men eager and able to fight for the proposition of *ein Volk, ein Reich, ein Führer*. Both sought to instill martial values, training youths to subordinate individualism to group dictates. For the generation coming of age during the Third Reich, both served as preludes to service in the Wehrmacht. Many of the 17 million who served in the German military during World War II, however, had reached adulthood before the Nazi consolidation of power, and they drew on older, more universal concepts such as duty, honor, *Kameradschaft*, and country to justify why they continued to serve under the most trying circumstances during World War II.

For officers and career noncombatants, the military virtues of duty and honor were pillars of their self-definition, with a great deal of ink spilled after the war on the inviolability of the oath they had given to serve the Führer unconditionally. Officers who survived the war likewise made reference to Prussian conceptions of honor which prohibited surrender or desertion. One might note that only a few paid much attention to oaths they had given to the Weimar constitution, and references to military honor did not stand in the way of the German Army's implementation of the commissar order or its intentional starvation of millions of Russian soldiers captured by the German Army in 1941/1942. A more convincing reason than oaths and honor for the reluctance of all but a tiny minority to desert is that most felt a bond to others in their unit.[31]

The German term *Kameradschaft* has been variously translated as comradeship, camaraderie, small group cohesion, or military bonding. The concept echoes across time and space as veterans have struggled to explain the relationship they formed with one another, with references to a "band of brothers," trench pals, shipmates, and the aircrew conveying an emotional, familial attachment and intense sense of community. Veterans speak of the difficulty of conveying the experience of battle, and of the bonds forged in the air, at sea, or at the front, groping for words to explain unit bonding. Wehrmacht veterans, seeking to explain to younger Germans in the 1980s and 1990s why so many of them fought to the bitter end for a regime whose ideology this newer generation believed was detestable, claimed they had done so because of *Kameradschaft* rather than because of Nazi ideology. One veteran, seeking to explain to a younger historian what *Kameradschaft* entailed, claimed that it was a notion the younger man could not understand; the term was meaningless without experience, floating in the air and incomprehensible to those who had not transitioned a "landscape of death" as part of a military group.[32] *Kameradschaft*, in short, was an almost mystical relationship that could not be explained. It had to be experienced.

One of the first postwar studies examining why the German Army had fought on tenaciously even when cut off, in retreat, or surrounded affirmed the importance of primary group relationship. Edward A. Shils and Morris Janowitz, two sociologists at the University of Chicago, drew upon frontline interrogations of Germans soldiers captured by US forces, POW camp assessments of Germans held by the United States, and captured German records to analyze why Wehrmacht forces had not disintegrated, surrendered, or deserted more frequently. Shils and Janowitz both served in the Intelligence Section of the Psychological Warfare Division of SHAEF (Supreme Headquarters, Allied Expeditionary Forces) during World War II and were intrigued by the limited success that Allied propaganda had in terms of undermining German military cohesion and stimulating disintegration among frontline units. Their 1948 study argued that Nazi ideology had contributed "only to a very slight extent...[to] the determined resistance of the German soldier."[33] Instead, the German soldier had fought because his small unit—the primary group—had "offered him affection and esteem from both officers and comrades, supplied him with a sense of power and adequately regulated his relations with authority."[34] Allied propaganda was unable to overcome bonds of loyalty to others in the unit, and efforts to unmask the criminality of the regime and the hopelessness of the war were "mainly unsuccessful" so long as the primary group remained intact.

Trevor Dupuy, an American officer and scholar, and Martin van Creveld, an Israeli military historian, went a step further than Shils and Janowitz to assert that the German military had been peculiarly adept at generating the sort of small-unit loyalty and cohesion that sustains fighting power. In Dupuy's *A Genius for War* (1977) and van Creveld's *Fighting Power:*

German and U.S. Army Performance, 1939–1945 (1982), both insisted that German training, its recruitment/replacement system, and small-unit leadership had been extraordinarily effective in generating cohesion and resilience within the German military. Focusing on the German Army, Dupuy and van Creveld concluded that its rigorous, realistic training coupled with geographic recruitment and unit reconstitution generated a remarkable resiliency.[35] Van Creveld, echoing Shils and Janowitz, asserted that the German soldier "did not as a rule fight out of a belief in Nazi ideology.... Instead he fought for the reasons that men have always fought: because he felt himself a member of a well-integrated, well-led team whose structure, administration, and functioning were perceived to be, on the whole... equitable and just."[36]

Omer Bartov's 1985 analysis of German troops on the Eastern Front challenged the idea that small-group dynamics lay at the core of Wehrmacht resilience. Bartov believed that ideology, racial worldviews, and anti-Semitism had been more important to German fighting power than Shils, Janowitz, Dupuy, and Creveld had recognized. Shifting focus from the Western Front to the Eastern Front in his tremendously influential *The Eastern Front, 1941–45: German Troops and the Barbarization of Warfare* (1985), Bartov insisted that anti-Semitism and Nazi ideology had been central to sustaining the will to fight. It was because of them that war in the East had been brutal, barbarous, and unconstrained from the start. Bartov pointed out that the tremendous casualty rates suffered by the German military in the East made building small-unit identity impossible after 1943, and he posited that high turnover rates made the sort of intense interpersonal relationship that may have existed earlier a relic of the past. The German Army was forced to cobble together formations from disparate units during the final years of the war, and still it fought on. Nazi ideology, the quest for German *Lebensraum*, annihilationist anti-Semitism, and anti-Bolshevism had sustained the determination of German soldiers to fight after the tide turned. Widespread knowledge that Germans had slaughtered Jews, communists, and partisans generated fear of retribution even among those who did not share Nazi values. Bartov's groundbreaking piece, soon joined by a gathering flood of literature exploding the myth of a clean Wehrmacht, projected a different, darker image of how *Kameradschaft* operated.[37]

Recent scholarship has provided a more synthetic view that recognizes that primary group loyalty and a commitment to and internalization of what Shils and Janowitz termed "secondary values"—politics, ideology, culture, ethics—are by no means an either/or proposition. Indeed, Shil and Janowitz had noted back in 1948 that the "stability and military effectiveness of the military primary group were in large measure a function of the 'hard core' [those imbued with Nazi ideology], who approximated about ten to fifteen per cent of the total of enlisted men," and ran higher and very much higher among noncommissioned officers and junior officers.[38] Shil and Janowitz based their assessment of Germans fighting on the Western Front; one might reasonably expect that the proportion of troops internalizing Nazi ideological worldviews was even greater on the Eastern Front where key elements of that ideology—*Lebensraum*, annihilationist anti-Semitism, anti-Bolshevism, and a racial ordering of peoples—were central to how and why the German military fought. Primary group bonding, in short, did not operate in a vacuum. So long as a "hard core" of men supported the regime and continued to be recognized as leaders by most of the group, these true believers set the boundaries of what could and couldn't be said within the sanctums of comradeship.

That many soldiers, sailors, and airmen remained with their units because of bonds of loyalty to one another is well-established. There was something to the idea of *Kameradschaft* that made desertion seem a personal betrayal to many. The German military services devoted a great deal of effort to doing away with some of the grievances that had enraged the common soldier and sailor of World War I: better food for officers than enlisted men, a class divide between the leader and the led, and martinet drill sergeants who delighted in humiliating their charges while avoiding frontline duty themselves. National Socialism, with its emphasis on the German community, pushed class pretensions into the background within the context of the primary group.

Two of the best studies of *Kameradschaft* to appear since Bartov's pioneering study contend that primary group loyalty and a Nazi *Weltanschauung* reinforced one another in fending off disintegration, desertion, or mutiny. *Kameradschaft*, in the words of German scholar Thomas Kühne, needs to be understood in its specific social fabric and setting. One must avoid essentializing the primary group and recognize that primary group loyalty need not be juxtaposed against higher-order values such as ideology and nationalism.[39] During World War II, the horizontal bonds of loyalty, affection, and respect that existed within Wehrmacht primary groups operated alongside vertical conceptions of *Kameradschaft* that embedded ideological conceptions of the Germanic people's community.

How, when, why, and whether men developed bonds of *Kameradschaft* with each other varied by organization (Wehrmacht or SS), service (Army, Navy, Air Force), branch (armor, infantry, submarine or surface, etc.), status (officer, noncommissioned officer, enlisted; frontline or support), time period, and region. Some men never experienced the sort of intimacy, bonding, warmth, and trust conveyed by the term, while for others, the unit became an almost sacred place. For some, *Kameradschaft* truly unfolded only in and after the experience of combat, while others succumbed to the mystique of the concept already in basic training. The SS, excluded from this analysis, certainly nurtured a unique, brutal, and highly ideological form of *Kameradschaft*, while the Navy and Air Force nurtured a *Kameradschaft* that made much of the sea and air domains where their combat power unfolded. Naval officers developed a special bond among each year-group of midshipmen that endured for years, and the U-boat branch claimed that the bonds between the crew and captain were exceptional.[40] The primary group itself and the vocabulary of *Kameradschaft* differed among frontline infantry units, panzer troops, aircrews, and fast attack boats. Those aspiring to become officers before the outbreak of war spent years acculturating themselves to military discipline and professionalism in cadet schools, academies, and officer programs, but for most Germans, the intense, rigorous basic training that turned civilian recruits into soldiers, sailors, or airmen laid the groundwork for *Kameradschaft*.

Some form of basic training served as the gateway to military life for most Germans who served in the Wehrmacht. The training regime differed by service, but all initial training entailed three elements: physical conditioning designed to make the recruit fit for combat; familiarization with basic military skills such as marching, shooting a rifle, throwing a grenade, and so forth; and developing habits of instinctive obedience, with individual needs and desires subordinated to the group's success. Basic training was meant to be arduous, realistic, and stressful, but pointless bullying and hazing—known as *Schikane*—were frowned on.[41] One veteran of the Hitler Youth remembered that "Our training was unbelievably hard, but basically fair. It passed quickly [because] we were drilled so hard from morning to night that we never got a moment to think."[42] Another recalled that harassment persisted but rationalized that it led his squad to stick together like "peas and carrots" in order to succeed. He and other recruits who had been total strangers at the outset emerged from basic training with an "amazing spirit of comradeship."[43]

The concept of creating unit solidarity during basic training by imposing stress was and is not unique to the German military. Recruits were forced to confront the fact that they needed to rely on one another, and that success was not an individual achievement. Drill, marching, and group exercise all sought to create a group "We" out of the individual "I's" that made up the unit. Max Momsen, a German academic of the era, described the process of transformation in the following terms: "When camp service seizes the body and compels it to a certain concise performance, it also forces the body into certain mental and emotional habits, which consist first of all in relinquishing all that is individual and selfish.... The private self, the individual, will be broken. This might be a hard and painful procedure. It is inevitable, though, for the sake of a higher and larger community."[44]

The hazing and chicanery of initial training served a purpose if kept in bounds. The drill sergeant became the adversary of each recruit, driving them together through the shared emotional testing and physical exhaustion. For young recruits already primed for the experience, basic training went a step beyond the camp life they had encountered in the Hitler Youth and during their Labor Service year. Its rigor hammered them together, and the realism of its training persuaded most that it served a purpose. The use of collective punishment for the derelictions or failures of an individual member of squad accelerated group cohesion. Since everyone might feel the wrath of the drill instructor for the failure of one individual, the strong began to help the weak, and the competent began to assist the less competent. On an uglier note, it also led to self-policing whereby nonconformists and individualists who did not contribute to group success would be taught a lesson by their peers. The lesson might range from peer admonitions and dirty looks to "blanket parties" (unauthorized beating by peers) communicating group expectations.[45] Few recruits relished the stress and exhaustion of basic training, but most recognized that the military's intense regime of realistic training might save their lives.

Basic training may have initiated recruits into the sphere of *Kameradschaft*, but the experienced veteran would scoff at the notion that shared training generated the intimate bonds associated with the term. For those who served at the front, it was the experience of combat that turned a fellow soldier, sailor, or airman into a *Kamerad*. It was facing death together and surviving. It was shared hunger, exhaustion, and exposure, coupled with the stark reality of one's own mortality. The German military's recruitment and replacement system helped create a sense of cohesion within units, but only when facing an enemy did the We/They of *Kameradschaft* fully develop.

The German Army associated its line units with specific geographical military districts, drawing replacements from that region when the unit was refitting and recovering. Rather than feeding in replacements individually, the unit would receive contingents of replacements when it was refitting and recovering from combat. Ideally, the replacements would be integrated into the unit seamlessly, with veterans of the unit instructing newcomers on how things were done while the unit was refitting. Once at the front, the experience of combat welded both veterans and green replacements together, with the process repeating itself once losses reached a certain level and the unit withdrew for refitting. The massive losses suffered by the German Army on the Eastern Front put increasing pressure on this pattern of refitting, replacing, and replenishing, with piecemeal and ad hoc replacements increasingly the norm for units that could not be withdrawn from frontline action. Bartov and others have therefore questioned the centrality of *Kameradschaft* as a motivational factor, arguing that ideology was more important. The latest scholarship argues that the two worked in tandem, and that the ideal of *Kameradschaft* enabled rapid bonding between men who may have only known each other for days. Attempting to explain how this was possible, one veteran remembered that when he returned to his unit after convalescence, most of his old comrades were dead, missing, or injured. But he rapidly reintegrated into the unit because he still felt loyalty to it. Writing to his family, he expressed this bonding as follows: "It is all the same, whether we know each other or not, we are all comrades here who all depend on each other."[46]

In seeking to reassure wives, parents, and loved ones in letters home, those at the front most frequently used the analogy of the family to express their relationship with one another. Fellow soldiers were like brothers, the company commander or ship's captain like a stern but benevolent father, and the cook, the chaplain, or someone else the caring mother figure.[47] A divisional chaplain assigned to an infantry division, wrote in his diary in 1942 that "one could feel that a company really was a sort of little family."[48] The shared tribulations of combat, of shared terror, and of survival drove men together. One gladly shared one's rations, a last cigarette, or a package from home with others, knowing that one's survival might rest on them. This level of trust did not develop in all units, and it depended on leadership and example.[49] But for many, *Kameradschaft* proved a difficult barrier to breach, transforming desertion from a personal or political decision to a betrayal akin to abandoning a brother.

The Wehrmacht drew on the vocabulary and narratives of a German military tradition reaching back centuries, and it very deliberately nurtured the idea of a special military bond known as *Kameradschaft*. In 1809, the German Romantic poet Ludwig Uhland penned a poem entitled *Der gute Kamerad* (The Good Comrade). Using a Swiss folk tune, Friedrch Silcher combined lyrics and melody, creating a moving piece of music that became associated with military funerals in Austria and Prussia in the nineteenth century. The melody and lyrics of *Der gute Kamerad* became fixtures of veteran meetings after World War I and were central to commemoration of the dead in World War II. They would have been instantly recognized to anyone serving in the German Army, Air Force, or Navy. The sense of loss and tenderness in the song reflected the intense personal bond forged in combat.

Der gute Kamerad
Ludwig Uhland (1809)

Ich hatt' einen Kameraden,	I once did have a comrade,
Einen bessern findst du nit.	No one better you would find.
Die Trommel schlug zum Streite,	The drum called us to battle,
Er ging an meiner Seite	He had marched there, at my side
In gleichem Schritt und Tritt. 2x	In perfect pace and stride. 2x
Eine Kugel kam geflogen:	A bullet came a-flying,
Gilt's mir oder gilt es dir?	Was it meant for me or you?
Ihn hat es weggerissen,	Then it swept his life away,
Er liegt zu meinen Füßen	He lies here at my feet,
Als wär's ein Stück von mir. 2x	As were he part of me. 2x
Will mir die Hand noch reichen,	He reached his hand out to me,
Derweil ich eben lad.	As I was trying to reload.
"Kann dir die Hand nicht geben,	"I cannot take your hand, right now
Bleib du im ew'gen Leben	May you rest there, in eternal life
Mein guter Kamerad!" 2x	My good comrade." 2x[50]

Intersecting with the habits of obedience nurtured in the Hitler Youth and the bonds of *Kameradschaft* that developed at the small unit level was the German soldier's perception of what was expected of a man.

Gender and Masculinity

Those contemplating desertion not only had to consider whether they were betraying their comrades in arms but also had to grapple with the notion that desertion was considered deeply unmanly. Social theories of gender posit that masculinity is a construct, and that the dominant, culturally accepted form of masculinity is hegemonic, suppressing and stigmatizing alternative interpretations of what it means to be a man.[51] Under the Third Reich, two levels of masculinity existed above the dominant interpretation of masculinity. The dominant, prevalent form can be labeled traditional masculinity. In essence, it was not substantially different than conceptions of masculinity elsewhere in Europe. It associated certain traits with the male and others with the female. Men were strong, brave, disciplined, and in control of their emotions, while women were gentle, fearful, submissive, and emotional. Politics and war were male domains, while the domestic sphere, the family, and child-rearing were female matters.

Layered upon this traditional form of masculinity was a heroic version of masculinity. Though it was not unique to Germany, this militarized conception of manhood resonated deeply in nationalist, middle-class circles in Germany following defeat in World War I. Believing that defeat could only have been possible because of betrayal, and interpreting the terms of the Versailles Treaty as a humiliation, German nationalists embraced a hard, aggressive, and misogynist version of masculinity that went beyond traditional masculinity. Klaus Theweleit, a German sociologist, examined what Free Corps paramilitary members wrote and read during the early years of the Weimar Republic and concluded that their conception of manhood was fascist at its core.[52] The male should be not only strong but aggressive, not only brave but fearless, not only action-oriented but disdainful of intellectualism. This hard new man did not cringe from violence, but embraced it. War unleashed the man of action from the restraints of civilization, transforming men into heroes. Contrasting strength and maleness against weakness and femininity, this heroic, militarized vision of manhood veered toward homoeroticism in its misogyny. Hitler's decapitation of the SA and his execution of Ernst Röhm reinforced heterosexuality as the accepted version of masculinity, as the state and military prosecuted and persecuted overt homosexuality in society and in the ranks.[53] Drawing from the Spartan model of militarized pederasty, the heroic vision of the aggressive, dominant man of action proved appealing to wide swathes of the German population.

Nationalists and Nazis found Erich Maria Remarque's *All Quiet on the Western Front*, released as a book in 1929 and as a film in 1930, deeply disturbing because it undermined their conception of manhood. SA troopers picketed movie theaters showing the film, and after coming to power, the Nazis banned the book as degenerate, pacifist, and subversive. In contrast, Ernst Jünger's *Storm of Steel* (1920) attracted the accolades of nationalist and Nazi commentators throughout the Weimar period, and it was republished during the Third Reich though Jünger warded off attempts by the Nazis to co-opt him. The memoir recalled the horrors of World War I but gave them meaning as selfless, heroic sacrifice. Its 1934 edition was dedicated "to the fallen."

The heroic, militarized ideal of manhood accentuated traits already present in the traditional conceptions of what it meant to be a man. Men should not only be strong and brave but also action-oriented, decisive, and aggressive. Sentiment and introspection needed to be pushed aside at the front. *Kameradschaft*, patriotism, and self-sacrifice defined the best of men, whereas self-interest, individualism, and moral squeamishness were weaknesses that had to be overcome. Men were hard, not compassionate; bold, not hesitant; and brave, not fearful. Those prone to self-reflection, humanistic musings, and moral doubts were weak and feminine.

Resting above traditional and heroic conceptions of manhood was the Nazi construction of the "German man." The Nazis emphasized that the German male was part of a racially (rather than politically) defined Germanic community. This German identity based itself on völkisch conceptions of the nation, and it was defined in its opposition to the Other, chiefly the Jew but also the Bolshevik, the socialist, the democrat, and the pacifist. The German man, according to this construct, stood opposed to all of these. Blending patriotism, nationalism, notions of maleness, and anti-Semitism, the Nazis associated additional traits and characteristics to masculinity. The male was held to be loyal, but loyal to the Führer and the German *Volksgemeinschaft* rather than simply his brothers in arms. The notion of the *Kamerad* was transformed into the notion of the *Volkskamerad*.

The centrality of gender expectations to military discipline becomes apparent in the pervasive references to the need to uphold *Manneszucht* in the military.[54] Usually translated simply as "discipline," the gendered term *Manneszucht* reveals the connection between manhood and discipline. As war loomed, the Nazi government put into effect the sweeping Order Imposing Extraordinary Wartime Laws and Penalties (*KSSVO*).[55]

Paragraph 5 of the *KSSVO* focused on the charge of undermining the military willpower (*Zersetzung der Wehrkraft*). Anyone who encouraged desertion, unauthorized absence, and subversion of discipline (*Manneszucht*) in the Wehrmacht committed a capital crime. The revised wartime edition of German Military Penal Code, released in October 1940, duly incorporated this gendered phrasing into its hitherto gender-neutral construct of "Instigating Dissatisfaction."[56]

The linkage between masculinity and military order, and the explicit connotation that the deserter was acting in an unmanly manner, became increasingly clear as the tide of war turned against Germany. Three illustrations make this explicit, defining service at the front in terms of the German man's duty to protect German women and children.

Luftwaffe pilots and aircrew, once at the cutting edge of Germany's wars of aggression and domination, increasingly were drawn back to the Reich as Britain's Bomber Command and the US 8th Air Force began to strike the German homeland with increasing effectiveness in 1944 and 1945. This enforced shift to the defensive, at odds with the ethos of airpower, was challenging at multiple levels. Luftwaffe pilots and Hitler Youth antiaircraft gunners were constantly reminded that they were protecting German women and children from Allied bombs, even as an increasing number of young German women were drawn directly into the enterprise, "manning" antiaircraft guns as personnel shortages became acute.[57]

German U-boat crews in the Atlantic, facing the high likelihood that they would not return from their next mission after mid-1943, were exhorted that their engagement at sea still served a purpose. As German men, they had a duty to sink Allied tankers and freighters since every loss inflicted on the enemy would save German lives. Every torpedoed oil tanker meant fewer Allied aircraft able to fly over Germany, and every ammunition freighter sent to the bottom of the Atlantic meant fewer bombs available to drop on Germany. As late as April 1945, long after any hope of turning the tide had dissipated, Grand Admiral Dönitz continued to exhort his men that "We soldiers of the navy know how we have to act. Our military duty, which we unerringly fulfill, whatever happens around us, leaves us standing as a rock of resistance, bold, hard and loyal. Anyone not acting in this way is a scumbag and must be hanged with a notice around his neck saying 'Here hangs a traitor who from the most base cowardice has helped German women and children to die instead of protecting them like a man.'"[58]

Goebbels and his propaganda ministry painted the grimmest images of what was in store for German women as Allied forces pushed toward the Reich in 1944–1945. German soldiers fighting in the East had no doubt that the Red Army would exact terrible revenge for the atrocities Germans had inflicted against Russian civilians. On October 21, 1944, Red Army units pressed into the Reich and occupied the town of Nemmersdorf in East Prussia. Two days later, the German military regained the town and discovered that the Russians had executed every German they had encountered, raping most of the women, and nailing several naked captives to barn doors before evacuating the town.[59] Goebbels and the German High Command made sure that German soldiers fighting in the East learned of the incident, painting lurid pictures of what was in store for German women if the Red Army managed to conquer the Reich. German soldiers were urged to fight to the end with explicit references to their role as the male protector of their wives, fiancées, and daughters. More than a few understood the Wehrmacht had treated the wives, fiancées, and daughters of their opponents brutally and anticipated the worst.

The record indicates that these misgivings were not misplaced. The soldiers of the Red Army raped German women of all ages as they moved into the Reich in 1945 and during the first months of occupation.[60] Few Soviet officers intervened, and a good number joined in the orgy of retribution. The mass rape of German women by Red Army forces during the last months of the war and the first months of occupation went beyond sexual release and revenge. It had a political undercurrent, signaling to all Germans that the "German man" had been unable to fulfill the most basic obligation of husband and father, the protection of his wife and daughter. It was meant to discredit an ideology built on racial hierarchies and German dominance, illustrating that the German superman was utterly helpless. So long as German units had the means to resist, however, stories of impending Russian revenge and rape made desertion a difficult choice for German soldiers.

The habits of obedience instilled in the Hitler Youth, the construct of *Kameradschaft*, and the narratives of masculinity made desertion distasteful or unthinkable for the most German soldiers, sailors, and airmen. Adding another barrier to desertion was the belief that desertion meant betraying the nation and the German people. Only a few could differentiate between loyalty to the Fatherland and the German people and loyalty to the regime and its leader. After World War II, polls revealed that many Germans continued to regard Stauffenberg and those involved in planning the July 20th attempt on Hitler's life as traitors. Well into the 1980s, many characterized Wehrmacht deserters as cowards who had abandoned their comrades, betrayed their loved ones at home, and turned their back on the Fatherland.

Patriotism, Nationalism, and the *Volksgemeinschaft*

The notion that soldiers fight for country and nation is too often taken for granted without adequate introspection. Warriors, legionnaires, knights, militias, and mercenaries have fought for honor, empire, liege lord, town, and profit over the course of history. The idea of fighting for the nation is a relatively modern concept that begs the question "What is the nation?" Peoples throughout history have defined themselves in different ways, identifying themselves by village, town, or locale; by religion, faith, or creed; by the chief, lord, or king they serve; or by a myriad of other associations. Benedict Anderson's notion of the nation as an "imagined community" remains influential because it succinctly captures the notion of the nation as a constructed identity created at different rates and in different ways over time.[61]

Notions of a German people or *Volk* can be detected before Napoleon, but prior to the French Revolution, most people residing in what became Germany still defined themselves in terms of social status (peasant, townsman, noble), work/guild (farmer, merchant, craftsman), religion (Catholic, Protestant, Jew), and town/region/state (Hamburger, Rhinelander, Bavarian) rather than as German. As Enlightenment ideas began to question tradition and the established order, figures such as the philosopher Johann Gottfried Herder led the way in conceptualizing a German nation that extended beyond the stifling provincialism of the myriad political entities that existed. Interested in language, literature, and the philosophy of history, Herder posited that language, culture, folk songs, and shared historical experiences defined the essential communities that together make up humanity, the folk group or *Volk*. Herder and other German Enlightenment figures posited a broader German nation and defined it not in political terms but in terms of language and culture.

Herder was not alone in thinking about a Germany above and distinct from the myriad political entities that constituted the Germanic community.

He initially welcomed the French Revolution as a manifestation of the French people's free will, and his views on Slavs, Latvians, and other peoples stayed clear of the chauvinism that later colored German nationalism.

The Napoleonic Wars, the dissolution of the Holy Roman Empire, and the experience of French occupation greatly accelerated the growth of German nationalism. German philosophers, writers, and activists ranging from Johann Gottlieb Fichte to Friedrich Ludwig Jahn to Ernst Moritz Arndt reacted to the exploitation of French occupiers and the military humiliation of the two leading German states (Prussia, Austria) by Napoleon's army by appealing to the German nation as a whole. Fichte, a giant of the German Enlightenment who like Herder had initially welcomed the French Revolution, delivered a series of addresses to the German nation criticizing the "foreign spirit" (French influence) prevailing.[62] Friedrich Ludwig Jahn, founder of the German gymnastics movement, sought to instill a sense of German nationalism among its youth. Railing that "Poles, French, priests, aristocrats and Jews are Germany's misfortune," Jahn played a role in founding the Lützow Free Corps fighting Napoleon's armies. The Corps drew on volunteers from the multiple states constituting Germany as an "imagined community," and its colors would later be adopted by the Weimar Republic and the Third Reich's successor states, West and East Germany.

Ernst Moritz Arndt, historian and poet, was among the loudest voices arguing that Germany needed to rise up and throw out the French occupiers. Best known for his song "What is the German Fatherland?," penned in 1813 at the height of nationalist efforts to drive French forces out of Germany, Arndt was relentless in arguing the superiority of German *Kultur* over French *civilisation*. The song, first performed in 1814, resonated deeply among German nationalists and reveals the basic conundrum facing German nationalists throughout the nineteenth century: how to reconcile the linguistic and cultural community of the German peoples with the notion of a nation-state. Four stanzas illustrate how aspirations dating back to the German awakening of 1813–1814 resonated with German nationalists and defined Germany in a maximalist way. Arndt repeated the question he posited in the first stanza multiple times, naming a particular region of Germany (including German-speaking Switzerland and Austria) and insisting that this region was not the German fatherland. Germany, per Arndt, was made up of *all* the regions in Europe that spoke German.

Des deutschen Vaterland
Ernst Moritz Arndt 1813

1	1
Was ist des Deutschen Vaterland?	What is the German's fatherland?
Ist's Preußenland? Ist's Schwabenland?	Is it Prussia, is it Swabia?
Ist's, wo am Rhein die Rebe blüht?	Is it where the vines blossom on the Rhine?
Ist's, wo am Belt die Möwe zieht?	Is it where the gull moves on the Belt?
O nein, nein, nein!	Oh no! No! No!
Sein Vaterland muss größer sein!	His fatherland must be bigger!
…	…
3.	3.
Was ist des Deutschen Vaterland?	What is the German's fatherland?
Ist's Pommerland? Westfalenland?	Is it Pomerania, Westphalia?
Ist's, wo der Sand der Dünen weht?	Is it where the sand of dunes blows?
Ist's, wo die Donau brausend geht?	Is it where the Danube rushes along?
O nein, nein, nein!	Oh no! No! No!
Sein Vaterland muss größer sein!	His fatherland must be bigger!
…	…
6	6
Was ist des Deutschen Vaterland?	What is the German's fatherland?
So nenne endlich mir das Land!	So name the great land to me, finally!
So weit die deutsche Zunge klingt	As far as the German tongue sounds
Und Gott im Himmel Lieder singt:	And sings songs to God in heaven:
Das soll es sein! Das soll es sein!	That shall it be, shall it be!
Das, wackrer Deutscher, nenne dein!	That, brave German, call that yours!
…	…
8	8
Was ist des Deutschen Vaterland,	What is the German's fatherland,
Wo Zorn vertilgt den welschen Tand,	Where rage wipes out the foreign junk,
Wo jeder Franzmann heißet Feind,	Where every Frenchman is called enemy,
Wo jeder Deutsche heißet Freund.	Where every German is called friend.
Das soll es sein! das soll es sein!	That shall it be,
Das ganze Deutschland soll es sein!	The whole of Germany it should be.[63]

Arndt's anti-French rhetoric and his insistence that Germany was more than Prussia, Bavaria, and Austria needs to be understood in the context of his time, as does the more famous *Deutschlandlied* (Song of the Germans) written a generation later by August Heinrich Hoffmann von Fallersleben and adopted as Germany's national anthem in the 1920s.[64] Both songs argue against the small state particularism that divided Germans into Wurtemburgers, Saxons, Bavarians, and so forth, and stressed that patriotism was owed to a broader German identity. But it was not a giant leap to connect the idea of a cultural German nation (Herder) to a German political state (nineteenth-century nationalism, Second Reich) to fantasies about bringing all Germans "home into the Reich" (Free Corps, National Socialism).

Early nineteenth-century German nationalists would be bitterly disappointed by the political arrangements put into place following Napoleon's defeat. No unified German nation emerged from the war of liberation (1813), but rather a weak German confederation dominated by its two most powerful states, Prussia and Austria. Their rulers carefully monitored any expressions that threatened the establishment's hold on power, sharply curtailing freedom of expression and stifling political reform. Forced to either emigrate or redirect their energy back to cultural definitions of what it meant to be German, German nationalists reengaged in the project of defining Germany in terms of ethnicity. The Brothers Grimm followed the path blazed by Herder, focusing on culture from below as they collected folktales on the verge of disappearing. In Bavaria, King Ludwig constructed the Walhalla memorial monument celebrating great Germans ranging from medieval King Henry the Fowler to Romantic-era Johann Wolfgang Goethe.

Politically, the grand story of German nationalism revolved around who and how the German nation would be defined. The failure of the 1848 revolution and dissolution of the Frankfurt parliament brought an abrupt end to the dreams of liberal, bourgeois Germans that Germany would be united from below and governed as a parliamentary democracy. Instead, Bismarck united Germany using "Blood and Iron."[65] Prussian-led victories over Denmark, Austria, and France in 1864, 1866, and 1870 determined the geographical contours of a united German nation, excluding the millions of German speakers in the Austro-Hungarian Empire.

Nationalism is based both on inclusion and exclusion, and German nationalism was created by both of these.[66] Defining Germany as a cultural community allowed one to include Rhineland Catholics, East Prussian Protestants, Frisian-speaking fishermen, and even dour Swiss Germans in a cultural community, but translating that constructed cultural community into a political entity was immensely difficult. Defining Germany in terms of what it was not—in terms of its opposition to the Other—proved essential to the creation of German nationalism. For Fichte, Jahn, Arendt, and others of the Romantic era, the German stood in contrast to the Frenchman. During German unification, Bismarck manipulated feelings against the Danes and French as part of his agenda to secure Prussian leadership of a Germany that excluded Austria. His successors in turn made the Other a key part of defining Germany, contrasting German *Kultur* against French *civilisation*, English commercialism, and Russian backwardness. Defining Germany required an Other precisely because Germans had been historically divided, spoke various dialects, followed different creeds, and had different traditions.

In addition to the external Other, German nationalists also pointed to an internal Other, the Jew. The roots of German anti-Semitism run deep, tracing back past the Reformation and Martin Luther's condemnation of the Jews to the Middle Ages, when German crusaders believed it right and godly to slaughter Rhineland Jews before embarking on their journey to the Holy Land. But most observers would have pointed out that Russia was far more intolerant of its Jewish population in the nineteenth century than Germany was, and that civilized France was torn apart by the Dreyfus Affair in the 1890s. Anti-Semitism was more central to the political program of German nationalists in Austro-Hungary than to the political parties in the German Empire, as Georg Ritter von Schönerer's Pan-German movement railed against Jews and Slavs.

Hitler imbibed the populist anti-Semitism rampant in Vienna during his years in that city and made anti-Semitism a pillar of the German Workers' Party he joined in 1919. Renamed the National Socialist German Workers' Party in 1920, the party drew upon and exploited nationalist definitions of Germany as the people's community (*Volksgemeinschaft*) rather than merely a state. Hitler appealed to nationalists by rejecting the borders imposed on the German people by the Versailles Treaty, demanding that German borders be redrawn to match the areas where Germans lived, and making anti-Semitism, "racial science," and the quest for living space the essence of his program. National Socialists demonized the Jew as both the internal and foreign Other, associating everything they loathed from Bolshevism to modernism to parliamentarianism to pacifism to cosmopolitanism with the Jew. They insisted that the true German was not only different and superior to the Frenchman, the Pole, and the Slav, but that Germany was at war with international Jewry.

Hitler came to power in coalition with German nationalists and conservatives who thought they could co-opt and control him. Instead, he co-opted and controlled them as became glaringly apparent when none lifted a finger as his henchmen "cleaned house" in June 1934, executing the SA leadership along with former chancellor General Kurt von Schleicher and the personal aide to Vice-Chancellor von Papen. Equally important, Hitler and the National Socialists co-opted and appropriated the main pillars of German nationalism. They appropriated the vocabulary, symbols, songs, and arguments of German nationalists who had created the "imagined community" that was Germany. The continuous reference to *das Volk*, the use of German folk melodies and marching songs, the celebration of poets, authors, and composers deemed German, and the exclusion of those who had been cosmopolitan, left-leaning, or Jewish echoed Napoleonic era efforts to define the German nation as a people rather than state. Culture and ethnicity determined who was a German, not borders.

National Socialism had made significant inroads into the German universities, the teaching profession, and the professional strata before Hitler's appointment as chancellor. And just as nationalism had proved more powerful than international socialism in 1914, Hitler's remilitarization of the Rhineland, his annexation of Austria, and his incorporation of the Sudeten region of Czechoslovakia appealed to Germans across the class divide. For many working-class Germans, National Socialism meant jobs, access to leadership positions once reserved for a social elite, and public displays affirming that the state recognized their worth within the constructed German community known as the *Volksgemeinschaft*.

The creation of the National Socialist *Volksgemeinschaft* rested on the violent decapitation of the left and the suppression of alternative worldviews. Once this was accomplished, the state turned its attention to confronting the domestic Other it had manufactured, the Jew. Soon after coming to power, the National Socialists passed laws excluding Jews from civil service positions and curtailing their access to university education, the legal profession, and other areas. In 1935, the Nuremberg Laws defined who was a Jew, declared that they were not German citizens, and prohibited sexual relations between [Aryan] Germans and Jews.[67]

The intermingling of patriotism, nationalism, and anti-Semitism resulted in a toxic brew that constituted a potent centripetal barrier to desertion. Many shared nationalist dreams dating to the nineteenth century of a greater Germany uniting one people in one state. Many became convinced that Hitler's foreign policy successes in the 1930s substantiated his claims to have unique leadership traits, buying into Nazi rhetoric of *ein Volk, ein Reich, ein Führer* (one people, one empire, one leader). Too many bought into the Nazi core ideas of anti-Semitism and a racial order where Germans dominated "lesser" races. The murderous agenda of the Nazis was already apparent during the Polish campaign, accelerating and embracing the wholesale genocide of all Jews after Hitler launched Operation Barbarossa in June 1941. How many German soldiers embraced this genocidal program is unknowable, but what we do know is that the mobile killing groups (*Einsatzgruppen*) that slaughtered millions of civilians were made up of "ordinary men."[68] We also know that knowledge of the killings became widespread and that Wehrmacht units assisted *Einsatzgruppen* by isolating villages, providing logistical support to them, and directly engaging in the effort to eradicate the Jewish population behind the front line under the guise of antipartisan warfare.[69] The string of German victories during the first years of the war did more than anything to motivate the troops, but as the conflict turned, the German government paid growing attention to ensuring the troops understood and embraced Nazi ideology.

In December 1943, the Führer directed the establishment of a National Socialist Leadership Staff at the High Command. Its task, as Hitler explained to those around him, was to ensure the "complete unification and slow penetration of the entire Wehrmacht with the National Socialist body of ideas" so that all its members internalize Nazi ideology.[70] That Hitler felt it was necessary to establish a staff charged with this task suggests that only a portion of the Wehrmacht had internalized Nazi ideology to the extent he felt desirable. Postwar accounts and contemporary memoirs indicate that some found the new *Nationalsocialistischer Führungsoffiziere* (NSFOs or National Socialist Leadership Officers) annoying, adding little to unit morale.[71] But they certainly did their best to conflate patriotism, nationalism, and National Socialism. They served as checks against war weariness, defeatism, and efforts to differentiate between regime and Fatherland.

Many of the soldiers, sailors, and aircrews of the Wehrmacht fought for the same second-order motives as had the soldiers, sailors, and aircrews of Imperial Germany. Patriotism and nationalism continued to convince millions that they owed military service to the Fatherland. They fought not only for one another (*Kameradschaft*) and because males were perceived to be the sword and shield of society (masculinity), but because of a belief in an "imagined community" called Germany. A portion of the Wehrmacht embraced National Socialism's construction of a *Volksgemeinschaft* that had a destiny to rule, of a German "imagined community" free of Jews, reaching far into the East, and founded on the principle of German domination. These true believers suppressed criticism of the regime and were vigilant in keeping watch against any activities that threatened the military's will to fight. Individual soldiers might have found mass killings troubling, and morale declined as a growing number began to realize that Germany could not win the war. But for the vast majority, the forces of conformity made desertion seem disgraceful.

7
Reasons for Desertion

Franz Mattersberger was a twenty-nine-year-old Tyrolean from a small Alpine village. He had only completed elementary school, and apparently he was not particularly bright or quick thinking. He was mustered into the German Army in October 1940, and decided he wanted to go home less than six months later. He was apprehended, charged with unauthorized absence, and court-martialed in October 1941. The court sentenced him to six months of confinement, and after serving his time, Mattersberger again left for home. This time he was charged with desertion. A letter from his father to the head of the military prison where Mattersberger awaited trial gives insight into the farmer's motivation:

> **To the Military Prison in Freiburg in Breisgau, Johaniterstrasse 8, 25 February 1943**
> I would like to make the following request to the authorities:
>
> I am the father of Franz Mattersberger, currently imprisoned and sentenced to eleven years for desertion. I know that my son never had the intention to permanently evade military service, but acted because he was homesick. When Franz was drafted into the military, I immediately began to worry that he wouldn't be able to stay away from home. He has never been able to stay away from his hometown... [letter continues elaborating on son's homesickness, asking permission to send the son an occasional parcel with food, asserting that the son was honest and never a cause for concern]. I cannot tell you how much it would mean, if you could tell me how I could seek a revision to his punishment. It is terrible for me as a father to know I cannot help my son since I know he suffers from homesickness to such a degree that it is clinical. If he had acted for any other reason, I wouldn't lift a finger to help him.
>
> With German Greetings
> Heil Hitler!
> Peter Mattersberger[1]

Two times, military courts apparently weighed the argument that Mattersberger was simple-minded and suffered from what we might now diagnose as some sort of separation anxiety. His wife pleaded for his life. Twice, courts-martial convicted Mattersberger for desertion and recommended long prison terms, only to have the reviewing authority insist that deserters deserved the death penalty. A third court-martial convicted the slow-witted farmer of desertion and sentenced him to death. His wife's desperate last-minute telegram emphasizing her husband's utter inability to function outside his familial and home environment had no effect. He was executed by a firing squad on June 1, 1943.[2]

German soldiers, sailors, and airmen decided to desert for a variety of reasons. Determining why some German soldiers chose to desert despite the strong forces of military bonding, ideological indoctrination, masculine identity, and a radicalized, Nazified form of nationalism is less straightforward than the wealth of source material would suggest. The documentary record, though it encompasses tens of thousands of pages, is incomplete and biased. Four distinct avenues of inquiry are available, each with its advantages and limitations.

The first avenue of inquiry is to analyze the court-martial records compiled by the German military services and *Reichskriegsgericht* in Berlin. The German Army, by far the largest service, sent completed court-martial records to the Heeresarchiv in Potsdam, and many of these records went up in flames when the building burned down when the Allies bombed it in April 1945. The Luftwaffe went one step further, burning most of its records preemptively to prevent them from falling into enemy hands. But thousands of Army and Air Force legal files survived the war, as did most of the German Navy's records, which had been stored elsewhere. More than 180,000 court-martial records, often fragmentary, have been preserved. Of these, 14,245 are associated with the charge of desertion and/or unauthorized absence.[3] Though many extant cases are incomplete and shed little light on *why* those on trial deserted, other case files contain a lengthy collection of sworn statements from the accused; from fellow soldiers, relatives, and neighbors; from supervisors and commanders; and from the physicians and psychologists who examined the accused.

In many cases, one can reconstruct when and how the deserter left his unit; where he traveled and stayed; what sort of assistance he received; who informed or alerted authorities about known or suspicious persons; how the deserter was apprehended; and what the apprehended suspect said under interrogation or to the court. The latter must be treated as problematic: those apprehended had every incentive to claim they intended to rejoin the military at some point, as this constituted the crucial distinction between desertion and unauthorized absence, between the death sentence and some other form of punishment. Although some individuals attributed their refusal to join the military or their decision to abandon it to personal convictions, moral objections, principled opposition to National Socialism, or a frank confession that they feared death or injury at the front, these explanations increased the probability of facing a firing squad and were best left unsaid by anyone wishing to avoid execution. The military files provide insight into the motives that the lawyers, judges, commanders, doctors, and psychologists attributed to the defendant, but the internal deliberations that prompted desertion are known only by the deserter.

In some cases, thick files provide descriptions of the background, education, and upbringing of the accused, his political leanings, his attitude toward National Socialism, and his civil and military derelictions. In other cases, the files are much smaller, containing little more than the military biography of the individual and the court procedures. In many cases, no files remain at all. The historian has to evaluate the extant records with an awareness that interests and biases make ascertaining internal motivations difficult. Taking this into account, one researcher who examined more than 450 Wehrmacht desertion court-martial cases found that the most frequent reasons for desertion were fear of punishment; flight from military prisons, punishment battalions, or detention centers; poor treatment by the unit; fear of injury or death; doubt over Germany's ultimate victory; political reasons; and family reasons.[4]

The interrogations and evaluations of German deserters who successfully managed to cross the border into neutral states constitute a second, invaluable window into the causes of desertion. Bias and self-interest still factor into deserter statements, but the immediate threat of execution had disappeared, and savvy interrogators sensed that many deserters unburdened themselves once they were beyond the reach of the German military. Germany's northern and western campaigns in 1940, its attack on Yugoslavia and Greece in spring 1941, and its assault on the Soviet Union in the summer of 1941 reduced the number of neutral states bordering the Reich, its allies, and occupied territories to five: Switzerland, Sweden, Vichy France, Spain, and Turkey. Of these, Switzerland was the favorite destination because German was an official language, Switzerland was easier to reach for those on home leave than were other neutral destinations, and in contrast to Sweden, Vichy France, Spain, and Turkey, the Swiss government had not committed itself to a policy of returning German deserters to the Reich.[5]

Swiss police and military personnel conducted interrogations of foreign military personnel who crossed their border, passing the interrogations on to judicial authorities who then determined whether or not the detainee should be interned, returned, or imprisoned. The Swiss national archive in Bern has more than 500 case files preserving Swiss military interrogation and judicial proceedings related to Wehrmacht deserters. Swiss interrogators routinely asked about their motivations, and German deserters could speak more freely than was the case when under examination or on trial before a German military court. If deserters being tried by the Wehrmacht had every incentive to downplay opposition to the regime and cowardice as motivating factors, one might expect that once in Switzerland they had an incentive to claim that political and ethical considerations had played an important role in their decision to desert.

Two independent studies of the Swiss records found that despite this incentive, war weariness and fear of punishment were more frequently listed for desertion than was political opposition to National Socialism. Most deserters provided multiple, overlapping explanations of what had inspired them to seek refuge in Switzerland. The reasons for desertion, listed in order from most to least frequent, were fear of future punishment and/or flight from confinement/penal battalions; war weariness; opposition to National Socialism; fear of being sent to the Eastern Front; not considering themselves German; poor treatment in the unit and dislike of military life; personal or family reasons; encouragement by girlfriends; support for resistance groups/organizations; and revulsion over atrocities.[6]

Historian Magnus Koch has conducted an extensive analysis of a sampling of German deserters who made it to Switzerland and constructed a detailed explanations for why these individuals deserted.[7] One must recognize that those who made it to Switzerland constituted only a sliver of the much greater number of German deserters who failed to reach a neutral safe haven. Far more German deserters were apprehended by German police than made it to Switzerland, and explanations for deserting varied over time and place. Nonetheless, the Swiss records are invaluable in offering a different perspective from that found in Wehrmacht court cases. Political motivations rise from sixth place when only drawing on Wehrmacht records to third place when using Swiss sources.

A third source that provides some insights on motivation is the trove of Allied interrogations of captured German soldiers. If "submarining" in the Reich became increasingly difficult and reaching Switzerland, Sweden, or another neutral country was unfeasible for many, then deserting across the front lines was another option. British, American, and Soviet propaganda leaflets and loudspeakers encouraged German military personnel to surrender rather than fight. Drawing on a survey of 230 Germans who had crossed over to the British lines in Italy in the spring of 1943, Lieutenant Colonel H. W. Dicks of the Directorate of Army Psychiatry compiled a psychological study of the German deserter submitted to the British War Office in May 1944.[8]

Dicks approached his analysis by first identifying predisposing and precipitating causes to desertion, and then describing the factors that deterred the act. He identified two major predisposing causes. The first was cultural, which ranged from the social background of the subject to oppositional convictions based on their religious, political, and idealistic convictions to the subject's sense of national identity. Poles, Czechs, Alsatians, and others conscripted in the Wehrmacht after their home regions had been incorporated into the Reich were most predisposed to desertion.[9] The second was the individual's personality, with Dicks identifying those who were highly individualistic, obstinate, rebellious, fearful, touchy, impulsive, or hysterical as predisposed to desertion.[10] With the exception of national identity, cultural and personal factors were usually insufficient to trigger desertion without some sort of precipitating cause. These included the military situation itself (front conditions favorable to desertion), poor personal relationships with superiors and peers, or some sort of internal crisis.

Dicks's assessment was that "Oppositional background or experience of other cultures does not of itself produce disloyal conduct or desertion... we must look to the combination of background and personality for the secret of the deserter's mentality and conduct." As for the trigger to desertion, "By far the most striking factor in the precipitation of the decision to desert appears to be an acute *climax of hate* for the milieu as a whole, or for some special authority-figures like an officer or N.C.O. in the group."[11]

Dicks ended his psychological study of the German deserter with some cautionary advice about the utility of German deserters to the British after capture. He concluded that while the majority of anti-Nazi deserters no doubt felt relief that they were now in British hands and had a "genuine wish to be helpful," there were also "socio-pathetic" self-seekers who would no doubt be troubling wards who would challenge British supervisors.[12]

The last comment connects to a phenomenon often overlooked in the literature on Wehrmacht desertion, namely the issue of collaboration between captors and captured. As the number of Germans held in POW camps swelled in 1944 and 1945. Western and Soviet authorities became aware of a silent war within the POW camps between German prisoners who remained steadfastly devoted to the Reich, the Führer, and the cause, and German POWs who were willing to work with their Western or Russian captors. This collaboration ranged from direct assistance in propaganda and espionage endeavors while the war was being waged to postsurrender assistance in reeducation and denazification efforts. German collaborators were treated as deserters by their fellow POWs, who stigmatized, ostracized, and if possible, punished these men for aiding the enemy. Only gradually did it dawn on some POWs that the enemy may well have been the Hitler regime, not those dedicated to resisting and overthrowing that regime.

A final source for understanding why some German soldiers, sailors, and airmen chose to desert is the postwar memoirs and speeches of those who survived. Following a spate of trials related to wartime military justice, a deadening silence prevailed in West Germany and Austria on the topic of Wehrmacht deserters and military justice until the 1970s. First-person accounts of desertion, such as Alfred Andersch's autobiography *The Cherries of Freedom*, published in 1952, attracted a great deal of attention because they were so rare. In East Germany, much attention was showered on German deserters and POWs who joined the Soviet-created National Committee for a Free Germany (NKFD) and the League of German Officers (BDO). These accounts were so heavily ideological that they received little attention in the West. They provide a monocausal, political explanation for German desertion, ignoring the multifaceted reality that politics ranked below war weariness and fear of punishment as an explanatory factor. The thawing of the Cold War and the coming of age of a new generation in West and united Germany opened a new window for deserters willing to speak out, but by then some forty years had passed. The first-person accounts that began to appear in the 1980s and 1990s shed some light on individual motivations, but for a broader view of why tens of thousands deserted, the Wehrmacht records, Swiss interrogations, and Allied studies of morale remain indispensable.

Fear of Punishment

Fear of punishment was the reason most frequently cited by soldiers for desertion. Some had overstayed their home leave by more than the twenty-four hours that differentiated unauthorized absence in time of war from desertion. They feared returning to their units, given warnings that deserters would be shot without any consideration of mitigating circumstances. Others had committed military derelictions such as sleeping on watch, stealing from fellow soldiers, or losing their weapons, and feared that they might be sent to a punishment battalion or one of the notorious labor camps filled with those expelled from the Wehrmacht for military, criminal, and political reasons. In some cases, deserters feared punishment for offenses that now seem admirable, as in the case of an enlisted man who waved through a truck at a border checkpoint knowing that the families of three Jews who worked for him were hidden aboard. The Jewish stowaways were detected by a noncommissioned officer who berated the soldier and scolded that his actions would "cost him his head." The enlisted man fled rather than waiting to see if his supervisor's threats were real or bluster.[13] In other cases, deserters fled after committing crimes that can only be termed heinous, such as the case of a naval gunner stationed in the Netherlands who broke into a civilian house, murdered a Dutch couple, and then raped their young daughter before killing her as well.[14] He deserted, was apprehended, and was executed.

Transgressions could range from relatively minor military violations to very serious charges. One out of two military personnel charged with desertion had some sort of military or civil infraction on their record.[15] Some, it appears, reckoned that deserting was preferable to facing a military justice system that condemned thousands to death, imprisonment, or service in punishment battalions.

The harsh penalties of German military justice prompted some men to desert rather than risk the outcome of a looming court-martial. Others, already convicted on some sort of charge, sought to escape before they were sent into the Reich's concentration camp system or transferred to one of the Wehrmacht's punishment battalions. Karl-Heinz Leiterholdt was not alone in deserting from the punishment battalion to which he was assigned when the opportunity presented itself. Two soldiers of the 4th Company of the Penal Detachment 5 explained to the judge overseeing their court-martial that they had deserted only because "We cannot understand why German soldiers should be beaten by German soldiers. We no longer could bear our treatment." Another military convict who managed to escape from a military labor camp explained that he had no choice. "Everyone in the camp was starving."[16] The treatment accorded German military personnel sentenced to labor camps and punishment battalions was brutal, and those who could do so sought to save themselves when possible before they succumbed to starvation, beatings, or became cannon fodder.

War Weariness

The second most common motivation for desertion cited by those who made it to Switzerland, Sweden, or across enemy lines was war weariness. Admitting that one no longer believed in the German cause or the Reich's ultimate victory would have been suicidal in front of a German court-martial, and it is remarkable how many Germans continued to believe in victory (*Endsieg*) until the final months of war. But from 1942 on, and greatly accelerating in the second half of 1944, growing numbers of German soldiers recognized that victory had become chimerical.[17] Most fought on stubbornly despite this realization, and postwar surveys on German sentiment toward the July 1944 attempt on Hitler's life reflect how deep loyalty to the regime remained embedded among the German people.

Desertions increased most dramatically in the final months of the war. Thousands began to desert, not just individually but in groups. Swiss authorities, who had been meticulous about asking why German soldiers were deserting earlier in the war, no longer bothered asking.[18] General Georg Ritter von Hengel, after inspecting German units on the Western Front in spring 1945, reported that "An unwelcome discovery, becoming ever more widespread, is the prevalence of apathetic and tired soldiers who only fight under the direct supervision of their officers. Neither military tribunals nor sharp reprimands can motivate them."[19] Field Marshall Keitel, assessing the deteriorating military situation around Berlin in March/April 1945 advocated "shooting a couple thousand deserters."[20] As the war reached its final stage, the German regime responded to growing war weariness in the ranks by doubling down on its calls to fight to the end, with the dead bodies of German soldiers accused of desertion or cowardice hanging from trees and lampposts as a warning to others.

Poor Treatment

A third, frequently encountered reason for desertion was poor treatment by one's comrades or commander. For some soldiers, this could be the perception that the sergeant in charge of the platoon or the officer in charge of the company had it out for them.[21] The Ludwig Metz case, discussed in Chapter 1, provides one example of a junior officer chafing under the command of someone he felt was unqualified and vindictive. For enlisted men, it could be a particular sergeant who made their life hell. More broadly, the loner or outsider who did not fit in tended to contemplate desertion more than those under the spell of *Kameradschaft*. For some soldiers, religiosity played a role. The rough and tumble of male bonding, the use and abuse of alcohol, the coarse humor of the barrack, and boasts of sexual exploits alienated some. For others, religion played no role. Instead, what alienated them was the demand for constant subordination, the suppression of individualism, and the dictates of conformity. The Third Reich placed an enormous amount of effort on instilling martial values, equating masculinity with hardness and the readiness to use force. Individuals who chafed at subordination and direction found military service difficult to bear.

The case of radioman Helmut Gustav Gaebelein illustrates how multiple motivations drove his decision to desert. As a teenager, Gaebelein was attracted by the teachings of the Confessing Church and was repulsed by the group dynamics he encountered in the Hitler Youth. Yet a close read of his memoir and the sources suggests that by the time he deserted, what bothered Gaebelein was military life, with all its regimentation. He explicitly ruled out political concerns as a motivation for desertion, and ethical conundrums barely surface in his memoir. He served well behind the front line, so combat fatigue or the shock of action played no role in his decision to desert. Gaebelein acknowledged that he had difficulty dealing with criticism, and others described him as sensitive. His parents and doctors noted that he had weak nerves. By his own account, it seems that he was simply an outsider who never bonded with his peers. Gaebelein complained that he was not valued, and that he was treated poorly. Perhaps. But what one senses is that he simply did not adjust well to military life, and never felt at ease with its regimentation and command climate.

Identity, Ethnicity, and the *Volksgemeinschaft*

Those who did not consider themselves part of the constructed *Volksgemeinschaft* (German people's community) experienced an even profounder sense of alienation and isolation. The Nazis and other Germans before them had defined the *Volksgemeinschaft* as an ethnic rather than political community. For the Nazis, the German community was not defined by politics, cultural self-identification, or service to the Fatherland, but by race. They believed that Jews could not be Germans and set about excluding Jewish Germans from the German community as soon as they came to power. Once in control of the German state, the Nazis passed a series of laws that restricted Jews from the civil service, limited their numbers in higher education, and excluded them from various professions.

The Reich Citizenship Law passed in September 1935 took away the citizenship of German Jews, deprived them of any civic rights, barred them from public office, and excluded them from the military. Jewish officers already in the military were expelled. Implementing these anti-Semitic laws required defining who was a Jew, and further legislation specified degrees of Jewishness, from a full-blooded Jew to a *Mischling* (mixed race) of the first degree to a *Mischling* of the second degree. Since there was no biological basis for distinguishing Jew from German, these gradations of Jewishness were determined based on the religion of one's grandparents, whether the individual practiced the tenets of Judaism, and whether he or she was married to a Jew. Courts subsequently specified that the same scheme of categorization applied to Germany's Roma and Sinti communities.

Following the introduction of mandatory military service, the Wehrmacht was confronted with the question of what to do with the tens of thousands of Germans who fell into the category of *Mischlinge*. Jews were excluded from military service, but what about converted *Mischlinge* or *Mischlinge* whose fathers had fought for Germany in World War I? Determining whether one was a Jew, a *Mischlinge*, or a German turned out to be problematic as it involved finding baptism records that might have been burned in a church fire or could not be located. The decision of whether to draft a young man or expel a long-serving officer or civil servant often came down to a matter of judgment, pitting ideologues and anti-Semites against those who argued that a trace of Jewish or non-German blood in one's ancestry should not exclude a German patriot from serving. By one account, perhaps as many as 150,000 Wehrmacht soldiers may have had a Jewish ancestor.[22] While some of these *Mischlinge* denied and suppressed their mixed ancestry, others were undoubtedly deeply disturbed by the Third Reich's racial agenda. Always suspect and increasingly threatened, German soldiers considered racially inferior by their peers had to consider how to respond. The number of *Mischlinge* who deserted is unknown, but one can assume that some took the opportunity to desert when it presented itself.

Perhaps the best-known example of a Jewish German forced to serve in the German military against his will is that of Solomon Perel, whose autobiography inspired the film *Europa, Europa* (1990). Born in Germany to Jewish parents, Perel and his family moved to Poland in the 1930s. German occupation officials identified the young man as a *Volksdeutsche* after eastern Poland was occupied by the Wehrmacht in 1941, and Perel ended up serving in the Wehrmacht on the Eastern Front.[23] Constantly worried that he would be identified as a Jew because he was circumcised, Perel survived the war and emigrated to Israel.

The ethnic dimension of desertion in the Wehrmacht becomes clearer when one turns to other groups designated as German over their objections. Hitler and the Nazis viewed interwar Austria as part of the German People's Community idolized in their mythology. Following Austria's incorporation into the Reich, the same process of discrimination, classification, and dehumanization that isolated Germany's Jewish community from the German *Volksgemeinschaft* unfolded in Austria, albeit at a more accelerated pace. After World War II, Austrians sought to distance themselves from the Third Reich by claiming that Austria was Germany's first victim. The Reich certainly crushed what remained of Austria's socialist and union movements, and Austrian monarchists and nationalists were sent the same message delivered to German conservatives in 1934. The Austrian military was incorporated into the Wehrmacht with only minor resistance and few resignations.

In a few cases, Austrians resisted conscription. Alpine farmer Franz Jägerstätter made a principled decision against joining the Wehrmacht after he received his conscription notice. But Jägerstätter, a devout Catholic, justified his refusal to join in ethical terms rather than because he was Austrian. He paid with his life.[24] Approximately 4,000 Austrians were charged with desertion over the course of World War II, of whom between 1,200 and 1,400 were executed.[25] Several Wehrmacht deserters who made it over the border to Switzerland claimed that they had deserted because they felt more Austrian than German.[26] Whether this explanation was heartfelt or provided to persuade Swiss authorities to intern rather than return them is unknown. Austrians deserted at the same low rates as Germans born in the pre-1938 borders of the Reich for most of the war; their desertion rates rose significantly above the norm only in the final year of the war.

The situation was quite different for Polish speakers from those areas of Poland annexed into the Reich. Days after German troops crushed the last Polish army still resisting Germany's assault in October 1939, Hitler issued a decree annexing large parts of western Poland and the Free City of Danzig into the Reich. Hitler appointed Heinrich Himmler as the Reich's Commissioner for the Strengthening of Germandom (*Reichskommissar für die Festigung deutschen Volkstums* [RKF]). The RKF staff, working through various SS departments and in parallel with the Gauleiter of the Reich districts created from or enlarged by annexed Polish regions, engaged in a massive expulsion of Jews, "Congress Poles," and those viewed as potential leaders of the Polish community.[27] Himmler's plan was to extinguish the Polish majority population in the annexed areas and to replace them with German settlers from the Reich and from ethnic German communities in Eastern Europe. The Jewish population was slated for immediately expulsion, and it would be murdered as part of Nazi Germany's program to eradicate every Jew in territories under Germany's control or influence.

Himmler's long-range plan of replacing the Polish majority population in the Warthegau and Upper Silesia required time. It entailed converting "ethnically valuable" Poles into Germans through forced adoptions, German language instruction, and the eradication of Polish symbols, culture, and elites. In the short term, hundreds of thousands of former Poles now inside the boundaries of the Third Reich became liable to conscription. The reaction was defiance. In the Upper Silesian town of Kattowitz, the German police reported that as recruits were loaded for transportation to their muster depots in April 1942, they "demonstratively spoke Polish, sang Polish songs, and refused to pledge allegiance to the German flag stating that they did not consider themselves German."[28] In Graudenz, West Prussia, authorities complained of desertion and even sabotage as conscripts were mustered into service in April 1943. German authorities executed recalcitrants and threatened their families with expropriation, imprisonment, and the concentration camp.

Wehrmacht soldiers from former Polish territories exhibited a very high rate of desertion. Many clearly did not identify with the German people's community and continued to consider themselves Polish. The Western Allies captured 89,300 Wehrmacht soldiers who identified themselves as Poles in the course of the North African, Italian, and French campaigns. More than half volunteered to join the Free Polish forces fighting against Germany under British command.[29] The Soviets likewise recruited captured Wehrmacht soldiers of Polish origins into the Polish People's Army created under their supervision in 1943.[30]

The German Army was alarmed by the high rates of desertion among soldiers from ethnically Polish majority districts. In February 1943, a German Army report noted that soldiers recruited from these areas exhibited the proclivity to avoid military service or desert once in service. "German citizens of Polish ethnicity justify the latter on the grounds that they had been born Poles and had been forcibly incorporated into the German community.... The OKH intends to transfer Wehrmacht personnel of Polish origins from the Eastern Front to the Balkans or the Western Front."[31]

The case of rifleman Stefan Hampel narrated earlier illustrates how race, ethnicity, and identity motivated some German soldiers to desert. Polish Germans, responsive to the virulence of anti-Polish sentiment in Germany, understood that they stood outside the German community and many suspected that the bonds of *Kameradschaft* would never truly extend to them.

The same sentiments and motivation pertained to the French-speaking populations of the Alsace-Lorraine. The French departments of Moselle, Bas-Rhin, and Haut-Rhin were annexed into the Reich after Germany's defeat of France in the summer of 1940. In 1941, service in the Reich Labor Service (RAD) became mandatory for those reaching the age of eighteen, and in August 1942, conscription was introduced to the annexed provinces of Alsace-Lorraine and the occupied principality of Luxembourg. The court-martial files of ten Alsatians indicate that the young men had sung the French national anthem and shouted anti-German slogans such as "*Vive la France*" and "*Merde la Prusse*" out of their train window en route to the Wehrmacht recruit depot. The court sentenced the young men to seven years of imprisonment and warned that should similar incidents take place in the future, harsher penalties would be imposed.[32]

Desertion rates steadily rose among conscripts who identified more with France than Germany. In the first five months of 1943, 6 Alsatians and 70 Lorrainers deserted or failed to show up when drafted; by September, the number had risen to 156 and 171, respectively.[33] Groups of young men attempted to flee to Switzerland to escape the draft. In February 1943, a group of young deserters exchanged gunfire with German border guards. They were outgunned, surrendered, and were tried by a German military tribunal. Thirteen of the eighteen young men were sentenced to death and executed.[34]

Around 130,000 men from Alsace-Lorraine were drafted into the German military. Of these, 25,000 died at the front, 14,000 were listed as missing in action, and 40,000 deserted.[35] German units slated to participate in the Ardennes offensive in December 1944 were instructed to screen their personnel and detach Alsatians and Lorrainers for rear area duty. The German High Command suspected that these men would desert if given the opportunity.[36]

Recruits from those regions of Slovenia (Carniola, Carinthia, Styria) incorporated into the Austrian districts of the Reich after Germany invaded Yugoslavia in 1941 were likewise unenthusiastic about fighting and dying for their new German fatherland. A Reich Commission for the Consolidation of German Nationhood (Reichskommissar für die Festigung deutschen Volkstums) memo from early 1943 complained that one out of five conscripts in Upper Carniola failed to report for muster. "They simply disappeared into the woods."[37] The Reich had incorporated the region into Greater Germany and had banned Slovenian language instruction and signs, but the locals clearly did not identify with the Commission's imposed Germanization. As the war progressed, more and more Wehrmacht recruits from the region chose to slip over to Tito's partisans rather than fight for Germany.

Luxembourg serves as another example of a people who refused to subordinate their identity to one that defined them as Germans. The Reich extended conscription to Luxembourg at the same time as it did to Alsace and Lorraine. Luxembourgers responded by staging a general strike, which was crushed by executions, sending organizers to camp, and forcing thousands to work in Germany. Of the 10,211 Luxembourgers drafted into the Wehrmacht, 2,800 deserted.[38] Some of them slipped away and joined the French Maquis, and others sought to hide until the Allies arrived. Eduard Juncker, a twenty-two-year-old Luxembourger sent to fight on the Eastern Front, deserted while on leave in June 1943. He spent over a year hiding in the barns, storage sheds, and at an abbey. He survived the war.[39]

As Allied troops surged into Luxembourg in late summer 1944, Gustav Simon, Gauleiter of Mosel district and Chief of the Civil Administration of

Luxembourg, advised combing through the Reich's concentration camps to ensure that any Luxembourg deserters sentenced to hard labor would not survive the war. The idea that these men might somehow survive the war while other Luxembourgers fighting for the Reich were dying enraged Simon. Other Nazi fanatics shared the sentiment. In January 1945, more than 800 military convicts from the Emsland camps were shot by guards as camp inhabitants were relocated. Among them were 90 Luxembourgers.[40]

Austrians, Poles, Slovenes, Frenchmen, and others serving in the Wehrmacht were all considered German by the Reich and consequently subject to conscription. An even larger number of foreigners served in special formations organized by the German Army and the SS. The German Army established special "legions" of Georgian, Azerbajani, Armenian, Tatar, and other ethnic groups keen to fight against Moscow. It also recruited and employed large numbers of Ukrainians and Russians who served as auxiliaries (HiWis) on the Eastern Front. Around 500,000 foreigners served in or alongside the Wehrmacht as legionnaires or auxiliaries. These soldiers were subject to German military courts, but records related to desertion and discipline for these formations are largely missing or destroyed. Another quarter million non-German volunteers from the Baltic states, Scandinavia, the Low Countries, Albania, Bosnia, Croatia, Romania, Ukraine, and elsewhere served in the SS.[41] Disciplinary matters in the Waffen SS and among SS foreign legions lay outside the Wehrmacht's purview. The quality of special legions, auxiliary formations, and SS divisions recruited outside the Reich varied widely. Ascertaining when and why non-Germans fighting for the Reich decided to give up or desert is speculative. Once it became clear that Germany was losing the war, desertion became endemic in all but a few foreign formations.

Homesickness and Family Reasons

Homesickness and family reasons most certainly played a role in prompting desertion on the part of some Wehrmacht personnel. Statistically, these reasons come in as the fourth or fifth most common motivation cited. They probably were more important than the selective samplings indicate. Soldiers, sailors, and airmen were constantly reminded that homesickness, love worries, and family problems were no excuse for overstaying leave, let alone deserting. Apprehended deserters and their defense counsels (when they had one) would have known that these explanations would hold no water with a military jury, and probably would have decided to emphasize other explanations. In the exit interviews to Swiss officials or Allied captors, deserters had reason to emphasize political factors or ethical concerns rather than homesickness and family matters as the cause for desertion. Going to Switzerland or over to the other side brought them no closer to family and home.

What is striking, however, is how often deserters returned to their hometowns and cities despite understanding that the first place authorities would check to find them was their residence of record. This suggests that homesickness, family matters, and a longing for loved ones drew many deserters home like moths to a flame. The Kanzenbach case of an enlisted man attempting to bicycle all the way from western France to his hometown in Pomerania is not unique. One again and again encounters accounts of the deserter showing up at the doorstep of family and friends. Often, they would realize that their presence was endangering their loved ones and decide to move on, as was the case with Ludwig Metz. In other cases, the deserter would seek to hide in place with the assistance of his wife, parents, siblings, or friends until the war ended, as was the case with Wilhelm Hanow, whose wife managed to hide and feed him for two years before a neighbor alerted police that she suspected Hanow was at home. The nosy neighbor eager to report suspicious activity and denounce disloyal behavior was essential to the system of surveillance and control. More often than not, it was a neighbor, work acquaintance, or relative who alerted authorities that someone was not doing their duty. Military justice depended on informers and denunciation to apprehend deserters and identify those suspected of "undermining the military spirit."[42]

Fear of Injury or Death

Some deserters who made it to Switzerland were quite frank that they had deserted because they feared injury or death. Those who had fought on the Eastern Front realized that the scale, level, and boundless violence of the type of war being waged there meant that there was a high likelihood they would be gravely injured or killed. Some made the decision to desert while on leave or while their unit was being rested and refitted. Others stationed in the West or in the Reich had heard stories about the violence and found rumors of an impending transfer to the Eastern Front unbearable. Once the Western Allies had landed in France and had broken out of the Normandy pocket, some decided that the war was lost and that death or injury served no purpose. At the front, desertion could take the form of quietly abandoning an outpost and seeking to surrender to the enemy. The line between desertion and surrender blurred as the Allied forces in the East and West broke through the German front. One did not need to go over to the other side; one could simply wait for the other side to roll over one's unit.

Though a significant number of German deserters admitted to their Swiss interlocutors that they deserted because they feared they were about to be sent to the Eastern Front, acknowledging that fear and self-preservation had motivated desertion was humiliating. Deserters did not want to be called cowards, and those who survived the war tended to stay quiet or point out how dangerous it was to desert.[43]

Moral Reservations and Political Motives

A more acceptable motivation, particularly in the postwar period, was to claim that one had acted on higher grounds than self-preservation. How important were moral or political reservations in deciding to desert? The answer varies depending on the time, locale, and destination. The Third Reich did not recognize any conscientious objections to military service. When the Order Imposing Extraordinary Wartime Laws and Penalties went into effect on August 26, 1939, those who failed to answer conscription notifications were treated as deserters. Jehovah's Witnesses and pacifists framed their refusal to serve in religious or ethical terms. The number of conscientious objectors in Germany was never high, and Jehovah's Witnesses account for many of those who refused to serve in the Wehrmacht. More than 2,000 would be sent to concentration camps, and more than 1,000 would perish due to starvation and mistreatment.[44] Germany's Protestant and Catholic establishments provided little support to the few mainstream Protestants and Catholics who embraced pacifism.[45] Catholic farmer Franz Jägerstätter's story is so striking because he refused to follow the advice of his priest and report for duty.[46]

Reservist officer Hermann Stöhr, a Protestant, likewise took a principled stand against supporting the Third Reich's wars of aggression. Stöhr, who had joined the German Navy in 1914 as a sixteen-year-old, had pondered about his responsibilities as a German, as a Christian, and as a man. He had been deeply troubled by the anti-Semitism and bellicosity of the Nazi movement, and he refused to report for military training when called up in the spring of 1939. Further infuriating his superiors, he refused to swear an oath of loyalty to Hitler. Stöhr was tried by a court-martial in March 1940 and executed in June at the Berlin-Plötzensee prison. His letter to the Military District Commander dated March 2, 1939, makes his position clear:

> I reject armed service for reasons of conscience. Christ instructed me and my people that "all they that take up the sword shall perish by the sword" (Matthew 26:52). I believe that military service does not protect the German community but endangers it. I will not participate in activities that threaten to destroy my people.[47]

One can find examples of brave individuals who rejected military service or deserted from it for pacifist or Christian reasons. But the number was relatively small. In addition, one can find numerous examples of officers and men executed on the charge of "undermining the military spirit." Within the confines of the small unit, antigovernment jokes and critical remarks might be tolerated, but those who pushed the boundaries eventually discovered *Kameradschaft* did not ensure freedom to be openly critical. Lieutenant Michael Kitzelmann, a Catholic officer stationed on the Eastern Front who was troubled by the atrocities he witnessed, was denounced by his own men. Several of them had heard Kitzelmann describe Nazis as "brown dogs" and complain about Russian civilians being starved to death. The comment that apparently provoked the denunciation was Kitzelmann's public rebuke that one could not put too much stock in the idea of fighting godless Bolshevism when back home the Nazis were taking crucifixes out of the school. Kitzelmann was tried by a divisional court-martial (262nd Infantry Division) on the charge of "undermining the military spirit." He was found guilty and was executed on June 11, 1942.[48]

Even in the confines of the U-boat community, renowned for its sense of group cohesion and crew camaraderie, criticism of the regime could prove fatal. The example of U-boat captain Oskar Kusch illustrates the limits of acceptable regime critique. Kusch's former first watch officer, Dr. Ulrich Abel, lodged a complaint in January 1944 denouncing his former commander as exhibiting an unacceptable attitude toward Germany's political and military leadership. According to Abel, an avid National Socialist, as first watch officer under Kusch, he had witnessed his commander remove a picture of Hitler from the wardroom, and heard him mock the Hitler Youth organization, remark that the global Jewish conspiracy was pure propaganda, and describe Hitler as a mentally disturbed megalomaniac.[49] Abel and Kusch had clashed a number of times during the cruise, and Abel's denunciation sprang from professional grievances as well as political conviction. Yet once lodged, the complaint spiraled into a court-martial on the charge of "undermining the military spirit." Kusch was found guilty of the charge and sentenced to death. Admiral Karl Dönitz declined to intervene. On May 12, 1944, a naval firing squad in Kiel carried out the sentence. News of the execution spread throughout the U-boat community by word of mouth.[50]

The linkage between politics and the charge of "undermining the military spirit" is clear, but neither Kitzelmann nor Kusch had thought of deserting themselves, nor had they encouraged desertion. Opposition to the regime and political motivations should, however, be included among the factors that contributed to desertion. Court-martial records indicate that investigating officers were vigilant in ferreting out whether deserters came from left-leaning families or had been critical of the regime at some point.[51]

Deserters who made it to Switzerland listed opposition to National Socialism as one of the reasons they deserted, with only war weariness and fear of punishment more frequently cited as the root cause for their desertion.[52] There are substantiated cases of German deserters in France who joined the Maquis, of Wehrmacht Slovene deserters who joined Tito's partisans, and of scores of German deserters who joined communist partisan groups in Greece, Italy, and the Balkans. These men never internalized the ideology of the Third Reich, and while equating desertion with resistance seems to stretch the meaning of the latter, for these men political convictions appeared to have played a role in their decision to desert from the Reich's military machine.

Political motives for desertion seem to have been particularly significant among deserters from the Wehrmacht's rehabilitation battalion 999. Shortly after the introduction of conscription in 1935, the Wehrmacht set up several "special battalions" (*Sonderbataillone*) for soldiers deemed problematic. Alcoholics, "asocials," draft resisters, petty thieves, and homosexuals in the ranks were transferred to these reeducation units where a mix of heavy manual labor, physical exercise, military drills, and ideological instruction was used to create the desired attitude toward the regime, military life, and discipline. Those deemed incorrigible were stripped of the right to serve in the military and transferred to the Reich's concentration camp system. An estimated 3,000–6,000 military personnel were sent to these "special battalions" between 1936 and 1939, where their brutal treatment prompted numerous attempts to desert. At least 180 "reeducation soldiers" were sent to Sachsenhausen, where hard labor, constant physical abuse, and undernourishment killed half of them within a year.[53] Following the outbreak of the war, the Wehrmacht reorganized the special battalions into "special field battalions" that eventually evolved into two variants: twenty-two military penal work units (*Feldstrafgefangen-Abteilungen*) tasked with performing especially difficult and dangerous noncombatant duties and two probationary units (*Bewährungstruppe*) assigned extremely dangerous combat tasks.[54]

The first probationary unit, *Bewährungstruppe* 500, was created by a Führer directive in December 1940, allowing soldiers convicted of minor offenses to serve out their sentences at the front with the promise that those who proved themselves would be eligible to return to their military units as rehabilitated soldiers.[55] By October 1942, manpower shortages in the German military prompted the government to comb through the camp system searching for Germans convicted by civilian courts and deemed "unworthy of military service" who might yet prove useful at the front.[56] Top-level communists, socialists, and union leaders continued to be incarcerated, but lower-level political prisoners and common criminals were given the opportunity to "redeem" themselves by volunteering for service in a *Bewährungstruppe* 999. The 999th probationary unit, modeled after the probationary unit set up in 1940, was known as the Africa Brigade, as the Wehrmacht intended to dispatch the unit to Tunisia to reinforce the deteriorating Axis position there. Two of its regiments, the 961st and 962nd, made it to Tunisia in the spring of 1943. A number of soldiers deserted at the first opportunity; others fought on until the surrender of German and Italian forces in June.

Other elements of the 999th Africa Brigade never made it to Africa; instead, they were posted to the southern section of the Eastern Front. Desertion rates were high, and on April 13, 1943, two companies of the 999th brigade went over to the Red Army en masse.[57] The Wehrmacht decided that former leftists could not be trusted, subsequently sending politically unreliable soldiers assigned to probationary units back to work camps in the Reich or assigning them to unarmed military penal units.

One of the political deserters who survived the war wrote of his experience decades later.[58] Wolfgang Abendroth was born into a social-democratic family in 1906 and had joined a communist youth organization in high school, only to be expelled from the KPD for efforts to bridge the socialist-communist divide in the late 1920s. He was dismissed from his position as a law clerk when the Nazis came to power and was among those arrested during the first wave of incarcerations targeting communists, socialists, and union activists. On release, Abendroth emigrated to Switzerland only to return to Germany in 1935. He engaged in antigovernment activities and in 1937 was again sent to a concentration camp. In February 1943, he and other political prisoners were recruited out of the Reich's camp system. He was assigned to a detachment of the 999th brigade garrisoning the Greek island of Lemnos. When the Wehrmacht evacuated the Aegean islands in 1944, Abendroth and several like-minded leftists defected to the Greek communist partisans (ELAS). They survived. Others, such as Franz Schneider, were less fortunate. Schneider, likewise posted to Greece as a member of the 999th brigade, was turned in by a fellow soldier who overheard him discussing the idea of a group surrender with other former camp inmates. Following a quick court-martial, he and five others were shot for treason, undermining the military spirit, and failing to report treasonous activities.[59] By September 1944, an estimated 500 former political prisoners serving in the 999th had deserted to communist partisan groups in Greece, Albania, and Yugoslavia.[60]

Wolfgang Abendroth would later become a political scientist in West Germany, serving as the *Doktorvater* (doctoral adviser) to Jürgen Habermas, a prominent thinker, activist, and critic of the postwar West German system. German deserters who went over to the Red Army or joined Soviet-sponsored POW camp organizations such as the National Committee for a Free Germany (NKFD) and the League of German Officers (BDO) would be rewarded with important positions in the East German establishment. Partly because of West Germany's aversion to East Germany, until the 1980s the West German establishment paid far more attention to the conservative, nationalist political opposition to Hitler than to deserters who defected to the Russians and subsequently helped build a repressive, communist East Germany.

The Female Dimension

Overlapping the factors of homesickness, political reasons, and war weariness are the roles played by wives, mothers, girlfriends, and romantic liaisons. If the deserter was a married man, the first place authorities would look for him was his home of record. Gustave Hanow was not the only wife to risk her life by hiding her deserter husband during the war, nor was Emmy Zehden the only female Jehovah's Witness to be executed for sheltering a family member who refused to report for military service when conscripted.[61] Girlfriends, mothers, and sisters could also be drawn into desertion attempts.

Lieutenant Ludwig Metz, after deserting from the Eastern Front in 1942, had shown up at an old girlfriend's apartment in Munich and had appealed to his mother to bring him clothes and money when he planned his escape to Switzerland. Rifleman Kanzenbach, longing to see his pregnant girlfriend, attempted to bicycle all the way from Western France to Pomerania, apparently assuming that his "bride" would be delighted to hide and support him when he showed up unannounced. Once they turned their back on the gendered, masculine community of comrades and *Kameradschaft*, many deserters seemed to instinctually turn to the women in their lives for help, love, and support. This put these women in great danger, as Germany's Order Imposing Extraordinary Wartime Laws and Penalties made assisting and hiding deserters a capital crime. Civilian courts, rather than military tribunals, charged German wives, mothers, and girlfriends with "undermining the military spirit" when they assisted husbands, sons, and boyfriends who had deserted. How many German women were charged, tried, and sent into the camp system is unknown. Just as most German soldiers, sailors, and airmen fought to the bitter end, domestic support for Hitler remained strong until the final months of the war. For most of the war, most German women urged their men to be brave, do their duty, and defend the Reich. As the war entered its final, desperate end phase, one hears of mothers yelling out the windows that child soldiers should go home and of low-level resistance to pointless fighting. Even then, the structures of conformity and control made supporting desertion dangerous for the deserter and the women who risked their lives sheltering them.

This leads to a sensitive and controversial subtopic, that of girlfriends and romantic liaisons in France, the Low Countries, and Scandinavia. German racial attitudes, policies, and brutality did not prevent sexual relations between German soldiers and local women in the occupied East, the Balkans, and North Africa. But sexual relations in the East reflected the war Germany was waging and the new order that the Nazis were seeking to impose. At best, relationships between German military personnel and local women were exploitative and transitory, while rape, violence, and murder were common in the East.[62] In occupied Western Europe and Scandinavia, a different dynamic unfolded as thousands of occupiers established personal relationships with local women. Germans did not view Norwegians and Danes as racially inferior and, while more critical toward the French, accepted them as part of a future German-dominated Europe. This created a certain space for fraternization. Relationships between German military personnel and female civilians in Western and Northern Europe could range from work relationships to the exchange of sexual favors for money and goods to friendships and flirtations to love relationships. An estimated 20,000 French women formed personal relationships with German soldiers, and around 50,000 Norwegian women did the same.[63] After liberation, the French Resistance castigated French women who had entertained personal connections with German occupiers as "horizontal collaborators," publicly shaving their heads and marching them through French cities and towns to shame them. In Norway, Norwegian women who had supported the occupation or slept with Germans were ostracized. The postwar Norwegian government interned many "German girls" and passed a law allowing the government to forcibly deport these women to Germany.[64]

There are sufficient examples of German deserters in France and in Norway who sought refuge with girlfriends to make note of the phenomenon. The story of Rifleman Schewe's desertion and execution near Carcassone in 1943 began with his disappearance after a New Year celebration the evening of December 31, 1942. Military police found Schewe hiding at his girlfriend's house, arrested him, and shot the nineteen-year-old soldier. Whether Schewe's girlfriend had encouraged his desertion or merely let him stay at her place is unknown, as are the consequences for her.

In another case, the details are clearer.[65] Twenty-seven-year-old Sergeant Willi Jutzi was stationed in Gardermoen, north of Oslo, after the German conquest of Norway. Though married, Jutzi became romantically involved with a local Norwegian girl named Ragna Fevik who worked on base. Their relationship deepened over the course of thirteen months, with Jutzi telling Fevik he planned to divorce his German wife and marry her after the war. After much discussion, the two decided to sit out the war in Sweden.

Both agreed that they disliked the German occupation and hoped that once in Sweden, they might be granted work and residence permits. This shows a naive ignorance of Swedish policies toward German deserters on their part. After traveling to a sparsely populated area well north of Oslo, the two were able to slip across the border near Fisktjärnet on the night of June 23, 1941. They hid in a forest hut with the tacit permission of its owner, but once Swedish authorities heard of the couple, their romantic adventure came to a tragic end. Swedish police arrested Jutzi, informing the couple that he would be deported and turned over to the German military. Fevik was told she could stay in Sweden, but she replied that if Jutzi was to be deported, then she wanted to return to Norway as well. While in transit to the Norwegian border, Jutzi attempted to flee. He realized that he would be shot by the German military once handed over and concluded he had nothing to lose. Swedish police shot at him as he fled into the woods, but he disappeared. A year later, two Swedish boys found Jutzi's decomposed body in a nearby river.

Fevik was turned over to Norwegian authorities. A German military court subsequently tried her on the charge of aiding and abetting desertion. She was found guilty and sentenced to one year of imprisonment. The story of illicit love (a married German man, a single Norwegian woman), Swedish-German collaboration (Sweden would adjust its policies as the war progressed, but through 1943 returned German deserters to the tender mercies of the Wehrmacht), and Wehrmacht justice provides one of the few examples where we know what happened to both girlfriend and wife. Fevik ended up in prison, and Jutzi's German wife divorced him.[66]

Norwegian historian Eivind Heides has studied the topic of Wehrmacht deserters in Norway in depth. Heides concludes that German deserters were utterly dependent on the support of Norwegian civilians, more often than not women. German deserters often had only the vaguest notion of how to get to neutral Sweden, and they needed civilian clothes, food, directions, and shelter en route. As for "submarining" in the civilian population, few Germans spoke Norwegian well enough, and deserters were entirely dependent on friendly Norwegians willing to risk their lives to help them. The interplay among fraternization, collaboration, and desertion stands out in the statement that one deserter provided to German military police when apprehended in February 1942. He explained that he had received a letter from his wife in Germany the previous June that made him suspicious she had been seeing other men.

> This upset me so much that I ran away in the pouring rain on Sunday evening, June 15th. I then spent the night in a small mountain farm and continued the next day in the direction of Dombaas [a rural, mountainous area in central Norway]. On the second day of my escape, I found a set of old civilian clothes, which I put on. I buried my uniform in the hills. I stayed in the mountains until July 2nd. Since I spoke Norwegian fairly well, I could beg for groceries and always received them. On July 2nd I met Lina Ohlsen on a small farm in Skjaak, where I became part of the community. At first she thought I was Norwegian, but little by little I told her of my situation. Since then, we've always been together. I made some money doing carpentry work and Lina Ohlsen [whose real name was Lina Böyeie] made money milking. Recently, we stayed near Maehlum-Gaard by Biri [near Lillehammer]. We lived on one ration card. I tried several times to contact German authorities, but Lina Böyeie persuaded me against doing so. She was pregnant with my child, and was afraid that she would lose me.[67]

Sexual and romantic relationships between German military personnel and French, Low Country, Norwegian, and Danish women have usually been viewed through the lens of collaboration. Yet in at least some cases, these relationships contributed to desertion or served to shelter and support German deserters in occupied France, the Low Countries, and Scandinavia. More broadly, Wehrmacht deserters, largely male, appear to have almost instinctively reached out to the other sex and gender when seeking help, assistance, and comfort.[68] Romantic liaisons influenced or supported some of those who deserted from the Wehrmacht.

One might wish that war crimes, mass executions, and the Holocaust had been important factors motivating Wehrmacht desertion. Unfortunately, moral concerns about atrocities lagged far behind other motivations given to Swiss authorities. They rarely crop up in the interviews of fellow soldiers and commanders conducted by German authorities investigating cases of desertion.[69] The fact that desertions in 1941 and 1942—that is, during the peak period when many Wehrmacht personnel became aware of the activities of *Einsatzgruppen* in the East—were far lower than desertions in 1944 and 1945 leads to the conclusion that war weariness, self-preservation, and diminishing faith in Germany's ultimate victory played a larger role in motivating desertions than did distress caused by knowledge of mass shootings, war crimes, and the mistreatment of civilians.

Some deserters stated that what they had witnessed in the East contributed to their decision to desert. The cases of rifleman Stefan Hampel and Lieutenant Ludwig Metz illustrate how moral outrage interacted with other factors as individuals contemplated whether to remain at their posts or desert. In Hampel's case, his mixed background (his mother was Polish) made the mass execution he witnessed at Wassiliski in May 1942 particularly traumatic. Hampel believed that his mother had been executed by the Red Army during its occupation of eastern Poland in 1939/1940. He was deeply troubled that civilians were being massacred solely on the basis of class, ethnicity, and religion. His empathy with Wassiliski's Jewish victims probably sprang from an awareness that he would never be considered fully part of the German people's community. Disentangling and weighing the importance of various motives is impossible, as personality, ethnicity, and outsider status all contributed to Hampel's decision to desert.

Very few German soldiers actively opposed the mass killings of civilians by *Einsatzgruppen* and Wehrmacht units engaged in antipartisan operation. Instead, thousands pitched in to help in some capacity or other. For Hampel, witnessing the execution of Wassiliski's Jewish community was searing and painful. He made a point of describing the scene to the German military police who arrested him in Freiburg im Breisgau eleven months after deserting from his unit in Poland. Hampel was court-martialed for desertion, found guilty, and the court recommended the death sentence. In an unexplained departure from normal practice, the general in charge of confirming the sentence, Friedrich Fromm, commuted it to fifteen years of heavy labor.[70] In spring 1945, Hampel and other military convicts at the Börgermoor penal camp were given the opportunity to volunteer for service in Bewährungsbattalion 500.[71] Hampel again deserted, and he was eventually taken prisoner by the Russians.

As discussed in Chapter 1, Ludwig Metz was another deserter who explicitly linked his decision to desert to his distress over German extermination policies targeting Jewish and Russian civilians in the East. In both his written answers to Swiss queries as to why he deserted, and in an unpublished memoir he wrote after his internment, Metz expressed outrage over the mass shootings of Jews in areas under military control. When invited to dinner by the military commandant of Simferopol, who confided that an SS group had just finished executing the town's Jewish population, Metz asked why the commandant could not have intervened as he was the commanding officer responsible for the town. The commandant sighed that he had been powerless to do anything and insisted that his hands were tied. A chance encounter with a fellow officer on a train likewise distressed Metz. Returning from convalescence leave, he had struck up a conversation with a fellow officer in his train compartment. The officer was a veterinarian from Bavaria, and his demeanor was that of a jovial country animal doctor. The friendly man then described how much fun it had been helping a mobile killing squad execute Jewish civilians. The man's evident gratification at having shot unarmed old men and middle-aged women appalled Metz.

Metz's decision to desert sprang from a combination of reasons, of which distress over German extermination policies was only one. Metz also told his Swiss interrogator that his relationship with his commander had been about as bad as it could get. He felt his commander, a reservist, had no idea how to lead a unit and was squandering the lives of his subordinates for no good reason. In his unpublished biography, Metz devoted as much attention to his unit's dysfunctional leadership, the relentless sacrifice of battle, and growing war weariness as he did to concerns about mass shootings and the Nazi persecution of the church. But he included these reasons, connecting the stress of combat to his moral concerns, and posing the question, What had he been fighting for? Was his cause just? Many considerations interacted with each other as Metz contemplated what he should do, causing a growing sense of internal distress that culminated in his decision to desert.

Only a few deserters listed atrocities and moral outrage as the primary reason for desertion. Even fewer military personnel actively refused to carry out orders that would be classified as war crimes and crimes against humanity. But a small number did. In the summer of 1942, army lieutenant Albert Battel, a fifty-one-year-old reservist and a lawyer by trade, convinced the German Army commandant of Przemysl, Major Max Liedtke, to block an SS execution squad tasked with rounding up and executing the town's Jewish inhabitants.[72] Battel, though a member of the Nazi Party, had never embraced its anti-Semitism, and Liedtke had lost his job as the editor of a small-town paper during the 1930s for publishing comments critical of the Nazi Party. Both found the idea of simply letting the SS round up and execute Jews under their protection reprehensible. Liedtke, showing moral courage, authorized Battel to use army troops to block SS units from entering the ghetto, joking that "the worst they can do to us is to shoot us."[73] Neither was shot, but their efforts were in vain. Within hours, Liedtke was ordered to lift the "state of siege" he had used as a pretense for blocking access to the ghetto. The next day SS units began to clear the ghetto, sending the first of many thousand Jews to the extermination camp at Belzec. Neither Battel nor Liedtke were executed, nor were they brought up on military charges or demoted. Himmler vowed that he would personally see to it that Battel was kicked out of the party and arrested after the war, a threat never carried out. The military reprimanded the two officers and transferred them from rear area assignments to the front. Battel developed a heart condition and was discharged from German Army in 1944, only to be drafted into the *Volksturm* during the final months of the war. He survived. Liedtke served at the front, was captured by the Red Army, and died in a Soviet POW camp in the 1950s.[74]

During the postwar trials of Germans accused of war crimes and crimes against humanity, defense lawyers spent a great deal of effort trying to find examples of German military personnel executed for refusing to shoot POWs, civilians, or Jews. They found none. During the 1980s and in reaction to controversies related to the traveling exhibit "Crimes of the Wehrmacht: 1941 to 1944," scholars and historians reexamined the issue and came to the same conclusion. Very few military personnel refused to carry out illegal executions or participate in mass shootings. Those who did suffered consequences ranging from reprimands to transfers to demotions to house arrest, but none were executed.[75] Since then, three cases have been discovered in which military personnel who helped Jews or POWs were executed for their actions. These cases are exceptional. But precisely because they are exceptional, one of their stories deserves to be told.

Army Sergeant Anton Schmid was both an ordinary man and an exceptional individual. He was born in Vienna, raised in the Catholic faith, and apparently had some friends who were Jewish. Schmid helped get them across the Czechoslovakian border after Germany annexed Austria. He was almost forty when he was drafted into the German military in 1939. In 1941, he was assigned to *Feldkommandantur* 814, a German Army unit stationed in Vilnius that had the responsibility of collecting soldiers who became separated from their units. From his window at work, Schmid witnessed how Jews were brutally rounded up. He knew that they were being marched out of the city and slaughtered. He felt a moral responsibility to help Jews who worked for him, eventually helping others with whom he had no personal connection. He is credited with smuggling 300 Jews out of the ghetto. An unknown *Kamerad* denounced Schmid, who was court-martialed. In his final letter to his wife and daughter, dated April 9, 1942, Schmid tried to explain why this would be his last letter to them. He wrote:

> Unfortunately, I have been sentenced to death by a court-martial in Wilna, something I never wished for.... But cheer up my dear ones. I am resigned to it, and fate wills it.... I want to tell you how this came about: there were many Jews gathered together here [Wilna] by the Lithuanian military, who execute them in a field outside the city, two or three thousand at a time. On the way [to the execution spot], they bash the children against trees, you can only imagine how horrible it is. I was assigned to take over the [Wehrmacht] collection site for [German military] stragglers... 140 Jews worked there; they asked me to take them away from here or arrange for one of our drivers to take them away. I was persuaded to help, you know how soft my heart is. The court didn't like this. Believe me, my dear Stefi and Gertha, it [Schmid's pending execution] is a hard blow for us but please, please forgive me. I was just acting like a human being and didn't want to hurt anyone.[76]

Schmid was not a deserter, nor can his actions be interpreted as some sort of military resistance aimed at toppling the regime. He only wanted to be a human being, and he showed compassion for other human beings. He was unwilling to be passive and do nothing.

This same sense of humanity percolates in another, controversial case of desertion driven by a moral imperative. In April 1941, naval gunner's mate Heinz Stahlschmidt was assigned shore duty in Bordeaux after surviving three ship sinkings, the last of which damaged his lungs. Stahlschmidt spoke some rudimentary French and became friendly with several French workers at the dock. He shared an occasional drink and Gaulois cigarette with them at the L'Ancre d'or cafe near the Quai des Queyries. His German colleagues teased him for his tolerant attitude toward the French, dubbing him the "little Frenchman." In 1943, Stahlschmidt was assigned to the weapons depot in Bordeaux where the Kriegsmarine stored its ammunition. In the spring of 1944, the Kriegsmarine began planning how to destroy Bordeaux harbor facilities should it become necessary. Preparations shifted into high gear once the Allies landed in Normandy. The German Navy wanted to blow up the entire harbor and planned to set off explosives every fifty meters along the entire harbor front. Stahlschmidt, as a weapons expert, was involved in preparing the demolition. He heard estimates that carrying out the demolition would cost the lives of 3,000 French civilians living near the harbor. Stahlschmidt faced a moral dilemma. By August, the Allies had broken out of the Normandy pocket, and Stahlschmidt expected that the order to blow up the harbor was imminent. Stahlschmidt believed that the war was all but lost and questioned the morality of blowing up the harbor and killing thousands of civilians. Through one of his French acquaintances, Stahlschidt passed on information to the French Resistance about where the Kriegsmarine was storing its demolition caps and explosives. He warned his Resistance contact that French civilian casualties would be very high if the Germans blew up the harbor.

Stalhlschmidt waited for something to happen, but nothing did. On August 21, Stahlschmidt heard rumors that the demolition plan was about to be put into effect. That night, he set fire to the munitions depot himself, causing an enormous explosion that cost the lives of fifteen Germans guarding it. Stahlschmidt deserted and was sheltered by his French friends, who hid him from the Germans and then prevented overzealous Maquis liberators from shooting him once the Germans withdrew. Stahlschmidt survived the war, returning to Bordeaux and becoming a French citizen in 1947. He married a French woman, adopted a new name (Henri Salmide), and became a harbor firefighter.

In postwar Germany, Stahlschmidt was despised as a traitor who had killed Germans in order to ingratiate himself with the French Resistance. In postwar France, he disappeared from memory for decades. Prominent French Resistance members preferred to take credit for saving Bordeaux, insinuating that the Resistance had set off the explosion. Only in the 1990s did his story become known. After years of being ignored or despised, Salmide became something of symbol of Franco-German reconciliation. He was awarded the French Légion d'Honneur in 2000 and Bordeaux's port authority named its headquarters after him in 2012.[77] In Germany, where progressives sought to characterize desertion as a form of resistance, Salmide's role in saving thousands of civilians began to overshadow earlier characterizations of him as a traitor who had killed his own comrades to curry favor with the French. Frenchman André Moga, a member of the local French Resistance, described Salmide in these terms: "Heinz was our fifth brother. He was certain that he was doing the right thing and had a remarkable mind. He acted out of principle, never thinking of personal advantage. Neither titles nor money meant anything to him. On that day, he put himself on the side of humanity, and afterwards both sides rejected him. As far as I'm concerned, he was a resistance fighter."[78]

Equating desertion with resistance is a stretch in most cases. One certainly should acknowledge that some deserters, such as conscientious objectors, regime opponents, and those appalled by its murderous execution of Jews, Poles, and captured Russians, acted out of principle. In addition, many of those who deserted did so because they never felt themselves to be German and had no desire to fight for a world where their chosen forms of identity would be suppressed or exterminated. Others deserted because they were nonconformists who could not or did not want to fit into the military world with its ethos of conformity, obedience, and enforced camaraderie. Many deserted because of homesickness, war weariness, fear of injury or death, fear of punishment, or because they felt mistreated. They did not actively oppose Hitler and the Third Reich, and desertion was an escape from participating in and contributing to the war. Multiple factors intermingled in personal decisions about duty and desertion. Regardless of motivation, the Wehrmacht believed that desertion was a threat that could metastasize and undermine its fighting effectiveness. The German military and the Third Reich, transfixed by the experience of mutiny and desertion in the final months of 1918, stood side by side in their shared determination that no smidgen of mercy should be shown to German deserters irrespective of individual motivations.

8

Avenues of Desertion

The reasons for deserting were varied, with multiple factors often contributing to the decision to abandon the military. The destinations that beckoned deserters likewise varied. If the main reason for deserting was homesickness or family matters, then deserters were drawn to their hometown, city, or region. If the main concern of the deserter was self-preservation, a diminishing faith in victory, and war weariness, then going over to the other side made sense. Soldiers posted to observation posts might slip over under the cover of night or bad weather, or they might fall out as German forces were retreating. Alternatively, deserters could seek refuge in rear areas or occupied territories, avoiding the dangers of getting shot when attempting to cross lines but having no long-term plan for survival. Most deserters understood that hiding in the Reich or in occupied territories was possible for a short time, but that their chance of evading detection decreased the longer one was on the run. Military police constantly checked identification and travel papers, and submarining in the Reich or occupied territories put family and friends in danger. All the state's instruments of surveillance, control, and coercion were employed to find deserters. Many deserters dreamed of escaping to a neutral country, but German alliances, its occupation of the Low Countries, Luxembourg, Denmark, and Norway in 1940, and the conquest of Yugoslavia and Greece the following year reduced the number of accessible neutral countries to two main destinations: Switzerland and Sweden.[1]

The leading quantitative study of Wehrmacht courts-martial for desertion provides a general sense of when and where desertion happened. In one out of five cases, desertion was a frontline phenomenon in which deserters attempted to go over to the other side. In another one out of five cases, desertion was a rear-area phenomenon happening behind the front. Eighteen percent of desertions happened when a unit was being transferred somewhere else, and another 10 percent occurred when the deserter was on leave. Almost a quarter of the cases have to do with desertion from military posts far from the fighting front. Sixteen percent of the cases dealt with military convicts who attempted to desert from military prisons, penal camps, and punishment or probationary units.[2]

Wehrmacht court-martial records provide a skewed metric for determining the total number of Wehrmacht personnel who deserted or attempted to do so. The legal department of the High Command compiled quarterly summaries of military charges, convictions, and sentences from August 1939 to December 1944. The pattern is clear: the number of German military personnel charged and convicted for desertion increased over time. If one compares convictions for desertion in 1940/1941 to convictions in 1943/1944, the increase is tenfold.[3] Convictions for desertion skyrocketed during the final year of the war. As the military situation deteriorated, many records never made it back to Berlin. In March 1945, Hitler directed the military to institute "flying tribunals" that could execute German soldiers without confirmation from above. How many soldiers were executed by these flying tribunals is unknown.[4]

Furthermore, equating the number of German military personnel who deserted to the number charged, tried, and sentenced for desertion is misleading. In 1944, for example, the Wehrmacht's legal department noted judicial proceedings had not yet been initiated for more than 200,000 charges related to unauthorized absence or desertion.[5] This is a far higher figure than the number charged, tried, and convicted of desertion. If it could be confirmed that a member of the German military was in Switzerland, Sweden, or cooperating with the other side, the Wehrmacht commenced proceedings even though the accused was outside the military's grasp. If someone saw a soldier desert, or if his commander had good reason to suspect desertion, the man would be charged and show up in the records. But in the fluid combat environment associated with encirclements by the enemy, attempted breakouts, and forced retreats, determining if someone had deserted, been killed or wounded, or had been captured was challenging. Even during relatively calm times, it was difficult to determine if a soldier had been captured by an enemy patrol, seized by partisans, or deserted, as the Gaebelein case examined in chapter 5 illustrates. Once morale began to collapse in March and April 1945, the line between deserting and surrendering became fuzzy. One did not have to cross over into enemy lines; one could simply wait for enemy formations to roll forward and surrender.

At Stalingrad and in Tunisia, German officers signed instruments of surrender against Hitler's instructions to fight to the last man. As the tide turned, German officers might take it upon themselves to surrender units under their command when their troops were surrounded, were out of ammunition, and commanders deemed resistance pointless. Neither the Western Allies nor the Soviet Union systematically distinguished between Germans who had deserted and Germans who had surrendered in their POW statistics. Frontline intelligence officers were more interested in gleaning information of tactical use to their unit than recording whether the soldier interrogated had deserted or been captured. Prisoners of war were subjected to more thorough questioning at the divisional level and at reception points on their way to POW camps, but more attention was directed to their political orientation (Nazi or anti-Nazi) than to whether they had deserted or been captured.[6] The Red Army captured far more German soldiers than did the Western Allies through 1944, reflecting the scale of land combat on the Eastern Front compared to the Mediterranean and Western Front during this period. During the final three months of the war, however, the balance shifted as millions of German military personnel did all they could to surrender to Western forces rather than the tender mercies of the Red Army (see Figure 7).[7]

Pinning down the precise number of German military personnel who deserted is impossible, though one can say with certainty that desertion rates were low until the final weeks of the war.[8] One can paint a better picture of where deserters headed. The four main destinations were to the

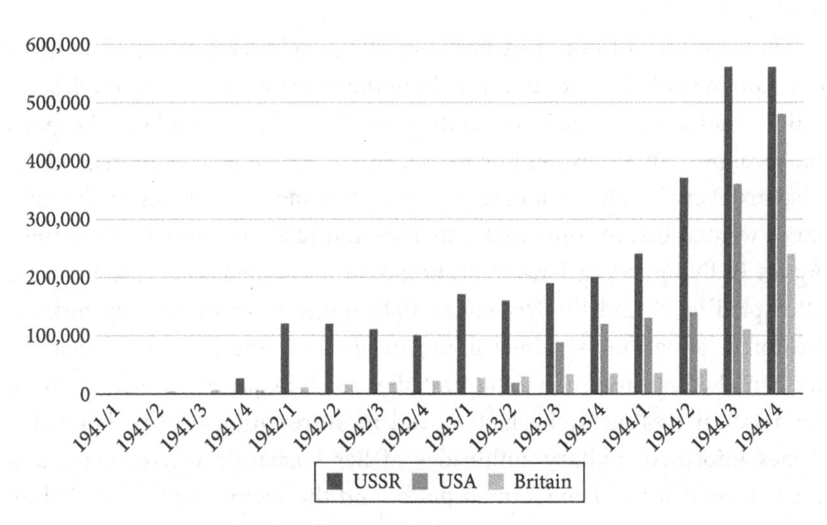

Figure 7. German POWs held by Allied Powers, 1941–1944

Reich and rear areas; to neutral states, in particular Switzerland and Sweden; and across front lines.

Desertions in the Reich and to the Rear

Many deserters from the Wehrmacht simply wanted to go home or to stay home when their home leave expired. Some, such as rifleman Hans Kanzenbach, had no clear conception of how they would evade detection once they made it back home, nor how they would feed themselves. They simply headed home, counting on spouses, wives, and family to hide and feed them. Wilhelm Hanow's wife, Gustave, managed to hide her husband for almost two years until a suspicious neighbor turned them in. Others, who either did not want to endanger loved ones or had no one willing to hide and support them, forged new identification papers and tried to fend for themselves. Deserters tried to pass themselves off as agricultural workers or urban laborers, but soon enough someone would question why they were not in the military, inform authorities, and identification papers would be scrutinized. In occupied Europe, deserters might try to survive by earning a living on the black market. But identification checks, police crackdowns, roundups, arrests, and scarcity meant that living off the bureaucratic grid was extremely difficult. In a number of cases, deserters were able to connect to resistance groups, but they were wary of German deserters who might betray them.

The deserter not only had to worry about military police and military checkpoints but also had to worry about the reaction of the shop clerk scrutinizing ration cards, the train conductor checking tickets and travel papers, the local policeman responding to reports of suspicious neighbors, and the phalanx of civil, military, and secret police looking for fugitives on the military's wanted list. In some cases, spouses and relatives turned in deserters. Agnes P., living in Marienwerder, became exasperated when her husband attempted to extend his December 1941 home leave by seeking medical treatment for an unexplained injury to his foot. She discovered that her husband had not returned to his unit after receiving a three-week extension for medical treatment; he had moved in surreptitiously with her sister. Agnes informed military authorities of her husband's whereabouts, and they arrested him.[9] The German police and the Wehrmacht depended on civilians to report deserters, and statistically speaking, deserters who attempted to disappear into the civilian population were liable to be caught and tried before long. In the Austrian provinces of the Reich, for example, nine out of ten who deserted in 1940 while on leave or on duty there were eventually caught, tried, and sentenced.[10]

The German Army issued a circular on "Measures to be taken against desertion and unauthorized absence" in December 1944. It admonished increased vigilance behind the front, claiming that

> Again and again, deserters have been able to spend weeks and even months loitering in rear areas. They have been able to get food, lodging, even pay and travel papers, despite having no or insufficient identification. Often they use forged papers. Claiming that they have become separated from their unit, they attach themselves to reserve formations and support detachments in order to avoid attention. They particularly like to use medical facilities and ambulances to proceed to the rear. It has come to attention, that in some cases deserters have acquired orders, travel papers, and medical forms which they fill out themselves, using official stamps and seals [to validate].[11]

German military leaders feared a reprise of 1918 as Western and Soviet armies pushed toward the Reich in 1944 and 1945. They became intensely suspicious of soldiers who had become separated from their unit or had lost their identification papers and equipment. Field Marshall Ferdinand Schörner, one of Hitler's favorite generals and commander of Army Group North (July 1944–January 1945) and Center (January–April 1945), sought to dissuade anyone thinking of deserting by making an example of those caught. Enraged by reports of malingerers, Schörner was notorious for hanging soldiers in his command suspected of intentionally becoming detached from their units. Goebbels noted admiringly that Schörner "lets them be hanged from the next tree with a notice attached saying 'I'm a deserter and have refused to protect German women and children.' That naturally has a good deterrent effect on other deserters or those who think of deserting."[12] Schörner was not alone, though he was more outspoken in his admiration of the Führer than some. Other commanders were just as draconian, convinced that leniency would open the floodgates to dissolution.

Hitler and high-ranking Nazis drew upon the narrative they had created about Germany's defeat in World War I. They refused to admit that Germany had been defeated militarily, and they blamed defeat on revolution, desertion, and internal enemies. In February 1945, Martin Bormann, Hitler's deputy, ranted that over half a million German soldiers were avoiding service and demanded that the military take harsher measures against these shirkers.[13] Bormann, like his leader, was transfixed by the memory of 1918. The number of German shirkers and deserters in February 1945 was nowhere near 500,000, and German formations were still fighting on doggedly.[14] Nonetheless, Bormann urged Heinrich Himmler, Reichsführer SS and Commander of the Replacement Army since July 1944, to organize "interception squads" to round up stragglers. Himmler did so, authorizing SS and police in these units to shoot looters and stragglers on the spot. In addition, Bormann established emergency courts (*Sonderstandgerichte*) that could try anyone from the military, the Waffen-SS, or the police accused of desertion. The guiding principle for these courts was to enforce Hitler's sentiment that "whoever is not willing to fight for the German people at this most dangerous hour is unworthy of living and should be executed."[15]

Flying tribunals and fanatical commanders sought to send a signal to anyone who wavered. At Frankfurt on the Oder, hanged deserters dangled from a still intact bridge as a warning to others. Lampposts and trees served similar functions elsewhere; a young refugee from East Prussia remembered how she had stared at the sign attached to one of these hanged men. The sign read "I am a deserter. I was a coward in the face of the enemy."[16] Across the German landscape, whether in the rubble of its cities or in relatively unscathed villages in the country, hanged deserters became ubiquitous.

Some of these hanged soldiers were young boys, others old men. Many thought the war was over, only to discover that the German military was employing summary lynch justice as the war Hitler had launched came home to roost. The home front was never a safe haven for deserters. For many, it became even more dangerous as the death spasms of the German Reich manifested themselves in a crescendo of violence directed against concentration camp inmates, foreign workers, and German soldiers abandoning a lost cause.

Willi Herold

How many deserters were hanged by flying tribunals or summarily shot in March and April 1945 is unknown, but certainly in the hundreds. The horrifying story of Willi Herold, a young German paratrooper who became separated from his unit near Arnhem, Holland, in April 1945 illustrates the chaos and murderous fanaticism of the final days of the Reich.[17] It provides compelling confirmation of Ernst Fraenkel's argument that the Third Reich was a "Dual State" with laws, procedures, and designated authorities (the "normative state") that could be overridden by Hitler, the Nazi Party, and the bureaucracies of coercion (Gestapo, SA, SS) when legal constraints stood in the way of accomplishing their purpose (the "prerogative state").[18] Herold, though only nineteen, claimed that he had been delegated authority from the Führer himself when he "liquidated" 192 German military personnel held at one of the Wehrmacht's prison camps in April 1945 without trial. He was able to do so only because he was backed by local Nazi Party officials and the Gestapo who chafed at legal formalities and an array of fellow soldiers, camp guards, and *Volkssturm* troopers who blindly followed Herold's orders without questioning his authority.[19]

One might empathize with Wilhelm Hanow hiding in a barn, with Stefan Hampel who could not forget that his mother was Polish, with Jakob Bug and his stubborn refusal to serve in the military because of his religious convictions, or even with Gustav Gaebelein and his weak nerves. Willi Herold's actions after he became separated from his unit can only elicit repugnance and condemnation.

Willi Herold was born in Lunzenau near Chemnitz, Saxony, in 1925, and attended middle and high school in Chemnitz. He would have been seven when Hitler became chancellor, and like that entire generation would have been indoctrinated with Nazi worldviews in school and in the Hitler Youth. Herold claimed that he and his friends grew tired of the organized activities of the *Jungvolk* (the Hitler Youth's junior division for ages ten to thirteen) preferring to play cowboy and Indian games inspired by the adventure books of Karl May. At age eleven, he was kicked out of his *Pimpfe* (HJ Cub Scout) pack for missing meetings and activities. At fifteen, he ran away from home intending to stow away on an Italian ship bound for the New World. He was apprehended by Italian authorities in Northern Italy, turned over to the German police, and sent back home after being thrashed soundly.[20] He completed his apprenticeship as a chimney sweep, and at age seventeen he was sent to France to work on the Atlantic Wall in fulfillment of the mandatory Reichs Labor Service duty. Shortly after his eighteenth birthday, he was conscripted into the military. Physically fit and good-looking, he was selected for paratroop training after completing the German Army's three-month basic infantry course.[21] Herold was then sent to Italy, where he saw action at Nettuno (Anzio) and Monte Cassino in 1944. His unit was transferred to the Western Front in 1945. Sometime in late March 1945, Willi Herold lost contact with his unit, Battalion 1 (*Kampfgruppe Gramse*) of the 32nd Fallschirmjäger Regiment, as it was withdrawing from its position near Gronau on the Dutch-German border.

Tens of thousands of soldiers lost contact with their units during combat operations, and the Wehrmacht did not habitually shoot stragglers who did their best to return to their unit or turned themselves in to the nearest military police as soon as possible. But during the final weeks of the war, the German military police (the *Feldgendarmerie*) were on the lookout for deserters, and Himmler's interception squads were meting out summary executions to anyone they suspected of intentionally malingering.

What Herold did after losing contact with his unit would have raised questions and, at the very least, resulted in military charges under normal circumstances. Wandering behind the lines, Herold discovered an abandoned military vehicle containing a suitcase with the uniform of an Air Force paratrooper captain, complete with decorations.[22] Herold changed uniforms, hid his papers, and assumed the identity of a German officer. Though only nineteen, he projected the self-confidence and commanding demeanor of a decorated war hero when he encountered two other stragglers who had lost their unit or deserted. Wearing the Iron Cross First and Second Class on his breast alongside a decoration for close combat, Herold demanded that they salute him before ordering them to report back to their unit immediately. The next day, the two encountered Herold again at a military checkpoint where the fake captain was regaling the major in command of the checkpoint with tales of his exploits in Crete and boasting that he was the youngest Luftwaffe officer to be promoted to captain. Herold managed to persuade the major to put five of the stragglers he had collected at his disposal, which the major duly did, annotating in their papers that they were now part of "Detachment Herold."

"Detachment Herold" proceeded along the way, and other lost men joined the unit, which commandeered an abandoned light truck equipped as a field kitchen. Stopped a second time by a military police patrol, Herold ordered his men to show their identity papers, but no one insisted that Herold show his own. When "Detachment Herold" reached the town of Meppen, Herold followed procedures and reported his unit's arrival to the military commander. Herold informed the commander that he had a battery of guns, including a 15 cm howitzer that might be useful in defending the town. This was complete fiction, but it got his men fed, the light truck refueled, and bought "Detachment Herold" some time. Herold sent some of his men out to reconnoiter the front and helped blow up a bridge as the German troops withdrew from Meppen. He was able to convince others to provide his unit with a heavier truck and a car. His men managed to mount a light antiaircraft gun taken from a naval riverboat about to be sunk on the truck. By the time "Detachment Herold" reached Papenburg in the Emsland, Harold commanded thirteen men equipped with a truck, a car, and a light antiaircraft gun. He again reported his arrival to the local military commander, who introduced him to the town's mayor and the Nazi Party district leader.[23]

Up to this point, the story of Willi Herold echoes the story of the "Captain of Köpenick." Prior to World War I, a recently released convict and con man had donned the uniform of a Prussian officer, ordered some enlisted men to fall in behind him, and marched them to the Köpenick city hall, where he confiscated 4,000 marks from the treasurer on "orders from Berlin." Newspapers critical of German infatuation with the military had used the incident to poke fun at the instinctive subordination of Prussian civil servants and much of its bourgeoisie to military authority. During the Weimar era, the incident became the topic of both a film and play. Yet Herold's story takes a much darker turn than the tale of the Captain of Köpenick.

Whether Herold was aware that the German region around Papenburg, known as the Emsland, had one of the densest networks of labor camps in Germany is unknown. Over lunch, Papenburg's mayor and the Nazi district leader regaled him with stories about escaped convicts who were allegedly terrorizing the area. The Third Reich had established numerous work camps for political prisoners in the Emsland, a thinly populated, isolated region of moors and farms, during its consolidation of power. By 1944, the Emsland camp network encompassed fifteen labor, penal, and POW camps, six of them filled with German military personnel who had been sentenced to heavy labor and declared "unworthy of military service" by Wehrmacht military tribunals. As Allied forces pushed the Wehrmacht out of the Low Countries and into the Reich in 1945, these Emsland military convicts joined the much larger trek of concentration camp inmates forced to march under appalling conditions away from approaching Allied forces in the East and West.[24] Jan Budde, the Nazi district leader, let Herold know that hundreds of prisoners had escaped while being marched from camps near the front to ones further away. He described the prisoners as swine who had taken advantage of the situation and were roaming about the area plundering and raping while Germany faced an approaching enemy. Something had to be done. Sensing an opening and an alternative to joining the fight at the combat front, "Captain" Herold demanded that Budde take him to Camp Aschendorfermoor, which was overflowing with 2,500 to 3,000 prisoners who had been kicked out of the Wehrmacht and sent to prison camps by military tribunals. Among those at the camp were convicts who had escaped during the march from other camps, been captured, and were now detained pending further instructions.

Budde, Herold, and a sergeant named Werner Freitag arrived at the camp around noon on April 11, 1945. Budde introduced Herold to the commander of the SA detachment guarding the camp, Karl Schütte. Schütte had joined the SA in 1931 and had worked his way up the camp hierarchy since 1939, starting as a guard and now in charge of the guard detachment. Commenting on the influx of recaptured prisoners over a bottle of schnapps, Schütte complained to Herold and Budde that the camp commander, who worked for the Ministry of the Interior, paid too much attention to the niceties of procedures. The commander was in the midst of organizing a trial for these returned men, when it was patently clear to Schütte that they should simply be shot. Schütte then escorted Herold into the camp, where the captain informed the commander that he had special orders from the Führer and was now in charge. Herold arranged a meeting with the local Nazi district leader as well, who after checking with the region Gauleiter and the Gestapo, wished Herold best success ("Hals und Beinbruch") with his mission.

Over the next week, Herold's group—assisted by camp guards and members of the local Volkssturm—would murder nearly 200 prisoners. Herold set the example by personally shooting German deserters in the back of the head immediately after his arrival at the camp. The next day, he ordered all camp inmates to fall in for muster. Walking down the line, he asked if anyone was from his home district. Those who said yes were summarily shot. Herold then ordered all military convicts wearing an F or V on their uniform to step forward.[25] These men, identified deserters and escapees, were ordered to dig a pit outside the camp. They were then lined up and gunned down. Herold's group used a light antiaircraft gun as well as rifles to shoot these men, tossing hand grenades into the pit to complete the job. *Schnellgericht Herold* (flying tribunal Herold), camp guards, and local volunteers celebrated their brutality that evening with beer, champagne, music, and women. Over the next several days, more prisoners would be shot. One of the survivors claimed that the executioners did not "do it because they had to, but because they enjoyed doing so." They were seen laughing as they shot prisoners and exhibited "*Lust und Freude*" (pleasure and joy) in killing defenseless men.[26] Herold decided that other camp prisoners were fit for military service and marched them out of the camp toward the front under escort. How many of these men arrived at the front is unknown.

On April 19, 1945, RAF bombers attacked German artillery positions near the camp, destroying many buildings and the perimeter fence. Herold's group slaughtered escaping prisoners and those desperately looking for food in the ruins. After leaving the destroyed camp, Herold's group hanged a German farmer who had hoisted a white flag and killed five Dutch civilians they encountered while retreating from the front. Herold's triple-game as straggler, self-appointed task group commander, and executioner came to an end as April drew to a close. The German naval commander at Aurich questioned Herold's authority when his "special command" showed up in town. The naval officer demanded identification papers and initiated military court proceedings against Herold. An SS officer, Untersturmführer Urbanek, intervened in the proceedings. He insisted that Herold, while guilty of impersonating an officer, had not betrayed the Third Reich. The local Nazi district leader and the naval judge in charge of the proceedings agreed. The naval judge, quite contrary to normal procedures, convinced the naval commander to stop the court-martial before it went any further. Herold was given the opportunity to prove himself at the front. The SS was organizing a special Battalion Emsland near Wilhelmshaven. Its purpose was to continue the fight, with wild talk of sending the unit to Berlin if possible. Assigned to the special battalion, Herold deserted the night after he arrived. He headed to Wilhelmshaven, forging discharge papers under his real name, and seeking work as a certified chimney sweep.

The particulars of Willi Herold's killing of fellow Germans who had once served in the Wehrmacht and had fled or deserted from it are unique, but the resort to summary executions without trial during the last days of the war was unexceptional. For most of the war, the Wehrmacht followed established procedures in dealing with German deserters and military personnel who were "undermining the military spirit." They were charged with violations of the military penal code (the *Militärstrafgesetzbuch*) and/or the Wartime

Criminal Law Special Ordinance (the *Kriegssonderstrafrechtsverordnung*), and tried in accordance with military courts-martial regulations and established wartime criminal processes. Thousands would be executed using these "regular" processes. But as the Allies closed in on Germany, fanatical supporters of the regime argued that desperate times required desperate measures. Herold was able to do what he did because party, Gestapo, SS, and military fanatics provided cover and support for his irregular mass executions.

Deserting back to the Reich was dangerous throughout the war, culminating in the fanatical spree of summary killings as the ground war came home to roost in 1945. Those contemplating a safer destination might have daydreamed about deserting to a neighboring neutral country, but that, too, had its challenges.

Deserting to Neutral Neighbors Switzerland and Sweden

One can determine with some certainty how many German deserters made it to Switzerland and Sweden over the course of World War II. Switzerland was the preferred destination of German deserters seeking refuge in a neutral state. The country was geographically accessible, its people spoke or understood German, and it had served as a haven for thousands of deserters during World War I. German deserters from incorporated Austria felt particularly drawn to Switzerland. Some knew the Alpine high country of Tyrol and Voralberg well; others convinced themselves that they might get special treatment. More broadly, German deserters who crossed the Swiss border hoped that Swiss neutrality precluded their forcible return.

The Nazi seizure and consolidation of power had generated a wave of political and Jewish refugees in 1933–1934, followed by a wave of German Jews in 1937–1938 as life for them in Germany and annexed Austria became increasingly oppressive. During this period, Switzerland attempted to distinguish between political refugees and German Jewish refugees, accepting the former but turning back the latter.[27] As of 1935, Switzerland was confronted with another issue: what to do with German conscientious objectors who refused to serve in the military or draftees who deserted across the border. Their number was small in comparison to the thousands of Jews who were denied entry to Switzerland during the 1930s. The Swiss military was not particularly interested in the few dozen German military conscientious objectors and deserters who crossed the Swiss border, telling the Ministry of Justice that this was a police and refugee matter beyond its jurisdiction.[28]

Germany's attack on Poland on September 1 and the declarations of war by the United Kingdom and France on Germany two days later radically changed the situation. Europe was again at war. Switzerland mobilized its military to signal the belligerents that it would defend itself. It spelled out its obligations as a neutral power in a diplomatic note sent to belligerent and interested parties on September 31. Internally, the Military Department and the Department of Justice and Police clarified who would be responsible for dealing with military deserters, conscientious objectors, and aircrews landing in Switzerland. If foreign military personnel crossed the border or landed in Switzerland, they became the responsibility of the Military Department. If someone crossed the border in civilian clothes and asserted that they had done so in order to evade military service, Swiss civil and police authorities would determine the appropriate course of action.

During the first nine months of the war in Europe, only a trickle of German and French military personnel crossed the Swiss border illegally. Border guards and police turned border crossers in uniform over to the Swiss military, which conducted interrogations focusing on unit dispositions, equipment, and so forth. In October 1939, the seven-member Swiss Federal Council decided that Switzerland would not forcibly repatriate foreign military personnel if severe punishment could reasonably be expected. This covered Wehrmacht deserters, and while incidents of border guards forcing deserters to turn around occurred, the Swiss military generally did not force German deserters back to the Reich. In certain cases, this policy could be overruled but doing so required approval from the Federal Council.

From the outbreak of war in Europe until May 1940, only a handful of German and French military personnel crossed the Swiss border. They were interrogated, sent to work on farms in the interior, and ordered to report to the local police every eight days. Swiss military officers had little sympathy for foreign deserters, and little effort was made to supervise them once interrogations were completed. The situation changed dramatically in May 1940, as Sitzkrieg turned to Blitzkrieg in the West. The German breakthrough at Sedan and the subsequent encirclement of French, Belgian, and British forces at Dunkirk shattered French morale. When German formations began to attack and overrun the Maginot Line from the rear in June, the French VL Corps positioned in Alsace crossed over into Switzerland on the night of June 19. Twelve thousand Frenchmen and 16,000 Poles decided that internment in Switzerland was preferable to surrendering to the Wehrmacht. Over the course of the war, thousands of additional foreign military personnel would land or cross over into Switzerland without authorization. These ranged from American airmen whose long-range bombers had sustained damage to Italian soldiers crossing the border after Italy's surrender to POWs escaping from prison camps. More than 100,000 foreign military personnel would be interned in Switzerland at some point during World War II (see Figure 8).[29]

German deserters made up only a small portion of the 7,000 Germany military personnel interned in Switzerland at the close of the war, as entire units had crossed over the Swiss border in the last months. And Germans made up only a portion of the foreign military personnel interned, with French, Italians, Poles, and Russians more numerous. Yet the Swiss military was mainly concerned about the threat posed by Germany until the tide turned in 1943. It devoted more effort to debriefing and interrogating German deserters than it did to questioning French and Italian soldiers who fled into Switzerland in 1940 and 1943.

Swiss records indicate that more than 100 German deserters were in Swiss custody by July 30, 1942, increasing to 535 by the fall 1944.[30] Thousands of German soldiers crossed the border in the final eight months of the war, some individually and others under the command of their officers. Determining whether the former were deserters while the latter were not became a legal distinction without practical consequences. Swiss

Nation	Number of Military Personnel Interned in Switzerland
France	32,621
Italy	29,213
Poland	14,972
Soviet Union	8,415
Germany	7,532
Britain and Commonwealth	5,139
Yugoslavia	2,921
USA	1,742
Belgium	783
Greece	846

Figure 8. Number of military internees in Switzerland

interrogations became perfunctory as interest shifted from gathering intelligence to preparing for a wave of border crossers once Allied troops pushed into Northern Italy and broke into Germany.

The most dangerous time for the deserter was the border crossing itself. German units stationed near the border were well aware that disgruntled soldiers might decide to flee to Switzerland and, as a consequence, restricted access to border areas. Military police set up moving checkpoints to inspect identification and travel paper, and customs officers inspected goods crossing the border. Most daunting to a potential deserter, German border police in guard towers and roving patrols were well armed and had orders to shoot anyone fleeing from the Reich. or attempting to slip into it. Swiss border guards were also armed and were authorized to use deadly force if threatened.

Once across the border, German deserters who sought internment usually turned themselves in to Swiss border guards or the nearest police station. Border guard officers from the intelligence section would conduct initial screenings, asking how, where, and why a deserter had crossed the border. If a deserter was in uniform, border guards were supposed to turn him over to the Swiss military. Weeks or even months might go by before this transfer was completed. During this interlude, German deserters were kept in police confinement. The Swiss military's intelligence branch, N.S. 1 (*Nachrichten- und Sicherheitsdienst*), was headquartered in the Schweizerhof Hotel in Lucerne. N.S. 1's main office conducted multiday interrogations in Lucerne, but as the number of deserters mounted, branch offices took on the task as well.

Switzerland's Federal Council (its seven-person executive) had decided in October 1939 against returning deserters who might be shot. But this decision was not publicized, and Swiss military intelligence officers could warn deserters that they would be sent back to Germany if they were uncooperative, refused to answer questions, or lied. It appears, however, that interrogators generally did not attempt to browbeat those they interviewed. They instead sought to nurture trust by engaging in extended conversations. Several of the officers working in N.S.1 were critical of National Socialism, and coupled trade-craft with sympathy as they elicited information.[31]

Interrogations served several purposes. During the first years of World War II, when the Swiss feared that the conflict might somehow embroil Switzerland militarily, the main purpose was to gather intelligence about German dispositions, plans, capabilities, tactics, techniques, and procedures.

Denmark, Norway, the Netherlands, Belgium, and Luxembourg had all discovered that neutrality meant nothing to Hitler if he reckoned there was a military advantage to be gained by occupying or overrunning a neutral state. Once it became clear that Germany had underestimated the Soviet Union and that the war in the East would be long and costly, assessing German military and civilian morale became equally important. Lastly, understanding why someone had deserted provided a basis for evaluating conditions in the Wehrmacht and in the Reich.

An internal memo listed nine areas that should be addressed during interrogation. Intelligence officers were given latitude in terms of specific questions and tone. Topics of interest included information about the individual, his unit, his superiors, and the manner and path of flight; information about home leave and transportation; military assessments; economic information; information about Germany's domestic conditions; data about food and rations; insights into the mood of the German people; observations about the Reich; the detainee's attitude toward Switzerland; and any specifics insights the deserter had about the German state, the Nazi Party, and the Wehrmacht.[32] The memo was undated, but it probably was written midway through the war as earlier interrogations were focused heavily on German dispositions, capabilities, and tactics.

Once N.S.1 had completed interrogating a deserter, he was sent to an internment camp. The fall of France and the influx of thousands of foreign military personnel resulted in a reexamination of Switzerland's initial treatment of deserters. Sending them to farms to help with agricultural work and instructing them to report weekly to the local police was judged no longer practical. German deserters were gathered at the Witzwil penitentiary in July 1940 and then sent on to one of the labor camps for interned military personnel. Most German deserters were sent to Murimoos in Canton Aargau.

German deserters who had turned their backs on the Wehrmacht because they disliked the discipline and regimentation of military life discovered that internment had its own strictures of control and supervision. They were mustered three times daily and had to render military salutes. Food was adequate but alcohol prohibited. Internees had to work long hours performing strenuous manual labor, chiefly peat work. They correctly sensed that Swiss officers overseeing the internment program thought poorly of them. Lieutenant Colonel Bossari, commandant of military internment camps in Aargau, was accused of calling them bastards and bums ("*Schweinekerle und Saukerle*"). Colonel Probst, head of the overall internment program, left no doubt about his attitude toward the inhabitants of Camp Murimoos. He characterized one-third of them as criminals, one-third as rotten moral weaklings, and believed that only one-third were decent humans who had earned the respect of his Swiss guards through hard work and good behavior.[33]

The hostile attitude of the camp commandant toward his wards prompted one concerned Swiss citizen to write to the editor of a local paper, observing that "We are talking about people who proved by their actions that they disassociated themselves with the Third Reich, and refused to continue to fight for its national-socialist regime."[34] The writer complained that it was a scandal that conditions at Murimoos were worse than at any of the other camps.

A handful of German deserters requested to be repatriated to the Reich during the war. This struck Swiss authorities as odd, since they were fully aware of the Führer directive of April 1940, which specified that desertion abroad was punishable by death. Officials who received these requests speculated that German diplomatic personnel had somehow established contact and convinced these deserters that they would not be executed if they returned. Or they might have been spies who had been using desertion as a cover story. But if Swiss intelligence had no reason to believe these deserters were playing a double game, they were allowed to return to the Reich. Some German deserters held in Switzerland disappeared from internment camps, either not returning from work assignments or slipping out of work camps undetected. Some may have simply merged into the Swiss population, particularly those with Swiss relatives. But as an internal Swiss memo dated March 9, 1943, remarked, not all German deserters were content with internment. A few wanted to fight against National Socialism and headed to the French border to join the Resistance or approaching Allied armies.[35]

Internment is Switzerland may not have lived up to the idyll that some deserters had envisioned. For most, however, it was a safe haven. Food and shelter were adequate, even if regimentation and restrictions were part of camp existence. Recalcitrants were treated roughly, but they were not starved or worked to death as would have been the case if they had been sent to German military penal camps and detachments. Swiss intelligence officers extracted what information they could, but since most deserters were young enlisted men, the value of the information they provided was limited. German deserters in Switzerland were sent back to Germany in late 1945 and 1946, merging into the mass of refugees, POWs, and camp inmates confronting the challenge of starting new lives in postwar Germany.

Sweden became the destination of almost as many Germany deserters as Switzerland, but. Sweden's policy toward German deserters fluctuated more sharply. Its policy reflected a less principled position on neutrality and what one might term a more accommodationist position toward the Third Reich following the fall of France and continuing into 1943.

From a Swedish perspective, the German conquest of Norway and Denmark in the spring of 1940, followed by the fall of the Low Countries and France that summer, meant that Germany had all but won the war. Britain's new Prime Minister Winston Churchill might pledge that His Majesty's Government would never surrender and would carry on the struggle from Britain's empire across the sea "even if, which I do not for a moment believe, this island or a large part of it were subjugated and starving," but the reality was that Sweden was isolated in a Europe under control or allied with a very powerful and self-confident Germany.[36] The Swedish government decided it could not afford to alienate the Third Reich. When the German government requested permission to use Swedish railroads to move German officers and men on leave across Swedish territory in July 1940, the Swedish government quietly acceded without putting the matter before parliament. This was a clear violation of neutrality, as the Hague Convention explicitly forbade neutral states from permitting belligerents to move troops, munitions, and supplies across their territory.[37]

The extent over German "leave traffic" across Sweden illustrates how far Sweden went in accommodating German requests. According to an April 1943 report, one special military train per day went from Oslo to ferry ports in Scania (Sweden) connecting to Denmark and Germany; three trains a week went from Narvik to these same ports; two trains a week went from Trondheim to Narvik and vice versa across through Swedish territory; and additional trains from Northern Norway to Finland crossed Swedish territory.[38] The German military was certainly not this generous in granting its members leave, and one can infer that the Wehrmacht used the cover of "leave trains" to rotate personnel, move equipment, and supply its forces in Norway and Northern Finland via neutral Sweden. Sweden was sensitive to Allied complaints that it was grossly violating the obligation of neutral powers to prevent movement across its territory, but until the tide of war turned in 1943, it was unwilling to alienate Germany. During Germany's period of military dominance, Sweden opted to accommodate rather than confront its powerful neighbor. This went well beyond supplying Germany with raw materials (iron ore) and manufactured goods (ball bearings, trucks) important to its war effort, or allowing Germany to move military personnel across Sweden (leave traffic). It extended to suppressing critical comments of the Nazi regime in newspapers, books, the theater, and the cinema.[39]

Sweden's overall policy of accommodating Germany after the fall of France influenced its treatment of German deserters. One or two Wehrmacht deserters might have made it to Sweden during the period of September 1939 to April 1940 (during the Polish campaign and Phony War), but it would have been far easier to desert across the land frontiers to Switzerland, Luxembourg, Denmark, the Netherlands, or France than across the Kattegat to Sweden. The German invasion of Denmark and Norway brought tens of thousands of German military personnel into geographic proximity, but the number of soldiers attempting to flee to Sweden was minuscule. During the course of the Norwegian campaign, several dozen German soldiers, sailors, and airmen landed or crossed into Sweden as a result of damage to their aircraft, parachute landings on the wrong side of the border, or in order to evade surrendering to Norwegian and Allied troops. These men were interned by the Swedes, who noted that most enthusiastically echoed National Socialist worldviews and could not wait to rejoin their units.[40] When Sweden began to repatriate interned German military personnel later that summer, five of the interned Germans confided that they had deserted and wanted to stay in Sweden. They hadn't stated this before because they feared that their fellow internees would react negatively. These men remained in Sweden when the far larger group of German military personnel who wished to go back to Germany were repatriated later in the summer. The Swedes did not disclose their presence to the German foreign ministry and kept these German deserters confined out of sight in Kalmar prison.

Over the course of the following months, a few additional German military personnel slipped across the Norwegian-Swedish border or absconded from the "leave trains" that began to operate. The number was exceedingly small. Sweden allowed Germany to operate these leave trains until August 1943. An estimated 2 million German military personnel crossed through neutral Sweden during this time. Only forty are recorded as having jumped train and deserted.[41]

Even a handful of German deserters might negatively affect German–Swedish relations. Sweden denied that it was harboring any deserters as summer turned to fall. On November 1, 1940, State Secretary Tage Erlander, in charge of Sweden's internment camps, directed that henceforth German deserters would not be allowed to stay in Sweden while authorities decided if they had acted out of political reasons. Instead, he ordered, "People belonging to the German armed forces who have absconded from service and arrived in the country shall be returned immediately."[42] In at least fifteen cases, Swedish authorities returned deserters to the Wehrmacht, which promptly put them on trial. Swedish border guards preferred to order German deserters intercepted at the border to turn back. How many German deserters were forced back without arrest and formal turnovers is unknown.[43]

Once it became clear that Germany was not on the cusp of winning the war, Sweden appears to have altered its policy first in practice and then officially. In practice, Sweden began to intern rather than return German deserters in the fall of 1942; the last recorded case of a German deserter turned over to the Wehrmacht occurred in November. The German defeat at Stalingrad forced Swedish authorities at the highest level to reconsider Sweden's obligations as a neutral. On April 9, 1943, King Gustaf V signed a letter repealing the directive of November 1, 1940. Henceforth, German deserters would not be automatically turned over to German authorities. Instead, police were to detain the deserter, notify the Ministry of Foreign Affairs, and keep the deserter in Swedish custody. Each individual case would be reviewed by the king.[44]

Sweden's decision to turn over deserters in November 1940 and its reversal of this policy in April 1943 were internal government decisions. The government apparently assured the German embassy at some point that Sweden would not harbor deserters, because in June 1941 one of Germany's diplomats visited the Swedish Ministry of Health and Social Affairs and inquired if there had been a change in policy. The German embassy had information that a German deserter named Josef Linke was working on a farm near Vingaker, and that two deserters were working on Count Carl Gustaf von Rosen's estate in Sörmland. The German requested the names of any deserters Sweden was harboring. The Swedish Foreign Ministry replied to the German diplomat that he was misinformed and that these reports were false. It furnished no names or numbers.

The April 1943 decision prompted Swedish authorities to establish internment camps for German deserters, alongside the internment camps already in existence. Deserters were sent to Klostersagen and Sövdeborg initially, and another site was set up at Vägershult in 1944.[45] As in Switzerland, internees wore uniforms and mustered every morning and evening. They had to observe military courtesies and were required to salute Swedish officers. During the week, they were assigned to work details that built roads, repaired bridges, cut wood, and so forth. Wardens were instructed to treat internees humanely, and the postwar Sandler commission concluded that food was adequate.

The number of German military personnel who deserted to Sweden was around 700. Five hundred deserted from Norway, another 150 from Denmark, and 50 from Finland. During the final chaotic weeks of the war, boatloads of German troops left East Prussia and other enclaves encircled by the Red Army and headed to Sweden. Hundreds of German troops retreating before the Red Army in Northern Norway chose to flee over the border to Sweden. They had burned and destroyed homes, bridges, and infrastructure in Russia and Northern Norway as they retreated, and many feared surrendering to the victims of their scorched earth operations. Sweden registered 3,200 military internees during the last weeks of the war.[46]

This final surge of German troops seeking internment in Sweden posed problems. Russian diplomats insisted that high-ranking Nazis, SS murderers, and war criminals were seeking to escape justice by fleeing to Sweden. They were correct about this. Bowing to Soviet demands, Sweden repatriated German internees who had arrived from East Prussia, the Baltics, and Finmark (Norway's northernmost province) in the last months of the war to Poland and the Soviet Union. Germans who had fled to Sweden from the rest of Norway, from Denmark, or had fought against the Western Allies were sent to the British zone of occupation. German internees, including deserters, were repatriated between December 1945 and January 1946.

Deserting across Enemy Lines

Deserting across enemy lines presented another, particularly dangerous option. It was dangerous at two levels. At the practical level, deserters understood that the units they were abandoning would try to shoot them to prevent them from betraying information and to set an example. Enemy troops might not see their raised hands or the white handkerchiefs they were waving, and they might kill an approaching enemy deserter if they were unsure about the situation.

Deserting across lines was dangerous at a different level as well. In addition to being charged with desertion, those who crossed lines faced the charges of treason, high treason, and aiding the enemy.[47] All of these were capital crimes. Crossing lines, even more than absconding to home, rear areas, or abroad, was a fundamental violation of *Kameradschaft*. It was a rejection of group solidarity and the bonds of individual trust that made small units cohesive. Those contemplating deserting to the other side knew that German military law, their superiors, and their erstwhile comrades would show no mercy if the attempt was detected and prevented. They would be dead men if caught.

This generalization applies both to those who went over the lines in the East and those who did so in the West. But ideology and character of the war in the East made the calculus of desertion different there. While the war in the West began two years before the war in the East, the fall of France meant going over to the other side was mainly an Eastern Front phenomenon until Western forces landed in Italy and France in 1943 and 1944.

The Wehrmacht had been a willing partner in Hitler's attack on the Soviet Union, and many of its men accepted the explanation that they were on a crusade to fight Bolshevism and International Jewry. As German armies advanced into Russia, the primitive living conditions of Russian and Ukrainian peasants reinforced widespread perceptions of German superiority and Slavic inferiority. Summary executions of Red Army commissars, the starvation of captured Soviet soldiers, reports of Soviet atrocities, and Germany's mass executions of Jews in the East made desertion to the other side unthinkable for most German military personnel in the East. Desertion rates were very low during the first year of the war in the East. Of those who crossed over to the Red Army, most came from neighborhoods that had once supported Germany's communist or socialist parties. Leftists who had reached adulthood during the Weimar era may have endured a stint in a concentration camp, and many had little desire to fight for an ideology they had not internalized. Their children had witnessed what the Nazi consolidation of power meant for friends and family, and the best efforts of schoolteachers and Hitler Youth leaders to transform young leftists into convinced National Socialists did not always succeed.

Immediately after the German invasion, the Soviet Union established a Bureau for Military-Political propaganda. As in the West, one of its mandates was to convince German soldiers that their cause was unjust and that the Red Army would treat them well if they deserted. The Bureau drew on exiled German communists steeped in Marxist ideology to assist them, such as Arthur Pieck, Peter Florin, and Konrad Wolf.[48] The results were disappointing. German troops found the language of class warfare off-putting, and efforts to pit soldiers against officers transparent. Claims that the Soviet Union was a workers' and farmers' paradise did not match what they had seen of living conditions in the East. Assertions that could easily be disproved undermined the effectiveness of early Russian propaganda. And during the first months of the war, Soviet propaganda sent mixed messages to potential deserters, lambasting the German soldier for being a murderous brute while reassuring him he would be well received if he crossed enemy lines.[49]

Increasingly, the Red Army used German deserters to send personalized, targeted messages to the units they had left, urging them to switch sides. In the short term, this accomplished little other than making German officers in targeted units more vigilant. But in the long term, it planted seeds of doubt. It disproved German claims that the Red Army took no prisoners, while making hungry, dejected, and demoralized soldiers wonder how bad treatment in Soviet captivity really was.

On August 20, 1941, a German light bomber went down behind enemy lines. Within days, paper leaflets were released behind German lines addressing all German airmen. The leaflets, signed by the entire crew, indicated that the captured airmen were being well treated and urged all aviators to abandon Hitler the murderer and come over. Another leaflet, signed by Private First Class Max Peinert, explained to his comrades why he had deserted. "I feel that I have only betrayed National Socialism. This war was not one that the people desired, but one that was forced on them by Hitler."[50]

In addition, the Soviets enlisted German communist writers who had fled the Third Reich to write poems and short stories that urged desertion. Erich Weinert's "Come Over" is typical of this sort of literary propaganda. Its first stanza, one of five, reads:

> German solider, you march towards Death,
> For Swindlers and Profiteers!
> Here you will live, Here there is bread.
> Come over![51]

Weinert would have been a familiar name to German soldiers who had once been communist. He had joined the German Communist Party in 1929, had contributed to its newspaper *Rote Fahne*, and had left Germany in 1933. After interludes in Switzerland and France, he went to Moscow, where he worked for Radio Moscow. His literary output and poems may have stirred dormant leftist sentiments among Wehrmacht soldiers from districts in Germany that had once been communist strongholds, but Goebbels, the German educational system, and the Hitler Youth had been quite successful in convincing many who once leaned to the left that National Socialism was creating a better future for them. The appeal of a classless German community built around one people, one Reich, one leader extended well beyond the middle class by 1941. The rank-and-file German soldier distrusted anything penned by German communists working Moscow's agenda.

German troops felt the heady exhilaration of victory as the German Army pushed deep into the Soviet Union in the summer and fall of 1941. But the Red Army's ability to stop the German Army's forward momentum before Moscow and push it back made some realize that German victory was far from certain. As German casualties mounted in 1942, and particularly following the defeat at Stalingrad, war weariness began to set in. A court-martial conducted by the 177th Division in December 1943 illustrates how war weariness and a loss of faith in victory led one officer to cross over:

> The accused was a member of the Panzer Grenadier Regiment 11. The 2nd battalion of the regiment had been engaged in heavy combat in late June and early July 1943. Around noon on the 8th of July 1943, the commander of the 2nd battalion fell in combat. During the ensuing confusion, the battalion began to retreat. The regiment command ordered the accused [Lieutenant Frankenfeld], as the battalion's senior officer, to take over command and stop the battalion's retreat, which he did.
>
> During the night of 8/9 July, the accused ordered motorcyclist private first class Fe. to drive him to the front lines in order to inspect the forward positions. Once at the front line, Lieutenant Frankenfeld urged the driver to desert, informing the private that early next morning he [Frankenfeld] intended to broadcast a call to the whole battalion encouraging them to go over to the other side. The accused then went over to the Red Army lines. As he had indicated to the private he intended to do, in a leaflet dated

> 10 July 1943 the accused urged his comrades in the 2nd Panzer Regiment to give up the fight and either desert individually or surrender as a unit. In addition, *Krasnaja Swesda* [*Red Star*, the Soviet military newspaper] published a piece by Lieutenant Frankenfeld on 15 July in which he sought to justify his desertion and reiterated his call to his former comrades to come over to the Soviet lines.[52]

Among the court records is a statement from one of the junior lieutenants in the unit:

> First Lieutenant Frankenfeld had private first-class Fe. use the side-carriage of his motorbike to take him to the front for the purpose of establishing contact with Group Schulz. The driver returned in great agitation, explaining that Frankenfeld had gone over to the other side. This development astounded me, as Lieutenant Frankenfeld was known to be a good National Socialist and was recognized throughout the battalion as *the* leader. He was always hard on himself and worked unselfishly all day for his company.[53]

On December 17, 1943, the military court of Division 177 sentenced Lieutenant Frankenfeld to death in absentia. The court declared that Frankenfeld was to be hanged as soon as he fell into German hands.

The German military captured far more Soviet troops than the Red Army captured Germans during the first eighteen months of the war in the East. Stalingrad was not just a military victory for the Red Army, but a tremendous psychological shock to German troops. Over a quarter million Germans, Romanians, and Italians became trapped in Stalingrad when Soviet troops launched attacks that encircled the Sixth Army at the end of November 1942. Hitler, on the advice of Field Marshall Erich von Manstein and Reich Marshal Hermann Göring, refused to authorize an attempt to break out of the encirclement.[54] Göring promised that the Luftwaffe would be able to supply the Sixth Army with food and ammunition until Manstein, appointed commander of the newly formed Army Group Don, could mount a relief effort. The Luftwaffe failed to deliver anywhere near the required food, ammunition, and medical supplies, and Manstein's relief effort in December failed to reach the city.

Soviet loudspeakers and leaflets urged Wehrmacht troops trapped in Stalingrad to recognize that their situation was untenable. The Red Army ensured that German troops in Stalingrad heard that Manstein's relief effort had been repulsed and urged them to surrender. A leaflet dropped in early January implored officers to order their men to give up. It appealed to them as follows:

4 January 1943
To the officers of the German Wehrmacht! The hour is near when the life or death of those in your charge will be decided upon. The Führer's HQ have not left you in doubt about the hopelessness of the situation at Stalingrad. Your men are starving and freezing.... Tens of thousands of young Germans will meet a senseless and inglorious death if your conscience does not compel you in this twelfth hour to lay down your arms before the Red Army is forced to annihilate you.[55]

On January 7, Marshall Konstantin Rokossovsky sent envoys to the German commander, General Friedrich Paulus, pointing out the German position was untenable and asking that Paulus surrender to avoid further bloodshed. Paulus asked Hitler for permission to surrender, which Hitler refused. On January 23, Rokossovsky again asked Paulus to order his command to surrender. Paulus again sought permission to do so from Hitler, who once again refused. Hitler instead instructed his commander that the Sixth Army should defend its position "to the last soldier and last bullet." Paulus knew that his troops were suffering dreadfully and informed Hitler on January 25 that he had "18,000 wounded without the slightest aid of bandages and medicine."[56]

That same day, General Walther von Seydlitz-Kurzbach, commander of what remained of the LI. Army Corps, told his subordinate commanders that they should decide for themselves whether to surrender to the Russians. When Paulus heard of this, he sacked von Seydlitz on the spot and placed his three divisions under the command of General Walter Heitz. Heitz issued an order to shoot anyone seen surrendering. On January 31, Red Army troops penetrated the bunker where von Seydlitz and others were sheltering. As Seydlitz and sixteen others—including another corps commander and two divisional commanders—were being led away by their Russian captors, they were sprayed with machine gun fire from German positions. Two were killed.[57] Friedrich Paulus, promoted to field marshal by Hitler on January 30, surrendered the same day. He never issued an order permitting others to do so. Hitler had appointed him field marshal the day before and had expected Paulus to commit suicide, just as he wanted German troops at Stalingrad to fight to the death. Hitler was furious that Paulus let himself be taken alive. Left to their own devices, isolated German groups continued to resist from basements and bunkers while others surrendered. By March the last holdouts had been liquidated. More than 90,000 Germans, many of them wounded or desperately sick, were captured alive. Among them were twenty-one generals and one field marshal.

The capture of thousands of Germans during the Soviet counteroffensive outside Moscow in January 1941 and more than 100,000 over the course of the Stalingrad campaign from November 1942 to February 1943 opened new avenues for Soviet propaganda and diplomacy. In July 1943, a manifesto appeared proclaiming the establishment of the National Committee for a Free Germany (NKFD). The manifesto, in work since June, called for the creation of a German government that would end the war, withdraw German troops to the border of the Reich, and initiate peace talks on the basis of returning all conquered territories. Twenty-one German POWs and twelve members of the German Communist Party in exile signed the manifesto, appealing to Germans of all political and ideological persuasions who were concerned that Hitler was leading the German people toward disaster. The manifesto made efforts to frame its call to overthrow Hitler in a way that might appeal to German nationalists, referencing the examples of Stein, Arndt, Clausewitz, and Yorck, who had disobeyed their monarch's orders.

Soviet political officers and German communists in the Soviet Union had combed through POW camps to recruit suitable military personnel willing to sign the manifesto and work toward its goals. Eleven German officers signed the Krasnogorsk manifesto, but none were senior in rank. Three majors, two captains, three lieutenants, and three second lieutenants signed on, along with ten enlisted men. Second Lieutenant Heinrich Graf von Einsiedel was one of the signatories. He was Otto von Bismarck's great-grandson and had been awarded the German Cross in Gold for his bravery as a pilot flying the Messerschmitt Bf 109. After postings in the West, he had been transferred to the Eastern Front and had been forced to land behind Soviet lines after his plane was damaged in combat. Though he was only a second lieutenant, his lineage and status as a war hero made his signature stand out.

The NKFD had a larger agenda than inciting desertion and instead aimed to convince Wehrmacht leaders to turn against Hitler and the Nazi

Party. Affiliated branches were established in Switzerland, liberated Greece, and elsewhere. But the makeup of the committee shows how limited its appeal was to German generals who had risen to the top of an institution deeply distrustful of leftists in general, and of communists in particular. No captured general was willing to work alongside German Communist Party functionaries such as Wilhelm Pieck, Anton Ackermann, Hans Mahle, and Walter Ulbricht.

The NKFD had more success recruiting enlisted German POWs. These assisted Red Army psychological operations designed to encourage desertion, persuade German units to surrender, and convince German soldiers that they would be well treated if they crossed lines. Well aware that German troops had been warned that the Bolsheviks would mistreat, starve, and send any captured Germans to Siberia if they were lucky enough not to be shot, Soviet and NKFD propagandists used German deserters to appeal directly to their former comrades in arms. They used loudspeaker trucks, dropped leaflets, and printed a weekly paper *Freies Deutschland* that was smuggled across front lines and left where German soldiers might find it.[58]

The impact of these publications was limited, largely because the German military nipped any hint of organized military resistance in the bud. In the summer of 1943, Private Hugo Ruf and another member of Sturmpanzer Abteilung 216 formed a two-man "soldiers council." After reading a leaflet designed by the NKFD, they recruited several other members to participate in the activities of a Free Germany committee. The group drank beer, vented frustrations, and apparently tore down a picture of Hitler. Someone in their unit reported them, and in December 1943 military police arrested seventeen members of Sturmpanzer Abteilung 216. They were charged with "planning to commit high treason" and "undermining the military spirit." The military court found eleven of them guilty. Two men were hanged, seven beheaded, and two were shot.[59]

Germany's military and political leaders were far more concerned about a different organization formed under Soviet tutelage, the League of German Officers (Bund Deutscher Offiziere [BDO]). Disappointed that not a single senior German officer had been willing to join the NKFD, the Soviets persuaded several of those captured at Stalingrad to participate in an organization that would be restricted to German officers. General Walther von Seydlitz-Kurzbach, who had commanded the LI. Army Corps, was the senior ranking POW to join the League, followed by Lieutenant General Alexander Edler von Daniels, commander of the 376th Infantry

Division. The organization's objectives were the replacement of the National Socialist government by a German government willing to end the war based on a return to the borders of 1937.[60]

The German Army and government initially tried to simply ignore the League of German Officers, brushing off the signatures of those who joined as forgeries. When it became clear that von Seydlitz, von Daniels, and others were cooperating with their Soviet captives, the German Army hierarchy insisted that they must have succumbed to intense pressure. They characterized those collaborating with the Soviets as weak men who had been forced to sign statements drafted by German-speaking Jewish Bolshevik emigrants working for Moscow.[61]

Several developments made it impossible to simply ignore the League of German Officers. In February 1944, Red Army troops encircled six German divisions in a bend of the Dnieper River near Cherkasy. Loudspeakers urged German troops to desert or surrender, and leaflets were dropped urging the same. The Red Army transmitted radio messages from generals Seydlitz and Korfes, who urged their counterparts to remember Taugoggen and Yorck, Rapello, and Weimar-era military cooperation. The German High Command was particularly alarmed when it heard that von Seydlitz had written personal letters to German commanders in the Cherkasy pocket urging them to surrender.[62] German Minister of Propaganda Joseph Goebbels raged in his diary that von Seydlitz's behavior made it utterly clear that he was not acting under duress but of his own will. There was no excusing his behavior. Von Seydlitz, according to Goebbels, was an unpatriotic swine and traitor. The German officer corps, he said, should be ashamed that he had ever belonged to it.[63]

Whether Stalin would have entertained the notion of making peace with Germany on the basis of the borders of 1938 if the German military had overthrown Hitler is doubtful, but the limited success of the NKFD and BDO confirmed that there was no daylight between the German High Command and the Nazi regime. The success of the Red Army in 1943 and 1944, along with satisfactory agreements at the Tehran Conference, made the notion of a negotiated agreement moot. Stalin and his Western counterparts had no interest in negotiating peace with a German government that Nazi diehards might later charge with stabbing Germany in the back. Stalin, Churchill, and Roosevelt aimed to defeat Germany militarily.

The main utility of the NKFD and BDO by 1944, from a Soviet perspective, was to encourage desertion, undermine German military morale, and—for a few handpicked volunteers—engage in sabotage and espionage. Von Seydlitz and other Germans who had gone over to the Reds failed to convince trapped Germans in the Cherkasy pocket to surrender in early 1944. The Wehrmacht was able to break through and relieve the pocket. That summer, however, a massive Soviet offensive crushed German Army Group Center, capturing or killing almost half a million German troops. Among those who surrendered was General Vincenz Müller, commander of the XII Army Corps. Müller joined both the NKFD and the BDO, and graduated from an antifascist school the Soviets had established at Krasnogorsk. After the war, Müller helped organize East Germany's military and was appointed chief of staff of the GDR's People's Army in 1956.[64]

Alarmed by the activities of the League of German Officers and aware of Hitler's mounting distrust of generals the Führer blamed for German military setbacks, General Rudolf Schmundt, head of the personnel department, and Goebbels, minister of propaganda, came up with the idea of an Army circular signed by all its field marshals denouncing Seydlitz and pledging loyalty to Hitler. Issued on March 19, 1944, the circular was signed by von Rundstedt, Rommel, von Kleist, von Manstein, and every other field marshal. It was categorized as a Secret Commander Eyes Only dispatch (*Geheime Kommandosache*) and sent out to German commanders in the field. Along with the field marshal's pledge of loyalty to Hitler, an attached note informed commanders that Seydlitz had been court-martialed for treason and condemned to death. His wife had been arrested, and his children had been placed in an orphanage. Even in captivity, the dispatch warned, commanders had to remember their oath to Hitler and remain fanatical defenders of National Socialism.[65] Following Stauffenberg's attempt on Hitler's life, the dependents of other German officers known to have joined the League of German Officers were arrested and detained.[66]

At a lower level, the German Army's personnel department sent out a booklet entitled "Why we fight" to every officer in January 1944. It explained to every officer how international Jewry, Bolshevism, and Anglo-American Plutarchy were one and the same thing, all seeking to destroy Germany.[67] Training material for National Socialist Leadership Officers became almost hysterical in tone about not reading NKFD propaganda. It encouraged anyone, including German POWs, to immediately strike down defeatists and collaborators whenever encountered.[68]

During the final days of the war in the East, rumors circulated that German soldiers working for the Red Army were sowing misinformation and engaging in sabotage behind the German lines. German commanders were warned to be on the lookout for "Seydlitz troops." Seydlitz had raised the idea of organizing some sort of German volunteer corps with Stalin in February 1944, recruited from German POWs held in the East. By then, the tide had turned decisively in Russia's favor and Stalin had expressed no interest in the concept.[69] The Soviet dictator was confident that the Red Army and the Allies could defeat Germany without the assistance of German deserters. There was no Seydlitz Army, but the League of German Officers and the NKFD had done their best to convince some Germans to come over. German veterans of the NKFD, acting under close Soviet supervision, would play an important role in setting up the East German People's Police and its successor, the [East German] National People's Army, after the war.

The fall of France in 1940 and the expulsion of British troops from Greece and Crete in 1941 made going over to the Western side impossible for most German military personnel until British and American forces reentered Europe in 1943 (Sicily, Italy) and 1944 (France).This does not mean that Britain, supported by its Empire, the Commonwealth, and various governments in exile, paid no attention to sowing distrust and inciting desertion among German military forces between 1940 and 1943. Days before the French government agreed to Germany's terms for a ceasefire and armistice, Prime Minister Winston Churchill set up the Special Operations Executive (SOE) on July 22, 1940. The new organization, an amalgam of three existing organizations under different ministries, took on the task of using sabotage, propaganda, and secret armies to "set Europe ablaze."[70] It directed its main effort during this difficult period toward organizing resistance movements in occupied Europe, inserting SOE agents into occupied Europe, and delivering arms, radio equipment, and explosives behind enemy lines.

The following year, six weeks after Hitler launched Operation Barbarossa, most of the staff of the propaganda section of the Special Operations Department were reassigned to the newly created Political Warfare Executive (PWE). There they, alongside staff from the Ministry of Information and the BBC, crafted black and white propaganda to subvert the German war effort. Sefton Delmar, a fluent German speaker, led the black propaganda section that created various radio stations purporting to be German. The PWE also created counterfeit German documents, letters, and newsletters. The white propaganda section ran a parallel effort through officially acknowledged broadcasts, pamphlets, and booklets.

Through black, gray, and white propaganda efforts, Britain sought to undermine German morale while sustaining the morale of Allied forces and resistance movements in occupied Europe. Encouraging desertion was a small but important element of this broader effort. *Soldatensender Calais*, which started broadcasting in November 1943 and remained on the air until the end of the war, reached a wide audience. Its signal went out on medium wave, with a special shortwave broadcast (*Kurzwellensender Atlantik*) targeting U-boat crews. The station masqueraded as part of the German military broadcasting network. Its content was mainly musical, with short news announcements and commentaries interspersed between the popular music. The broadcasts sought to subtly instill anxiety or doubt by reporting on Allied air raids back home, reading greetings from family members, and providing news on developments in other theaters. A black propaganda version of *Nachrichten für die Truppe* provided the same news, with the radio and print formats reinforcing each other's legitimacy. *Soldatensender Calais*, renamed *Soldatensender West* after D-Day, had to be entertaining and believable.[71] It was part of the broader effort to "soften up" the enemy by creating doubt and confusion, but as one PWE veteran would later concede, black propaganda was not a war winner. It was most effective after its listener had lost faith in his military commander, the Nazi movement, and the Führer. For many, that moment only came after Germany's last offensive in the West was beaten back in December 1944.[72]

Efforts to demoralize the German military through radio transmissions were supplemented by tangible aids to desertion. Britain's Political Warfare Executive forged leave slips, ration cards, and "bomb damage" papers that allowed those visiting home to use shelters and food kitchens on a temporary basis.[73] The PWE also dropped copies of a small booklet that described in detail how to feign disease or injury. The booklet, known internally as publication H 312–Malingering, was dropped into occupied Europe with harmless book jackets such as *Sport Instructions for the German Navy* or *1000 French Words*.[74]

Churchill had high expectations that propaganda, commando raids, and resistance groups in Europe, coupled with Bomber Command attacks on German cities, would seriously undermine German civilian and military morale. This was not to be the case until very late in the war. Yet one little-known episode illustrates how deserters contributed to British propaganda and intelligence efforts notwithstanding the small numbers involved.

On Sunday, May 9, 1943, Ju 88 of the Luftwaffe's 10th Night Fighter Squadron stationed in Aalborg, Denmark, took off for a patrol mission over the Skagerrak. After refueling in Norway, the aircraft sent a signal at 1725 to its controlling station that its starboard engine was on fire. The plane dropped below radar detection range, threw three lifeboats into the sea, and then proceeded across the North Sea to Scotland. The German military launched a search and rescue effort. Scout planes sighted empty lifeboats near the location where the aircraft had sent out its final distress call. The Luftwaffe assumed the night fighter had crashed into the sea and sunk.

It had not. Instead, the airplane's pilot, flight engineer, and wireless operator/gunner had deserted, using the Luftwaffe's night fighter as the vehicle for their defection. As the Ju 88 neared Scotland, two RAF Spitfire fighters intercepted it. The Junker lowered its landing carriage, waggled its wings, and dropped flares to indicate that it was friendly. The Spitfires escorted the airplane to Dyce airfield, where the German fighter landed. Its three-man crew informed RAF officers that they wanted to defect. They despised Hitler and his agenda and were convinced that the Nazi Party was leading Germany down a disastrous path. The Germans cooperated fully with their RAF interrogators, and the Royal Air Force was delighted to get its hands on the Luftwaffe's latest airborne radar set, the FuG 202 Lichtenstein B/C.[75] British scientists were able to calculate the optimal length for metal strips dropped to blind enemy radar thanks to the defection.

Britain granted the three members of the aircrew refugee status rather than endangering their lives by sending them to a POW camp. All three assisted the Political Warfare Executive branch to interrogate other prisoners, and in the case of the pilot, worked on the team that created the material for *Gustav Siegfried Eins* and *Soldatensender Calais*. The flight engineer and gunner contributed to the white propaganda efforts of the PWE.[76]

Once the United States joined the war, it poured resources into its equivalent of Britain's Political Warfare Executive. The US counterpart to the PWE was the Office of Strategic Services' Morale Operations Branch, started in March 1943. Drawing from the British experience, it also set up radio stations, forged documents, and air-dropped leaflets. Operating from North Africa, Britain, Italy, and Sweden, the Morale Operations Branch carried out psychological warfare across Europe.[77]

The Supreme Headquarters Allied Expeditionary Force (SHAEF) established its own Psychological Warfare Division in February 1944. Cobbling together personnel from the Office of Strategic Services, the US Office of War Information, and Britain's Political Warfare Executive, SHAEF's Psychological Warfare Division mounted a major effort before and after D-Day to undermine German military morale in France. The Americans designed special leaflet canisters that could be dropped from the air, dropping more than 3.2 million leaflets and safe conduct passes on German positions. Leaflets, radio broadcasts, and fliers informed German troops that their situation was hopeless, and the accompanying safe conduct passes assured Germans who deserted or surrendered that they would be well treated.

Much to their disappointment, the British and Americans discovered in North Africa, Italy, and Normandy that the German soldier had not internalized Germany's inevitable defeat. Only a trickle of Germans deserted. German units in the West continued to fight rather than surrender as long as they had food, ammunition, and leadership. After the fall of Rome, desertions in Italy began to tick up, with the G-2 Section of Headquarters Fifth Army estimating that perhaps around 3 percent of surrendered German personnel captured since May were deserters. This would have equated to around 1,200 men. As the Fifth Army pushed northward, prisoners fell into three categories: stragglers who made no attempt to keep up with their unit during withdrawal, Germans left behind without leadership and cut off, and deserters.[78] In Normandy, however, though more than a million broadsheets were dropped over Cherbourg after it was cut off in mid-June, its German garrison forced the Allies to clear them out bunker by bunker.[79] Other German Atlantic fortresses such as Lorient, La Rochelle, and Saint-Nazaire held out until Germany's unconditional surrender in May 1945.

The barrage of fliers and safe conduct passes clearly alarmed German commanders in France who feared a repeat of 1918. The commander of the 91st Infantry Division sent out the following order: "Recognizing that in this final battle for the Fatherland Germany depends on every single soldier, the enemy is attempting to persuade German soldiers to forget their sacred duty and desert using a flood of propaganda fliers. Remarks and observations that give reason to suspect someone is contemplating desertion are to be immediately reported to one's superior."[80] The commander of the 2nd Panzer division echoed the sentiment: "The enemy, unable to break through our positions despite a superiority in men and firepower, is utilizing a barrage of leaflets to persuade German soldiers to desert using lies. We must be vigilant in preventing this poison from falling into the hands of wavering comrades. I forbid reading these enemy fliers. Anyone who finds one should immediately tear it up and turn over the torn-up flier to his immediate superior."[81] In more colorful language, the commander of Grenadier Regiment 713 instructed: "Unfortunately, a few weaklings, whom we once called comrades, have gone over to the other side. Only a rotten, inferior swinish lout is capable of abandoning his comrades when danger looms.... Whoever thinks they will speed up their return home by going to the other side, or assumes he will be able to sit out the war in warm quarters, is wrong!"[82]

Far fewer Germans deserted during the bitter fighting at Normandy than SHAEF's Psychological Warfare Division had hoped. Instead, under intense aerial bombardment and almost encircled at Falaise, tens of thousands of German soldiers sought to escape rather than surrender. The German military was able to reconstitute itself and fought hard as Allied forces approached the Reich's borders near Aachen in October. Desertion did not become a significant phenomenon in the West until after the Ardennes offensive, accelerating in February 1945. Desperate to escape surrendering to the Red Army, German forces streamed to the West in the last weeks of the war. More than a million German soldiers, sailors, and airmen surrendered to Western forces in the final month of the war (see Figure 9).[83]

By mid-April 1945, Russian troops had encircled Berlin. In the West, German troops were surrendering to Western troops at an unprecedented

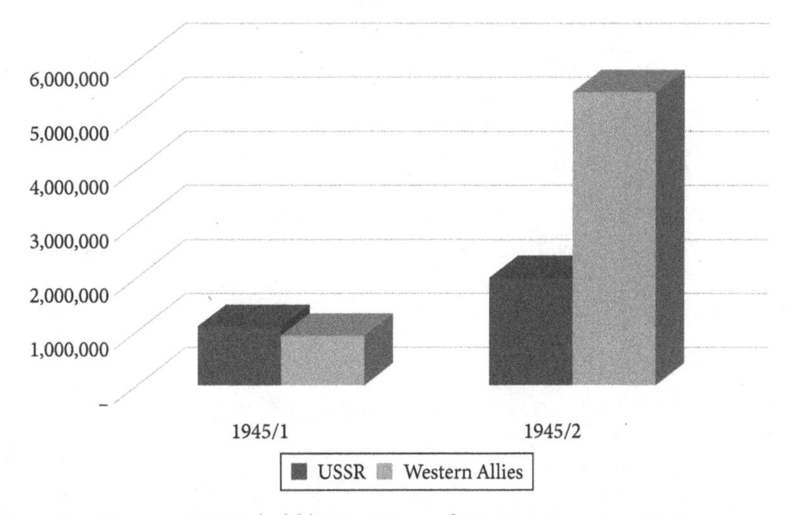

Figure 9. German POWs held by Soviets and Western Powers, 1945

rate. On April 29, Adolf Hitler dictated his last will, married his long-term mistress Eva Braun, and appointed the ever-loyal Grand Admiral Dönitz as his successor. The next day Hitler committed suicide. Dönitz ordered the German military to continue fighting, hoping to negotiate some sort of partial surrender to the West while continuing the mass evacuation of desperate German civilians and troops trapped on the Hela peninsula and in the Courland pocket by the Red Army.[84] German Army commanders in Italy, northwest Germany, and Bavaria capitulated to American and British forces on April 29, May 4, and May 5, respectively. On May 6, the German emissary dispatched to SHAEF in Reims informed Grand Admiral Dönitz that Eisenhower was insisting on an "immediate, simultaneous and unconditional surrender on all fronts."[85] Germany would not be able to play off the members of the Grand Alliance against one another at the last minute. On May 7, General Alfred Jodl, chief of the Operations Staff of the German Armed Forces High Command, signed an instrument of unconditional surrender instructing all German military forces to cease operations at 2301 Central European time the next day. The Soviets insisted that surrender proceedings should be repeated in Berlin. Redrafting pushed the final signing of the surrender document to 1 a.m. on the morning of May 9, 1945.[86] The Third Reich was destroyed, but the battle over how to remember the Wehrmacht, its military justice system, and the role of deserters had only begun.

9
Situating the Deserter in Postwar German Consciousness

In 1952, Alfred Andersch published *The Cherries of Freedom: A Report.* Written in the first person, the essay tells the story of a German soldier's desertion from his unit north of Rome in June 1944. Andersch insisted that the piece was nonfictional but preferred to characterize it as a report rather than as an autobiographical essay. *The Cherries of Freedom* earned Andersch critical acclaim, establishing the thirty-eight-year-old West German's reputation as an author. The essay equated desertion with freedom, juxtaposing the group mentality of those German soldiers who continued to fight against the protagonist's personal decision to quit the war. Andersch painted the act of desertion in these terms:

> I climbed down into the valleys, finding it difficult to strike a path through the dense macchia [bushes]. I was sweating profusely.... Late in the afternoon, I grazed the skirts of an immense wheat-field that idled gently down a hillside. Beyond the trees, on the opposite side of the valley, I could see houses and make out the sound of tanks in motion, a higher and more evenly pitched sound than that of the German tanks I was familiar with.... And at that point I made a gesture of tremendous pathos—but I made it nonetheless: I took my carbine and flung it into the rippling tide of wheat. I undid the ammunition pouch and bayonet from my belt, took my helmet, and threw the lot after the carbine. Then I walked across the field.[1]

As the narrator crossed the field, he encountered a wild cherry tree. He reached up and ate a handful of its fruit, christening them "the wild desert cherries of my freedom."

More than fifty years would elapse before the parliament of a united Germany overturned Wehrmacht convictions related to desertion, subversion of the military spirit, and treason. Assessing the crime of desertion in the context of the Third Reich's war of aggression took decades of debate, changing and evolving over time. It would be debated between the two Germanies. It pitted different segments of society against one another: survivors and perpetrators, playwrights and judges, those who had stayed in the ranks and those who had not. Andersch's voice was one of many seeking to define the act of desertion and the character of deserters. Were deserters cowards and criminals who fully deserved the outcast status they were accorded in the postwar period? Were they victims of an unjust military justice system, or guilty of a crime uniformly condemned by militaries around the world? Were they individualists who refused to subordinate themselves to a military discipline they could not tolerate, or egoists who abandoned comrades and community? Was desertion the resistance of the little man, worthy of admiration? Was the deserter an outcast, a victim, or a role model?

In the West, left-leaning individuals and the conservative establishment battled over how Wehrmacht deserters should be treated during the occupation period and in Adenauer's West Germany. Progressive authors, particularly those associated with Gruppe 47, provoked the reading public with plays, short stories, and memoirs that sought to destigmatize the deserter. In the courts, a handful of survivors and the mothers and fathers of deserters executed during the last days of the war demanded justice. Kriegsmarine jurists and commanders were hauled into court during the late 1940s and punished, only to have their verdicts overturned or reduced on appeal in the 1950s. The disconnect between the positive assessment of Wehrmacht deserters by West Germany's literati and the negative outcome of judicial proceedings was glaring.

In the East, Wehrmacht deserters who had joined the National Committee for a Free Germany (NKFD) discovered that the Red Army had little use for them after the war. A few deserters contributed to communist-led efforts to establish people's police formations during the occupation era, and after the establishment of an East Germany state, NKFD veterans assisted in training what became the East German military. But Wehrmacht deserters and those who had joined the NKFD had to wait until the late 1950s before the East German state began to circulate stories celebrating their actions during World War II. In 1958, East Germany organized a "Working Group of Former Officers." The working group was encouraged to analyze the roots of World War II and the role of the Wehrmacht in the Third Reich in a scholarly manner. The West held the group's output in low regard for their heavily ideological slant. Nonetheless, East German historians addressed several topics that generated debate and attention in the Federal Republic a decade before they entered the mainstream of scholarship in the West. One of these was the role of deserters in World War II.

In 1972, West Germany's *Der Spiegel* published an interview with a Kriegsmarine veteran who claimed that one of the Federal Republic's leading politicians, Hans Filbinger, had sentenced a sailor to six months of imprisonment for criticizing the Nazi regime three weeks after Germany's surrender. Filbinger sued, and he succeeded in suppressing certain statements before the matter flared up again in 1978. The Filbinger affair, as it came to be known, launched a final round of West Germany's efforts to come to terms with the past, which continued through German unification and into the twenty-first century. Peace activists latched onto the figure of the Wehrmacht deserter to prompt discussions about conscription and the duties of the "citizen in uniform." They questioned why Stauffenberg should be honored while the wartime deserter remained stigmatized. This activism encouraged and in turn fed upon new scholarship that explored the role of the German military justice system in World War II and the position of the Wehrmacht in the Third Reich. Stimulated by activism and informed by scholarship, courts and the German parliament took up the issue of whether to overturn wartime verdicts related to desertion, subversion of the military spirit, and treason. Commencing before the fall of the wall, the debate persisted throughout the 1990s and only reached resolution in 2009. A new consensus emerged that the Wehrmacht military justice system had been flawed, its verdicts suspect, and that desertion from the Wehrmacht had been neither criminal nor dishonorable.

Origins of the Dialogue in the Decade after the War

The Allied Powers faced a host of challenges as supreme authorities in Germany after its defeat. The situation in the defeated country was desperate. Around 11 million displaced persons needed to be fed and housed. They ranged from concentration camp survivors to forced foreign laborers to German refugees who had fled the advance of the Red Army or were being driven out of the Sudetenland, Silesia, and East Prussia by Czechs, Poles, and others. Allied POWs needed to be repatriated. Germany's infrastructure had been smashed, its cities reduced to rubble, and food stocks were insufficient to feed the population. Equally important, after twelve years of Nazi rule and decades more of right-wing agitation against democracy, Marxism, and the Jews, changing German thinking and attitudes was imperative for the recovery of Europe.

The European Advisory Commission (EAC), established as a result of the Moscow and Tehran Conferences of November 1943, worked up recommendations for administering postwar Germany the following year. The EAC drew up various proposals regarding future occupation zones, policies, and mechanisms. At Yalta and Potsdam in February and July/August 1945, Allied political leaders hammered out the boundaries between their occupation zones in Germany and agreed to the common goals of demilitarizing, denazifying, decentralizing, and democratizing Germany. Germans who had committed war crimes were to be put on trial, and an International Military Tribunal would be established to try the leading figures of the Third Reich and its military. Germans who had committed crimes specific to certain occupied countries or regions were to be tried by authorities from that country. Occupation authorities would arrest, intern, and try tens of thousands. How occupation authorities determined who should be interned and who should be put on trial varied enormously from zone to zone. More than 400,000 Germans would be interned after the war, and one-third of the estimated 130,000 arrested by the Soviets died in captivity.[2] The Western Allies were quicker to release those they detained and, in contrast to the Soviets, made some effort to determine individual guilt.

In this context, the treatment of German deserters during the war seemed unimportant, as did the question of whether and how deserters returning from abroad should be integrated into a society that had been deeply hostile to them. German civilians were concerned with day-to-day survival, such as finding food, shelter, and work. Once these needs were satisfied, their thoughts turned to those still missing. These might be daughters who had served as Flak helpers (antiaircraft gun crew helpers) or sons reported as missing during the war or fathers held in POW camps far from home. Families who knew that their son, husband, or brother had deserted or been convicted by a German court-martial generally remained silent, cowed by neighbors who still viewed these men as cowards, traitors, or weaklings.

Desertion, the German court-martial system, and the crime of "insubordination of the military spirit" did crop up as themes in a few postwar trials. In addition, some deserters and POW collaborators were drawn into the process of denazification, demilitarization, and democratization in various ways. How the occupying powers went about implementing the guiding principles agreed upon at Potsdam varied from zone to zone, as did the perception, role, and status of Wehrmacht deserters.[3]

In the East, German soldiers who had joined the NKFD and the League of German Officers (BDO) had hoped to play some role in building up a new Germany. They discovered that the Red Army and returning German communists did not share this view. NKFD operatives assigned to the front to support the Russian army were prohibited from establishing direct contact with the antifascist committees that sprang up in Potsdam, Berlin, Greifswald, and Leipzig in the last weeks of the war. Composed of low-level communists, socialists, and progressive democrats, these committees served as the first interface between the Red Army and local communities. Returning German Communist Party (KPD) members rapidly gained leading roles in these committees, and many were suspicious of any German who had fought for Hitler. Neither the NKFD nor the BDO had a role to play in occupied Germany.[4] In November 1945, Stalin dissolved both organizations since he no longer had any use for them.

Indirectly, however, members of the NKFD would contribute to the Soviet military administration in eastern Germany. When KPD exiles in Moscow, at Stalin's direction, began to recruit German deserters and POW converts for the NKFD, they did so out of an office known as Institute 99. Composed of émigré German communists, Institute 99 conducted political work, supported the NKFD administratively, and organized antifascist schools for German POWs. Institute 99 continued to function after the dissolution of the NKFD and BDO. By May 1946, more than 8,000 German POWs had graduated from these antifascist schools in the Soviet Union.

Most of the core group of German communists sent from Moscow to Germany in May 1945 had worked at Institute 99 during the war. Walter Ulbricht, Anton Ackermann, and Gustav Sobottka had all spent time supporting the NKFD, and they took on the task of organizing communist cadres in the Berlin region, Saxony, and Mecklenburg after the Third Reich's defeat. They would emerge as key players in the Soviet occupation zone over the period 1945–1946 and were central to the foundation of Socialist Unity Party (SED) in April 1946.

A few of the military members of the NKFD, that is, Wehrmacht soldiers who had joined the anti-Hitler organization, contributed to demilitarizing, democratizing, and denazifying the Soviet Occupation Zone, as these terms were interpreted by Soviet military authorities. Bernhard Bechler, for example, had commanded the 1st Battalion, Infantry Regiment 29, 3rd Infantry Division, Sixth Army. Like so many other military members of the NKFD, his experience at Stalingrad had generated profound disillusionment toward the Third Reich's political and military leadership. He had been one of the few officers to sign the founding charter of the NKFD, had subsequently joined the BDO, and had contributed to the NKFD newspaper *Free Germany*. He graduated from the antifascist school in Krasnogorsk in 1944 and was awarded the Soviet Union's Order of the Patriotic War for his contributions to the war. Bechler led the way in denazifying Brandenburg, impatiently lecturing an assembly of approved mayors and provincial leaders that "It is impossible that a single member of the NSDAP can remain [employed]...all remaining [Nazi] party members will have to be released from service....I know that this or that man will say, I haven't got replacements for this or that employee. This viewpoint would be incorrect. We can find the replacements with the necessary intensity of effort."[5] The Soviets appointed Bechler as director of Brandenburg's provincial commission for denazification and land reform in July 1945. He joined the SED in 1946, became Brandenburg's Minister of the Interior shortly thereafter, transferred to the People's Police in October 1949, and was appointed deputy chief of staff of the "Barracked People's Police," the precursor to East Germany's National People's Army, in 1952.

Rather than elevating Wehrmacht deserters and members of the NKFD into figures of resistance to the Third Reich, the Soviets and their German protégés preferred to highlight the contributions of the KPD in the fight against Hitler. But Bechler was hardly the only Wehrmacht veteran who decided to put his talent at the disposal of the Soviet Military Administration in Germany. In 1952, four out of seven "alert detachment" chiefs of staff, eleven out of twenty deputy chiefs of staff, and fourteen out of twenty school commanders in the "Garrisoned People's Police" were Wehrmacht veterans.[6] Many of these veterans had followed the same path as Bechler in that they had joined the NKFD, attended the antifascist school in Krasnogorsk, and then found jobs in the provincial administration and People's Police. When the Soviets decided to militarize the People's Police—a decision that preceded the Berlin Blockade—they drew on the expertise of Wehrmacht veterans who had gone over to their side at the front or as POWs.[7]

In the Western zones, the Wehrmacht deserter cropped up on the stage, in the media, in the courtroom, and as an element of literature during the occupation era and the first years of the Federal Republic. Max Frisch, a Swiss playwright, centered his 1945 play *Now They Sing Again: An Attempt at a Requiem* (*Nun Singen Sie Wieder. Versuch eines Requiems*) around the figure of Karl, a German soldier who refused orders to shoot hostages and then deserted. It opened in Zurich during the last month of the war in Europe, and US and British occupation authorities approved its stage performance in Munich and Hamburg the following year. The play consisted of eight scenes, confronting issues from duty to denunciation to death in war. It grappled with themes that would reemerge in the 1960s as elements of [West] Germany's attempt to come to terms with its past, and it portrayed Karl as a principled figure rather than an opportunist. Radio Bremen, Nordwestdeutscher Rundfunk, and Süddeutscher Rundfunk aired the play in 1946 and 1947, ensuring a broad audience for its message.[8]

US and British authorities authorized stage and radio performances of Frisch's play as part of their effort to demilitarize and denazify Germany culturally. They likewise sought to create a media landscape in their zones supportive of these goals. The first newspapers published in the US and British zones and sectors, Berlin's *Allgemeine Zeitung* and Hamburg's *Die Welt*, were under the direct control of the Western military governments. Within months, the Western Allies shifted their approach, granting press licenses to Germans. Although they generally refrained from direct censorship, the American and British military governments scrutinized the makeup of editorial boards before approving their licenses. They sought to screen out editors and journalists who had propagated Nazi and nationalist views during the Third Reich, providing an opening for liberal, democratic, and left-leaning viewpoints.

By the middle of 1946, Western occupation authorities began to reject licenses to outlets deemed too supportive of Soviet viewpoints. Mainstays of the West German press, such as the *Süddeutsche Zeitung*, the *Frankfurter Rundschau*, *Die Welt*, *Die Zeit*, and *Der Spiegel*, trace their roots to the occupation period. Several editors and journalists, such as Marion Gräfin Dönhoff and Heinrich Graf von Einsiedel at *Die Zeit*, had connections to Nazi opposition groups (Dönhoff to the July 20th group, Einsiedel to the NKFD), while others, such as Rudolf Küstermeier of *Die Welt* and Arno Rudert of the *Frankfurter Rundschau*, were concentration camp survivors. They were fully committed to denazifying and demilitarizing Germany and were critical of the Wehrmacht as an institution.[9]

The overlap between wartime collaboration, denazification, and the creation of a new (West) German media and cultural landscape is most apparent in the licensing of *Der Ruf* (*The Call*) by the Office of Military Government, US (OMGUS) in the American zone in August 1946. Committed to providing a socialist-humanist perspective, the paper was founded by returning German POWs who had been involved in the US Provost Marshal's effort to wean German prisoners in the United States away from Nazism by publishing a camp paper. The paper, also called *Der Ruf*, had provided German POWs with ongoing news about the war and had attempted to open their minds to new points of view. Alfred Andersch and Hans Werner Richter, the publisher and chief editor of the paper licensed by OMGUS in August 1946, had both contributed to the POW camp paper but had chafed at American supervision. Both had joined the KPD during the final years of the Weimar Republic, had been arrested and been detained by German authorities in the 1930s, and had been drafted into the Wehrmacht during the war. Captured in Italy, they had elected to put their literary talents at the disposal of the Americans while in captivity. Determined that the German version of *Der Ruf* would be an independent voice rather than a mouthpiece of the US military government, they published pieces critical of American policies and promoted the idea of a unified, socialist Germany. Given Soviet machinations in Europe, US authorities took a dismal view of *Der Ruf*'s editorial stance. The military government's Information Control Division reacted first by cutting the paper's production run and then by dismissing Richter and Andersch from their positions in 1947.

Hans Werner Richter and Alfred Andersch would shift their focus from journalism to literature after their departure from *Der Ruf*, founding (Richter) and participating in (Andersch) what came to be known as Gruppe 47. Starting as an informal group of young, progressive writers who met annually to discuss and critique each other's work, Gruppe 47 would become an enormously influential cultural institution though it eschewed fixed membership and formal organization. Heinrich Böll, Hans Werner Richter, Alfred Andersch, and others would grapple with the interplay between *Kameradschaft* and desertion in several works that appeared in the early 1950s. These public intellectuals would force the German public to think about the role and status of deserters as the narrative of a clean, apolitical Wehrmacht emerged in the newly established Federal Republic.

Heinrich Böll's first novel, *The Train Was on Time* (published 1949), was among the earliest German works of literature to broach the topic of desertion in World War II. Böll tells the story of a German soldier returning from leave and headed to the Eastern Front in 1943. The soldier travels by train and is seated in a compartment with two other Germans and a Polish prostitute. As the train rolls eastward, conversation turns to the horror of war, the likelihood of death, and the possibility of evasion by desertion. Böll paints a grim picture, suggesting that desertion was not an alternative to death but rather a different path to it, given the likelihood of capture and execution. Short, grim, and full of pathos, the novella was well received. It was the first of dozens of books unpacking the evils of war and bringing name recognition to an author who would become one of West Germany's literary giants.[10]

Hans Werner Richter explored the tension among *Kameradschaft*, collaboration, and desertion in a book that appeared the same year as Böll's novella. In *The Defeated* (*Die Geschlagenen*), Richter tells the story of Private Gühler, an enlisted German soldier captured by the Americans at Monte Cassino and sent to a POW camp in the United States. Drawing on his own experience, Richter depicted a bitter struggle between Hitler loyalists and the majority of the POW population for control of the camp, with American supervisors either oblivious or unsupportive of those who broke ranks with the German camp hierarchy. Both a critique of German POWs unwilling to abandon the cause and American supervisors who valued order above all else, *The Defeated* portrayed the ordinary German soldier as an apolitical misfortunate. At the front, Gühler and his comrades discussed desertion but rejected it. After they are captured, an American intelligence officer asks Gühler, who identified himself as a regime critic, to supply information about German artillery positions. Gühler refuses to comply. His interrogator chides that if Gühler really opposed Hitler, then he would help end the war as quickly as possible. Gühler objects that the men manning the German position are comrades, not Nazis.

For Gühler—read Richter—patriotism and the bonds of *Kameradschaft* made desertion objectionable. Gühler wearily explained to his American interrogator that "I am only a little gear in a machine, a gear that cannot extract itself." Asked why he did not emigrate, he responds that to do so would have been cowardly. Asked why he became a soldier, he answered that he had had no choice. Questioned why he did not resist, he retorted that if he had, he would be dead.

Richter, channeling his thoughts on duty, *Kameradschaft*, and desertion through Gühler, constructed a version of reality that appealed to a German public still struggling to come to grips with evidence presented at Nuremberg.

They insisted that ordinary German soldiers had been powerless against the coercive powers of the state and its military justice system. They asserted that German soldiers had not fought for Hitler, but for the nation and for each other. The common *Landser*, according to this narrative, was as much a victim of war as the Ivan, Tommy, or Yank he had so tenaciously fought against. Rank-and-file members of the Wehrmacht had simply done their duty and fought for Germany and their *Kameraden* rather than for Hitler and Nazism.

Richter's book became a bestseller in West Germany. It downplayed ideology as a reason Germans had fought to the bitter end, and it contributed to an emerging narrative of the Wehrmacht as an apolitical institution misused by Hitler and the Nazis. The book's dedication illustrates how Werner sought to reconcile his political opposition to Nazism with his service in the Wehrmacht and with his growing dissatisfaction about American influence in Germany. It read: "To my four brothers, opponents to and soldiers in war, who hated a system and nonetheless had to fight for it. They neither betrayed their beliefs nor their country."[11]

In 1952, Richter's colleague and literary competitor Alfred Andersch published what became the seminal piece of literature on Wehrmacht desertion, duty, and alienation in postwar Germany. Richter drew on his biographical experiences to write a novel he presented as fiction; Andersch, in contrast, insisted that his work was nonfictional.[12] Entitled *The Cherries of Freedom: A Report*, the memoir traces Andersch's life journey from son of a nationalist Munich businessman to member of the KPD in the 1930s to Wehrmacht soldier and deserter.

Written in the first person, the piece attracted a great deal of attention because Andersch was unapologetic about his desertion. Andersch shocked his readers by dismissing the notion of comradeship—"I was sick and tired of these so-called comrades. They made me want to puke. The worst thing about them was that they were always there. *Kameradschaft* meant that one was never by oneself, that one could never close the door and be alone."[13] He rejected arguments that the oath of loyalty had made desertion unthinkable, commenting that the oath "may have presented a problem to many officers, but I never heard a single soldier I met throughout the war even mention it."[14] Most off-putting to many readers was Andersch's explanation of why German soldiers refrained from deserting—"it never occurred to them that they could do anything other than stay with the group. Staying with the group was easy, in that terror and propaganda created a herd mentality...vague notions of comradeship and defense of the fatherland, or an inclination for combat led the individual to consign his fate to that of the collective."[15]

Andersch presented his desertion as the rebellion of the individual against group thinking, as the act of a leftist intellectual who had never internalized Nazi ideology, of a nonconformist no longer willing to conform to military subordination. The act of desertion was transformed from a cowardly act to one of bravery. One passage would resonate over the years, equating desertion to resistance. Andersch wrote that at the time of his desertion, "I had no idea that six weeks later a bomb would explode near Hitler. My very small, private 20th of July took place on the 6th of June."[16]

Andersch's autobiographical reflections on duty, comradeship, and desertion elicited an outpouring of commentary in the West German press and media. At the time of its publication, the United States was at war in Korea and was pressuring the West German government, Britain, and France to find some way of harnessing German manpower into the North Atlantic Treaty Organization (NATO). The West German public was deeply divided about remilitarization, and slogans of "Without Me!" and "Never Again War!" were gaining traction. Politicians and intellectuals on the left were particularly uneasy about remilitarization, and they were uncomfortable hearing that Wehrmacht generals were advising Theodor Blank, Adenauer's special adviser on defense matters.

Traumatized by their experience in the Third Reich and in its military, Heinrich Böll, Hans Georg Brenner, and other progressives praised the *The Cherries of Freedom* in the literary sections of papers and magazines ranging from *Die Zeit* to the *Frankfurter Allgemeine Zeitung* to *Der Spiegel*. They characterized Andersch as a brave man for acknowledging his desertion, applauded the book for its style, and encouraged readers to grapple with its implications. Böll asked why Germans were snapping up the memoirs of Wehrmacht generals while ignoring books that opposed war. He found Andersch's work "refreshing and candid."[17]

Reviewers on the right of West Germany's political spectrum were much more negative. An anonymous reviewer writing for the *Deutsche Soldaten-Zeitung*, a newspaper established in 1951 by Wehrmacht veterans who supported an "anti-bolshevik German contribution" to Europe's defense, had this to say about the *The Cherries of Freedom*:

> This book is written by a deserter who came up with the idea of transforming desertion into an act of honor. The man did not desert because he thought of his mother, wife, or children under bombardment or threatened by the Gestapo.... He deserted to save his own life, which he valued above the lives of [those the author maligned as] stubborn dummies dead or dying around him.[18]

Less polemical, but equally negative, is the assessment of the book by Andersch's superior at Radio Hesse, where he was employed as evening editor. Writing privately to Andersch, his superior recalled that he, too, could have deserted when his unit was overrun at Normandy, but instead he had crawled through a hollow in the ground to rejoin his comrades. He did so because he regarded desertion as an easy way out of a mismanaged war. If he were a judge, the man continued, he would condemn deserters even if he had doubts about the justice of the war itself.[19]

Andersch always claimed the account was autobiographical rather than fictional. After his death, however, researchers discovered an unpublished manuscript he wrote as a POW describing his capture by Italian partisans and his experience in American captivity. The manuscript, written in the first person, makes no mention of desertion but instead recounts that the writer had become separated from his unit and had blundered into a group of Italian partisans and an inebriated American soldier who had taken him prisoner. Selections from the manuscript, entitled "Americans—First Impression," had been published in the prison paper *Der Ruf* in 1945.

Five years later, Andersch published a different version of events, this time written in the third person, that appeared in serialized form in the *Frankfurter Allgemeine Zeitung* between August 11 and August 23, 1950. In this version, entitled *Flight in Etruria*, trusted friends within a unit discuss desertion. Two decide to take the plunge, while others decide that they cannot do so. *Kameradschaft* still exists. No one in the know betrays those contemplating desertion, and several even provide them with food and best wishes. Both accounts differ from the account in *The Cherries of Freedom*. In the 1945 manuscript, the author is captured but does not desert. In the 1950 version, a group of conspirators discusses desertion; the majority decides against it while two take the plunge together. Andersch's 1952 book circumvents the difficulty of abandoning one's comrades by making desertion a highly personal, liberating experience that distinguishes the individual from the pack.

In 2015, literary scholar Jörg Döring and historians Felix Römer and Rolf Seubert published the results of their effort to discover which account comes closest to the truth. After poring over archival records in Germany and the United States, and meticulously reconstructing the combat records of Andersch's unit, the American units operating in that region, and interrogations in Italy and in the United States, they believe that *Flight in Etruria* was the most accurate account of Andersch's "personal 20th of July." His company, part of Jäger Regiment 39 of the 20th Luftwaffe Field Division, was depicted as gung ho and elite in *The Cherries of Freedom.* In reality, it was a heterogeneous collection of Luftwaffe personnel with little combat experience. On June 6, a day *before* Andersch's company saw its first combat action in Italy, seventeen men went missing. Andersch's desertion most probably was not a solitary act breaking free of the bonds of conformity, but one planned and carried out alongside other demoralized soldiers.[20]

Progressive authors such as Heinrich Böll, Hans Werner Richter, and Alfred Andersch empathized and even identified with the Wehrmacht deserter during the occupation and Adenauer periods. In court, however, judges and juries in the West were less empathetic, thwarting efforts to overturn wartime military verdicts or punish Wehrmacht jurists. Several trials in occupied West Germany and the Federal Republic brought the interconnected topics of Wehrmacht justice, desertion, and "undermining the military spirit" to the public's attention.[21]

The most prominent case involving deserters pertained to a Kriegsmarine judge and commander who had ordered the execution of three naval deserters two days *after* Germany's unconditional surrender. Commodore Rudolf Petersen, the former commander of Germany's S-boats, a naval judge, and three others were charged with crimes against humanity.[22] Formal charges were first lodged in December 1946, but the case dragged on until February 1953 because of appeals and retrials. A Hamburg jury finally decided that Petersen and the others had been innocent of "second-degree murder" and "perversion of justice" (*Totschlag und Rechtsbeugung*). The court declared that the murder charge could not be substantiated since no "perversion of justice" had taken place. No one was punished.[23]

The Petersen case reveals how traditional, nationalist fears of leftist revolution intermingled with National Socialist radicalism in the closing days of the war. Petersen decided to execute German deserters ten days after Hitler's suicide and two days after Germany's unconditional surrender. On May 4, 1945, British Field Marshal Bernard Montgomery accepted the unconditional surrender of all German forces in the Netherlands, Denmark, northwest Germany, and surrounding waters. The following day, the Flensburg station in northern Germany broadcast news of the surrender, describing it as an "armistice." That evening (May 5), the commander of a naval infantry battalion recently scrapped together and awaiting transportation from the Danish island of Funen to Germany, held a *Kameradschaftsabend* (social evening) for his men. The battalion was a heterogeneous group composed of sailors and shore personnel cobbled together on Dönitz's order as a last show of loyalty to Hitler. Dönitz intended to put the men of the naval battalion, untrained in infantry combat, at the disposal of General Helmuth Weidling, who was in charge of the defense of Berlin.

By the end of April, Berlin had fallen, Hitler had taken his life, and the battalion remained stranded in Svendborg, Denmark, for lack of transportation. Lt. Albert Otto Sanders, commander of the naval infantry battalion, was determined that news of Hitler's suicide, the fall of the Reich's capital, and the surrender of German military forces in northwest Germany should not crush morale. He set the tone by declaring that his men needed to keep themselves ready. At the *Kameradschaftsabend*, he declared that National Socialist virtues such as camaraderie, loyalty, discipline, and nationalism remained essential, and speculated about making joint cause with the British against the Russians. Beer flowed freely, and the meeting hall rang with the chorus of a popular Nazi song whose refrain ("tomorrow the whole world belongs to us") was entirely out of touch with reality.[24]

Soon after the social evening ended, three sailors and a young soldier decided that as far as they were concerned, the war was over. The leader of the group, twenty-six-year-old Fritz Wehrmann, came from one of Leipzig's red neighborhoods, and thought he might do better in the East than the West. The other three simply wanted to go home and saw no reason to remain with the battalion. The men had only the vaguest notion of how they planned to get to Germany from Funen. They planned to steal a Danish fishing boat, sail it to the mainland, and then each go his separate way. Shortly after decamping from the barracks, they were intercepted by a Danish patrol, which promptly returned them to their unit. Sander was furious at the men. Sander's naval battalion embarked on the tender *Buéa* the next day, and after arriving in Gelting Bay, Sanders reported to the senior naval officer present that he had detained four men who had attempted to desert. The senior German officer, Commodore Petersen, had only recently arrived in Gelting Bay (*Geltinger Bucht*) after a perilous voyage with his fast attack boats from Holland. En route, he had been informed of incidents of sabotage, mutiny, and desertion in the fleet.[25]

Petersen did not have a reputation as one of the German Navy's Hitler enthusiasts, but he, like other German officers, was determined that there would not be a breakdown of discipline as had happened in November 1918. He ordered that a court-martial convene on the morning of May 9, that is, five days after the German surrender in northwest Germany and eight hours after Germany's unconditional surrender. The members of the court-martial deliberated whether the accused had been guilty of desertion, and what sentence to recommend. Sanders, acting as prosecutor, argued that the deserters needed to be "liquidated." Adolf Holzwig, the presiding judge, was the only member of the court with any legal training. He had joined the Nazi Party and SA in 1933, studied law at the University of Königsberg, and became a member of the German Navy's judge advocate branch in 1942.[26] The three members of the court rapidly agreed that the accused were guilty of desertion. Holzwig pointed out that the Führer guidance of April 14, 1940, specified the death penalty for deserters who had acted as a group and for those whose desertion threatened unit discipline.[27] They recommended that three of the accused be sentenced to death, and the youngest member be sentenced to three years of imprisonment. The accused had no defending attorney, as was their right, nor was any consideration given to the fact that Germany had surrendered unconditionally the day before the trial. Commodore Petersen confirmed the verdict and sentence recommendation on the morning of May 10. That afternoon a firing squad executed Fritz Wehrmann (age twenty-six), Alfred Gail (age twenty), and Martin Schilling (age twenty-two) on the afterdeck of the tender *Buéa*. Their bodies were taken out to sea, placed in weighted bags, and sunk near the entrance to Gelting Bay.

In December 1946, Petersen, Holzwig, Sanders, and four others were charged with "crimes against humanity" as laid out in Allied Control Council Law Nr.10. A Hamburg jury found Petersen and four others innocent for lack of evidence and sentenced Holzwig and Sanders to two years of imprisonment. The jury was sympathetic to Petersen's defense that he had a duty to uphold discipline given the ongoing effort to evacuate Germans from East Prussia and the Courland, and blamed Holzwig and Sanders for insisting on the death sentence. The prosecutor appealed the case, and the appeals court in the British zone ordered a retrial. It was unconvinced that Petersen had had no choice but to approve the death sentence, pointing out that the "discrepancy between the guilty verdict and the sentence was intolerable" given the circumstances. Petersen did have a duty to uphold discipline but not by methods that ignored human dignity and worth. As for Holzwig, the appeals court dismissed arguments that a judge could not be found guilty of misconduct so long as he upheld the law. The court countered that using law to commit inhumanities was one of the most dangerous and unacceptable violations of the law.

The case was retried, and on August 4, 1949, five of the defendants were convicted of crimes against humanity. Petersen was sentenced to two years of imprisonment, Holzwig to five years, Sanders to two, and the others received lesser sentences. The chief justice made note that the accused had "completely overlooked that the war was over." They had so obsessed with avoiding another November 1918 that they had lost perspective. The death sentence was grossly disproportionate to the charge since the war was over.[28]

The defendants appealed the verdict. The appeal now wound its way to the Supreme Court of the newly established Federal Republic of Germany. The head of the senate (the *Bundesverfassungsgericht* has two sections termed senates) had himself been a military judge during the war and directed that the case be retried.[29] The court found that "A judge who imposes a death sentence can only be held criminally liable if he violates the law. This requires a conscious and intentional violation of procedures, without which there would have been no death sentence.... Only when he deliberately proceeds against the law, that is violates it, does responsibility fall upon him."[30]

The case was returned to the lower court. In accordance with the guidance laid out by the German Supreme Court, on February 27, 1953, the Hamburg State Court ruled that the accused Kriegsmarine veterans on trial had not violated German military law as it then existed, nor had their decisions been influenced by National Socialist principles or ideology. The court concluded that Petersen had acted out of a sense of responsibility for order and discipline. Going beyond this, the court asserted that the German Navy's jurists had defended their independence from the encroachment of the party. All charges were dropped. Soon after the verdict was announced, Alfred Gail's mother killed herself.[31]

There were several other trials addressing military court-martial proceedings that had taken place at the very end of the war, and even after capitulation[32] The Heinrich Hagemann case provides another example of how postwar West German courts reacted to cases related to desertion and wartime military justice. The case received considerable attention in the postwar era and would later be referenced when the Federal Republic reexamined the topic of Wehrmacht justice in the 1980s and 1990s. It attracted and continues to attract attention because it concerned the wartime trial, conviction, and execution of a U-boat captain on the charge of "undermining the military spirit."

U-boat captain Oskar Kusch had been denounced by a fellow officer in January 1944 who claimed that he had "seen continuous, unmistakable evidence of an attitude strongly opposed to Germany's political and military leadership [and] I therefore consider him incapable of commanding a submarine."[33] The denunciation escalated into a court-martial that convicted Kusch on the ambiguous charge and sentenced him to death. The verdict and sentence were confirmed at the highest level.[34]

Oscar Kusch's parents, outraged over the execution of their son for comments deemed critical of the Nazi regime, were determined to clear his name of undermining the Wehrmacht. They believed that Kusch had been charged for ideological reasons, that the navy had failed to protect its own despite its constant references to *Kameradschaft*, and that the judge and confirming authorities had internalized Nazi worldviews.[35] Kusch's father asserted in his 1946 petition to the state prosecutor that:

> It was not my son who subverted the Wehrmacht, but rather all those criminals who are now sitting accused before the International Tribunal at Nuremberg, and those Hitler fanatics who, though they knew better, acted as judges and denouncers at the court martial held in Kiel on the 26th of January 1944, sentencing to death a completely innocent and morally superior young man who had done nothing more than recognize and tell the truth.[36]

It took a great deal of prodding from Kusch's parents and an attorney hired by the father before Schleswig-Holstein's chief prosecutor eventually lodged charges against the naval judge (Karl-Heinrich Hagemann) who had presided over Kusch's court-martial and had pressed for the death penalty. Former naval jurists, in particular Karl Helmut Sieber, used connections in the provincial judiciary to block charges against their colleague, fearing that any proceedings would have ramifications that could affect them all. One former naval jurist wrote to Heinrich Hagemann shortly before Christmas 1947 cautioning that "Colleagues in Kiel sometimes feel you are underestimating the seriousness of the matter and take it too lightly.... Preventing an arrest warrant against you is about as far as they can go in terms of doing you a favor."[37] It took the intervention of a German Jew, stripped of his citizenship by the Nazis and recently appointed attorney general in Schleswig-Holstein by the left-leaning government, before charges were finally lodged in 1948. Every member of the court, including the prosecutor, had been a member of the Nazi Party.[38] The charge was lengthy. Section 11 conveys its central thrust: "The severity of the sentence [recommended by the German naval court-martial] was a reaction to statements against Hitler's person and politics. The verdict should be understood as part of the national socialist state's system of terror. Kusch represented anyone who might dare to express similar thoughts."[39]

The final trial took place in Kiel from May 2 to 23, 1950. The defense called on witnesses who sought to deflect from the political dimensions of the charge to the military and moral qualities of Oskar Kusch. One witness even claimed that his fellow officers feared that Kusch might have been planning to desert or turn over the U-boat:

> Without any doubt the "re-education lessons" Kusch imparted to us officers implied the possibility of going over to the enemy with the entire boat. Kusch never proposed any concrete steps in this direction. He never used words like "desertion," "surrender" or "joining the other side," or anything like it. But did he think of it?... I spoke to the chief engineer several times about this subject. From him I know that we had a good number of handguns on board that were supposed to be distributed in a crisis. There was an actual list as to who was to be armed in this manner. The chief engineer manipulated this list in such a way that among our enlisted men only those would receive a gun who like himself had been leaders in the Hitler Youth and would have followed his orders rather than Kusch's in a desertion scenario. In reality the guns were never distributed.[40]

Desertion continued to carry a terrible stigma in postwar Germany, and the witness's insinuation that Kusch had contemplated the same reframed the issue. Kusch had not been charged with desertion during his wartime court-martial, and the matter had never come up. The same witness also suggested Kusch might be a homosexual, a charge likewise never brought up in his court-martial but one to which stigma continued to be attached in postwar Germany. The defense's effort to deflect away from the political and draw attention to the military and moral qualities of Kusch succeeded. While conceding that the death sentence may have been excessive, the court ruled that there was insufficient evidence to convict Hagemann of a crime against humanity.[41] He had acted within the bounds of the law of the time.

The disconnect between West Germany's judicial and political establishments, and its literati and the progressive press, was glaring when it came to assessing deserters and wartime military justice. Conservatives, most veterans, and much of the public embraced the myth of a clean Wehrmacht and a nonpolitical military justice system. They attributed blame for war crimes, mass shootings, and the Holocaust to the SS, and accepted the claims of Wehrmacht generals and admirals that they had maintained their distance from Hitler and the party. A few authors, many associated with Gruppe 47, continued to prick at this narrative. Left-leaning journals provoked their readers with reports that the Wehrmacht had been far closer to the Nazi regime than veterans cared to remember. Most West Germans, however, preferred to remember the Wehrmacht—as distinct from the SS and SA—as an honorable institution.

Adenauer's decision to dangle the promise of a (West) German contribution to NATO and the defense of Western Europe in exchange for greater sovereignty helped drive a critical assessment of the past to the political and literary fringes. As West Germany turned to its military veterans to organize a new German military supportive of parliamentary government and Western liberal values, it desperately looked for military role models. Those who had deserted from the military remained anathema, even as officers associated with the July 20, 1944, attempt to kill Hitler became epitomes of commendable military resistance to the Nazi regime.

Reassessing the Wehrmacht Deserter, 1956–2009

During the occupation era, the Soviet Military Administration Germany and its German communist helpers could combine antifascist and antimilitarist education efforts with a subtle pacifist message. Yet when the SED, at the direction of the Soviets, began to organize covert paramilitary forces in the late 1940s and early 1950s, the party had to provide Marxist military role models and tamp down on pacifist thinking.[42] As in all other things, German communist leaders held up the Soviet Union and its military forces as the preeminent model of how to organize, train, and sustain ideologically reliable military forces. In addition, the SED sought to draw on the German past to find progressive military exemplars and traditions.[43] The National People's Army and its service components were directed to commemorate the brave peasants of the Great Peasants War, the revolutionaries of 1848, the sailors who had initiated the November 1918 revolution, and communist resistance leaders who had opposed the Hitler regime and Nazism. Initially, Wehrmacht deserters and veterans of the NKFD and the BDO received no special recognition in this pantheon of heroes, and their contributions were downplayed. By the late 1950s, deserters and veterans of the NKFD became elements of this leftist military tradition, though old guard German communists still viewed anyone who had served in the Wehrmacht with a certain level of distrust.

This did not mean, however, that the East German state was ready to dispense with the service of Wehrmacht veterans altogether. The East German state, much like the USSR, decided that these officers could be instrumentalized as part of its propaganda war with West Germany. In 1957, East Germany's Politburo instructed Colonel Wolf Stern, deputy director of the National People's Army's Military History Research Division, to organize a "Working Group of former [Wehrmacht] Officers" for the following purposes: (1) to establish contact with veteran groups in West Germany, with Wehrmacht veterans who had joined the Bundeswehr, and with groups resisting the introduction of conscription in West Germany, and (2) to prepare scholarly and factual studies related to the military and military-political dimensions of World War II.[44]

On January 11, 1958, the East German press was invited to an event at the German-Soviet House of Friendship in Berlin, where the establishment of a "Working Group of former Officers" was formally announced. Thirty-one dignitaries attended, including five professors, newspaper and radio editors, a minister of state, and seven former Wehrmacht generals.[45] While almost all the Wehrmacht attendees had been members of the NKFD and the BDO, the event was not presented as some sort of reunion but rather as the establishment of a new organization by Wehrmacht veterans who were alarmed by what was taking place in West Germany.[46] The working group claimed that the Adenauer government, prompted by the United States, was building a new German military for purposes of waging war to reclaim lost territories. This new military was going to be led by Wehrmacht officers who had learned nothing from the previous war, and the working group felt compelled to speak out. Referring to the leaders of the Bundeswehr, the founding protocol stated:

> Members of the Hitler Wehrmacht, our former comrades, are laying the foundations for rearmament. Even worse, they are trying to win over the population of the West to the idea of a war of aggression. They do so by means of incitement against the Soviet Union, by instilling hatred towards the GDR, by idealizing the war and falsifying the history leading to World War II and about the war itself.[47]

That West Germany relied on Wehrmacht officers to an even greater extent than East Germany is beyond dispute, as is the fact that many of these veterans served into the 1970s. In 1957, almost all West German officers at or above the rank of major had served in the Wehrmacht, and forty-four generals and admirals had been appointed to lead the force after parliamentary screening.[48] But efforts on the part of the Working Group of former Officers to dissuade veterans in the West from building up the Bundeswehr went nowhere. The Working Group's deafening silence on the Red Army's behavior in Germany in 1945, and its support for the Red Army interventions in Hungary and Czechoslovakia, made it clear that the purpose of the group was not dialogue but subversion of Western efforts to strengthen the NATO alliance. Most veterans in the West continued to regard those who had joined the NKFD and the BDO as traitors who had simply swapped loyalty from one totalitarian system to another. The working group's commentaries on contemporary issues were part and parcel of East Germany's Cold War propaganda directed against West Germany. Its calls for an atomic-free zone in Central Europe, for German demilitarization, and for a united Germany failed to sway veteran opinion in the West.[49]

Every East German paper and radio station ran articles and editorials about the foundation of the new working group. The group was depicted as a spontaneous coming together of concerned veterans, with no admission that it was the brainchild of the Politburo. Wolf Stern's role in screening its members remained hidden, as did his editorial interventions as director of the Institute for German Military History. At its peak, the group had around 100 members.

Alongside engaging the West German public and veterans in the West on contemporary issues, the working group from its inception had a secondary purpose. Its members were encouraged to research and write on the Wehrmacht's role during the Third Reich and in World War II. The guidance was to be scholarly and factual, and gross distortions were usually avoided. But ideological orthodoxy determined the outcome of analyses, with Stern and his successor deleting, adding, and altering text as they deemed it necessary.[50]

At its opening meeting, Luitpold Steidle, one of those German officers taken prisoner at Stalingrad who joined the BDO, rejected the idea that the Wehrmacht had been apolitical. He commented that the German officer of the 1930s failed to recognize that by selecting a military career, he was making a deeply political decision. The issue was not individual guilt, but the role of the Wehrmacht as sword and shield of the Third Reich. The unwillingness of Wehrmacht officers to grasp the implications of Clausewitz's dictum that war is nothing more than the extension of politics was clear. Steidle remarked:

> This is precisely what makes the path of the German Wehrmacht a tragic one: the subjective innocence of many individuals does not offset the objective guilt of all, of all individuals together. Despite the bravery and camaraderie of many individuals, the path of the former German Wehrmacht inevitably led to dishonor and shame as it fought under Adolf Hitler's flag; this led to the national catastrophe of 1945, the cause of which—and one must finally see this—is much deeper and goes back further than the crime of Germany's war of aggression itself.[51]

Steidle's analysis was not off the mark. Others took up Steidle's line of reasoning. The working group's newsletter ran a series of reflections on the self-delusion of being "only a soldier." Arno von Lenski, who had commanded the 24th Panzer Division at Stalingrad, recalled that as a cadet and in military schools, he had been taught to carry out duties as ordered, to follow military regulations without question, and to obey the orders of one's superior without hesitation. He now recognized that this ethos had been wrong.[52]

The working group and historians at East Germany's Institute for Military History addressed a number of themes that would be picked up by West German activists and scholars in the 1970s and 1980s. Professor Otto Rühle of Greifswald University chided the group that nothing substantial had been written on the topic of the NKFD and the BDO since their dissolution in November 1945. By the mid-1960s, East Germany had shifted from downplaying the significance of the two organizations to celebrating their contributions as symbols of an alternative, progressive, and antifascist German military heritage. It would take another twenty years before a younger generation of West German historians began to question the orthodoxy of the Adenauer era which had stigmatized members of the NKFD and BDO as traitors and deserters.

In addition, the working group and historians associated with the [East German] Institute for Military History began to highlight incidents of mutiny and desertion from World War II. East German historians and journalists resurrected issues that had disappeared in the West, drawing upon the court proceedings of the late 1940s and supplementing these with survivor and eyewitness accounts. In a twenty-nine-part investigation published by *Junge Welt* between October 1966 and May 1967, an East German team of investigators publicized the outbreak of mutiny onboard the harbor patrol boats NO 13 and NO 21 in Oslo fjord during March and April 1945, the ocean mine sweeper M 612 on May 4, 1945, the destroyer Z-5 *Paul Jacobi* in Flensburg on May 6; and R 412 in Denmark on May 8.[53] The series—and a five part docu-drama broadcast by the East German television in January 1971—provided a fresh look at the Kriegsmarine system of military justice. The series sought to transform Wehrmacht deserters and mutineers into working-class icons of military resistance. East German historians and journalists argued that the Wehrmacht had been more fanatical and Nazi-penetrated than the West German establishment cared to admit, and they publicized that many officers in the West had once served the Third Reich. Some of these points were valid, but clumsy manipulation of the facts coupled with an all too apparent political agenda allowed West Germany's political establishment to dismiss anything that came from the East as propaganda and pseudo-history.

That the Working Group was instrumentalized as a cudgel in the Cold War propaganda war is beyond dispute. Charges and countercharges flew between East and West, and the hostility between Wehrmacht veterans in the two Germanies was intense throughout the 1960s. Formed at the direction of East Germany's politburo, the Working Group was dissolved at its direction as well. The 1969 federal elections in West Germany made the Social Democratic Party of Germany (SPD) the largest party in the Bundestag, and a coalition government elected Willi Brandt as chancellor. As part of his *Ostpolitik*, Brandt and his advisor Egon Bahr persuaded their

East German counterparts to reduce the level of inflammatory rhetoric between the two Germanies. Bahr suggested that a first concrete step would be to cease demonizing each other's militaries.[54] Erich Honecker, who had succeeded Walter Ulbricht as General Secretary of the SED in May 1971, decided that the 1971 newsletter of the Working Group of former [Wehrmacht] Officers would be its last. Detente was at hand, and the group had served its purpose.[55] East Germany would continue to exist for another eighteen years. The heated rhetoric of the 1960s was replaced by a calmer tone, but ideology remained central to its understanding of the past.

In April 1972, a firestorm of controversy broke out in West Germany when *Der Spiegel*, a widely read progressive periodical, published an interview with a Kriegsmarine veteran who had been convicted by a naval court after Germany's surrender for "undermining the military spirit." Hans Filbinger, a rising star in West Germany's Christian Democratic Party and minister president of Baden-Württemberg, had been the presiding naval judge. Filbinger sued *Der Spiegel* to block it from publishing comments he deemed defamatory. A West German court issued an injunction against publishing certain quotations, speculating that the Kriegsmarine veteran interviewed by *Der Spiegel* might have been mistaken about Filbinger's identity. Filbinger believed the matter was resolved, but he would discover that progressive authors, the liberal press, and historians in the West had only begun to explore his past. By the 1970s, the West German public, in particular its younger generation, were ready to reexamine topics that had lain dormant for years.

In 1978, a West German playwright named Rolf Hochmuth published a preview of his forthcoming novel *A Love in Germany* in *Die Zeit*. In it, Hochmuth described Filbinger as a "terrible jurist" who was "only a free man thanks to the silence of those who knew him."[56] Filbinger again sued, and West German media soon dubbed the accusations and denials that flew back and forth as the "Filbinger Affair." Hochhuth's accusation set lose a storm of controversy. Filbinger's poor memory, Hochhuth's tendency to polemics, and party politics combined to make the affair the dominant story of the year. *Der Spiegel*, *Die Zeit*, *Süddeutsche Zeitung*, *Panorama*, and broadcast media featured investigative stories, interviews, and commentaries about Filbinger's lawsuit against Hochhuth. Filbinger insisted that he had done nothing wrong, with *Der Spiegel* quoting him expounding that "What was right then cannot be wrong today."[57]

Over the spring and summer, archivists discovered cases that contradicted Filbinger's claim that he had never sentenced anyone to death. Public opinion shifted, and even supporters of Filbinger began to gripe that it would have been better if Filbinger had expressed some contrition over judicial rulings that now seemed excessive rather than insisting that he had only followed the law. Commentators noted that there was a distinction between what was right and what was legal. Following the discovery of another case that reflected poorly on Filbinger, in August 1978 Baden-Württemberg's Christian Democrats began to search for a new leader. Filbinger announced his resignation on August 7, 1978. He would spend the next thirty years trying to rehabilitate his name and reputation.[58] Shortly after Filbinger's resignation, the Institute for Contemporary History in Munich published a devastating sixty-five-page collection of primary documents and commentary in its well-respected *Vierteljahrshefte für Zeitgeschichte*.[59] After carefully looking at court-martial records, historian Lothar Gruchmann concluded that the Kriegsmarine's justice system had been both harsh and ideological in its rulings.

The Filbinger affair of the late 1970s unleashed a wave of interest in the Wehrmacht deserter. This manifested in three dimensions, each of which influenced and interacted with the other. At the first level, activists involved in the German peace movement began to extol desertion as a form of resistance, embracing *The Cherries of Freedom* as a progressive critique of involuntary military service. They devoted a great deal of effort to publicizing how many Germans had deserted from the Wehrmacht, how intricately that organization had been engaged in war crimes, and how few veterans had come to grips with this reality. The progressive press took note, ensuring that the debate about Wehrmacht justice was not pushed back into the shadows. At a second level, scholars began to look at desertion, insubordination of the military spirit, and military justice more deeply. Franz Seidler, Lothar Gruchmann, Fritz Wüllner, and Manfred Messerschmidt led the way, but others began to research and write on these topics, providing a scholarly foundation to public debates.[60] Lastly, the interrelated issues of compensation, convictions, and rehabilitation were taken up at the judicial and political judicial level. Public debates and activism spurred both scholarly research and political/judicial proceedings, and scholarship in turn redirected activism and informed policy over time.

The same peace activists, left-leaning literati, and grassroots Greens who rallied against the Euromissiles in the late 1970s and early 1980s initiated and promoted a public debate about deserters and military justice.[61] The Greens first raised the issue in Cassel at the communal level in 1978, with their local councilmember proposing a resolution in 1981 to fund an investigation into the topic of deserters. The investigation generated one of the first studies on the subject, Jörg Kammler's 1985 *I've Had Enough of the Butchery and Intend to Desert... The City of Cassel's Soldiers between Refusal and Resistance.*[62] Radical, pacifist, and alternative, the initiators of the deserter debate hoped to provoke discussion about military resistance and opposition to war and armaments, intentionally blurring lines between past and present. Alarmed and disturbed by the Kohl government's cautious embrace of German nationalism and German interests in the 1980s, activists sought to break taboos and to question the legitimacy of the military principle of obedience.[63] The introduction to a 1990 publication on desertion by the *Geschichtswerkstatt Marburg* asserted that scholarship and activism should not be viewed as contradictory: scholarship should reshape German social-historical consciousness so that future Bundeswehr soldiers might arrive at the appropriate lessons.[64] The groups most outspoken about rehabilitating the Wehrmacht deserter were also outspoken in their opposition to NATO, the Kohl government, and the Bundeswehr, and bore names such as "Reservists Who Refuse to Serve" ("*Reservisten verweigern sich*") and "The Campaign against the Draft, Mandatory Military Service, and Militarism" ("*Kampagne gegen Wehrpflicht, Zwangsdienste, und Militär*").

Ludwig Baumann, a Wehrmacht deserter who would go on to found the Association of Victims of Nazi Military Justice in 1990, recalled that he began his public activism protesting against Pershing II missiles, conscription, NATO, and consumerism.[65] He would show up at train stations to pass out pamphlets informing Bundeswehr conscripts how they could avoid service, relocate to West Berlin where there was no conscription, or request early release.[66] He was firmly entrenched in West Germany's peace movement, and only gradually embraced a different role, that of a Wehrmacht deserter who demanded recognition. Drawing upon literature and plays, organizing public appearances by former deserters, and engaging at the emotional level, peace activists drew attention to the fate of Wehrmacht deserters precisely because they wanted the German public to "Denk mal" (Think!) not just about the past but about the present and future.

As activists stoked interest in the issue of wartime deserters, they rediscovered Alfred Andersch, Heinrich Böll, Hans Werner Richter, and Werner

Kolbenhoff of the Gruppe 47 literary movement. Reaching further back, activists also drew on the antiestablishment works of Weimar-era playwrights such as Kurt Tucholsky, Carl von Ossietzky, and others associated with the *Weltbühne*, a left-leaning weekly literary magazine of the 1920s. In the struggle of imagery and symbol, Alfred Andersch's 1952 *The Cherries of Freedom* attained an almost cult-like status and the Weimar-era motto "Soldiers are Murderers" reentered the public dialogue.[67]

German activists successfully linked their cause to wider historiographical currents. They tapped into a growing interest in German resistance to Hitler. By the 1970s, July 20th as the dominant image of German resistance had come under attack. Conference organizers now included youth resistance, female forms of opposition, worker activism, and other forms of resistance on their programs.[68] Commemoration services acknowledged a wider spectrum of resistance. West Germany's Research Center for Military History ensured that its traveling exhibition on military opposition in the Third Reich included material about Munich's White Rose youth group, the "Red Orchestra," and the NKFD.[69] Latching onto these historiographical themes, proponents could convincingly argue that if Swing Kids, émigrés, and double agents fell within the rubric of German resistance, then surely deserters should.

By tapping into an existing discourse on German resistance, activists warded off objections about spotty records and the inability to know why deserters had acted as they did. From the very inception of the German deserter debate, activists made the point that determining individual motivation was unimportant, asserting, "Did not everyone who refused to participate in the war act honorably and correctly? How can one honor resisters—such as the men of the 20th July 1944—and simultaneously label as dishonorable criminals the little people who only could offer passive resistance?"[70] Others repeated the argument, equating desertion with resistance.

Activists made this connection explicit in the form of monuments and artwork. Concerned citizens set up monuments to honor Wehrmacht deserters in Bonn, Bremen, Darmstadt, Cassel, Karlsruhe, Ulm, and dozens of other municipalities. The earliest initiatives drew on, in the words of one participant, "little or no scholarly research."[71] In 1981, Ulrich Restat, a Green Party councilor in the city of Cassel, requested that public ceremonies honoring the war dead of the past should include tributes to those Germans executed by their own military for desertion, disobedience, and other forms of resistance. Following prolonged investigation and controversy, Kassel erected a plaque in honor of German soldiers who had been executed for "refusing to bow to the orders of the Nazi state." Bremen's monument to "the unknown deserter" was done at the initiative of a group called "Reservists Who Refuse to Serve" ("*Reservisten verweigern sich*").[72] The monument featured "a life-size soldier's head with lopsided and net-covered NATO helmet" and a plaque to "The Unknown Deserter" rather than to the "Wehrmacht Deserter."[73]

These often primitive monuments generated interest and controversy as conservatives lambasted them as "Schandmale" (sites of shame) rather than "Denkmale" (monuments). Commenting on these monuments, a Bundeswehr colonel described them as a disgrace to the "conception of law and justice." Deserters were men who had "ignored and violated their duty both to the state and—as I would like to emphasize strongly—to their comrades as well."[74]

Jürgen Schreiber, head of West Germany's Association of German Soldiers (*Verband deutscher Soldaten*), argued that making deserters into heroes was nothing less than "perfidious" in the organization's newsletter in 1992.[75] He clashed with Ludwig Baumann on NDR radio in 1994, where the two men presented diametrically different assessments of the Wehrmacht deserter.[76] For Schreiber, deserters remained soldiers who had abandoned their comrades and had been convicted of a crime all militaries abhorred. For Baumann, it was intolerable that military judges who had served the Nazi regime had never been punished and were now comfortably drawing retirement benefits. Bauman insisted: "We no longer will tolerate that the legal system continues to support those who served the Hitler regime and its criminal, genocidal war while denying us victims recognition and compensation. Military judges passed more terror and death sentences than did the *Volksgerichtshof* and all the special tribunals put together."[77]

As activists, veterans, public intellectuals, and survivors stirred up public interest, news outlets and public officials turned to historians for insights. They tapped into a lively scholarly debate sparked by the publication in 1978 of a controversial apologia by two former Wehrmacht jurists, Otto Peter Schweling and Erich Schwinge. Schweling and Schwinge had argued that German military justice had been firm but just, comparing it favorably to US military justice in World War II. This proved too much for two researchers who knew better.[78] Fritz Wüllner, an amateur historian who had lost a brother in World War II, was outraged by the effort of Wehrmacht jurists to whitewash the record. Wüllner worked as a business manager in Heidelberg but had spent years trying to track down what had happened to his brother during the war. His brother had been drafted into the Wehrmacht and had participated in the campaign against France. Shortly thereafter, the family was informed that the young man had been shot while attempting to flee from a punishment battalion.[79] Wüllner searched through the archives seeking information about his brother and becoming thoroughly acquainted with the primary documents. His research convinced him that the Wehrmacht justice system had been far harsher than Filbinger, Schweling, Schwinge, and other alumni of its military justice system cared to recall or admit. Wüllner teamed up with Manfred Messerschmidt, the chief historian at West Germany's Military History Research Office in Freiburg in Breisgau, to write a rebuttal.

Messerschmidt had made his reputation writing about the Wehrmacht as a pillar of the Nazi state, and he agreed that something was amiss about Schweling and Schwinge's scholarship.[80] Wüllner and Messerschmidt collaborated in researching and writing what became the definitive book on military justice in the Third Reich at the time of its publication.[81] The thoroughly researched monograph swept away any residual claims that the Wehrmacht justice system was apolitical and comparable to the military justice systems of the British, Americans, or French. Fritz Wüllner provided further material over the next decade, and with each revelation the number of executed soldiers increased, the examples of executions for "undermining the military spirit" multiplied, and evidence that many military jurists had internalized Nazi worldviews became harder to refute.[82]

In the decades that followed, scholars in Germany published more than twenty books on the topic of Wehrmacht military justice, desertion, and associated topics.[83] Historians associated with West Germany's Military History Research Office (the *Militärgeschichtliche Forschungsamt*, then located in Freiburg im Breisgau), the German Resistance Memorial Center (*Gedenkstätte Deutscher Widerstand* in Berlin), and the historical branches of memorial centers at Neuengamme, Emsland, Dresden, and Dortmund were particularly active. The topics they explored included region-specific examinations of deserters, broader assessments of desertion in the Wehrmacht, studies on the NKFD, monographs on judges in the Third Reich, and books on the refusal to render military service.[84]

Most of these studies were of high quality, resting on primary sources and archival records. These studies supported the conclusion of Messerschmidt and Wüllner that Wehrmacht military justice had been far harsher than the military justice systems of Britain, France, and the United States in World War II. Most empathized if not sympathized with German military personnel executed for desertion, with some explicitly making the connection between desertion and resistance.[85] Only a few scholars distanced themselves from this equation, most notably Franz W. Seidler at the Bundeswehr University of Munich. Seidler, who had been awarded West Germany's Federal Cross of Merit in 1978 for his contributions to professional military education, argued that most Wehrmacht deserters had acted out of personal rather than political or moral reasons. Critics lambasted Seidler for ignoring the context of desertion and understating the degree to which National Socialist ideas had influenced how the Wehrmacht had waged war and punished deserters.

Seidler's argument that militaries around the world viewed desertion as a criminal offense resonated with conservatives. He was called to provide expert opinion by conservative parliamentarians skeptical about efforts to rehabilitate Wehrmacht deserters, but Messerschmidt provided a compelling counterargument that it was high time to overturn the verdicts of the past. Seidler's willingness to speak to groups such as Danubia München and Germania, and his interviews with right-wing newspapers such as the *National-Zeitung* accomplished what progressive critics on the left had not been able to do. Seidler was not silenced, but his credibility was damaged and he was perceived to have moved to the fringes of the scholarly mainstream. Seidler had written one of the only works to date that explored deserter methods, motives, and destinations, but he uncritically accepted the characterizations and verdicts of the time without adequately recognizing how deeply they had been influenced by National Socialist worldviews.[86] Scholarship more empathetic toward Wehrmacht deserters and more critical of the Wehrmacht's justice system had greater influence on the political debates unfolding about rehabilitating and recognizing Wehrmacht deserters.

Launched by peace activists in the early 1980s and informed by two decades of scholarship, by the 1990s the topic of desertion and conscientious objection during the Third Reich moved into the political and judicial spheres. The first discussion of the topic at the Bundestag level was initiated by a representative of the Protestant Working Group for the Support of Conscientious Objectors (*Evangelische Arbeitsgemeinschaft zur Betreuung der Kriegsdienstverweigerer* [EAK]), a group founded in 1956 in opposition to then pending legislation mandating military or community service for young West German males who reached the age of eighteen. Using the opportunity of a public forum of the Bundestag's standing committee for domestic issues in June 1987, Günter Knebel of the EAK urged the committee to recognize that conscientious objection, desertion, and subversion of the military spirit during the Third Reich had been forms of resistance. Since West German courts had refused to accept this interpretation, he argued, the Bundestag should lead the way. These people, according to Knebel, deserved recognition, compensation, and rehabilitation.[87] The committee heard Knebel out, but it took no action on his petition.

Nonetheless, that petition coupled with the grassroots activism associated with protests, deserter monuments, and regional initiatives prompted action at the political level. In May 1990, Germany's major opposition party at the time, the SPD, organized a public forum in Bonn on the topic "the unknown deserter—provocation or necessary debate?"[88] Not to be outdone, Antje Vollmer of the Green Party made a speech in the Bundestag that September citing Wüllner and Messerschmidt's figure of over 20,000 executions for desertion from the Wehrmacht. She insisted that these soldiers should be recognized as victims, and deserved rehabilitation and compensation. The military justice system of the time, she continued, had put itself entirely at the service of the regime.[89]

To spur further action at the political and judicial levels, activists and concerned scholars urged surviving Wehrmacht deserters to come forward and organize. Ludwig Baumann, a Wehrmacht deserter who had found his purpose in the peace movement during the 1980s, recalled that Manfred Messerschmidt had chided him that Wehrmacht deserters needed to organize and become engaged if they wanted public rehabilitation. In October 1990, Baumann established the Association of Victims of Nazi Military Justice. Its initial membership was thirty-six old men and one woman. Baumann became a tireless advocate pushing the establishment to rehabilitate and compensate Wehrmacht deserters. The association eventually employed three part-time secretaries, paid for by the director of the Hamburg Institute for Social Research, Jan Philipp Reemtsma. It compiled a list of seventy members of parliament who might be amenable to taking on the cause, largely members of parties then in opposition to Helmut Kohl's conservative governing coalition.[90]

Baumann redirected his energy from the peace movement to the "necessary debate" about rehabilitating Wehrmacht deserters. He spoke to study groups, appeared at rallies, and pushed back against traditionalists who continued to view Wehrmacht deserters as weaklings who had betrayed their country. His public profile generated hate mail and denunciations. An anonymous writer sent Baumann a letter that conveys the reaction of some to the agenda of the Association of Victims of Nazi Military Justice. Dated December 1993, the letter reads:

> Dear Mr. Baumann!
> I can only regret that you were not shot or beheaded. How in the world have deserters convinced themselves that they deserve wreaths and accolades? They were scoundrels, good-for-nothings, cowardly rascals. These deserters have the lives of hundreds of thousands of their comrades on their conscience.
> That you dare even appear in public is a disgrace. You should burn in hell.
> In my eyes, you and other deserters are wretched, despicable scoundrels and bandits and murderers who left your comrades in the lurch. You didn't want to fight the system, but were a cowardly, back-stabbing wretch.
> Victims of military justice? I can only laugh at that.[91]

Somewhat surprisingly, the first break in the dam of conservative opposition to reexamining the status of Wehrmacht deserters was a legal ruling by the Federal Social Court in September 1991.[92] During the Adenauer period, West Germany had passed a series of laws authorizing damage payments to victims of Nazi persecution.[93] For over thirty years, West German courts had interpreted the law to exclude those whose claims for compensation rested on the verdicts of Wehrmacht courts. A 1961 ruling concluded that desertion, insubordination, and related military charges were punishable even in countries where the rule of law applied, and that those who had suffered because of courts-martial had not been victims of Nazi political or racial persecution. Those convicted of desertion consequently had been deemed ineligible for any sort of victim compensation, and their dependents had been denied military pension payments.

The Federal Social Court ruling of 1991 reversed these earlier rulings. The court explained that historical research now made it clear that German military justice could not be compared to the military justice systems of the British, French, or Americans. The Wehrmacht had executed many more of its own soldiers than had the Western powers, and claims that the German military justice system had operated like those of the Western powers had been thoroughly debunked.[94] It asserted that the Wehrmacht's military justice system had used law to terrorize its own soldiers, thus rendering it a perversion rather than a vehicle of justice. The court cleared the way for the claimant, the widow of a German soldier executed during the last days of World War II in Europe, to seek pension payments that had previously been denied.

The court ruling opened the way for individuals to seek compensation, but missing records made the process difficult. During the winter 1993/1994, both Bündnis 90/the Greens and the SPD proposed legislation to rehabilitate deserters and provide compensation. These proposals were blocked or voted down by the governing majority.[95] Norbert Geis, a leading Christian Democrat, adamantly opposed any sort of general rehabilitation, arguing that doing so would dishonor the much larger group of Germans who had served in the Wehrmacht out of a sense of loyalty to their fellow soldiers and the country.

Several developments in 1995 amplified the debate about whether Wehrmacht deserters deserved rehabilitation or compensation. In January, the Hamburg Institute for Social Research opened an exhibit that focused on the war crimes of the Wehrmacht. The exhibit provoked a storm of controversy, introducing the public to an uncomfortable truth that scholars had been exploring for decades: the Wehrmacht had abandoned all notions of law and restraint when waging war against Poland, the USSR, and partisans. It had known of the activities of SS *Einsatzgruppen*, and it had directly assisted in rounding up Jewish civilians and securing mass killing sites. It had murdered political commissars and had anticipated that its seizure of food would starve millions.

The traveling exhibit went on display in thirty-three German and Austrian towns over the course of the next five years and was viewed by 800,000 visitors. A proportion of the public was enraged by the exhibit, claiming it besmirched the honor of fathers and grandfathers who had served in the Wehrmacht out of loyalty to comrades and country.[96] Despite this backlash, the exhibit seems to have affected public attitudes toward Wehrmacht deserters. In 1990, fewer than one out of ten Germans polled supported the agenda of the Association of Victims of Nazi Military Justice. Five years later, seven out of ten supported the idea of rehabilitating and compensating Wehrmacht deserters. One in three felt that desertion had been a form of resistance, and one out of ten went so far as to characterize Wehrmacht deserters as heroes.[97] The tide of public opinion had shifted.

Further action at the political, judicial, and institutional levels generated additional momentum toward full rehabilitation of Wehrmacht deserters. Bündnis 90/the Greens and the SPD reintroduced motions they had previously made in the spring of 1995, leading to a full discussion of Wehrmacht courts-martial and the status of Wehrmacht deserters in the German Parliament. Parties on the left side of Germany's political spectrum again advocated for the full rehabilitation of all deserters, while parties on the conservative side of the spectrum resisted blanket nullifications of wartime convictions. Norbert Geis conceded that "without a doubt, many verdicts were unjust," but warned that military courts had also sentenced soldiers for heinous crimes such as murdering and raping civilians. He cautioned:

> Ladies and gentlemen, we should not go about declaring generally that the conduct of those who deserted was lawful because the war was a terrible war of aggression. We have to remember that doing so would be telling those who stayed that their decision was fundamentally wrong. We would be arrogant if we put our judgment today above the judgment of those who were out in the field at the time.[98]

The conservative governing coalition refused to endorse any sort of general overturning of Wehrmacht court-martial verdicts related to desertion. Geis insisted that "there are enough cases of Wehrmacht deserters who abandoned their comrades in a reprehensible and criminal manner to preclude any sort of general amnesty.... We remain committed to reviewing each case individually."[99]

Activists and politicians on the left were unable to push through political legislation that went beyond an individual right to seek rehabilitation and damages through the courts. At the judicial level, however, Germany's high court began to distance itself from positions courts had taken in the 1950s and 1960s. The high court explicitly criticized the failure to hold Nazi-era judges to account. After German unification, a former East German judge was hauled into court on the charge that he had perverted justice by condemning six GDR citizens to death on various charges of a political nature. The judge's defense attorney argued that West German courts had ruled in the 1950s that Nazi-era jurists could only be found guilty of perverting justice if they had ignored or bent the law then existing. The GDR judge's attorney made the same claim: if the sentence imposed had followed the law, no perversion of justice had occurred. The case ended up in the Federal Court of Justice, which rejected this line of reasoning. The court ruled that the failure to hold Nazi-era judges accountable had been a grave omission and did not provide a reason for failing to hold East German jurists accountable. While the case revolved around East Germany's justice system, the high court's commentary criticized Adenauer-era rulings that had allowed Nazi-era judges—including military judges—to escape accountability for their perversion of justice. The judiciary was changing its position.[100]

Two weeks after the court ruling, the Legal Committee of the Bundestag asked experts to comment on the opposition's motion to rehabilitate and compensate Wehrmacht deserters. Bündnis 90/the Greens and the SPD invited Prof. Manfred Messerschmidt of the German Military History Research Office and Dr. Traugott Wulfhorst from the Federal Social Court to provide statements that favored their motion, while the CDU/CSU invited Professor Franz Seidler from the Bundeswehr University of Munich. Messerschmidt and Wulfhorst reviewed their findings that German military justice had been harsh and more ideological than Wehrmacht jurists cared to remember. Seidler countered that few deserters had deserted for political or moral reasons. He argued that most had done so for personal reasons, and the act should not be interpreted as some sort of resistance to the Third Reich and its military.[101] The Bundestag majority did not approve the opposition's motion for a blanket rehabilitation of Wehrmacht deserters.

Advocates for rehabilitation did not give up. In November 1996, the German Protestant Church held its annual synod in Hannover. Ludwig Baumann, head of the Association of Victims of Nazi Military Justice, and Manfred Messerschmidt, chief historian of the German Military History Research Office, were both invited to comment on a resolution on the topic of Wehrmacht deserters. The resolution declared the following:

There still live among us fellow citizens who were sentenced by the Wehrmacht justice system between 1939 and 1945 for desertion, disobedience, or undermining the military spirit. They are still considered criminals. This is no longer acceptable. The Synod of the Protestant Church in Germany declares: The Second World War was a war of aggression and annihilation, a crime committed by National Socialist Germany. The Church, which did not recognize this at the time, must now recognize this. Anyone who refuses to take part in a crime deserves respect. Upholding convictions…is absurd. A rehabilitation of deserters does not demean German soldiers of the Second World War. Most soldiers believed that they were doing the duty they owed their country, or believed there was no way to refuse military service…

A rehabilitation of the victims of Wehrmacht justice does not affect the Bundeswehr. [The Bundeswehr] is the army of a democratic, constitutional state. The Basic Law of the Federal Republic of Germany prohibits any action aimed at a war of aggression. The soldiers of the Bundeswehr are forbidden by the Soldiers Act from following criminal orders. The Bundeswehr's draws inspiration from the men and women who resisted the Nazi dictatorship. The synod of the Protestant Church in Germany therefore asks Germany's parliament to declare that sentences passed by Wehrmacht courts pertaining to desertion, insubordination, and undermining the military spirit were wrong.[102]

In August 1998, the Bundestag passed a law repealing National Socialist judicial convictions that violated the basic idea of justice (*Gesetz zur Aufhebung nationalsozialistischer Unrechtsurteile in der Strafrechtspflege*). The law sought to invalidate convictions based on Nazi-era laws related to race, religion, politics, and ideology. The opposition parties sought to include military court-martial convictions among the verdicts repealed but could not persuade the governing coalition to include these in the package.

The September 1998 federal elections in Germany changed the political landscape in Germany. The SPD performed better than it had for over twenty years, while the CDU/CSU governing party suffered its worst defeat since 1949. The Social Democrats formed a governing coalition with Bündnis 90/the Greens, giving the center-left (red-green) coalition a strong majority. The Association of Victims of Nazi Military Justice looked forward to finally realizing its goal of rehabilitation, recognition, and compensation, but international developments put the issue on the back burner.

The German public and its political leaders focused on war and peace in the Balkans for much of 1999 and 2000, but Germany's new Minister of Justice, Herta Däubler-Gmelin, had not forgotten the various motions her party had put forward while in opposition to rehabilitate Wehrmacht deserters. The time was at hand to revise the verdicts of history. In the summer of 2002, the Red-Green governing coalition proposed a revision to the 1998 law repealing National Socialist judicial convictions. The revision repealed Third Reich military verdicts passed against deserters and homosexuals. The 1998 law had already overturned verdicts related to "subversion of the military spirit" and individuals who could prove they had deserted out of political or moral reasons had been able to claim compensation of DM 7,500. Fewer than half of those who had sought compensation had been able to provide the required documents to support their claims, as many records had been lost or destroyed. The Bundestag majority, now centrist-left, decided that requiring individual deserters to support their claims for rehabilitation and compensation was unjust. The government argued that deserters had acted honorably, and deserters should not continue to be labeled as criminals. Norbert Geis, now in the minority, was not pleased. He warned his colleagues that "The path to glorifying the Wehrmacht deserter is open.... When we characterize those who ran away and left others in the lurch as the real heroes of the war, we dishonor those who held out."[103]

A second revision of the 1998 law passed in September 2009. The first revision had not overturned treason convictions. The CDU/CSU and the FDP joined the SPD and Bündnis 90/the Greens in proposing a revision that would add treason to Wehrmacht convictions that were null and void. The entire parliament voted for second revision. A CDU parliamentarian conceded that "the way courts-martials had worked...and the exclusive threat of the death penalty 'did not correspond to the rule of law.'"[104]

The political debate was over. Sixty-four years after the end of World War II in Europe, the German parliament overturned all Wehrmacht military convictions related to desertion, subversion of the military spirit, and treason.

Epilogue

In the 1980s, German peace activists initiated what proved to be an extended debate about Wehrmacht deserters because they wanted their fellow citizens to think about military service, war, desertion, and resistance more broadly. They provoked a societal discussion because they were worried about an escalating arms race between the superpowers, by the deployment of intermediate-range nuclear weapons, and by the possibility of war in Europe. But when major war came to Europe, it was not one pitting NATO against the Warsaw Pact, as the peace activists of the 1980s had feared. Instead, in February 2022, Russia's president Vladimir Putin ordered a full-scale invasion of neighboring Ukraine. The purpose of the invasion was clear: the overthrow of Ukraine's government, the suppression of its sovereignty, and the subordination of its policies to those dictated by Moscow. In February and March, more than 3 million Ukrainian women, children, and old men fled their homes, seeking shelter in Poland, Romania, Moldavia, Hungary, and Slovakia. They were greeted with open arms, as Ukraine's neighbors offered food, shelter, and support to the refugees. Putin's partial mobilization of Russian reserves in September 2022 unleashed a smaller exodus, as thousands of young Russian men unwilling to fight in the Ukraine lined up at the borders to Georgia, Armenia, Kazakhstan, Finland, and Turkey.

The attitude of the Germans toward Russian deserters, reservists who refused mobilization orders and men leaving the country because they opposed military service, differed sharply from those of its neighbors. Reflecting positions developed during the debate about Wehrmacht deserters, German politicians equated desertion with resistance and argued that the German government should welcome these men with open arms. The parliamentary leader of the Green Party, Irene Mihalic, lectured the government that "Any soldier who refuses to participate in Putin's illegal and murderous war of aggression against the Ukraine should be given asylum in Germany."[1] Parliamentarians from the SPD, the FDP, and the Left Party likewise pressed the government to find ways to provide these men with asylum. The deputy chairman of the main parliamentary opposition party, the CDU/CSU, agreed, advising the government to be generous in granting humanitarian visas. Russian deserters, he asserted, should be included in a broad policy of welcoming Russians opposed to Putin's war.

German church groups issued statements sympathetic to Russians who refused to fight, and advocacy groups such as Pro Asyl pressed the government to ease visa requirements for Russians who had fled the country. Minister of Interior Nancy Faeser assured the press that Russians critical of their own government and facing persecution could already ask for asylum on political grounds. She cautioned, however, that each case needed to be reviewed individually, a requirement particularly relevant to Russian military personnel seeking asylum. The government's overall position was that refusal of many Russians to answer Putin's mobilization orders was a welcome development.

German openness toward granting asylum to Russian deserters, draft evaders, and protesters stood in marked contrast to attitudes expressed in Poland, Lithuania, Latvia, Estonia, Finland, and the Czech Republic. All these countries closed their borders to Russians seeking to flee Putin's draft. In response to images of military-age Russian men lined up at border crossings, Lithuania's foreign minister tweeted: "Russians should stay and fight. Against Putin."[2] Latvia's foreign minister rejected the idea that these men deserved to be treated as conscientious objectors, remarking that they hadn't protested when Russia invaded Ukraine in February. Poland, Finland, and other European Union countries cautioned that Russia security services would use the opportunity to infiltrate agents into the European Union if Europe opened its doors to Russians the same way it had to Ukrainian refugees.

Ukraine's ambassador to Germany left no room for doubt about his government's position on the matter. It would be catastrophic, the ambassador tweeted. He elaborated: granting asylum to Russians who simply wanted to avoid the war and enjoy the good life in the West was naive. If they did not like Putin's war, then they should overthrow his regime.[3] Kateryna Rietz-Rakul, a Ukrainian national who worked as a translator at the Humboldt Institute, remarked that when she first heard the news that Germany was considering granting asylum to Russian deserters, "I thought this can't possibly be true, I couldn't believe it at first. Until I watched the evening news." She argued, "These are not opposition figures or dissidents. These are men who just don't want to risk their own lives. They had no problem with Russian policy until just a few days ago, and now they have woken up. But it's not the West's job to protect these people."[4] She and other Ukrainians in Germany simply could not understand why so many Germans were favorably disposed to providing asylum to Russian deserters. Much like the ambassador, they believed that if these men really opposed the war, they should do so in Russia. They rejected the notion that desertion and draft evasion constituted a form of resistance.

An editorial in *taz*, Germany's leading leftist-alternative newspaper, made clear why many Germans were more sympathetic to welcoming Russian deserters than were their neighbors or Ukrainians in Germany. Pascal Beucker, the paper's editor for domestic news, argued that it would be a "civilizational failure" if Germany did not open its doors to Russian deserters. In his view, refusing to participate in war was a human right, even if it was not accorded that status by international law. Germany had executed more that 20,000 of its own in World War II for desertion, and it had taken years to correct this injustice. Beucker connected the ongoing debate about Russian deserters to Germany's recently concluded debate about Wehrmacht deserters. He cited Ludwig Baumann, who died in 2018. Baumann, who had become the face of the Wehrmacht deserter, had written that he had never claimed to be a resistance figure or a hero. He had deserted for the simple reason that he had not wanted to kill anyone. For Beucker, that was reason enough, "both then and now [2022]."[5]

taz and its editorial staff do not represent the mainstream of Germany's political establishment, but rather its left-leaning, alternative segment. Yet across the German political spectrum, from the Left Party to the CDU/CSU, Germans proved more sympathetic toward Russian deserters than their counterparts in Poland, Finland, the Baltic Republics, and elsewhere in Eastern Europe. They were more empathetic because part of the establishment had internalized the idea that desertion equated to resistance to an oppressive regime. They were more ready to consider asylum because some drew parallels between Putin's war and those Germany had waged, both in terms of their unjust cause and conduct. Others, particularly those with pacifist leanings, regarded the deserter as a victim, threatened with severe punishment if he refused to fight a war for reasons he did not understand or had rejected. Germans sympathized with those who refused to serve as military instruments of an oppressive state. Their East European and Ukrainian neighbors demanded more. They wanted these men to stand up, protest, and oppose the system, drawing upon their own historical experiences in the shipyards of Gdańsk (1980), outside Lithuania's Supreme Court building (1991), and in Kyiv's Maidan Square (2014).

The topic of desertion from the Third Reich's military also raises larger questions about duty, conscription, and the right to refuse military service. Popular films like *Cold Mountain* (2003) and *The Free State of Jones* (2016) prod Americans to think about why poor Southern whites fought for the Confederacy. Did those drafted into the Confederacy have the right to refuse?

If so, did the Irish Americans who rioted against the Union draft in New York weeks after Gettysburg have a right to object as they did? When and under what circumstances can citizens refuse to serve if conscripted, or leave the ranks if already in the military? Can conscripts refuse to serve in particular wars they find questionable, such as Vietnam? Or can they refuse to serve only if they have conscientious objections to *all* wars? Protest songs from the Vietnam era remind us of bitter discussions that tore apart American society in the late 1960s and early 1970s. Years after the Vietnam War ended, former Secretary of Defense Robert McNamara would concede that the war might have been a mistake.[6] But there are no monuments to Vietnam-era draft dodgers and deserters. Instead, by the mid-1980s, American society had begun to feel deep regret about how it had treated Vietnam veterans when they returned home.

A consensus emerged that one needed to differentiate between criticizing the war and criticizing the warrior. Yet if Carl von Clausewitz is correct that war is an instrument of policy, if one strongly objects to the policy and the war, does the soldier-citizen have the right to refuse to be instrumentalized? In the case of the Wehrmacht soldier in World War II or the Russian soldier in Ukraine, most readers probably would endorse a refusal to serve. But the picture becomes blurrier when one turns to wars waged by democratic states for reasons their governments assure the public are just and necessary.

In the aftermath of the Vietnam War, the United States abandoned the draft and shifted to an all-volunteer force. Many European nations did the same after the end of the Cold War and the dissolution of the Soviet Union and Warsaw Pact. In part, the shift from conscription to professional forces was a financial decision, but it is clear that that decision changed the dynamics of military intervention and war. There was considerable debate on college campuses and in the public square about President George W. Bush's decision to use military force against Iraq in 2003. But there were no images of young men burning their draft cards. This raises a new question: Do military professionals and those who join a military voluntarily abandon their right to refuse to serve in particular wars? Are there different standards of duty for the citizen-soldier conscripted and for the military professional who volunteered? Under what circumstances can the professional refuse to serve? Germany honors Stauffenberg and concluded that Wehrmacht professionals who deserted had not behaved criminally or dishonorably, but the context of their actions was so unusual that it constitutes a German exceptionalism. Richard Kohn, an American scholar of civil-military relations, argues that American officers—particularly those at the highest levels—have no right to threaten to resign when confronted with policies they deem foolish or wrong. They, like others, may refuse an illegal order but not an unwise one.

This leads to a final series of questions related to jus in bello concerns. When West Germany began to build the Bundeswehr using veterans from the Wehrmacht, the institution devoted a great deal of thought to making sure that "I was only following orders" would never again provide grounds for committing war crimes. The Nuremberg Trials and the Geneva Conventions of 1949 made clear that actions such as killing prisoners of war, taking and executing hostages, mass executions, and the intentional targeting of civilians constituted war crimes. Earlier conventions, including the Hague Conventions of 1899 and 1907 and the Geneva Convention of 1929, had been ignored by the Wehrmacht and the Red Army in the savage war of annihilation both waged in the East. Intent on making sure that future German soldiers internalize the right to defy illegal orders, the Bundeswehr developed the concept of "inner guidance" (*Innere Führung*). Germany turned its back to Prussian concepts of instinctual military obedience, embracing the idea that the soldier as citizen should be guided by a moral compass. Not only did one have the right to disobey illegal and immoral orders, one had the responsibility to do so.

German soldiers of the Federal Republic are now instructed to listen to their own moral compass and refuse to commit violence that is illegal or disproportionate. How well does the concept travel? Should soldiers, sailors, and airmen everywhere rely on their own internal moral compass when unsure whether something is illegal or disproportionate? At first glance, one might think yes. But the logic of nuclear deterrence rests on the "delicate balance of terror," according to one of its pioneering theoreticians, Albert Wohlstetter.[7] Should we expect missile crews and those manning the launch buttons of submarines armed with ballistic nuclear missiles to grapple with their consciences before responding to orders to launch these terrible weapons? Or does deterrence work because nuclear powers have confidence that orders will be followed unthinkingly?

Are the lessons Germany has learned from World War II in terms of military duty, obedience, and refusal broadly applicable? Or are they a case of German exceptionalism? The German establishment grappled with the question of whether Wehrmacht deserters were outcasts, victims, or role models for decades. Under what circumstances should deserters from other wars be condemned, pitied, or praised? It depends. The cause justify the war, the methods employed in the war, and the context of the conflict all need to be considered when assessing soldiers, sailors, and airmen who chose to desert rather than stay in the ranks.

Notes

Chapter 1

1. The following narrative derives from Norbert Haase's moving account of the incident, as told to him in 1987 by a sixty-three-year-old Berliner who wished to remain anonymous. Norbert Haase and Otl Aicher, *Deutsche Deserteure*, 1. Aufl. ed. (Berlin: Rotbuch Verlag, 1987), 50–52.
2. Haase and Aicher, *Deutsche Deserteure*, 51.
3. "Möge Gott Ihnen ein gerechter Richter sein." Haase and Aicher, *Deutsche Deserteure*, 51.
4. Ernst Jünger and Elliot Yale Neaman, *A German Officer in Occupied Paris. The War Journals, 1941–1945*, trans. Thomas S. Hansen and Abby J. Hansen (New York: Columbia University Press, 2018), 13–15.
5. Manfred Messerschmidt, *Die Wehrmachtjustiz, 1933–1945* (Paderborn: Schöningh, 2008), 168, 453.
6. Messerschmidt and Wüllner arrive at the figure of around 15,000 Germans executed for desertion, but it is an educated estimate. The precise number of people executed for subversion of the military spirit is even more uncertain, as the charge was used in both civilian and military courts. Messerschmidt's figure between 18,000 and 22,000 German military personnel executed by the German military (previous note) includes those executed for other charges such as subversion of the military spirit. Manfred Messerschmidt and Fritz Wüllner, *Die Wehrmachtjustiz im Dienste des Nationalsozialismus: Zerstörung einer Legende* (Baden-Baden: Nomos, 1987), 91; Messerschmidt, *Die Wehrmachtjustiz, 1933–1945*, 168, 453.
7. For a brief history and pictures of Gnoien in Mecklenburg, see the pamphlet put out by the town, *Leben, Wohnen & Arbeiten in Gnoien* (Gera: Wicker Druck, 2018), available at https://www.total-lokal.de/city/gnoien/data/17179_49_01_18.pdf.
8. My description of the arrest derives from the very detailed report submitted by the *Schutzpolizreidienststelle* Gnoien to superiors on July 22, 1942. See BAMA PER 15-2473, 89–90.
9. The officer investigating Hanow's case in 1943 ascertained that Hanow had been designated as 10 percent disabled in 1921 and had received a one-time payment. His physical examination revealed a scar at the top of his head, alongside a torn earlobe. He fell out of the train while relieving himself ("fiel...bei der Verrichtung seiner Notdurft aus dem fahrenden Zuge"). BAMA PER 15-2473, 118, 133, 146.
10. For the specific charges, penalties, and localities, see copies of Hanow's Strafregister at BAMA PER 15-2473, 178–179.
11. Barbara Bojarska, *Eksterminacja inteligencji polskiej na Pomorzu Gdańskim*, Wyd. 1. ed. (Poznań: Instytut Zachodni, 1972), 66. For a fuller picture of the brutality of the German conquest and occupation of Poland, see Richard J. Evans, *The Third Reich at War*, 1st American ed. (New York: Penguin Press, 2009), 1–105.
12. Klaus-Michael Mallmann et al., *Einsatzgruppen in Polen Darstellung und Dokumentation* (Darmstadt: WBG, 2008); Jochen Böhler, "Auftakt zum Vernichtungskrieg die Wehrmacht in Polen 1939" (PhD diss., Univ Köln, 2004, Fischer, 2006); Hannes Heer and Klaus Naumann, *War of Extermination: The German Military in World War II, 1941–1944* (New York: Berghahn Books, 2000).
13. For an example of the questions asked of Frau Hanow, see the letter from the Gericht handling the Hanow case to the police in Gnoien, dated March 31, 1942, in BAMA PER 15-2473, 77.
14. Oberstaatsanwalt bei dem Landgericht Rostock an das Gericht der Wehrmacht Kommando Berlin, October 8, 1942. BAMA PER 15-2473, 113.
15. Richtlinien Adolf Hitlers vom 14. April 1940 im Ulrich Baumann and Magnus Koch, "*Was damals Recht war...*" *Soldaten und Zivilisten vor Gerichten der Wehrmacht* (Berlin-Brandenburg: Bebra, 2008), 201.

16. "Es war der Auffassung, daß es das Deutsche *Volk* in seinem derzeitigen Schicksalskampf nicht verantworten kann, ein derartig lebensunwertes Leben weiterhin mitzuschleppen. Das Gericht war überzeugt daß der Angeklagte wie in der Vergaangenheit so auch in der Zukunft niemals und an keiner Stelle zu irgendwelcher positiven Betätigung verwendet werden könnte." BAMA PER 15-2473, 149.
17. The Zuchthaus Brandenburg-Görden turned over a detailed report listing who was present and the time of execution. See BAMA PERS 15 2473, 168–169.
18. The account of Metz's desertion rests on a manuscript Metz wrote shortly after his detention in Switzerland, along with additional research done by his brother-in-law Hans Böckler and German historian Magnus Koch. See Hans Böckler, *Der Entschluss: die Flucht eines aktiven deutschen Offiziers 1942 von der Krim in die Schweiz*, Reihe Helvetica im Novalis Verlag (Schaffhausen: Novalis, 2004); Magnus Koch, *Fahnenfluchten: Deserteure der Wehrmacht im Zweiten Weltkrieg—Lebenswege und Entscheidungen* (Paderborn: Schöningh, 2008), 213–276. In addition, Peifer viewed the pertinent records in the German and Swiss archives, specifically BAMA PERS 15 133617 and SFA E27 1000/721#9927, 9928 v.8.
19. Ltr Major Kohl to August Metz, May 5, 1942, in BAMA PERS 15 133617, 19.
20. I draw on a published version of the manuscript Metz began to write in the summer of 1942 while interned in the Lindenhof/Witzwil internment camp in Switzerland. Metz wrote the manuscript in third person, using the pseudonym of Lt Catt. Magnus Koch concludes that Metz may have originally intended to publish the piece and used the third-person cover to provide anonymity. The narrative parallels Metz's military experience as substantiated by archival sources, but it goes beyond the record in sharing the reflections and very personal experience of a German deserter in the midst of World War II. For details about Metz's reflections during the night of May 15/16, and of his manuscript, see Böckler, *Der Entschluss*, 194–199; Koch, *Fahnenfluchten*, 214–; Andreas Platthaus, "Was habe ich da noch hier verloren? Wie ein deutscher Offizier als Deserteur im Frühjahr 1942 in der Schweiz Zuflucht fand," *Frankfurter Allgemeine Zeitung* (Frankfurt), May 6, 2004.
21. Böckler, *Der Entschluss*, 22–23.
22. Einvernahmebericht, Abt. Nachrichtern- und Sicherheitsdienst, dated August 18, 1942, Bericht No. 8809/d.4532, SFA E27 1000/721; and Böckler, *Der Entschluss*, 177.
23. Beurteilung über den Obwchtm. und O.A. Ludwig Metz der 6./A.R. 132, October 21, 1940, to December 14, 1940, in BAMA PERS 15 133617.
24. Beurteilung über Leutnant d. Res. Ludwig Metz, III. Abt., Regt 132, June 1, 1941, in BAMA PERS 15 133617.
25. One of Metz's fellow officers in the 132nd Infantry Division, Gottob Herbert Bidermann, wrote a memoir of his experience on the Eastern Front, published by the University Press of Kansas in 2000. Bidermann and Metz present similar assessments of an initially rapid, uncontested advance into Russia and of the difficult fighting outside of Sevastapol. Bidermann provides no discussion about mass killings or ethical dilemmas. G. H. Bidermann and Derek S. Zumbro, *In Deadly Combat: A German Soldier's Memoir of the Eastern Front* (Lawrence: University Press of Kansas, 2000).
26. Magnus Koch presents a detailed assessment of the manuscript. While written in the third person and centered on a protagonist called Herbert Catt (probably an allusion to Frederick the Great's friend Hans Herrmann Katte, executed for helping Frederick plan an escape from his overbearing father), the persona of Catt is a twenty-nine-year-old artillery officer from Frankfurt whose assignment, background, and experience are identical to that of Metz. Koch assesses the piece as an "anonymized" memoir complete with an appendix providing the actual names of persons given alias names in the manuscript. Metz's sister and brother-in-law reworked the manuscript into publishable form because they believed it gave a unique perspective on Metz's experience in Russia and during his eight-week flight from the Crimea to Switzerland. Böckler, *Der Entschluss*, 12–13; Koch, *Fahnenfluchten*, 214–216.
27. Böckler, *Der Entschluss*, 155.
28. Böckler, *Der Entschluss*, 175; Bidermann and Zumbro, *In Deadly Combat*, 84.
29. Abt. Gef. St., den 7.7.1942, BAMA PERS 15, 133617.
30. The bulk of German equipment and supply on the Eastern Front depended on horses, so the course itself was not as ridiculous as it might first appear. See Richard L. DiNardo, *Mechanized Juggernaut or Military Anachronism? Horses and the German Army of World War II* (New York: Greenwood Press, 1991).
31. Beurteilungsnotizen über den Leutnant Ludwig Metz, February 12, 1942.

32. Koch, *Fahnenfluchten*, 244.
33. Böckler, *Der Entschluss*, 165–166.
34. Böckler, *Der Entschluss*, 168.
35. Koch, *Fahnenfluchten*, 256.
36. Einvernahmebericht No. 8809/d.4532, July 13, 1942, in SFA E27 1099 721.
37. For an analysis of the relationship between military operations and mass killings, see Stephen G. Fritz, *Ostkrieg: Hitler's War of Extermination in the East* (Lexington: University Press of Kentucky, 2011), 100–104. For details about the massacre at Simferopol, see the Simferopol entry in the Yad Vachim's database "The Untold Stories" at https://www.yadvashem.org/untoldstories/database/index.asp?cid=646.
38. Böckler, *Der Entschluss*, 198.
39. Böckler, *Der Entschluss*, 142–143.
40. Koch describes an essay that Metz submitted to a competition in 1934 that made the case that Christian faith and military service were interconnected. Metz's essay came in fifth place, with the award winner writing a piece entitled "Being a Soldier Means Being Tough." Koch, *Fahnenfluchten*, 259n104.
41. "Händchen falten, Köpfchen senken, und an Adolf Hitler denken, der uns gibt das täglich Brot und uns hilft aus aller Not." Einvernahmebericht, Abt. Nachrichtern- und Sicherheitsdienst, dated August 18, 1942, Bericht No. 8809/d.4532, SFA E27 1000/721.
42. Meldung über unerlaubte Entfernung, II./Art. Regt. 132, den 17.3.1942 in BAMA Metz PERS 15 133617.
43. The Böckler book provides a detailed reconstruction of the period between when Metz deserts on March 6 and crosses the Swiss border on May 16, 1942. Böckler, *Der Entschluss*, 184–199.
44. See the Haftbefehl der 132nd Infantrie Division, issued March 28, 1942, and various telegrams exchanged between the Kriminalpolizei and the military in BAMA Metz PERS 15 133617.
45. Böckler, *Der Entschluss*, 195.
46. Information about Kanzenbach's activities in the area derive from two reports compiled by the French police station in Laval, district of Mayenne, on June 2 and 5, 1942, and the German military police reports. BAMA PERS 15 2327, 20–30.
47. Meldung über unerlaubte Entfernung/Fahnenflucht, Infanterie Regiment 668, den 28.5.1943, in BAMA PERS 15 2327, 13.
48. Sworn statements by private Laube, taken by investigating officer Leutnant Weigel on May 28, 1942, in BAMA PERS 15 2327, 4.
49. Stellungsnahme der Kompanie Führer, 8.M.G.Kp./I.R. 668, May 28, 1942, in BAMA PERS 15 2327, 11.
50. BAMA PERS 15 2327, 49, 114.
51. Norbert Haase based his chapter "le Déserteur Allemand" on the Kanzenbach case, writing a vivid description of incident in his groundbreaking Haase and Aicher, *Deutsche Deserteure*, 16–20. The Haase chapter inspired me to examine the Kanzenbach file held at the Bundesarchiv in Freiburg i. Br., and my information stems from the three, slightly different accounts Kanzenbach gave to authorities while in detention. The Kanzenbach folder consists of over ninety pages of reports, warrants, statements, and court findings, and it can be found at BAMA PERS 15 2327.
52. Thionville is situated in the French department of Moselle, an area that had been annexed by the Germans after the fall of France. The 444th replacement battalion was part of the 148th Replacement Division, and the case therefore fell to the 148th Division's military court in Metz, Lorraine.
53. Kanzenbach was initially detained in Würzburg, where he provided his first explanation of his absence from his unit on July 31, 1942. He amended his initial statement in updated account available at BAMA PERS 15 2327, 49–51.
54. Gericht der Division Nr. 148, September 16, 1942, BAMA PERS 15 2327, 58.
55. The Germans made a distinction between imprisonment in a *Zuchthaus* and a *Gefängnis*. The former entailed imprisonment with heavy labor. See C. Meyer-Kretschmer, "Die Entwicklung des deutschen Strafgesetzbuches," in Rechtsgeschichte at http://www.juraindividuell.de/blog/die-entwicklung-des-deutschen-strafgesetzbuches/.
56. Gericht der Division Nr. 148, September 16, 1942, BAMA PERS 15 2327, 61.
57. "Abschliessend muss auch noch gesagt werden, dass der geistig wenig bewegliche Angeklagte auf das Gericht nicht den Eindruck eines gerissenen Lügners gemacht hat." Gericht der Division Nr. 432, Haupstelle Kattowitz, January 22, 1943, in BAMA PERS 15 2327, 116.

58. Gericht der Division Nr. 432, Haupstelle Kattowitz, January 22, 1943, in BAMA PERS 15 2327, 112.
59. Müller-Heß's evaluation, dated May 22, 1943, is available in the Kanzenbach file at BAMA PERS 15 2327, 144–148.
60. There is no indication or record that the third military court contacted the unit to verify that the regiment knew it was being transferred before the orders arrived on June 5. The author suspects that members of the court simply accepted the opinion of the legal review without verification.
61. Gericht der Wehrmachtkommandatur Berlin, May 25, 1943, in BAMA PERS 15 2327, 152–159.
62. The Zuchthaus Brandenburg-Görden turned over a detailed report listing who was present and the time of execution. See BAMA PERS 15 2327, 165–166.
63. Hampel joined the Hitler Jugend in 1932. His HJ Ehrenzeichen was included in the case materials. Hampel file, BAMA PERS 15 2285.
64. See Hampel's handwritten Lebenslauf, dated May 11, 1943, in Hampel file, BAMA PERS 15 2285, 28–31. Norbert Haase should be credited with bringing attention to the Hampel case decades ago, using a fictional name to provide anonymity. Baumann, Koch, and others have likewise written about the case. My account rests on these secondary materials along with the primary documents in the BAMA. See Baumann and Koch, *"Was damals Recht war,"* 160–161; Haase and Aicher, *Deutsche Deserteure*, 112–119.
65. The Nuremberg Laws defined used the term *Mischling* to describe those of German and Jewish ancestry. But the term was also used to describe those of mixed ethnicities. Stefan Hampel used it to describe himself as the son of a German father and Polish (Catholic) mother.
66. Wolfgang Oleschinski, "Ein Augenzeuge des Judenmords desertiert. Der Füsilier Stefan Hampel," in *Zivilcourage: Empörte, Helfer und Retter aus Wehrmacht, Polizei und SS*, ed. Wolfram Wette, Die Zeit des Nationalsozialismus (Frankfurt am Main: Fischer Taschenbuch, 2006), 52.
67. Dr Müller-Heß drew on and relayed the findings of the Staatsanwaltschaft Königsberg in the Gutachten he submitted to the Gericht der Wehrkommandatur Berlin dated February 10, 1944, in BAMA PERS 15 2285.
68. Later in the war, manpower shortages meant that Germany used all sorts of units and people for its war in the East. But at this point, one of his evaluations has the notation that "Hampel war immer bei der Ersatztruppe, nach einer Feldabstellung wurde er unmittlebar wieder zurürkgeschickt, da er als im früheren Russland geboren, nicht im Osten eingesetzt werden durfte." BAMA PERS 15 2285.
69. Stefan Hampel, Lebenslauf, Freiburg, May 11, 1943, BAMA PERS 15 2285. Yad Vasham has a brief entry about Wasiliszki's Jewish community and its destruction. See https://www.yadvashem.org/untoldstories/database/index.asp?cid=1169.
70. The original passes can be seen in Hampel's file PERS 15 2285 at the BAMA.
71. Hampel's defense lawyer put it as follows: "Er wurde auch entsprechend von der Kriminalpolizei als Ausländer behandelt, d.h. man ging nicht mit Glacé-Handschuhen bei der Vernehmung genegen ihn vor." BAMA, PERS 15 2285.
72. Hampel spoke out publicly about his desertion at a convention on the role of deserters in the Third Reich held at Aachen in 1991. His claim to have joined a Lithuanian-Polish underground group was accepted at face value, and the Stiftung Denkmal für die ermordeten Juden Europas incorporates Hampel's recollections in its exhibition. I have no reason to doubt the account, but I must note that the relationship among Lithuanians, Poles, Jews, and Red Army soldiers was more often antagonistic than cooperative. The underground cell was exceptional if it attracted both Lithuanians and Poles, as the relationship between their respective underground movements was generally antagonistic. See Bernd Müllender, "Deserteur in Deutschland—ein Leben lang Außenseiter," *TAZ* (Berlin), January 22, 1991; Baumann and Koch, *"Was damals Recht war,"* 160; Wolfgang Oleschinski, "Empörung über den weltanschaulichen Vernichtungskrieg im Osten" in *Zivilcourage: Empörte, Helfer und Retter aus Wehrmacht, Polizei und SS* (Frankfurt am Main: Fischer Taschenbuch, 2006), 55–56.
73. While there was a different presiding judge, the court was the same: the Gericht der Wehrkommandantur Berlin.
74. Hampel shunned publicity after the war, living quietly in West Germany until his death in 1999. Norbert Haase, "Desertion und Kriegsdienstverweigerung," in *Aufstand des Gewissens: militärischer Widerstand gegen Hitler und das NS-Regime 1933–1945*, ed. Heinrich Walle (Berlin: Mittler, 1994), 531.

Chapter 2

1. The German military began to think of total war well before the rise of the Nazi Party, with all the implications this had in terms of targeting civilians. See Roger Chickering and Stig Förster, *Great War, Total War: Combat and Mobilization on the Western Front, 1914–1918* (Washington, DC: German Historical Institute, 2000); Roger Chickering, Stig Förster, and Bernd Greiner, *A World at Total War: Global Conflict and the Politics of Destruction, 1937–1945* (Washington, DC: German Historical Institutes & Cambridge University Press, 2005).
2. See Stephen Fritz's discussion of the German Army's War Economy and Armaments Office prior to the invasion of Russia. These military bureaucrats coolly noted that "tens of millions of people will undoubtedly starve to death" if the German Army requisitioned foodstuffs from the conquered areas, but they recommended doing so nonetheless. Fritz, *Ostkrieg*, 59–63.
3. Raul Hilberg, *The Destruction of the European Jews* (New York: Holmes & Meier, 1985), 338, Table B-1.
4. Omer Bartov, *The Eastern Front, 1941–45: German Troops and the Barbarisation of Warfare* (Basingstoke, UK: Macmillan, 1985); Omer Bartov, *Hitler's Army: Soldiers, Nazis, and War in the Third Reich* (New York: Oxford University Press, 1991); Waitman Wade Beorn, *Marching into Darkness: The Wehrmacht and the Holocaust in Belarus* (Cambridge, MA: Harvard University Press, 2014); Wilhelm Deist, "The German Army, the Authoritarian Nation-State and Total War," in *State, Society and Mobilization in Europe during the First World War*, ed. John Horne (Cambridge: Cambridge University Press, 1997); Heer and Naumann, *War of Extermination*; Geoffrey P. Megargee, *War of Annihilation: Combat and Genocide on the Eastern Front, 1941* (Lanham, MD: Rowman & Littlefield, 2006); Christian Streit, *Keine Kameraden. Die Wehrmacht und die sowjetischen Kriegsgefangenen 1941–1945* (Stuttgart: Deutsche Verlags-Anstalt, 1978); Wolfram Wette, *The Wehrmacht: History, Myth, Reality* (Cambridge, MA: Harvard University Press, 2006).
5. Figures from Messerschmidt. Baumann estimates that death sentences were carried out at least 65 percent of the time; Wüllner estimates between 60 and 70 percent. Baumann and Koch, "*Was damals Recht war*," 63; Messerschmidt, *Die Wehrmachtjustiz, 1933–1945*, 152–153, 453; Fritz Wüllner, *Die NS-Militärjustiz und das Elend der Geschichtsschreibung* (Baden-Baden: Nomos, 1991), 233.
6. Rolf-Dieter Müller and Hans-Erich Volkmann, eds., *Die Wehrmacht: Mythos und Realität* (München: Oldenbourg, 1999), 39.
7. This comment pertains to the English-language literature. In Germany itself, a great deal of attention and debate has been paid to the figure of the Wehrmacht deserter, as will be elaborated in Chapter 9.
8. For broader studies of assent, consent, and coercion in Nazi Germany, see Robert Gellately, *Backing Hitler: Consent and Coercion in Nazi Germany* (Oxford: Oxford University Press, 2001); Robert Gellately, *Hitler's True Believers: How Ordinary People Became Nazis* (New York: Oxford University Press, 2020).
9. Messerschmidt and Wüllner, *Die Wehrmachtjustiz*, 179. For an excellent English-language overview comparing German military justice to US military justice, see Steven R. Welch, "'Harsh but Just'? German Military Justice in the Second World War: A Comparative Study of the Court-Martialling of German and US Deserters," *German History* 17, no. 3 (1999), 369–399.
10. For a detailed discussion of records relating to the German military justice system, particularly what records were kept and how many were destroyed, see chapter 3 of Wüllner, *Die NS-Militärjustiz*.
11. See record group RW 6 129 at the BAMA for the surviving Kriegs-Kriminalstatistik für die Wehrmacht.
12. Otto Heinicke, "Auszüge aus der Wehrmachtkriminalstatistik," *Zeitschrift für Militärgeschichte* 5 (1966); Wüllner, *Die NS-Militärjustiz*, 15. Messerschmidt uses the same record group but organizes his data by calendar year instead of war year. Messerschmidt and Forschungsamt, *Die Wehrmachtjustiz*, 163.
13. Wüllner, *Die NS-Militärjustiz*, 263–299.
14. Messerschmidt, *Die Wehrmachtjustiz*, 168, 453. Note that even Erich Schwinge put the number of Germans soldiers executed by the German military at around 10,000 in his controversial 1977 study which sought to defend the Wehrmacht's military justice system. Otto Peter Schweling and Erich Schwinge, *Die deutsche Militärjustiz in der Zeit des Nationalsozialismus* (Marburg: Elwert, 1977), 266.

15. BAMA RW 6 130 v.5, table 1.
16. Figures derived from the data in BAMA RW 6 130 v.5.
17. Figures derived from the data in BAMA RW 6 130 as compiled by Messerschmidt. Messerschmidt and Forschungsamt, *Die Wehrmachtjustiz*, 200.
18. Schweling and Schwinge, *Die deutsche Militärjustiz*, 31; Welch, "'Harsh but Just'?," 385.
19. Figures for Britain, France, and Germany from Messerschmidt; figures for Italy from Welch. For an insightful comparison of the British and German military justice systems in World War I, see Jahr. Messerschmidt and Forschungsamt, *Die Wehrmachtjustiz*, 172; Welch, "'Harsh but Just'?," 377; Christoph Jahr, *Gewöhnliche Soldaten: Desertion und Deserteure im deutschen und britischen Heer 1914–1918* (Göttingen: Vandenhoeck & Ruprecht, 1998).
20. In his large sample set, Welch did discover another case of an American shot for desertion, a Private Robert Donnelly. But as Welch explained, Donnelly had shot and killed a military policeman, and he was executed for murder rather than desertion. For a comparative discussion, see Welch, "'Harsh but Just'?"; Wüllner, *Die NS-Militärjustiz*, 77–79.
21. David French, "Discipline and the Death Penalty in the British Army in the War against Germany during the Second World War," *Journal of Contemporary History* 33 (1998): 535, 541; Gerard Oram, "Armee, Staat, Bürger und Wehrpflicht. Die britische Militärjustiz bis nach dem Zweiten Weltkrieg," in *Wehrmachtsjustiz: Kontext, Praxis, Nachwirkungen*, ed. Peter Pirker and Florian Wenninger (Wien: Braumüller, 2011), 197. See also Gerard Oram, *Death Sentences in the British Army* (London: Francis Boutle, 1998); Douglas C. Peifer, "The Past in the Present: Passion, Politics, and the Historical Profession in the German and British Pardon Campaigns," *Journal of Military History* 71, no. 4 (2007), 1107–1132.
22. Messerschmidt and Wüllner arrive at the figure of around 15,000 Germans executed for desertion, but it is an educated estimate. The precise number of people executed for subversion of the military spirit is even more uncertain, as the charge was used in both civilian and military courts. Messerschmidt later estimated that between 18,000 and 22,000 German military personnel were executed by the Wehrmacht, but this total includes those executed for other charges such as subversion of the military spirit. Messerschmidt and Wüllner, *Die Wehrmachtjustiz*, 91; Messerschmidt, *Die Wehrmachtjustiz, 1933–1945*, 168, 453.
23. Wüllner, *Die NS-Militärjustiz*, 155.
24. Messerschmidt estimates that Japan executed almost 20,000 of its own in World War II and cites an unverifiable estimate of 150,000 Soviet soldiers shot by the state during the course of the conflict. Messerschmidt, *Die Wehrmachtjustiz, 1933–1945*, 172.
25. The current US military justice system and that of the Wehrmacht rest on different principles; conveying the meaning of legal terms through verbatim translations can be difficult. The *Militärstrafgesetzbuch* (MStGB) equates to the legal code itself, while the *Militärstrafgerichtsordnung* (MStGO) relates to court processes and procedures. The United States likewise distinguished between codes (Articles of War, later Unified Code of Military Justice [UCMJ]) and courts-martial rules and procedures (the Manual for Courts-Martial [MCM]).
26. See Ilse Reiter-Zatloukal, "Militärgerichtsbarkeit und Staatsordnung. Zur Geschichte einer Sondergerichtsbarkeit in Deutschland und Österreich," in *Wehrmachtsjustiz: Kontext, Praxis, Nachwirkungen*, ed. Peter Pirker and Florian Wenninger (Wien: Braumüller, 2011), 21.
27. Minister of Defense Werner von Blomberg's proposal to the German cabinet to reintroduce the military judicial system, April 24, 1933, in Detlef Garbe, "Abschrekungsjustiz im Dienst der Kriegsführung," in *Wehrmachtsjustiz: Kontext, Praxis, Nachwirkungen*, ed. Peter Pirker and Florian Wenninger (Wien: Braumüller, 2011), 30 (Peifer translation).
28. Garbe claims that work on a new code commenced in early 1934, with Messerschmidt elaborating that a formal working group was appointed in early 1935. Garbe, "Abschrekungsjustiz im Dienst der Kriegsführung," 1934; Messerschmidt and Forschungsamt, *Die Wehrmachtjustiz*, 71.
29. Ministerrat Fritz Grau,"Gedanken über ein neues Wehrstrafrecht," *Zeitschrift der Akademie für Deutsches Recht*, vol. 3 (1936), 220–223 from Garbe, "Abschrekungsjustiz im Dienst der Kriegsführung," 31. For a broader discussion of German military justice prior to the Third Reich, see Messerschmidt and Forschungsamt, *Die Wehrmachtjustiz*, 1–44.
30. BAMA, RW 6 129 v.1, 14.
31. I have translated the legal language in terms familiar to English-language readers. Georg Dörken and Werner Scherer, eds., *Militärstrafgesetzbuch mit Erläuterungen. Neufassung von 10 Oktober 1940* (Berlin: Franz Dahlen, 1941).
32. Versions of the *Militärstrafgesetzbuch* published during the war included the *Kriegssonderstrafrechtsverordnung* in an appendix. See Dörken and Scherer, *Militärstrafgesetzbuch mit Erläuterungen*, 138–142.

33. For a detailed discussion of military proceedings against civilians and POWs, see Messerschmidt, *Die Wehrmachtjustiz, 1933–1945*, 233–320.
34. Messerschmidt, *Die Wehrmachtjustiz, 1933–1945*, 75.
35. Bartov, *The Eastern Front.*
36. For an examination of Imperial Germany's predilection to escalation and total war, see Chickering and Förster, *Great War, Total War: Combat and Mobilization on the Western Front, 1914–1918*; John Horne and Alan Kramer, *German Atrocities, 1914: A History of Denial* (New Haven, CT: Yale University Press, 2001); Isabel V. Hull, *Absolute Destruction: Military Culture and the Practices of War in Imperial Germany* (Ithaca, NY: Cornell University Press, 2005).
37. These nineteenth-century interpretations of Clausewitz may be dismissed as misreadings, but as Hugh Strachan points out, *On War* has been interpreted very differently at different times and by different audiences. Indeed, that enduring debate about how to interpret *On War* may be one of its attractions. See Hew Strachan, *Clausewitz's On War: A Biography* (New York: Atlantic Monthly Press, 2007), 16–21.
38. Erich Ludendorff, *Der totale Krieg* (München: Ludendorff Verlag, 1935).
39. Evans, *The Third Reich at War*, 11.
40. Evans, *The Third Reich at War*, 7.
41. Evans, *The Third Reich at War*, 14.
42. Evans, *The Third Reich at War*, 24.
43. Evans, *The Third Reich at War*, 26.
44. Evans, *The Third Reich at War*, 25.
45. Evans, *The Third Reich at War*, 25–26; Manfred Messerschmidt, "Das System Wehrmachtjustiz. Aufgaben und Wirken der deutschen Kriegsgerichte," in *"Was damals Recht war..." Soldaten und Zivilisten vor Gerichten der Wehrmacht*, ed. Ulrich Baumann and Magnus Koch (Berlin: Bebra, 2008), 239–241.
46. Evans, *The Third Reich at War*, 26.
47. Beorn, *Marching into Darkness*, 52; Norbert Müller, *Deutsche Besatzungspolitik in der UdSSR 1941–1944* (Cologne: Pahl-Rugenstein, 1980), 65.
48. Beorn, *Marching into Darkness*, 52.
49. Beorn, *Marching into Darkness*, 92–118.
50. The German Army and Navy were also renamed, with the Reichsheer becoming the Heer and the Reichsmarine renamed the Kriegsmarine.
51. Messerschmidt and Forschungsamt, *Die Wehrmachtjustiz*, 44. Note that the names of these departments changed over the course of time. The General Navy Office, for example, was called the *Allgemeines Marineamt* until 1936, when it became the *Allgemeine Marinehauptamt*, only to be renamed *Kriegsmarine-Wehr* in 1944.
52. Messerschmidt and Forschungsamt, *Die Wehrmachtjustiz*, 84–85.
53. Fritz Wüllner estimated that between 5,000 and 6,000 jurists rotated through the system. This seems too high an estimate, given Messerschmidt's later estimate of between 2,500 and 2,800 military jurists at the height of the war. Claudia Bade puts the number at around 3,000. Wüllner, *Die NS-Militärjustiz*, 43; Messerschmidt and Forschungsamt, *Die Wehrmachtjustiz*, 84–85; Claudia Bade, "Die Akteure der Wehrmachtsjustiz," in *Wehrmachtsjustiz: Kontext, Praxis, Nachwirkungen*, ed. Peter Pirker and Florian Wenninger (Wien: Braumüller, 2011), 80.
54. Messerschmidt estimates the size of the Luftwaffe as ~2 million, the Kriegsmarine as ~800,000, and the German Army as over 6 million in March 1943. Messerschmidt and Forschungsamt, *Die Wehrmachtjustiz*, 169.
55. Wehrkreis XVII and XVIII were created after Germany annexed Austria in March 1938. Existing districts were expanded after the occupation of the Sudetenland and Bohemia in the fall of 1938 and spring of 1939. After the conquest of Poland and France in 1939–1940, existing military districts were expanded to incorporate various annexations and two new districts (Wehrkreis XX and XXI) were created. The listing of standing military courts and branch locations as of August 1939 from Messerschmidt and Forschungsamt, *Die Wehrmachtjustiz*, 69.
56. Gruchmann notes that while the code recommended that all military personnel charged with capital crimes be provided a defense attorney, the absence of a defense attorney did not invalidate the court proceedings. Lothar Gruchmann, "Ausgewählte Dokumente zur Deutschen Marinejustiz im Zweiten Weltkrieg," *Vierteljahrshefte für Zeitgeschichte* 26, no. 3 (1978): 435; Heinrich Walle, *Die Tragödie des Oberleutnants zur See Oskar Kusch* (Stuttgart: Steiner, 1995), 97.

57. United States Army, Judge Advocate General's Corps., *The Army Lawyer: A History of the Judge Advocate General's Corps, 1775–1975* (Washington, DC: Government Printing Office, 1975), 88, http://www.loc.gov/rr/frd/Military_Law/pdf/lawyer.pdf.
58. Under the UCMJ passed after World War II, US commanders have the right to "disapprove findings of guilty and to disapprove, reduce, or suspend an adjudged sentence," but they do not have the right to disapprove findings of innocence or to increase an adjudged sentence. John S. Cooke, "Fiftieth Anniversary of the Uniform Code of Military Justice," *Military Law Review* 165 (Symposium Issue), September (2000): 9; Messerschmidt, "Das System Wehrmachtjustiz," 28.
59. Cooke, "Fiftieth Anniversary of the Uniform Code of Military Justice," 6; Messerschmidt and Forschungsamt, *Die Wehrmachtjustiz*, 168, 453.
60. Admiral von Friedeburg, Commander U-boot branch, to subordinates, September 30, 1944, in Gruchmann, "Ausgewählte Dokumente," 43.
61. In addition to Messerschmidt's opus, one should consult Gruchmann's very clear discussion of the relationship between the *Gerichtsherr* and the military judge. Paragraph 7 of the Order Imposing Wartime Criminal Procedures (the *Kriegsstrafverfahrensordnung* [KStVO]) specified that the *Gerichtsherr*, not the presiding military judge, held ultimate responsibility for proceedings. Gruchmann, "Ausgewählte Dokumente," 436.
62. Schweling and Schwinge, *Die deutsche Militärjustiz*, 163–164; Messerschmidt, *Die Wehrmachtjustiz, 1933–1945*, 74.
63. The civil rank structure has no direct English-language equivalent, and I use the term *judge advocate* throughout though the German system was quite different. Those desiring a detailed listing of the titles and ranks of German military jurists before and after May 1944 should consult Messerschmidt and Forschungsamt, *Die Wehrmachtjustiz*, 465–466.
64. Gruchmann, "Ausgewählte Dokumente," 441–442.

Chapter 3

1. Timothy Travers, "The Allied Victories, 1918," in *The Oxford Illustrated History of the First World War*, ed. Hew Strachan (Oxford: Oxford University Press, 2014), 279; see also Timothy Travers, "How the War Was Won" (London: Routledge, 1992).
2. Erich Ludendorff, *My War Memories, 1914–1918*, 2 vols. (London: Hutchinson, 1919), 683.
3. Wilhelm Deist and E. J. Feuchtwanger, "The Military Collapse of the German Empire: The Reality Behind the Stab-in-the-Back Myth," *War in History* 3, no. 2 (1996): 198.
4. Ludendorff, *My War Memories, 1914–1918*, 585.
5. Deist and Feuchtwanger, "The Military Collapse of the German Empire," 202; Wilhelm Deist, "Verdeckter Militärstreik im Kriegsjahr 1918?," in *Der Krieg des kleinen Mannes: eine Militärgeschichte von unten*, ed. Wolfram Wette (München: Piper, 1992), 146–167; Alexander Watson, *Enduring the Great War: Combat, Morale and Collapse in the German and British Armies, 1914–1918* (Cambridge: Cambridge University Press, 2008), 208.
6. Watson, *Enduring the Great War*, 72–80, 215–231. See also Messerschmidt, *Die Wehrmachtjustiz, 1933–1945*, 20.
7. Richard J. Evans, *The Coming of the Third Reich* (New York: Penguin, 2004), 61.
8. Evans, *The Coming of the Third Reich*, 61.
9. Seeckt's exact words to President Ebert have been recorded differently, but their meaning was clear. Seeckt had no intension of ordering Reichswehr units to put down the coup by force. For an excellent analysis, see Heinz Hürten, *Zwischen Revolution und Kapp-Putsch: Militär und Innenpolitik 1918–1920* (Düsseldorf: Droste, 1977); Heinz Hürten, *Der Kapp-Putsch als Wende: über Rahmenbedingungen der Weimarer Republik seit dem Frühjahr 1920* (Opladen: Westdeutscher Verlag, 1989).
10. Wolfram Wette, "Ideology, Propaganda, and Internal Politics as Preconditions of the War Policy of the Third Reich," in *The Build-up of German Aggression*, ed. Wilhelm Deist, Germany and the Second World War (Oxford: Oxford University Press, 1990), 27; Gerhard Weinberg, "Rollen- und Selbstverständnis des Offizierskorps im NS-Staat," in *Die Wehrmacht. Mythos und Realität*, ed. Rolf-Dieter Mueller and Hans-Erich Volkmann (Munich: R. Oldenbourg, 1999), 66–67.
11. See Messerschmidt and Forschungsamt, *Die Wehrmachtjustiz*, 19–21; Jörg Echternkamp, *German Wartime Society 1939–1945: Politicization, Disintegration and the Struggle for Survival*, ed. Militärgeschichtliches Forschungsamt, vol. 9/1, Germany and the Second World War (Oxford: Clarendon Press, 2008), 55–56.

12. Ludendorff, *My War Memories, 1914–1918*, 611–612.
13. Messerschmidt and Forschungsamt, *Die Wehrmachtjustiz*, 11, 21; Baumann and Koch, "*Was damals Recht war*," 67; David H. Kitterman, "The Justice of the Wehrmacht Legal System: Servant or Opponent of National Socialism," *Central European History* 24, no. 4 (1991), 450–462. Schwinge's commentary would go through six editions, and his post-World War II effort to whitewash the Third Reich's military justice system became notorious.
14. Messerschmidt, *Die Wehrmachtjustiz, 1933–1945*, 73. Schwinge continued to argue that German military justice had been too soft in World War I in his highly controversial 1977 study. For Schwinge's assessment and a discussion of the Schwinge and Schweling apologia, see Schweling and Schwinge, *Die deutsche Militärjustiz*, 30–40; Welch, "'Harsh but Just'?"
15. Messerschmidt, *Die Wehrmachtjustiz, 1933–1945*, 70.
16. Robert Gellately makes a related point in *True Believers*. Many of the Nazi movement's early leaders and militants had embraced its core tenets well before they joined the movement. And as others have pointed out, the German military's tendency toward extremist solutions likewise predates the Nazi seizure of power. Gellately, *Hitler's True Believers*.
17. East Germany would later name two Berlin streets after the executed ringleaders Albin Köbis and Max Reichpietsch. While many streets and plazas were renamed after unification in 1990, Köbisstrasse and Reichpietschufer remain. See Daniel Horn, *War, Mutiny and Revolution in the German Navy: The World War I Diary of Seaman Richard Stumpf* (New Brunswick, NJ: Rutgers University Press, 1967); Holger H. Herwig, *The German Naval Officer Corps: A Social and Political History, 1890–1918* (Oxford: Clarendon Press, 1973), 199–209.
18. Herwig, *The German Naval Officer Corps*, 208.
19. Daniel Horn goes as far as labeling Scheer's actions in October 1918 as "an act that can only be described as mutiny or rebellion" by the admirals against the Reich's government. See Daniel Horn, *The German Naval Mutinies of World War I* (New Brunswick, NJ: Rutgers University Press, 1969), 198–233.
20. See Leonidas E. Hill, "Signal zur Konterrevolution? Der Plan zum letzten Vertstoß der deutschen Hochseeflotte am 30. Oktlber 1918," *Vierteljahrshefte für Zeitgeschichte* 38, no. 1 (1988), 113–130; Horn, *War, Mutiny and Revolution*; Wilhelm Deist, "Die Politik der Seekriegsleitung und die Rebellion der Flotte Ende Oktober 1918," *Vierteljahrshefte für Zeitgeschichte* 14 (1966), 341–368.
21. Herwig, *The German Naval Officer Corps*, 258; Horn, *War, Mutiny and Revolution*.
22. See Chief of the Admiralty Admiral Adolf von Trotha's "Gedanken über die Zusamenbruch in der Marine" from February 1919 and Erich Raeder's *Mein Leben*, cited in Keith W. Bird, *Weimar, the German Naval Officer Corps and the Rise of National Socialism* (Amsterdam: Grüner, 1977), 255.
23. Adolf Hitler, Alvin Saunders Johnson, and John Chamberlain, *Mein Kampf* (New York: Reynal & Hitchcock, 1940), 275–276.
24. For the context behind the writing of *Mein Kampf*, as well as Hitler's actual experience during November 1918, see Ian Kershaw, *Hitler*, 2 vols. (New York: W.W. Norton, 1999), vol. 1, 102–105, 240–253; Hitler, Johnson, and Chamberlain, *Mein Kampf*, 275–276.
25. Michael Mueller, *Nazi Spymaster: The Life and Death of Admiral Wilhelm Canaris* (New York: Skyhorse, 2017), 78.
26. Martin Niemöller, *Vom U-boot zur Kanzel* (Berlin: M. Warneck, 1934), 133.
27. Bird, *Weimar*, 285. For excellent studies of the interwar German navy and its relationship to the government, see also Jost Dülffer, *Weimar, Hitler und die Marine; Reichspolitik und Flottenbau, 1920–1939* (Düsseldorf: Droste, 1973); Hans Gotthard Ehlert, ed., *Deutsche Militärhistoriker von Hans Delbrück bis Andreas Hillgruber* (Potsdam: Militärgeschichtliches Forschungsamt, 2010); Mueller, *Nazi Spymaster*.
28. For detailed analyses supporting this contention, see Gruchmann, "Ausgewählte Dokumente"; Dietrich Krause, "Marinerichter in der NS-Zeit," *Marine Forum*, no. 3 (1998), 23–27.
29. Welch, "'Harsh but Just'?," 378.
30. For a more developed discussion of the Kriegsmarine's ethos and postwar shaping of memories related to it, see Douglas Carl Peifer, "From Enemy to Ally: Reconciliation Made Real in the Postwar German Maritime Sphere," *War in History* 12, no. 2 (2005), 208–224; Douglas Carl Peifer, *The Three German Navies: Dissolution, Transition, and New Beginnings, 1945–1960* (Gainesville: University Press of Florida, 2002); Douglas Carl Peifer, "Selfless Saviours or Diehard Fanatics? West and East German Memories of the Kriegsmarine and the Baltic Evacuation," *War & Society* 26, no. 2 (2007), 99–120. The following section derives from Peifer, *The Three German Navies*, 10–17.

31. International Military Tribunal, *Trial of the Major War Criminals before the International Military Tribunal, Nuremberg, 14 November 1945–1 October 1946*, vol. 35 (Nuremberg: 1947), 106.
32. Rolf Johannesson, *Offizier in kritischer Zeit* (Herford: E.S. Mittler, 1989), 110. See also Sönke Neitzel, "Der Bedeutungswandel der Kriegsmarine im Zweiten Weltkrieg," in *Die Wehrmacht: Mythos und Realität*, ed. Rolf-Dieter Müller and Hans-Erich Volkmann (München: Oldenbourg, 1999), 259–263.
33. Author's estimate based on Hannemann and Wüllner figures. Ludwig Hannemann, *Die Justiz der Kriegsmarine 1939–1945* (Regensburg: S. Roderer, 1993), 72–74, 258, 90–92; Wüllner, *Die NS-Militärjustiz*.
34. Walle, *Die Tragödie*, 89. For a detailed English-language analysis of the Kusch case, building upon the Walle book using additional sources and correspondence, see Eric C. Rust, *U-boat Commander Oskar Kusch* (Annapolis, MD: Naval Institute Press, 2020).
35. Messerschmidt and Wüllner, *Die Wehrmachtjustiz*, 167–168.
36. Fietje Ausländer, Norbert Haase, and Gerhard Paul, *Die anderen Soldaten: Wehrkraftzersetzung, Gehorsamsverweigerung und Fahnenflucht im Zweiten Weltkrieg* (Frankfurt am Main: Fischer Taschenbuch Verlag, 1995), 119.
37. Hans Filbinger, *Die geschmähte Generation* (München: Universitas, 1987), 81.
38. Gruchmann, "Ausgewählte Dokumente," 449–456.
39. Gruchmann, "Ausgewählte Dokumente," 469.
40. Peter Hoffmann, *The History of the German Resistance, 1933–1945*, 3rd English ed. (Montreal: McGill-Queen's University Press, 1996), 15.
41. At the time (summer 1934), the SS was much smaller than the SA, and the German military did not view it as a threat.
42. For two rather different perspectives on the significance of the new oaths, see Jürgen Förster, "Ideological Warfare in Germany, 1919 to 1945," in *German Wartime Society 1939–1945: Politicization, Disintegration and the Struggle for Survival* (Oxford: Clarendon Press, 2008), 505–511; Hans-Erich Volkmann, "Vom Blomberg zu Keitel," in *Die Wehrmacht: Mythos und Realität*, ed. Rolf-Dieter Müller and Hans-Erich Volkmann (München: Oldenbourg, 1999), 59–61.
43. Reichgesetzblatt nr.153 (August 14, 1919), 1419; available at Austrian National Library, Historische Rechts- und Gesetztexte Online (Peifer translation) at https://alex.onb.ac.at/cgi-content/alex?aid=dra&datum=1919&size=45&page=1621.
44. Reichgesetzblatt nr.136 (December 2, 1933), 1017; available at Austrian National Library, Historische Rechts- und Gesetztexte Online (Peifer translation) at https://alex.onb.ac.at/cgi-content/alex?aid=dra&datum=1933&size=45&page=1142.
45. Reichgesetzblatt nr.98 (August 22, 1934), 785; available at Austrian National Library, Historische Rechts- und Gesetztexte Online (Peifer translation) at https://alex.onb.ac.at/cgi-content/alex?aid=dra&datum=1934&page=899&size=45.
46. Weinberg's assessment is far more persuasive than the apologetic portrayal of Kane. Weinberg, "Rollen- und Selbstverständnis des Offizierskorps im NS-Staat"; Robert B. Kane, *Disobedience and Conspiracy in the German Army, 1918–1945* (Jefferson, NC: McFarland, 2002).
47. Kershaw, *Hitler*, v.1, 530–591.
48. This is the central thrust of Gellately's analysis of senior and mid-level members of the party in Gellately, *Hitler's True Believers*.
49. Adolf Hitler et al., *Hitler's Second Book*, 1st English language ed. (New York: Enigma, 2003).
50. Hitler, Johnson, and Chamberlain, *Mein Kampf*, 773.
51. Hitler, Johnson, and Chamberlain, *Mein Kampf*, 775.

Chapter 4

1. See paragraph 26 of the Wehrgesetz of May 21, 1935, published in Reichgesetzblatt nr.52 (May 22, 1935), 613; available at Austrian National Libary, Historische Rechts- und Gesetztexte Online at https://alex.onb.ac.at/cgi-content/alex?aid=dra&datum=1935&page=755&size=45.
2. Jeremy Noakes and Geoffrey Pridham, *Documents on Nazism, 1919–1945* (London: Cape, 2001), 20–21.
3. Wilhelm Deist, "The Rearmament of the Wehrmacht," in *The Build-up of German Aggression* (New York: Oxford University Press, 1990), 521.
4. Von Blomberg decree, April 24, 1934, from Hans-Ulrich Thamer, "Die Erosion einer Säule. Wehrmacht und NSDAP," in *Die Wehrmacht: Mythos und Realität*, ed. Rolf-Dieter Müller and Hans-Erich Volkmann (München: Oldenbourg, 1999), 420.

5. Erlaß des Reichswehrministers, Generalobest v. Blomberg April 16, 1935 in Hans Meier-Welcker and Manfred Messerschmidt, *Offiziere im Bild von Dokumenten aus drei Jahrhunderten* (Stuttgart: Deutsche Verlags-Anstalt, 1964), 261.
6. Messerschmidt, *Die Wehrmachtjustiz, 1933–1945*, 29.
7. Note that the guidance on eligible spouses was issued eight months before passage of the Nuremberg Race Law. Erlaß des Chefs der Heeresleitung, General der Artillerie Frhr. v. Fritsch, December 21, 1934, in Meier-Welcker and Messerschmidt, *Offiziere im Bild von Dokumenten aus drei Jahrhunderten*, 259–260.
8. Förster, "Ideological Warfare in Germany, 1919 to 1945," 521.
9. Erlaß des Reichsministers der Luftfahrt, General der Flieger Göring, June 15, 1934, in Meier-Welcker and Messerschmidt, *Offiziere im Bild von Dokumenten aus drei Jahrhunderten*, 255.
10. Document 653-D Extract from Raeder's Address on Hero Memorial Day 12 March 1939 in *Trial of the Major War Criminals before International Military Tribunal*, vol. 35, 310–314.
11. Thamer, "Die Erosion einer Säule," 429.
12. Wette, *The Wehrmacht*, 133.
13. Messerschmidt, *Die Wehrmachtjustiz, 1933–1945*, 26.
14. Messerschmidt puts it like this: the ideal was the political soldier serving the Nazi people's community. Messerschmidt, *Die Wehrmachtjustiz, 1933–1945*, 23.
15. Thamer, "Die Erosion einer Säule," 420.
16. For a detailed discussion of the Blomberg-Fritsch scandals, see Kershaw, *Hitler*, v.2, 51–60.
17. That Beck had not yet come to grips with the nature of the Third Reich is apparent in the memorandum he wrote on July 19, 1938: the Wehrmacht needed to intervene "for the Führer! Against tyranny!... [and for] The rule of law again in the Reich!" Mueller, *Nazi Spymaster*, 129. When urged by a subordinate to assemble the Army's senior officers during the Fritsch affair, Beck replied that "Mutiny and Revolution are words not to be found in a German officer's dictionary." His views would subsequently evolve. Hoffmann, *The History of the German Resistance*, 46.
18. Beck to Brauchitsch, July 16, 1938, from Hoffmann, *The History of the German Resistance*, 75.
19. Kershaw, *Hitler*, v.2, 103.
20. See Hoffmann, *The History of the German Resistance*, 81–96; Klaus-Jurgen Muller, *Generaloberst Ludwig Becks Entwicklung vom regimebejahenden General zur Zentralfigur des Widerstandes* (Hamburg: Fuhrungsakademie der Bundeswehr, 1998); Klaus-Jürgen Müller and David N. Dilks, *Grossbritannien und der deutsche Widerstand 1933–1944* (Paderborn: Schöningh, 1994); Klaus Jürgen Müller, *Der deutsche Widerstand 1933–1945* (Paderborn: F. Schöningh, 1986).
21. One of the leading experts on the Abwehr cautions that only about fifty of its 13,000 military and civilian personnel actively opposed the regime. Most served it loyally until it became clear that Germany could no longer win the war. Mueller, *Nazi Spymaster*, 125.
22. In my view, the preliminary discussions between Franz Halder and Walther von Brauchitsch about overthrowing Hitler in November 1939 hardly elevate them into oppositional figures. After thinking about the matter, both abandoned the idea precisely because their opposition was about the timing of the Western offensive rather than about the nature and long-term objectives of the Hitler government. John Wheeler Wheeler-Bennett and R. J. Overy, *The Nemesis of Power: The German Army in Politics, 1918–1945*, 2nd ed. (New York: Palgrave Macmillan, 2005); Klaus Jürgen Müller, *Generaloberst Ludwig Beck: eine Biographie* (Paderborn: F. Schöningh, 2008); Klaus Jürgen Müller and Ernst Willi Hansen, *Armee und Drittes Reich, 1933–1939: Darstellung und Dokumentation* (Paderborn: F. Schöningh, 1987).
23. For an exhaustive, detailed assessment of Beck's path into opposition, see Müller, *Generaloberst Ludwig Beck*.
24. The best analysis of Canaris's double role in the Third Reich is Mueller, *Nazi Spymaster*.
25. For details of Canaris's double life and the price he paid, see Mueller, *Nazi Spymaster*. For a graphic description of the torture, starvation, and humiliation inflicted on those arrested, see Hoffmann, *The History of the German Resistance*, 521–523.
26. The Gestapo used the failed July 1944 assassination opportunity to round up thousands, many of whom were not directly involved. Peter Hoffman, a leading historian of military resistance to Hitler, puts the number of conspirators executed as a result of the July 20, 1944, coup attempt at around 200. Peter Hoffman, *German Resistance to Hitler* (Cambridge, MA: MIT Press, 1988); Hoffmann, *The History of the German Resistance*.
27. This book very intentionally does not focus on the opposition to Hitler on the part of generals, field-grade officers, and others. For a discussion of the military opposition to Hitler, see

Joachim Fest, *Plotting Hitler's Death: The Story of the German Resistance* (New York: Weidenfeld & Nicolson, 1996); Theodore S. Hamerow, *On the Road to the Wolf's Lair: German Resistance to Hitler* (Cambridge, MA: Belknap Press of Harvard University Press, 1997); Hoffman, *German Resistance to Hitler*; Hoffmann, *The History of the German Resistance*; Martyn Housden, *Resistance and Conformity in the Third Reich* (London: Routledge, 1997); Gerd R. Ueberschaer, ed., *Der 20. Juli. Das "andere Deutschland" in der Vergangenheitspolitik* (Berlin: Elefanten Press, 1998); Gerd R. Ueberschär, *Für ein anderes Deutschland: der deutsche Widerstand gegen den NS-Staat 1933–1945* (Frankfurt: Fischer, 2006).

28. See Chapter 9 for a more detailed discussion of the Schweling manuscript, completed in 1966, its rejection by the Institut für Zeitgeschichte, and the contentious interaction between Schweling's successor, Erich Schwinge, and Manfred Messerschmidt and Fritz Wüllner.
29. Schweling and Schwinge, *Die deutsche Militärjustiz*, 119–122.
30. Garbe, "Abschrekungsjustiz im Dienst der Kriegsführung," 29.
31. Messerschmidt, "Das System Wehrmachtjustiz," 27.
32. Messerschmidt, "Das System Wehrmachtjustiz," 53.
33. See, for example, the case of Max Heine, who refused to convict a group of Poles charged with attacking Germans given that no evidence was presented. Heinz was transferred to other duties, and a younger, more aggressive judge convicted the Poles without compunction. Bade, "Die Akteure der Wehrmachtsjustiz," 81–84.
34. Richard J. Evans, *The Third Reich in Power, 1933–1939* (New York: Penguin Press, 2005), 45; Ernst Fraenkel et al., *The Dual State* (New York: Oxford University Press, 1941); Ernst Fraenkel et al., *The Dual State: A Contribution to the Theory of Dictatorship*, 1st ed. (Oxford: Oxford University Press, 2017).
35. Messerschmidt, "Das System Wehrmachtjustiz," 53; Kristina Brümmer-Pauly, *Desertion im Recht des Nationalsozialismus* (Berlin: Berliner Wissenschafts-Verlag, 2006).
36. Garbe, "Abschrekungsjustiz im Dienst der Kriegsführung," 40.
37. Franz W. Seidler, *Fahnenflucht: der Soldat zwischen Eid und Gewissen* (München: Herbig, 1993), 295.
38. Messerschmidt, "Das System Wehrmachtjustiz," 178.
39. Author translation. Dörken and Scherer, *Militärstrafgesetzbuch mit Erläuterungen*, 55–.
40. The Military Penal Code provided additional elaboration and guidance on unauthorized absence. If a person was incapacitated due to an accident or sickness, the period of incapacitation was not to be reckoned toward the three-day/one-day absence. Those who voluntarily returned after absences shorter than a day might be dealt with by nonjudicial punishment. Dörken and Scherer, *Militärstrafgesetzbuch mit Erläuterungen*, 55–56.
41. Author translation. Dörken and Scherer, *Militärstrafgesetzbuch mit Erläuterungen*, 55–.
42. Data derived from a comparison of the entries in BAMA RW 6 129 v.1, 9 and RW 6 v.537, 4.
43. BAMA, RW 6 v.537, 3.
44. Richtlinien des Führers und Obersten Befehlshabers der Wehrmacht für die Strafzumessung bei Fahnenflucht vom 14. April 1940 in Dörken and Scherer, *Militärstrafgesetzbuch mit Erläuterungen*, 59–60.
45. Gruchmann, "Ausgewählte Dokumente," 469.
46. Messerschmidt, "Das System Wehrmachtjustiz," 174.
47. Messerschmidt, "Das System Wehrmachtjustiz," 175.
48. Anthony McElligott, Tim Kirk, and Ian Kershaw, *Working towards the Führer: Essays in Honour of Sir Ian Kershaw* (Manchester: Manchester University Press, 2003).
49. Heinicke, "Auszüge aus der Wehrmachtkriminalstatistik."; Wüllner, *Die NS-Militärjustiz*, 15. Messerschmidt uses the same record group, but organizes his data by calendar year vice war year. Messerschmidt, *Die Wehrmachtjustiz, 1933–1945*, 163.
50. Messerschmidt, *Die Wehrmachtjustiz 1933–1945*, 152–153, 453.
51. Wüllner, *Die NS-Militärjustiz*, 502, 504.
52. Author translation, Dörken and Scherer, *Militärstrafgesetzbuch mit Erläuterungen*, 141–142.
53. Those interested in the attitude of the Nazi state toward the mainstream Protestant and Catholic churches, the Confessing Church, and the Jehovah's Witnesses should start with Part 3 "Converting the Soul" of Evans tour de force, *The Third Reich in Power*. For a moving account of one Catholic farmer's refusal to serve, see the book and film about Franz Jägerstätter. Franz Jägerstätter, Erna Putz, and Robert Krieg, *Letters and Writings from Prison* (Maryknoll, NY: Orbis Books, 2009); Terrence Malick, *A Hidden Life* (Fox Searchlight Pictures, 2019);

Gordon C. Zahn, *In Solitary Witness: The Life and Death of Franz Jägerstätter* (London: Chapman, 1966).

54. Detlef Garbe and United States Holocaust Memorial Museum, *Between Resistance and Martyrdom: Jehovah's Witnesses in the Third Reich*, English ed. (Madison: University of Wisconsin Press, 2008), 64.
55. Garbe, *Between Resistance and Martyrdom*, 236.
56. Garbe, *Between Resistance and Martyrdom*, 289–290.
57. Garbe, *Between Resistance and Martyrdom*, 370.
58. I have slightly adjusted Garbe's translation for clarity's sake. Garbe, *Between Resistance and Martyrdom*, 362.
59. Garbe, *Between Resistance and Martyrdom*, 679n200.
60. BA-MA, RH 53-6/76, Bl.168 Chief OKW, December 1, 1939. Garbe, *Between Resistance and Martyrdom*, 363.
61. June 2, 1942, in Adolf Hitler and Henry Picker, *Hitlers Tischgespräche im Führerhauptquartier*, 3rd ed. (Stuttgart: Seewald, 1976). Translation from Dagmar Grimm in Garbe, *Between Resistance and Martyrdom*, 364–365.
62. For a detailed discussion of the specific charge leveled against conscientious observers—KSSVO para 5.1.3, see Messerschmidt, *Die Wehrmachtjustiz, 1933–1945*, 96–97.

Chapter 5

1. Brümmer-Pauly looked through 14,245 military files that had been flagged as records related to deserters. Many of these files relate to correspondence or preliminary investigations that were dropped, with the study concentrating on the 446 cases that culminated in a judicial verdict and sentence recommendation. Brümmer-Pauly, *Desertion im Recht des Nationalsozialismus*, 23–28.
2. The SS, in comparison, was 450,000 in 1943, ballooning to 830,000 by 1945. Brümmer-Pauly, *Desertion im Recht des Nationalsozialismus*, 47; Rolf-Dieter Müller and Janice W. Ancker, *Hitler's Wehrmacht, 1935–1945* (Lexington: University Press of Kentucky, 2016), 44.
3. Brümmer-Pauly, *Desertion im Recht des Nationalsozialismus*, 47.
4. See record group RW 6 129 at the BAMA for surviving Kriegs-Kriminalstatistik für die Wehrmacht.
5. The military file on Bug runs to 183 pages, enabling the author to go into considerable detail about Bug's arrest, his statements, and the legal proceedings. BAMA PERS 15 1571.
6. Jacob Bug Statement to Kriegsgerichtsrat Schultz, Mannheim, September 2, 1939, in BAMA PERS 15 1571, 4.
7. BAMA PERS 15 1571, 28–29.
8. BAMA PERS 15 1571, 43.
9. See letter from Katherina Bug to Kriegsgerichtsrat Schulz, October 30, 1939, in BAMA PERS 15 1571, 165–166.
10. BAMA PERS 15 1571, 66.
11. BAMA PERS 15 1571, 74.
12. BAMA PERS 15 1571, 102–103.
13. BAMA PERS 15 1571, 123.
14. Garbe, *Between Resistance and Martyrdom*, 484.
15. See the case of Franz Jägerstätter, an Austrian farmer who refused to serve, gained public attention with the release of Malick, *A Hidden Life*. For details regarding his case and those of other Austrians, see Walter Manoschek, "Österreichische Opfer der NS-Militärjustiz," in *Wehrmachtsjustiz: Kontext, Praxis, Nachwirkungen*, ed. Peter Pirker and Florian Wenninger (Wien: Braumüller, 2011); Zahn, *In Solitary Witness*.
16. Sworn Statement, NCO Johannes Peter, May 30, 1944, in BAMA Leiterholdt PER 15 3908.
17. Feldurteil, Gericht der Wehrmachtkommandantur Berlin, August 11, 1944, in BAMA Leiterholdt PER 15 3908.
18. Feldurteil, Gericht der Wehrmachtkommandantur Berlin, August 11, 1944, in BAMA Leiterholdt PER 15 3908.
19. BAMA Leiterholdt PER 15 3908, 52–54.
20. Letters dated 21 and 27 from Adolf Gaebelein to Generalmajor Erich Brandenberger, BAMA PERS 15 133155.
21. In a letter to the Gericht der Wehrmachtkommandatur dated November 11, 1943, father Gaebelein adds that he had been with the SA for years, his wife's two older brothers had served

in World War I and one had fallen at Ypers, and the youngest brother-in-law was with a tank division on the Eastern Front. BAMA PERS 15 133155.

22. Letter Adolf Gaebelein to German consulate in Bern, January 4, 1943, BAMA PERS 15 133155.
23. Magnus Koch's work was indispensable in guiding me to the archival sources concerning the Helmut Gustav Gaebelein case and in providing insightful analysis of those sources. Koch's study, published in 2008, utilized pseudonyms in the case studies he analyzed of deserters who made it to Switzerland. In the case of Helmut Gaebelein, Koch used the name Helmut Gravenstein as archival privacy rules still pertained. I thank and acknowledge Koch for his groundbreaking study. I have been influenced by its analysis and found its notes most helpful in locating the original documents in Freiburg and Bern. I cite the archival sources if I viewed the original sources myself, and I cite Koch for references to sources in other collections or archives that I did not exam. Koch, *Fahnenfluchten*.
24. See, for example, the Kripo interview of Gaebelein's sister who lived in Strassburg and a Gestapo interview of Gaebelein's seventy-nine-year-old maternal grandmother in Würzburg, both conducted in 1944. Court-martial proceedings may have been suspended, but the German Army continued to gather evidence to be used in a future court-martial throughout 1944. BAMA PERS 15 133155.
25. Gaebelein provided the Swiss military information about encryption procedures, codes, and communication as recorded in the Einverhahmebericht of July 24, 1942. Swiss Federal Archive, Bern E 27 1000 721.
26. Koch, *Fahnenfluchten*, 136.
27. Gaebelein self-report to Swiss authorities, Swiss Federal Archive, Bern E 27 1000 721.
28. Gaebelein, "Motive und Verlauf meiner Flucht von der Truppe," n.d. Swiss Federal Archive, Bern E 27 1000 721.
29. Direktor Gaebelein to Gericht der Wehrmachtkommandantur Berlin, May 28, 1943, in BAMA PERS 15 133155.
30. Dr. Klaesi report to the Polizeiabteilung des Eidg. Justiz- und Polizeidepartements, Bern, September 29, 1943.
31. Gaebelein ltr to parents, November 15, 1942, BAMA PERS 15 133155.
32. Gaebelein, "Meine persöhnliche Stellungnahme zur H.J," n.d. Swiss Federal Archive, Bern E 27 1000 721.
33. Swiss Verhörprotokoll, July 3, 1942, from Koch, *Fahnenfluchten*, 141.
34. Koch, *Fahnenfluchten*, 140.
35. See the entries for Unzucht unter Männer in the Kriegs-Kriminalstatistik für die Wehrmacht, BAMA RW 129 and 130.
36. Gaebelein, "Meine Einstellung zum Nationalsozialismus," n.d. Swiss Federal Archive, Bern E 27 1000 721.

Chapter 6

1. Evans estimates that at least seventy camps were set up during the first months of the new regime. Evans, *The Third Reich in Power*, 81.
2. Kershaw, *Hitler*, v.1, 515.
3. Kershaw, *Hitler*, v.1, 519.
4. Wette, "Ideology," 90.
5. Evans, *The Third Reich in Power*, 81.
6. Evans, *The Third Reich in Power*, 45.
7. Kershaw, *Hitler*, v.1, 521.
8. Gellately, *Hitler's True Believers*, 139.
9. Evans, *The Third Reich in Power*, 178–181.
10. A few exceptions to policies were made for Jewish veterans of World War I, but these ameliorations disappeared over time. For one of the best accounts describing the relentless and mounting assault on Jewish professionals and veterans, see Victor Klemperer, *I Shall Bear Witness: The Diaries of Victor Klemperer* (London: Weidenfeld & Nicolson, 1998).
11. Gellately, *Hitler's True Believers*.
12. Koehler quotes Simon Wiesenthal, who claimed "The Gestapo had 40,000 officials watching a country of 80 million, while the Stasi employed 102,000 officials to control only 17 million." The real discrepancy if one includes "unofficial workers" was even greater. At its height, the Stasi had over 90,000 employees with another 173,000 informants. John O. Koehler, *Stasi: The Untold Story of the East German Secret Police* (Boulder, CO: Westview Press, 1999), 8; Gary Bruce, *The Firm: The Inside Story of the Stasi* (Oxford: Oxford University Press, 2010), 10.

13. For a counternarrative to Gellately's argument, see Evans, *The Third Reich in Power*, 42–119.
14. Gellately, *Hitler's True Believers*, 6.
15. See Evans's discussion of the police state and instruments of terror, as well as his rebuttal of Gellately's thesis in Evans, *The Third Reich in Power*, 19–119.
16. Jürgen Förster, "Wehrmacht, Krieg und Holocaust," in *Die Wehrmacht. Mythos und Realität*, ed. Rolf-Dieter Mueller and Hans-Erich Volkmann (Munich: R. Oldenbourg, 1999), 948.
17. Gellately, *Hitler's True Believers*, 317.
18. See Rass's analysis of the 253rd Infantry Division Christoph Rass, "The Social Profile of the German Army's Combat Units, 1939–1945," in *German Wartime Society 1939–1945: Politicization, Disintegration and the Struggle for Survival* (Oxford: Clarendon Press, 2008), 708–709.
19. Evans, *The Third Reich in Power*, 267.
20. Evans, *The Third Reich in Power*, 269.
21. Evans, *The Third Reich in Power*, 270.
22. Michael H. Kater, *Hitler Youth* (Cambridge, MA: Harvard University Press, 2004), 16–19; Evans, *The Third Reich in Power*, 272.
23. Kater, *Hitler Youth*, 25.
24. Evans, *The Third Reich in Power*, 272.
25. I focus on the Hitler Youth rather the *Bund Deutscher Mädel* because almost all Wehrmacht deserters were male.
26. Kater, *Hitler Youth*, 37.
27. Jay W. Baird, *To Die for Germany: Heroes in the Nazi Pantheon* (Bloomington: Indiana University Press, 1990), 120.
28. Evans, *The Third Reich in Power*, 277.
29. Armin Nolzen, "The NSDAP, the War, and German Society," in *German Wartime Society 1939–1945: Politicization, Disintegration and the Struggle for Survival*, ed. Jörg Echternkamp and Militärgeschichtliches Forschungsamt, Germany and the Second World War (Oxford: Clarendon Press, 2008), 133.
30. Hitler's speech at the Nuremberg Rally of 1935 became a catechism of sorts to the Hitler Youth. Evans, *The Third Reich in Power*, 273.
31. One recent study of the Wehrmacht claims that desertion was a marginal phenomenon involving less than 1 percent of soldiers. Precisely because it was so rare, understanding how consent and coercion convinced millions to serve is important. Müller and Ancker, *Hitler's Wehrmacht, 1935–1945*, 30.
32. Thomas Kühne, *The Rise and Fall of Comradeship: Hitler's Soldiers, Male Bonding and Mass Violence in the Twentieth Century* (Cambridge: Cambridge University Press, 2017), 23.
33. Edward A. Shils and Morris Janowitz, "Cohesion and Disintegration in the Wehrmacht in World War II," *The Public Opinion Quarterly* 12, no. 2 (1948): 281.
34. Shils and Janowitz, "Cohesion and Disintegration," 281.
35. Trevor N. Dupuy, *A Genius for War: the German Army and General Staff, 1807–1945* (Englewood Cliffs, NJ: Prentice-Hall, 1977); Martin Van Creveld, *Fighting Power: German and US Army Performance, 1939–1945* (Westport, CT: Greenwood Press, 1982); Martin Van Creveld, "Die deutsche Wehrmacht: eine militärische Beurteilung," in *Die Wehrmacht: Mythos und Realität*, ed. Rolf-Dieter Müller and Hans-Erich Volkmann (München: Oldenbourg, 1999).
36. Van Creveld, *Fighting Power*, 163–164.
37. For a discussion of the books and exhibits that developed Bartov's thesis further in the 1990s, see his preface to the second edition entitled "The Barbarization of Warfare: Fifteen Years Later," in Omer Bartov, *The Eastern Front, 1941–45: German Troops and the Barbarisation of Warfare*, 2nd ed. (New York: Palgrave, 2001), xv–xxiv.
38. Shils and Janowitz, "Cohesion and Disintegration," 286.
39. Kühne, *Rise and Fall*.
40. For discussions of *Kameradschaft* in the German Navy, see Peifer, *The Three German Navies*; Eric C. Rust, *Naval Officers under Hitler: The Story of Crew 34* (New York: Praeger, 1991); Eric Topp, "Manning and Training the U-boat Fleet," in *The Battle of the Atlantic, 1939–1945*, ed. Stephen Howarth and Derek G. Law (Annapolis, MD: Naval Institute Press, 1994).
41. Fritz claims that there may even have been less petty, personal harassment of troops in the German training pipeline than in the Anglo-American one. Stephen G. Fritz, *Frontsoldaten: The German Soldier in World War II* (Lexington: University Press of Kentucky, 1995), 25.
42. Fritz, *Frontsoldaten*, 16.

43. Kühne, *Rise and Fall*, 115.
44. Kühne, *Rise and Fall*, 92.
45. Kühne, *Rise and Fall*, 116.
46. Kühne, *Rise and Fall*, 164.
47. Thomas Kühne, "Gruppenkohäsion und *Kameradschafts*mythos in der Wehrmacht," in *Die Wehrmacht: Mythos und Realität*, ed. Rolf-Dieter Müller and Hans-Erich Volkmann (München: Oldenbourg, 1999), 539.
48. Echternkamp, *German Wartime Society*, 9/1, 58.
49. Evans, *The Third Reich in Power*, 253–256.
50. Text and translation from entry "Ich hatt' einen Kameraden" at https://en.wikipedia.org/wiki/Ich_hatt'_einen_Kameraden
51. Raewyn Connell introduced the term *hegemonic masculinity* in his influential 1995 study, updated in 2005. Mosse, Theweleit, and Herzog are essential studies of the construction of masculinity in Germany after World War I and during the Third Reich. R. W. Connell, *Masculinities* (Berkeley: University of California Press, 2005); Dagmar Herzog, *Sexuality and German Fascism* (New York: Berghahn, 2005); George L. Mosse, *The Image of Man: The Creation of Modern Masculinity* (New York: Oxford University Press, 1996); Klaus Theweleit, *Male Fantasies*, 2 vols. (Minneapolis: University of Minnesota Press, 1987).
52. Theweleit, *Male Fantasies*.
53. Eleanor Hancock, *Ernst Röhm: Hitler's SA Chief of Staff* (New York: Palgrave Macmillan, 2008); Karen Hagemann and Stefanie Schüler-Springorum, *Heimat-Front: Militär und Geschlechterverhältnisse im Zeitalter der Weltkriege* (Frankfurt am Main: Campus, 2002); Claudia Neusüss and George L. Mosse, *Der Homosexuellen NS-Opfer gedenken* (Berlin: Heinrich-Böll-Stiftung, 1999).
54. Maria Fritsche, "Proving One's Manliness: Masculine Self-Perceptions of Austrian Deserters in the Second World War," *Gender & History* 24, no. 1 (2012), 35–55.
55. The *Verordnung über das Sonderstrafrecht im Kriege und bei besonderem Einsatz*, usually shortened to the *Kriegssonderstrafrechtsverordnung* (KSSVO).
56. See the explanatory note to the October 1940 revision of the Military Penal Code incorporating the KSSVO terminology. Para 102 "Erregen von Mißvergnügen" was extended to include an additional subparagraph (a) condemning the "Untergraben der Manneszucht" (sic).
57. For a discussion of the tens of thousands of young female antiaircraft crew (*Flakhelferinnen* or *Blitzmädel*), see Kater, *Hitler Youth*, 233–238.
58. Ian Kershaw, *The End: The Defiance and Destruction of Hitler's Germany, 1944–1945* (New York: Penguin Press, 2011), 306.
59. Kershaw, *The End*, 112–113.
60. Antony Beevor, *The Fall of Berlin, 1945* (New York: Viking, 2002); Norman M. Naimark, *The Russians in Germany: A History of the Soviet Zone of Occupation, 1945–1949* (Cambridge, MA: Belknap, 1995).
61. Benedict R. O'G Anderson, *Imagined Communities: Reflections on the Origin and Spread of Nationalism* (London: Verso, 1983).
62. Johann Gottlieb Fichte and Gregory Moore, *Addresses to the German Nation*, Cambridge texts in the history of political thought (Cambridge: Cambridge University Press, 2008).
63. Lisa Feurzeig and Josef Gersbach, *Deutsche Lieder für Jung und Alt* (Middleton: A-R Editions, 2002), 68–69.
64. The Weimar Republic adopted the song as Germany's national anthem in 1920. During the Third Reich, only its first verse "Deutschland, Deutschland über alles" was sung, followed by the Horst-Wessel Lied. The Federal Republic of Germany adopted the melody and song as its national anthem in 1952, specifying that only the third stanza be sung on official occasions.
65. Bismarck's 1862 speech to the Prussian House of Representatives asserted that "Not through speeches and majority decisions will the great questions of the day be decided—that was the great mistake of 1848 and 1849—but by iron and blood." The final phrase was inverted in popular memory.
66. See Gellately, *Hitler's True Believers*; Kühne, *Rise and Fall*.
67. The fundamental shallowness of Nazi racial science becomes apparent in the Nuremberg Laws, which resorted to defining Jews and Germans in terms of the faith practiced by their grandparents rather than by any inherent biological traits or differences.

68. Christopher R. Browning, *Ordinary Men: Reserve Police Battalion 101 and the Final Solution in Poland* (New York: HarperCollins, 1992).
69. Beorn, *Marching into Darkness.*
70. Förster, "Ideological Warfare in Germany," 615.
71. For a discussion of morale in the troops and the role of NSFOs, see Echternkamp, *German Wartime Society*, 9/1; Förster, "Ideological Warfare in Germany."

Chapter 7

1. BAMA PERS 15 2486.
2. BAMA PERS 15 2486.
3. Brümmer-Pauly, *Desertion im Recht des Nationalsozialismus*, 23. As explained in Chapter 2, the number of cases concerning desertion and unauthorized absence was higher than the number of case files which survived the war.
4. Brümmer-Pauly, *Desertion im Recht des Nationalsozialismus*, 52–57.
5. The Swedish government, in contrast, returned German deserters apprehended in Sweden to the German military in Norway until November 1942, when the certainty of a German victory receded, and the policy was reexamined. For a discussion of Sweden's policy of returning German deserters to the Wehrmacht, see Lars G. Petersson, *Hitler's Deserters: When Law Merged with Terror* (Stroud: Fonthill Media, 2013), chapter 10. As for the other three neutrals, the official policy of their governments was to return German deserters to German military authorities.
6. Seidler and Koch disagree on the most frequent reason, but both agree that fear of punishment and war weariness were more frequently given as motivations than political opposition. Seidler, *Fahnenflucht*, 316; Koch, *Fahnenfluchten*, 398.
7. See the important study conducted by Magnus Koch which selects a sampling of cases from the Bern collection and cross-references them with the Wehrmacht files assembled in preparation for court-martial proceedings never completed. I have drawn on the Koch study throughout, using archival sources wherever possible in the individual case stories presented in Chapters 1 and 4. Koch, *Fahnenfluchten*; Magnus Koch, "Das Stigma Fahnenflucht. Überlegungen zur Bedeutung männlicher Selbstbilder von Wehrmachtsdeserteurnen," in *Wehrmachtsjustiz: Kontext, Praxis, Nachwirkungen*, ed. Peter Pirker and Florian Wenninger (Wien: Braumüller, 2011).
8. LtCol H. V. Dicks, "The German Deserter: A Psychological Study," Directorate of Army Psychiatry, Research Memorandum 45/03/9, British Archives WO 241/2.
9. Dicks, "The German Deserter," 5.
10. Dicks lists twelve psychological traits that he believed predisposed individuals to desertion, subordinating them to the broader categories of narcissim, aggressiveness, ambivalence, and "neurotics." "The German Deserter," 3.
11. Underlined in the original. Dicks, "The German Deserter," 32.
12. Dicks, "The German Deserter," 32.
13. Brümmer-Pauly, *Desertion im Recht des Nationalsozialismus*, 52.
14. BArch-MA, RM 123/10265.
15. Brümmer-Pauly, *Desertion im Recht des Nationalsozialismus*, 47; Messerschmidt, *Die Wehrmachtjustiz, 1933–1945*, 175; Dieter Knippschild, "Deserteure im Zweiten Weltkrieg: Der Stand der Debatte," in *Armeen und ihre Deserteure: vernachlässigte Kapitel einer Militärgeschichte der Neuzeit*, ed. Ulrich Bröckling and Michael Sikora (Göttingen: Vandenhoeck & Ruprecht, 1998), 229.
16. Brümmer-Pauly, *Desertion im Recht des Nationalsozialismus*, 54; Knippschild, "Deserteure im Zweiten Weltkrieg," 231.
17. Ziemann asserts that Stalingrad served as a key inflection point in terms of belief in Germany's ultimate victory. Yet desertion rates accelerate most markedly in the summer of 1944. Benjamin Ziemann, "Fluchten aus dem Konsens zum Durchhalten," in *Die Wehrmacht: Mythos und Realität*, ed. Rolf-Dieter Müller and Hans-Erich Volkmann (München: Oldenbourg, 1999), 602.
18. Seidler, *Fahnenflucht*, 314.
19. Messerschmidt and Forschungsamt, *Die Wehrmachtjustiz*, 178.
20. Knippschild, "Deserteure im Zweiten Weltkrieg," 233.
21. Seidler, *Fahnenflucht*, 316.

22. Bryan Mark Rigg, *Hitler's Jewish Soldiers: The Untold Story of Nazi Racial Laws and Men of Jewish Descent in the German Military* (Lawrence: University Press of Kansas, 2002).
23. Solomon Perel, *Ich war Hitlerjunge Salomon* (Munich: Heyne, 1993).
24. Jägerstätter, Putz, and Krieg, *Letters and Writings from Prison*; Zahn, *In Solitary Witness*. Jägerstätter's moral opposition was celebrated in Malick's 2019 film, *A Hidden Life*.
25. Manoschek, "Österreichische Opfer der NS-Militärjustiz," 50.
26. Koch, *Fahnenfluchten*, 398.
27. The Reichsgau Wartheland and Reichsgau Danzig-West Prussia were created wholesale from former Polish territories, while Reichsgau East Prussia and Upper Silesia were enlarged by annexed Polish territories.
28. Norbert Haase, "Von 'Ons Jongen,' 'Malgré-nous' und anderen. Das Schicksal der ausländischen-Zwangsrekruierten im Zweiten Weltkrieg," in *Die anderen Soldaten: Wehrkraftzersetzung, Gehorsamsverweigerung und Fahnenflucht im Zweiten Weltkrieg*, ed. Fietje Ausländer, Norbert Haase, and Gerhard Paul (Frankfurt am Main: Fischer Taschenbuch Verlag, 1995), 159.
29. Haase, "Von 'Ons Jongen,'" 159.
30. The story of Polish soldiers fighting against Germany is complicated by the reality that the Soviet Union attacked and occupied East Poland as part of the Ribbentrop-Molotov Agreement. The first Polish formation organized by the Red Army, Anders's Army, was recruited from Polish forces interned by the NKVD. Anders was loyal to the Polish government in exile in London, and his unit was eventually evacuated to the Mediterranean theater. The later Berling Army or Polish People's Army drew upon both forcibly removed Poles and Polish and Jewish refugees, and captured Wehrmacht soldiers of Polish origin.
31. Haase, "Von 'Ons Jongen'," 160.
32. Haase, "Von 'Ons Jongen'," 167.
33. Seidler, *Fahnenflucht*, 200.
34. Seidler, *Fahnenflucht*, 200.
35. Haase, " "Von 'Ons Jongen'," 165; Seidler, *Fahnenflucht*.
36. Haase, "Von 'Ons Jongen'," 169.
37. Haase, "Von 'Ons Jongen'," 163. See also Lisa Rettl, "Fahnenflucht in den Widerstand. Kärntner Slowenen als Deserteure und Partisanen," in *Wehrmachtsjustiz: Kontext, Praxis, Nachwirkungen*, ed. Peter Pirker and Florian Wenninger (Wien: Braumüller, 2011); Walter Manoschek, *Opfer der NS-Militärjustiz: Urteilspraxis, Strafvollzug, Entschädigungspolitik in Österreich* (Wien: Mandelbaum, 2003).
38. Haase, "Von 'Ons Jongen'," 168.
39. Haase, "Von 'Ons Jongen'," 169.
40. Eight hundred Emsland camp convicts were sent to Sonnenland and executed by the SS. Among these were eighty Luxembourgers. For details, see Haase, "Von 'Ons Jongen'," 172.
41. See Bernd Wegner, *The Waffen-SS: Organization, Ideology, and Function* (Oxford: Basil Blackwell, 1990); David Littlejohn, *Foreign Legions of the Third Reich*, 4 vols. (San Jose: R.J. Bender Publishing, 1979).
42. Ela Hornung, "Denunziation als soziale Praxis. Eine Fallgeschichte aus der NS-Militärjustiz," in *Wehrmachtsjustiz: Kontext, Praxis, Nachwirkungen*, ed. Peter Pirker and Florian Wenninger (Wien: Braumüller, 2011), 100–117.
43. See Maria Fritsche, "'Meinen Mann hab ich gestellt!' Geschlechtsidentitäten österreichischer Wehrmachtsdeserteure im Kontext des militärischen Männlichkeitsdiskuses der NS Zeit," in *Wehrmachtsjustiz: Kontext, Praxis, Nachwirkungen*, ed. Peter Pirker and Florian Wenninger (Wien: Braumüller, 2011), 141–146. For a specific example of this insistence, see Baumann and Koch, "*Was damals Recht war*," 152–153.
44. Garbe, *Between Resistance and Martyrdom*, 484.
45. Haase, "Desertion und Kriegsdienstverweigerung," 525.
46. Jägerstätter's case is undoubtedly the most well-known case of Catholic conscientious objection to service, but one can find a few others as well, such as Alfred Andreas Heiß. For more information, consult Jägerstätter, Putz, and Krieg, *Letters and Writings from Prison*; Zahn, *In Solitary Witness*; Haase, "Desertion und Kriegsdienstverweigerung," 527.
47. Stöhr's case is probably the best-known example of a mainstream Protestant conscientious objector sentenced to death. Messerschmidt lists a few others, but the number seems to have been in the double digits rather than the hundreds. Haase, "Desertion und Kriegsdienstverweigerung," 525; Messerschmidt and Forschungsamt, *Die Wehrmachtjustiz*, 104–105; Eberhard Röhm, *Sterben für den Frieden: Spurensicherung, Hermann Stöhr (1898–1940) und die ökumenische Friedensbewegung* (Stuttgart: Calwer, 1985).

48. Jakob Knab, "Empörung über den weltanschaulichen Vernichtungskrieg im Osten. Der katholische Leutnant Michael Kitzelmann, " in *Zivilcourage: Empörte, Helfer und Retter aus Wehrmacht, Polizei und SS*, ed. Wolfram Wette (Frankfurt am Main: Fischer Taschenbuch, 2006), 43–45.
49. Walle, *Die Tragödie*, 90.
50. Walle, *Die Tragödie*, 89. For a detailed English-language analysis of the Kusch case using additional sources and correspondence, see Rust, *U-boat Commander*.
51. See, for example, the complicated case of Hans Demblowski, BAMA PER 15 2576.
52. Ziemann estimates that only 15 percent of desertions were politically motivated. This seems puzzling, in that he cites Seidler's study where political motivations are third in terms of frequency. Since Ziemann published his essay, an outpouring of literature suggests that political considerations were more important than Ziemann estimated. Ziemann, "Fluchten," 602; Seidler, *Fahnenflucht*, 316; Peter Pirker and Florian Wenninger, *Wehrmachtsjustiz: Kontext, Praxis, Nachwirkungen* (Wien: Braumüller, 2011); Messerschmidt, "Das System Wehrmachtjustiz"; Koch, *Fahnenfluchten*.
53. Geoffrey P. Megargee, Rüdiger Overmans, and Wolfgang Vogt, eds., *Camps and Other Detention Facilities under the German Armed Forces* (Bloomington: Indiana University Press, 2022), 593.
54. The SS also established a probationary unit, the infamous SS-Sturmbrigade Dirlewanger. That unit included convicted rapists and murderers in its ranks and became known for its brutality. My discussion here focuses on Wehrmacht penal and probationary units. Megargee, Overmans, and Vogt, *Camps and Other Detention Facilities*, 595.
55. See the detailed discussion of Bewährungstruppe 500 in Messerschmidt and Forschungsamt, *Die Wehrmachtjustiz*, 366–379.
56. See Messerschmidt and Forschungsamt, *Die Wehrmachtjustiz*, 379–391.
57. Seidler, *Fahnenflucht*, 188–189.
58. Barbara Dietrich, Joachim Perels, and Wolfgang Abendroth, *Wolfgang Abendroth: ein Leben in der Arbeiterbewegung* (Frankfurt am Main: Suhrkamp, 1976).
59. Baumann and Koch, "*Was damals Recht war*," 158–159.
60. Seidler, *Fahnenflucht*, 190; Gottfried Hamacher and André Lohmar, *Gegen Hitler: Deutsche in der Résistance, in den Streitkräften der Antihitlerkoalition und in der Bewegung "Freies Deutschland"* (Berlin: Karl Dietz, 2005), 76; Knippschild, "Deserteure im Zweiten Weltkrieg," 237.
61. Emmy Zehden's story is one of the exhibits at the German Resistance Memorial Center, available online at https://www.gdw-berlin.de/en/recess/biographies/index_of_persons/biographie/view-bio/emmy-zehden/.
62. Regina Mühlhäuser, *Eroberungen: Sexuelle Gewalttaten und intime Beziehungen deutscher Soldaten in der Sowjetunion 1941–1945* (Hamburg: Hamburger Edition, 2012); Sonja M. Hedgepeth and Rochelle G. Saidel, *Sexual Violence against Jewish Women during the Holocaust* (Hanover: University Press of New England, 2010); Regina Mühlhäuser, "Sexual Violence and the Holocaust," in *Gender: War*, ed. Andrea Pető (Farmington Hills, MI: Macmillan, 2017).
63. Hanna Diamond, *Women and the Second World War in France, 1939–1948: Choices and Constraints* (London: Longman, 1999); Kjersti Ericsson and Eva Simonsen, *Children of World War II: The Hidden Enemy Legacy* (Oxford: Berg, 2005).
64. In 2010, the Norwegian prime minister issued an apology for the postwar treatment of these "German Girls." See Erna Solberg, "Official Apology to Girls and Women Who Had Relationships with German Soldiers during the Second World War," Office of the Prime Minister, October 23, 2018, available at https://www.regjeringen.no/en/historical-archive/solbergs-government/Ministries/smk/speeches-and-articles/statsministeren/talerogartikler/2018/app/id2616005/.
65. Note that Ernst Jünger's account of witnessing the execution of a deserter likewise revolves around a French girlfriend.
66. D. V. Andersson, *Jutzi. Ett drama vid gränsen* (Arvika: Tänk, 1961); Eivind Heide, *Deserteringer fra den tyske okkupasjonshæren i Norge 1940–1945* (Atnbrua: Sollia forlag, 1994).
67. Translated from the German by the author, quote from Seidler, *Fahnenflucht*, 267–268. For a more detailed discussion of the case, see Heide, *Deserteringer*.
68. Ziemann, "Fluchten," 598.
69. This assertion is based on overviews of the reasons given for desertion to Swiss authorities. The cross section of German deserters who made it to Switzerland may not be representative of all deserters, but studies of court-martial records compiled by the Wehrmacht likewise only occasionally reference moral outrage as the reason the deserter absconded. Koch, *Fahnenfluchten*, 393; Seidler, *Fahnenflucht*, 316.

70. Fromm would himself later be executed by a firing squad on the allegation that he had supported the July 20th plot. Fromm played a noncommittal role in the plot, aware of it but neither supporting nor stopping it during the planning phase.
71. In February 1945, Himmler directed another sweep of camp inmates in search of men capable of military service. The goal for the Emsland complex of camps, for example, envisioned sending 80 percent of German prisoners to probationary battalions at the front, though Jews, gypsies, Mischlinge, homosexuals, and political prisoners were not to be considered eligible. See Heinrich Peters and Inge Peters, *Pattjackenblut: Antreten zum Sterben-in Linie zu 5 Gliedern* (McFarland, WI: Books on Demand, 2014), 114–118.
72. Battel and Liedtke entries, Yad Vashem database, available at https://righteous.yadvashem.org/.
73. Liedtke entry, Yad Vashem database, available at https://righteous.yadvashem.org/.
74. The Holocaust Remembrance Center at Yad Vashem would later recognize both as being Righteous Among the Nations.
75. David H. Kitterman, "Those Who Said 'No!': Germans Who Refused to Execute Civilians during World War II," *German Studies Review* 11, no. 2 (1988): 241, 50.
76. Author's translation from the original German in Wolfram Wette, "Ein Judenretter aus der Wehrmacht. Feldwebel Anton Schmid (1900–1942)," in *Menschen mit Zivilcourage* (Luzern: Bildungs- und Kulturdepartement, 2015), 79. For full details, see Wolfram Wette, *Feldwebel Anton Schmid: ein Held der Humanität* (Frankfurt am Main: Fischer, 2013).
77. Dominique Lormier, *Bordeaux brûle-t-il?, ou, La Libération de la Gironde, 1940–1945, Mémoires de France* (Bordeaux: Dossiers d'Aquitaine, 1998); Maia de la Baume, "Henri Salmide, 90, Dies; German's Defiance Saved a French Port," *New York Times*, March 7, 2010; Christian Seguin, "Allein gegen Résistance und Wehrmacht," *taz*, August 20, 1994.
78. Seguin, "Allein gegen Résistance und Wehrmacht," 19.

Chapter 8

1. Italy only became a belligerent in June 1940, and Spain never became a belligerent. But both had agreements to turn over German deserters to German authorities, and these were unattractive options. As for the handful of other neutral powers in Europe following the conquest of the Balkans and invasion of Russia (Portugal, Turkey), they were few and far away.
2. Brümmer-Pauly, *Desertion im Recht des Nationalsozialismus*, 27–45.
3. Heinicke, "Auszüge aus der Wehrmachtkriminalstatistik"; Wüllner, *Die NS-Militärjustiz*, 15. Messerschmidt uses the same record group but organizes his data by calendar year instead of war year. Messerschmidt and Forschungsamt, *Die Wehrmachtjustiz*, 163.
4. See "Führerbefehl" über die Bildung eines "Fliegenden Standgerichtes" vom 9.3.1945 in Gerd R. Ueberschär, Rolf-Dieter Müller, and Rolf-Dieter Müller, *1945: das Ende des Krieges* (Darmstadt: Primus, 2005), 165.
5. Seidler, "Die Fahnenflucht," 30.
6. Jörg Döring, Felix Römer, and Rolf Seubert, *Alfred Andersch desertiert: Fahnenflucht und Literatur* (Berlin: Verbrecher Verlag, 2015), chapter 5.
7. Rüdiger Overmans and Ulrike Goeken-Haidl, *Soldaten hinter Stacheldraht: deutsche Kriegsgefangene des Zweiten Weltkriegs* (München: Propyläen, 2000), 272–273.
8. Overmans provides two superb studies, one addressing the number of German POWs, the other estimating overall German deaths. Neither provides insights on the number of deserters who may have been killed when attempting to go over nor the number of POWs who fall into the category of deserter. The number was relatively low, but impossible to quantify precisely. Rüdiger Overmans, *Deutsche militärische Verluste im Zweiten Weltkrieg*, Beiträge zur Militärgeschichte (München: R. Oldenbourg, 1999); Overmans and Goeken-Haidl, *Soldaten hinter Stacheldraht*.
9. Brümmer-Pauly, *Desertion im Recht des Nationalsozialismus*, 39. For a fascinating discussion of the sociology of denunciation in the Third Reich, see Hornung, "Denunziation als soziale Praxis."
10. Manoschek, "Österreichische Opfer der NS-Militärjustiz," 50.
11. Seidler, "Die Fahnenflucht," 37.
12. Kershaw, *The End*, 219.
13. Kershaw, *The End*, 220.
14. See assessments by Martin van Creveld, Benjamin Ziemann, and Rolf-Dieter Müller in Müller and Ancker, *Hitler's Wehrmacht, 1935–1945*; Müller and Volkmann, *Die Wehrmacht*.
15. These *Sonderstandgerichte* were to include a civilian judge, a ranking party member, and an officer from the service or branch of the accused. Messerschmidt and Forschungsamt, *Die Wehrmachtjustiz*, 412.

16. Kater, *Hitler Youth*, 191.
17. In August 1946, the British Military Administration tried Willi Herold and thirteen others for the murder of 125 prisoners held at the Aschendorfermoor military prison camp during the last weeks of the war in Europe. Like so many other cases, his story faded from memory until a television documentary and a major film introduced a new generation to this case of sadistic cruelty. See Robert Schwentke, *Der Hauptmann* (Germany, France & Poland: Filmgalerie 451; Alfama Films; Opus Film, 2017); Rudolf Kersting and Paul Meyer, *Der Hauptmann von Muffrika—Eine mörderische Köpenickade* (documentary) (Germany: Filmförderung Hamburg, Filmförderung Niedersachsen, Paul Meyer Filmproduktion, 1997).
18. Ernst Fraenkel et al., *The Dual State* (New York: Oxford University Press, 1941); Ernst Fraenkel et al., *The Dual State: A Contribution to the Theory of Dictatorship* (Oxford: Oxford University Press, 2017).
19. Erich Kosthorst and Bernd Walter, *Konzentrations- und Strafgefangenenlager im Emsland 1933–1945: Zum Verhältnis von NS-Regime und Justiz* (Düsseldorf: Droste, 1985), 486.
20. The author consulted the primary records of the case at the British National Archives, FO 1060/1674 Military Government Court Case Willi Herold and thirteen others and WO 311/247 Emsland Group of Concentration Camps. Herold Statement, CIC Esterwegen, January 26, 1946, British National Archives FO 1060/1674. William Bönitz, "Ein Henker von Lunzenau," 2002.
21. Peters claims that Herold volunteered for military service; Pantcheff claims that he was drafted. The distinction is immaterial in that military service was mandatory. I have elected to rely on the account compiled by the British military intelligence officer who interrogated him, T. X. H. Pantchefll For an overview of Herold's background and service, see T. X. H. Pantcheff, *Der Henker von Emsland. Dokumentation einer Barbarei am Ende des Krieges 1995*, 2nd ed. (Schuster: Leer, 1995), 87–89; and Peters and Peters, *Pattjackenblut*, 169–170.
22. The Luftwaffe captain's uniform had Narvik shield and Crete armband on its sleeve, meaning that the captain had been a paratrooper. Pantcheff, *Der Henker von Emsland*, 13.
23. Heinrich and Inge Peters assert that "Detachment Herold" participated in a counterattack against advancing British forces near Lathen before retreating to Papenburg. They provide no documentation, and the British officer who interrogated Herold while putting together evidence for his trial, T. X. Pancheff, suggests these "heroic engagements," along with Herold's claim he had been wounded during one of them, were made up. Medical officers could find no sign of any recent wounds. When asked by Pancheff why Herold and his men engaged in the mass shootings at Emslager II Aschendorfermoor, Herold had remarked, "I don't really know why I had all those people shot. The only reason was that neither me nor my men cared about the war anymore, and [staging] the executions was an alternative to returning to the front." Peters and Peters, *Pattjackenblut*, 177; Pantcheff, *Der Henker von Emsland*, 62, 91.
24. Goldhagen describes these treks in detail, though his overall thesis is controversial. See Michael Klundt, *Geschichtspolitik: die Kontroversen um Goldhagen, die Wehrmachtsausstellung und das "Schwarzbuch des Kommunismus"* (Cologne: PapyRossa, 2000); Koch, *Fahnenfluchten*; Daniel Jonah Goldhagen, *Hitler's Willing Executioners: Ordinary Germans and the Holocaust* (New York: Knopf, 1996).
25. The F stood for Flüchtling (escapee) and the V for Verstärkter Straffvollzug (enhanced punishment). Interogation of PW Anton Hensel and PW Joseph Winkelmüller, Kempton Park Camp, May 12, 1946, in WO 311/247.
26. Interview with survivor, Kersting and Meyer, *Der Hauptmann von Muffrika.*
27. For a good introduction to Swiss refugee policies, in particular the decision to bar the entry of German Jews fleeing persecution, see Jürg Stadelmann, *Umgang mit Fremden in bedrängter Zeit: schweizerische Flüchtlingspolitik 1940–1945 und ihre Beurteilung bis heute* (Zürich: Orell Füssli, 1998).
28. Seidler notes that after the introduction of conscription, only forty German conscientious objectors/deserters crossed over into Switzerland in 1935. Seidler, *Fahnenflucht*, 213.
29. Schlußbericht des Eidesgenössischen Kommissariats für Internierung und Hospitalisierung, vol. 8, from Seidler, *Fahnenflucht*, 206.
30. Brümmer-Pauly, *Desertion im Recht des Nationalsozialismus*, 44, 55.
31. Brümmer-Pauly, *Desertion im Recht des Nationalsozialismus*, 50.
32. Brümmer-Pauly, *Desertion im Recht des Nationalsozialismus*, 52.
33. Seidler, *Fahnenflucht*, 227.
34. Seidler, *Fahnenflucht*, 230–231.

35. Brümmer-Pauly references the case of Peter Schilling who joined the French resistance. Brümmer-Pauly, *Desertion im Recht des Nationalsozialismus*, 53.
36. Quote from Churchill's famous speech to Parliament pledging to fight the Germans on the beaches, in the fields, in the streets and in the hills. Text available at https://winstonchurchill.org/resources/speeches/1940-the-finest-hour/we-shall-fight-on-the-beaches/.
37. For a discussion of the July 8, 1940, agreement for continuous Wehrmacht traffic across Sweden, see Gerd R. Ueberschaer, "The Involvement of Scandinavia in the Plans for Barbarossa," in *Germany and the Second World War* (Oxford: Oxford University Press, 1996), 473–474.
38. Joesten, "Phases in Swedish Neutrality," 327.
39. Joesten, "Phases in Swedish Neutrality," 327.
40. Seidler, *Fahnenflucht*, 254.
41. Seidler, *Fahnenflucht*, 246.
42. Parliamentary Investigation Commission on Refugees and Security Services (Sandler Commission), *Report on Treatment of Refugees*, Swedish government (Stockholm, 1946), 248; Petersson, *Hitler's Deserters*, chapter 10 (no page number).
43. Seidler, *Fahnenflucht*, 249.
44. Parliamentary Investigation Commission, *Report on Treatment of Refugees*, 250.
45. Seidler, *Fahnenflucht*, 255.
46. Seidler, *Fahnenflucht*, 245–247, 59–61.
47. Gerhard Paul, "'Die verscwanden einfach nachts.' Überlaufer zu den Allierten und den europäischen Befreiungsbewegungen," in *Die anderen Soldaten: Wehrkraftzersetzung, Gehorsamsverweigerung und Fahnenflucht im Zweiten Weltkrieg*, ed. Norbert Haase and Fietje Ausländer (Frankfurt am Main: Fischer, 1995), 139.
48. Seidler, *Fahnenflucht*, 73.
49. Seidler, *Fahnenflucht*, 73–74.
50. Seidler, *Fahnenflucht*, 76.
51. Sowjetisches Absurd-Flugblatt mit einem Gedicht von Erich Weinert, from Deutsche Digitale Bibliothek, available at https://www.deutsche-digitale-bibliothek.de/item/SMCF733KAZ2ZJRCYZR2YDIJ64WYQC4SI.
52. Translation mine, proceedings from Wüllner, *Die NS-Militärjustiz*, 472–473.
53. Translation mine, proceedings from Wüllner, *Die NS-Militärjustiz*, 472–473.
54. Weinberg, "Rollen- und Selbstverständnis des Offizierskorps im NS-Staat," 450–451.
55. Erich Weinert, *Stalingrad Diary*, trans. Egon Larsen (London: I.N.G Publication, 1944).
56. Wilhelm Adam, Otto Rühle, and Tony Le Tissier, *With Paulus at Stalingrad* (Barnsley: Pen & Sword Military, 2015), 193.
57. Walther von Seydlitz, *Stalingrad, Konflikt und Konsequenz: Erinnerungen* (Oldenburg: Stalling, 1977), 252; Antony Beevor, *Stalingrad* (New York: Viking, 1998), 382.
58. For a full discussion of the evolving thrust of NKFD propaganda, see the contributions by Nikolaj Bernikov and Vladmir Vsevolodov in Gerd R., Ueberschär, ed., *Das Nationalkomitee "Freies Deutschland" und der Bund Deutscher Offiziere. Originalausg* (Frankfurt am Main: Fischer Taschenbuch Verlag, 1995), 112–132.
59. The different forms of execution stemmed from whether the court found them guilty of treason or merely guilty of undermining the military spirit. Baumann and Koch, *"Was damals Recht war,"* 178–179.
60. Gerd R. Ueberschär, ed., *Das Nationalkomitee "Freies Deutschland" und der Bund Deutscher Offiziere* (Frankfurt am Main: Fischer Taschenbuch Verlag, 1995), 34; Bodo Scheurig, *Freies Deutschland: das Nationalkomitee und der Bund Deutscher Offiziere in der Sowjetunion 1943–45* (Cologne: Kiepenheuer & Witsch, 1984), 58.
61. Paul Heider, "Reaktionen in der Wehrmacht auf Gründung und Tätigkeit des Nationalkomitees 'Freies Deutschland' und des Bundes Deutscher Offiziere," in *Die Wehrmacht: Mythos und Realität*, ed. Rolf-Dieter Müller and Hans-Erich Volkmann (München: Oldenbourg, 1999), 619.
62. Heider, "Reaktionen," 621; Seydlitz, *Stalingrad*, 336–339.
63. Heider, "Reaktionen," 622.
64. For a detailed discussion of the NKFD and BDO, see Sabine R. Arnold and Gerd R. Ueberschär, eds., *Das Nationalkomitee "Freies Deutschland" und der Bund Deutscher Offiziere* (Frankfurt am Main: Fischer Taschenbuch Verlag, 1995).

65. Heider, "Reaktionen," 624.
66. Ueberschär, *Das Nationalkomitee*, 40.
67. Heider, "Reaktionen," 628.
68. Heider, "Reaktionen," 629.
69. Ueberschär, *Das Nationalkomitee*, 36.
70. Hugh Dalton and Ben Pimlott, *The Political Diary of Hugh Dalton, 1918–40, 1945–60* (London: Cape, 1986), 62.
71. The British ran other stations and broadcasts aimed at the German military, occupied populations, and the resistance. For details about the Nachrichten für die Truppen project and Sefton Delmer's role, see Peter Pomerantsev, *How to Win an Information War*, 182–187.
72. Howe, *The Black Game*, 6.
73. Howe, *The Black Game*, 216, 22; Seidler, *Fahnenflucht*, 64.
74. Howe, *The Black Game*; Peter Pomerantsev, *How to Win an Information* War, 174–178.
75. "The Defection of Oblt. Herbert Schmid with Ju 88 to the United Kingdom," n.d., accessed June 30, 2022, http://aircrewremembered.com/schmid-herbert-defection.html; Jerry Scutts, *German Night Fighter Aces of World War 2* (Oxford: Osprey, 1998), 47.
76. I would be remiss if I didn't thank the research team who tracked down the details of this story: Laura Elliott (Researcher), David Flanagan (London Academic Services Researcher), Willi "Barnaby" Weiss (Researcher), Tom Kracker (Kracker Luftwaffe Archive), Franek Grabowski (Researcher and Author), Stefan Pietrzak Youngs (Aircrew Remembered), Kate Tame (Aircrew Remembered Researcher), Georg Winter (Aircrew Remembered Researcher). Elinor Florence, "The Defection of Oblt. Herbert Schmid with Ju 88 to the United Kingdom." n.d., available at https://aircrewremembered.com/schmid-herbert-defection.html [accessed August 8, 2024].
77. Clayton D. Laurie, *The Propaganda Warriors: America's Crusade against Nazi Germany* (Lawrence: University Press of Kansas, 1996).
78. Periodic Summary of Headquarters Fifth Army G2 Section 21 July 1944, NARA, Entry 427, RG 407, Box 1767 from Jörg, Römer, and Seubert. *Alfred Andersch desertiert*, chapter 4.
79. Seidler, *Fahnenflucht*, 64.
80. Seidler, *Fahnenflucht*, 67.
81. Seidler, *Fahnenflucht*, 68.
82. Seidler, *Fahnenflucht*, 68.
83. Overmans and Goeken-Haidl, *Soldaten hinter*, 274–275.
84. Kershaw, *The End*, 354.
85. Kershaw, *The End*, 370.
86. The Soviet backdated the signing of the surrender protocol to 2243 Central European time to be consistent with the surrender protocol signed at Reims.

Chapter 9

1. Alfred Andersch, *The Cherries of Freedom: A Report*, trans. Michael Hulse (New Milford, CT: Toby Press, 2004), 87–88.
2. Andrew H. Beattie, *Allied Internment Camps in Occupied Germany: Extrajudicial Detention in the Name of Denazification, 1945–1950* (Cambridge: Cambridge University Press, 2020).
3. Historians disagree on how many "Ds" to list, with some adding in decartellization. One most commonly reads of four Ds, but one can make a case for six if disarmament and decartellization are included.
4. Ueberschär, *Das Nationalkomitee*, 43.
5. Timothy R. Vogt, *Denazification in Soviet-Occupied Germany: Brandenburg, 1945–1948* (Cambridge, MA: Harvard University Press, 2000), 42–43.
6. Rüdiger Wenzke, "Das unliebsame Erbe der Wehrmacht und der Aufbau der DDR-Volksarmee," in *Die Wehrmacht: Mythos und Realität*, ed. Rolf-Dieter Müller and Hans-Erich Volkmann (München: Oldenbourg, 1999), 1121.
7. For a detailed analysis of the shift from demilitarization to remilitarization, see Peifer, *The Three German Navies*.
8. Döring, Römer, and Seubert, *Alfred Andersch desertiert*, location 336 of 4408 Kindle ebook.
9. For an overview of Allied media policies and the creation of a new media landscape in the West, see Dennis L. Bark and David Gress, *A History of West Germany. From Shadow to Substance, 1945–1963* (Oxford: Blackwell, 1993), 155–164.
10. Döring, Römer, and Seubert, *Alfred Andersch desertiert*, location 3564 of 4408 Kindle ebook.

11. Hans Werner Richter, *Die Geschlagenen* (München: K. Desch, 1949), 5.
12. Alfred Andersch, *Die Kirschen der Freiheit. Ein Bericht* (Frankfurt: Frankfurter Verlagsanstalt, 1952); Andersch, *Cherries of Freedom*; Alfred Andersch, *Die Kirschen der Freiheit. Ein Bericht* (Zurich: Diogenes Verlag, 2012). I have used the 2012 version, all translations mine.
13. Andersch, *Die Kirschen der Freiheit*, 48.
14. Andersch, *Die Kirschen der Freiheit*, 75,79.
15. Andersch, *Die Kirschen der Freiheit*, 71–75.
16. Andersch, *Die Kirschen der Freiheit*, 53.
17. Döring, Römer, and Seubert, *Alfred Andersch desertiert*, 3579 of 4408 Kindle ebook.
18. Döring, Römer, and Seubert, *Alfred Andersch desertiert*, location 3375 of 4408 Kindle ebook.
19. Döring, Römer, and Seubert, *Alfred Andersch desertiert*, 3389 of 4408 Kindle ebook.
20. See chapters 3, 5, and 12 of Döring, Römer, and Seubert, *Alfred Andersch desertiert*.
21. Interestingly enough, all three pertained to the smallest of the Wehrmacht's services, the Kriegsmarine. This was probably because occupation, municipal, and provincial authorities in Hamburg, Schleswig-Holstein, and Wilhelmshaven leaned more to the left than those in the US zone of occupation and southern Germany, because Kriegsmarine judicial records were better preserved than those of the Heer and Luftwaffe, and because the families of personnel condemned to death by naval tribunals were angered by ongoing efforts to paint the Kriegsmarine and the grand admirals tried at Nuremberg as apolitical.
22. The full record of the proceedings can be found in file N623/v.65 of the Bundesarchiv Militärarchiv in Freiburg.
23. Full details can be found in *Justiz und NS-Verbrechen. Sammlung Deutscher Strafurteile wegen Nationalsozialistischer Tötungsverbrechen 1945–1966* (Amsterdam: University Press Amsterdam, 1973), 10: 445–511 and BAMA N623/v.65.
24. The song "Es zittern die morschen Knochen" was written during the 1920s and became the official anthem of the Hitler Youth. The final verse ends with the bombastic boast that "tomorrow, the world belongs to Germany."
25. Günther Gribbohm, "5. Mai 1945: Meuterei auf M 612 - Zeitgeschichtliches in rechtlicher Sicht," *Militärgeschichte* 10 (2000); Hans Constabel and Siegfried Stölting, *Hol nieder Flagge: Ereignisse um ein Standgericht* (Bremerhaven: Nordwestdeutsche Verlagsgesellschaft, 1989); Douglas Carl Peifer, "Selfless Saviours or Diehard Fanatics? West and East German Memories of the Kriegsmarine and the Baltic Evacuation," *War & Society* 26, no. 2 (2007): 99–120.
26. Biographical details from the 1952 verdict on the Petersen case, found in the Bundesarchiv-Militärarchiv, N623/v.65.
27. Bundesarchiv-Militärarchiv, N623/v.65.
28. Gerhard Paul, "Die Erschießungen in der Geltinger Bucht. Das blutige Geschäft der NS-Militärjustiz und ihre justitielle Bearbeitung nach 1945," *Demokratische Geschichte* IX (1995): 176–177.
29. Ingo Müller, *Furchtbare Juristen: die unbewältigte Vergangenheit unserer Justiz* (München: Kindler, 1987), 218–.
30. Paul, "Die Erschießungen," 177.
31. "Geltinger Todesurteile," 2021, https://geschichte-s-h.de/sh-von-a-bis-z/g/todesurteile/.
32. See, for example, the Carl Lüder case pertaining to the execution of four Kriegsmarine sailors for desertion on May 4, 1945, in Justiz und NS-Verbrechen, 10: 647–660.
33. Report submitted by Lieutenant Dr. Ulrich Abel to the commander of the 3rd U-boat Instructional Division at Neustadt, January 12, 1944, from Bundesarchiv-Militärarchiv, PER 15 71334, 2. Translation mine.
34. Rust cites a letter from Dönitz to Karl Helmut Sieber from 1946/47 where Dönitz recalls discussing the case with Admiral Warzecha and Admiralty Staff Judge Rudolphi. Rust, *U-boat Commander*, 236–237.
35. For two excellent analyses of the case, see Rust, *U-Boat Commander* and Walle, *Die Tragödie*.
36. I have translated the German text differently than Rust, drawing on the German original in Walle. *Neue Zeitung* (Stuttgart), July 8, 1946; Rust, *U-Boat Commander*, 259; and Walle, *Die Tragödie*, 185–186.
37. Rust, *U-boat Commander*, 262. For a detailed discussion of how the network of former naval jurists delayed prosecution and then assisted the defense, see Walle, *Die Tragödie*, 194–199.

38. Walle, *Die Tragödie*, 215–216.
39. Walle, *Die Tragödie*, 218.
40. Rust, *U-boat Commander*, 265–266.
41. Rust, *U-boat Commander*, 268, 70–71.
42. Bruno Thoß, ed., *Volksarmee schaffen—ohne Geschrei! Studien zu den Anfängen einer "verdeckten Aufrüstung" in der SBZ/DDR 1947–1952* (Munich: R. Oldenbourg, 1994).
43. Edgar Doehler and Horst Haufe, *Militärhistorische Traditionen der DDR und der NVA* (East Berlin: Militärverlag der DDR, 1989), H. Hafenstein, "Die revolutionären Traditionen der Volksmarine," *Marinewesen* (1965), 1045; Peter J. Lapp, *Traditionspflege in der DDR* (Berlin: Holzapfel, 1988).
44. Paul Heider, "Die Arbeitsgemeinschaft ehemaliger Offiziere (AeO)—Propaganda—und Diversionsinstrument der SED," *Militaergeschichtliche Zeitschrift* 61, no. 2 (2002): 463–464.
45. The seven former Wehrmacht generals were Rudolf Bamler, Arthur Brandt, Walter Freytag, Rudolf Hähling, Dr. Otto Korfes, Wilhelm Kunze, and Martin Lattmann. Heider, "Die Arbeitsgemeinschaft," 465.
46. For an overview of the debates in West Germany about acquiring nuclear weapons, see Dennis L. Bark and David Gress, *A History of West Germany*, 2nd ed., 2 vols. (Cambridge: Blackwell, 1993), 386–410.
47. Heider, "Die Arbeitsgemeinschaft," 465.
48. Heider, "Die Arbeitsgemeinschaft," 474.
49. Heider, "Die Arbeitsgemeinschaft," 481.
50. Heider, "Die Arbeitsgemeinschaft," 470.
51. Heider, "Die Arbeitsgemeinschaft," 468.
52. Lenski made no mention of his appointment as an honorary member of the infamous *Volksgerichtshof*, which dealt with cases of treason, defeatism, and subversion of the military spirit. Quotation from his contribution to the 1966 *Mitteilungsblatt*, translated from the German in Heider, "Die Arbeitsgemeinschaft," 480.
53. The East German articles, to be treated with caution due to their mixture of fact and propaganda, are as follows: series "Rottenknechten," *Junge Welt*, December 30, 1966–May 26, 1967; *Neues Deutschland*, March 2, 1967; *Berliner Zeitung*, January 10, 1971.
54. Egon Bahr, *Zu meiner Zeit*, 1. Aufl. ed. (München: K. Blessing, 1996), 400.
55. For a full discussion of the working group, see Paul Heider, *Offiziere der Wehrmacht beim Aufbau der Bewaffneten Organe der DDR und die Rolle der Arbeitsgemeinschaft ehemaliger Offiziere* (Potsdam: Militärgeschichtliches Forschungsamt, 2000) and Peter Joachim Lapp, *Arbeitsgemeinschaft ehemaliger Offiziere—DDR-Propaganda gegen die Bundeswehr* (Aachen: Helios, 2000).
56. *Die Zeit*, February 17, 1978.
57. "Affäre Filbinger: 'Was Rechtens war…'" *Der Spiegel*, nr. May 14, 1978.
58. Heinz Hürten, "Die Tätigkeit Hans Filbinger als Marinerichter," in *Hans Filbinger. Der "Fall" und die Fakten*, ed. Bruno Heck (Mainz: Hase & Koehler, 1980); Wolfram Wette, *Filbinger, eine deutsche Karriere* (Springe: Klampen,, 2006).
59. Gruchmann, "Ausgewählte Dokumente."
60. Franz Seidler, a professor of modern history at the Bundeswehr University in Munich, published an article on desertion from the German Wehrmacht in the *Militärgeschichtliche Zeitschrift* the year before the Filbinger Affair. He and Messerschmidt would later be called as expert witnesses as the Bundestag debated various resolutions regarding deserters. Seidler's article did not resonate in the same manner as Messerschmidt and Wüllner's book, with Seidler publishing a book length monograph on Wehrmacht desertion six years after Messerschmidt and Wüllner had reframed the interpretive narrative. Messerschmidt and Wüllner, *Die Wehrmachtjustiz*; Seidler, "Die Fahnenflucht"; Seidler, *Fahnenflucht.*
61. The characterization stems from Jörg Kammler, "Deserteure. Zeitgeschichtliche und aktuelle Anmerkungen zu einer antimilitaristischen Leitfigur," in *Deserteure—Eine notwendige Debatte* (Hamburg: Ergebnissen Verlag, 1990), 5. Ausländer characterizes early participants along the same lines in Fietje Ausländer, ed., *Verräter oder Vorbilder? Deserteure und ungehorsame Soldaten im Nationalsozialismus* (Bremen: Ed. Temmen, 1990). For a broader discussion of the Euromissile controversy and the German peace movement, see Jeffrey Herf, *War by Other Means: Soviet Power, West German Resistance, and the Battle of the Euromissiles* (New York: Free Press, 1991).

62. Jörg Kammler, *Ich habe die Metzelei satt und laufe über…Kasseler Soldaten zwischen Verweigerung und Widerstand (1939–1945): Eine Dokumentation* (Fuldabrück: Hesse, 1985).
63. See editorial in Stefan Beck, Klaus Schönberger, and Jürgen Roth, eds., *Deserteure—Eine notwendige Debatte* (Hamburg: Ergebnissen Verlag, 1990).
64. Editorial in Stefan Beck, Klaus Schönberger, and Jürgen Roth, eds., *Deserteure*.
65. Ludwig Baumann and Norbert Joa, *Niemals gegen das Gewissen: Plädoyer des letzten Wehrmachtsdeserteurs* (Freiburg: Herder, 2014), 14, 20–21, 26.
66. The pamphlet was entitled "Informationen für unzufriedene Soldaten." Baumann describes its contents and his role in the peace movement in Baumann and Joa, *Niemals gegen das Gewissen*, 26–28.
67. For an example of Zwerenz's outlook and approach, see Gerhard Zwerenz, *Soldaten sind Mörder: die Deutschen und der Krieg* (Munich: Knesebeck & Schuler, 1988). For a candid discussion of the impact of literature on the early deserter debate in Germany, see Kammler, "Deserteure," 5–17.
68. For a detailed discussion of West German historiography on resistance, see Gerd R. Ueberschär, "Von der Einzeltat des 20. Juli 1944 zur 'Volksopposition'? Stationen und Wege der westdeutschen Historiographie nach 1945," in *Der 20. Juli. Das "andere Deutschland" in der Vergangenheitspolitik*, ed. Gerd R. Ueberschär (Berlin: Elefanten Press, 1998), 125–157.
69. See Heinrich Walle, "Ein Rundgang durch die Ausstellung," in *Aufstand des Gewissens. Militärischer Widerstand gegen Hitler und das NS-Regime 1933–1945*, ed. Heinrich Walle (Herford: E.S. Mittler & Sohn, 1994), 17–205.
70. Kammler, "Deserteure," 13.
71. Quote from Kammler as follows: "Diese Initiativen arbeiten in aller Regel ohne Verbindung mit der akademischen Forschung, erhalten nur selten und in geringem Umfang öffentliche Mittel und sind überwiegend eher am aktuellen Bezug des Themas, als an seiner zeitgeschichtlichen Dimension interessiert." Kammler, "Deserteure." For full details on the monument movement, see Fritz Soergel, "Deserteure-Initiativen," in *Deserteure—Eine notwendige Debatte* (Hamburg: Ergebnissen Verlag, 1990): 43–.
72. Fietje Ausländer, "Veranstaltung in Burlage. 'Der Metzelei und Hitlers Armee den Rücken gekehrt,'" *Ostfriesen Zeitung*, February 24, 1988, 9.
73. Description from the *Manchester Guardian Weekly*, March 15, 1987, 8. Fritz Soergel includes a photo of the monument in his article "Zur Geschichte der lokalen Deserteurs-Initiativen in Deutschland," in Wette, *Deserteure der Wehrmacht*, 42–56.
74. Steven R. Welch, "Commemorating 'Heroes of a Special Kind': Deserter Monuments in Germany,"*Journal of Contemporary History* 47, no. 2 (2012): 379.
75. Welch, "Commemorating," 380. For a sense of Schreiber's grievance, see the title of his 1998 polemic *Wider den geistigen Terror linker Gesinnungspäpste. Aufsätze und Vorträge gegen heuchlerische Vergangenheitsbewältigung und das Diktat der "politischen Korrektheit"* (Bonn: Verlag Soldat im Volk, 1998).
76. "Verdienen die Deserteure von damals heute unsere Anerkennung?" Streitgespräch zwischen Ludwig Baumann und Generalmajor a.D. Jürgen Schreiber," NDR, March 2, 1994, in Wolfram Wette, "Verweigerung und Desertion im Wandel der öffentlichen Meinung (1980–1995), in Die anderen Soldaten, ed. Norbert Haase and Gerhard Paul (Frankfurt am Main: Fischer, 1995), 293–314.
77. Baumann and Joa, *Niemals gegen das Gewissen*, 37.
78. For a full description of the controversy surrounding the Schweling and Schwinge apologia, see Schweling and Schwinge, *Die deutsche Militärjustiz*; Welch, "'Harsh but Just'?"
79. Baumann and Joa, *Niemals gegen das Gewissen*, 37–38.
80. Manfred Messerschmidt, *Die Wehrmacht im NS-Staat. Zeit der Indoktrination* (Hamburg: R. v. Decker, 1969).
81. Messerschmidt and Wüllner, *Die Wehrmachtjustiz*. Messerschmidt would later publish an even more exhaustive work, but its findings support and elaborate rather than weaken his earlier assessment. Messerschmidt, *Die Wehrmachtjustiz, 1933–1945*.
82. Wüllner, *Die NS-Militärjustiz*.
83. For a fine overview of the major scholarly publications on the topic, see Kristina Brümmer-Pauly, *Desertion im Recht des Nationalsozialismus* (Berlin: Berliner Wissenschafts-Verlag, 2006), 1–26.

84. Arnold and Ueberschär, *Das Nationalkomitee*; Ausländer, *Verräter oder Vorbilder?*; Ausländer, Haase, and Paul, *Die anderen Soldaten*; Beck, Schönberger, and Roth, eds., *Deserteure*; Ulrich Bröckling and Michael Sikora, *Armeen und ihre Deserteure*; Hans Frese and Fietje Ausländer, *Bremsklötze am Siegeswagen der Nation: Erinnerungen eines Deserteurs an Militärgefängnisse, Zuchthäuser und Moorlager in den Jahren 1941–1945* (Bremen: Ed. Temmen, 1989); Haase and Aicher, *Deutsche Deserteure*; Haase and Ausländer, *Die anderen Soldaten*; Hannemann, *Die Justiz der Kriegsmarine 1939–1945*; Kammler, *Ich habe die Metzelei*; Kammler, "Deserteure; Hans-Peter Klausch, *Die Bewährungstruppe 500. Stellung und Funktion der Bewährungstruppe 500 im System von NS-Wehrrecht, NS-Militärjustiz und Wehrmachtstrafvollzug* (Bremen: Temmen, 1995); Müller, *Furchtbare Juristen*; Gerhard Paul, *Ungehorsame Soldaten: Dissens, Verweigerung und Widerstand deutscher Soldaten (1939–1945)* (St. Ingbert: Röhrig, 1994); Stefanie Reichelt, *"Für mich ist der Krieg aus!" Deserteure und Kriegsverweigerer des Zweiten Weltkriegs in München* (München: Buchendorfer, 1995); Martin Schnackenberg, *"Ich wollte keine Heldentaten mehr vollbringen" Wehrmachtdeserteure im II. Weltkrieg Motive und Folgen untersucht anhand von Selbstzeugnissen* (Oldenburg: BIS, 1997); Franz W. Seidler, "Die Fahnenflucht in der deutschen Wehrmacht während des Zweiten Weltkrieges," *Militärgeschichtliche Zeitschrift*|22, no. 2 (1977): 23–42; Seidler, *Fahnenflucht*; Peter Steinbach, *Kriegsdienstverweigerer Widerstandskämpfer in den "Bewährungseinheiten" 999* (Berlin: Gedenkstätte Deutscher Widerstand, 1992); Heinrich Walle, *Aufstand des Gewissens: militärischer Widerstand gegen Hitler und das NS-Regime 1933–1945*, 4th ed. (Berlin: Mittler, 1994); Wolfram Wette, *Der Krieg des kleinen Mannes: eine Militärgeschichte von Unten*, Originalausg. ed. (München: Piper, 1992); Wolfram Wette, *Deserteure der Wehrmacht: Feiglinge—Opfer—Hoffnungsträger? Dokumentation eines Meinungswandels* (Essen: Klartext, 1995); Wüllner, *Die NS-Militärjustiz*; Hermine Wüllner, *"... kann nur der Tod die gerechte Sühne sein" Todesurteile deutscher Wehrmachtsgerichte eine Dokumentation* (Baden-Baden: Nomos-Verlag, 1997); Ziemann, "Fluchten."
85. See, for example, Ausländer, *Verräter oder Vorbilder?*; Baumann and Koch, *"Was damals Recht war"*; Haase and Ausländer, *Die anderen Soldaten*; Wette, *Der Krieg des kleinen Mannes*.
86. Ziemann, "Fluchten," 593.
87. Günter Knebel, "Wiedergutmachung für Wehrmacht-Deserteure," in Wolfram Wette, *Deserteure der Wehrmacht*, 31–41.
88. Haase and Ausländer, *Die anderen Soldaten*, 197.
89. Proposal put forward by Antje Vollmer, Green Party, in Wette, *Deserteure der Wehrmacht*, 140–144.
90. Baumann and Joa, *Niemals gegen das Gewissen*, 45.
91. Baumann and Joa, *Niemals gegen das Gewissen*, 5.
92. Baumann and Joa, *Niemals gegen das Gewissen*, 46; Wette, *Deserteure der Wehrmacht*, 234–261; Haase and Ausländer, *Die anderen Soldaten*, 194–195.
93. The Bundesgesetz zur Entschädigung für Opfer der nationalsozialistischen Verfolgung (BEG) was passed in 1956, revising an earlier 1951 law. It would be expanded in 1965, 1980, and after unification.
94. The court explicitly cited the works of Wüllner, Messerschmidt, and Hennicke Wette, *Deserteure der Wehrmacht*, 244; Kristina Brümmer-Pauly, *Desertion im Recht des Nationalsozialismus* (Berlin: Berliner Wissenschafts-Verlag, 2006), 6.
95. Haase and Ausländer, *Die anderen Soldaten*, 232n35, n36.
96. Jan Philipp Reemtsma, director of the Hamburg Institute for Social Research, would suspend further exhibitions in November 1999 in reaction to criticism that the exhibit had identified pictures of atrocities committed by the Red Army, Ukranian forces, and the SS as crimes of the Wehrmacht. A scholarly commission examined these charges and found that only twenty of the 1,433 photographs in exhibition misattributed atrocities committed by others to the Wehrmacht. For a full account of the controversy, the commission, and the second exhibit, see Christian Hartmann, Johannes Hürter, and Ulrike Jurei, *Verbrechen der Wehrmacht. Bilanz einer Debatte* (Munich: C.H. Beck, 2005).
97. Baumann and Joa, *Niemals gegen das Gewissen*, 47.
98. Bundestagsdebatte vom 16. März 1995 über die Anträge der Fraktionen von BÜNDNIS 90/DIE GRÜNEN und der SPD vom 30. Januar 1995 in Wette, *Deserteure der Wehrmacht*, 191–223.
99. Baumann and Joa, *Niemals gegen das Gewissen*, 58; Brümmer-Pauly, *Desertion im Recht des Nationalsozialismus*, 7.

100. Tatbestand der Rechtsbeugung bei Mitwirkung eines DDR-Strafrichters an Todesurteilen, BGH StR 747/97—Urteil vom 16. November 1995 (Berlin), available at https://www.hrr-strafrecht.de/hrr/5/94/5-747-94.php.
101. Baumann and Joa, *Niemals gegen das Gewissen*, 59.
102. Baumann and Joa, *Niemals gegen das Gewissen*, 61–62.
103. Baumann and Joa, *Niemals gegen das Gewissen*, 76.
104. Quote from Jürgen Gehb (CDU) in Bernard Bode, "Einstimmige Entscheidung. NS-Unrecht. Bundestag rehabilitiert 'Kriegsverräter'" in *Das Parlament*, nr. 38 (2009), available at https://www.das-parlament.de/2009/38/Innenpolitik/27027296-302550.

Epilogue

1. "Bund offen für russische Deserteure," *Tagesschau*, September 23, 2022, available at https://www.tagesschau.de/inland/russland-deserteure-101.html.
2. "EU divided on Response to Russians Fleeing Military Service," *PBS News Hour*, September 25, 2022, available at https://www.pbs.org/newshour/world/eu-divided-on-response-to-russians-fleeing-military-service.
3. "Ampel will Asyl für Deserteure," *taz*, September 23, 2022, available at Kriegsdienstverweigerer aus Russland: Ampel will Asyl für Deserteure-taz.de.
4. Oliver Pieper, "Ukrainians in Germany Fear Russian Deserters," *DW in Focus*, September 27, 2022, available at https://www.dw.com/en/ukrainians-in-germany-oppose-asylum-for-russian-deserters/a-63251172.
5. Pascal Beucker, "Streit über russische Deserteure. Zivilisatorisches Versagen," *taz*, November 10, 2022, available at https://taz.de/Streit-ueber-russische-Deserteure/!5890226/.
6. Robert S. McNamara and Brian Van De Mark, *In Retrospect: The Tragedy and Lessons of Vietnam* (New York: Times Books, 1995).
7. Albert Wohlstetter, "Delicate Balance of Terror," *Foreign Affairs* 37, no. 2 (January 1, 1959): 211–234.

Bibliography

Primary Sources

German Federal Archive, Military Division Freiburg im Breisgau (BAMA)
E 27 1099 721, 9928 bd 8

PERS 15/1571, 2285, 2327, 2473, 2486, 2576, 4470, 71334, 133155, 133617
RW 6 129 v.1–5, 130 v.1–5, 527, RW 20–19, MStGB October 1940, May 1944

British National Archives, Kew
WO 311/247, WO 219/335, WO 219/4716, WO 219/4905B, WO 219/1483, WO 204/6647, WO 241/2, FO 371/49525, FO 1060/1674, KV 6/33, CAB 122/1267

Swiss Federal Archives, Bern (SFA)
E27#1000/721#9927 E27#1000/721#9928—v.3, 6–9

Secondary Sources

Abenheim, Donald. *Reforging the Iron Cross: The Search for Tradition in the West German Armed Forces.* Princeton, NJ: Princeton University Press, 1988.

Adam, Wilhelm, Otto Rühle, and Tony Le Tissier. *With Paulus at Stalingrad.* Barnsley, UK: Pen & Sword Military, 2015.

Andersch, Alfred. *Die Kirschen der Freiheit. Ein Bericht.* Frankfurt: Frankfurter Verlagsanstalt, 1952.

Andersch, Alfred. *The Cherries of Freedom: A Report.* Translated by Michael Hulse. New Milford, CT: Toby Press, 2004.

Anderson, Benedict R. O'G. *Imagined Communities: Reflections on the Origin and Spread of Nationalism.* London: Verso, 1983.

Andersson, David Verner. *Jutzi. Ett drama vid gränsen.* Arvika: Tänk, 1961.

Arnold, Sabine R., and Gerd R. Ueberschär. *Das Nationalkomitee "Freies Deutschland" und der Bund Deutscher Offiziere.* Frankfurt am Main: Fischer, 1995.

Ashcroft, Michael. *In the Shadows. The Extraordinary Men and Women of the Intelligence Corps.* London: Biteback Publishing, 2022.

Ausländer, Fietje. *Verräter oder Vorbilder? Deserteure und ungehorsame Soldaten im Nationalsozialismus.* Bremen: Ed. Temmen, 1990.

Ausländer, Fietje, Norbert Haase, and Gerhard Paul. *Die anderen Soldaten: Wehrkraftzersetzung, Gehorsamsverweigerung und Fahnenflucht im Zweiten Weltkrieg.* Frankfurt am Main: Fischer Taschenbuch Verlag, 1995.

Barth, Boris. *Dolchstosslegenden und politische Desintegration. Das Trauma der deutschen Niederlage im Ersten Weltkrieg 1914–1933.* Düsseldorf: Droste, 2003.

Bartov, Omer. *The Eastern Front, 1941–45: German Troops and the Barbarisation of Warfare.* Basingstoke, UK: Macmillan, 1985.

Bartov, Omer. *Hitler's Army: Soldiers, Nazis, and War in the Third Reich.* New York: Oxford University Press, 1991.

Baum, Walter. "Der Zusammenbruch der oberstern deutschen militärischen Führung 1945." *Wehrwissenschaftliche Rundschau* 10, no. 4 (1960): 237–266.

Baumann, Ludwig, and Norbert Joa. *Niemals gegen das Gewissen: Plädoyer des letzten Wehrmachtsdeserteurs.* Originalausgabe. ed. Freiburg: Herder, 2014.

Baumann, Ulrich, and Magnus Koch. *"Was damals Recht war..." Soldaten und Zivilisten vor Gerichten der Wehrmacht.* Berlin-Brandenburg: Bebra, 2008.

Beattie, Andrew H. *Allied Internment Camps in Occupied Germany: Extrajudicial Detention in the Name of Denazification, 1945–1950.* Cambridge: Cambridge University Press, 2020.

Beck, Stefan, Klaus Schönberger, and Jürgen Roth, eds. *Deserteure—Eine notwendige Debatte.* Vol. 22, Geschichtswerkstatt. Hamburg: Ergebnissen Verlag, 1990.

Beevor, Antony. *The Fall of Berlin, 1945.* New York: Viking, 2002.

Beevor, Antony. *Stalingrad.* New York: Viking, 1998.

Beorn, Waitman Wade. *Marching into Darkness: The Wehrmacht and the Holocaust in Belarus.* Cambridge, MA: Harvard University Press, 2014.

Bergh, Hendrik. *Deserteure: Fahnenflucht von und nach Deutschland.* Pfaffenhofen: Ilmgau-Verlag, 1971.

Bernett, Hajo, ed. *Internationales Jahn-Symposium Berlin 1978.* Leiden: Brill, 1979.

Bird, Keith W. *Weimar, the German Naval Officer Corps and the Rise of National Socialism.* Amsterdam: Grüner, 1977.

Bischof, Günter, Stephen E. Ambrose, and Eisenhower Center (University of New Orleans). *Eisenhower and the German POWs: Facts against Falsehood.* Baton Rouge: Louisiana State University Press, 1992.

Böckler, Hans. *Der Entschluss: die Flucht eines aktiven deutschen Offiziers 1942 von der Krim in die Schweiz.* Schaffhausen: Novalis, 2004.

Bredemeier, Karsten. *Kriegsdienstverweigerung im Dritten Reich.* Baden-Baden: Nomos, 1991.

Bröckling, Ulrich, and Michael Sikora. *Armeen und ihre Deserteure: Vernachlässigte Kapitel einer Militärgeschichte der Neuzeit.* Göttingen: Vandenhoeck & Ruprecht, 1998.

Browning, Christopher R. *Ordinary Men: Reserve Police Battalion 101 and the Final Solution in Poland.* New York: HarperCollins, 1992.

Bruce, Gary. *The Firm: The Inside Story of the Stasi.* Oxford: Oxford University Press, 2010.

Brümmer-Pauly, Kristina. *Desertion im Recht des Nationalsozialismus.* Berlin: Berliner Wissenschafts-Verlag, 2006.

Buruma, Ian. *The Wages of Guilt: Memories of War in Germany and Japan.* New York: Farrar Straus Girous, 1994.

Carell, Paul, and Günter Böddeker. *Die Gefangenen: Leben und Überleben dt. Soldaten hinter Stacheldraht.* Frankfurt: Ullstein, 1980.

Carlgren, W. M. *Swedish Foreign Policy during the Second World War.* New York: St. Martin's Press, 1977.

Carlson, Lewis H. *We Were Each Other's Prisoners: An Oral History of World War II American and German Prisoners of War.* 1st ed. New York: Basic Books, 1997.

Chickering, Roger, Stig Förster, and Bernd Greiner. *A World at Total War: Global Conflict and the Politics of Destruction, 1937–1945.* Washington, DC: German Historical Institute & Cambridge University Press, 2005.

Citino, Robert Michael. *The German Way of War: From the Thirty Years' War to the Third Reich.* Lawrence: University Press of Kansas, 2005.

Citino, Robert Michael. *The Path to Blitzkrieg: Doctrine and Training in the German Army, 1920–1939.* Boulder, CO: Lynne Rienner, 1999.

Citino, Robert Michael. *The Wehrmacht's Last Stand: The German Campaigns of 1944–1945.* Lawrence: University Press of Kansas, 2017.

Connell, Raewyn. *Masculinities.* Berkeley: University of California Press, 1995.

Constabel, Hans, and Siegfried Stölting. *Hol nieder Flagge: Ereignisse um ein Standgericht.* Bremerhaven: Nordwestdeutsche Verlagsgesellschaft, 1989.

Cooke, John S. "Fiftieth Anniversary of the Uniform Code of Military Justice." *Military Law Review* 165 (Symposium Issue), September (2000): 1–21.

Costelle, Daniel. *Prisonniers nazis en Amérique.* Paris: Acropole, 2012.

Culler, Dan, Rob Morris, and Dwight S. Mears. *Prisoner of the Swiss: A World War II Airman's Story.* Rev. ed. Philadelphia: Casemate, 2017.

Dalton, Hugh Dalton, and Ben Pimlott. *The Political Diary of Hugh Dalton, 1918–40, 1945–60*. London: Cape, 1986.
Deist, Wilhelm. *The Build-up of German Aggression*. New York: Oxford University Press, 1990.
Deist, Wilhelm. "Die Politik der Seekriegsleitung und die Rebellion der Flotte Ende Oktober 1918." *Vierteljahrshefte für Zeitgeschichte* 14 (1966): 341–368.
Deist, Wilhelm. "The German Army, the Authoritarian Nation-State and Total War." In *State, Society and Mobilization in Europe during the First World War*, edited by John Horne, 144–160. Cambridge: Cambridge University Press, 1997.
Deist, Wilhelm. "The Military Collapse of the German Empire." *War in History* 3, no. 2 (2001): 186–207.
Deist, Wilhelm. "The Rearmament of the Wehrmacht." In edited by the Militärgeschichtliches Forschungsamt (Research Institute for Military History) *The Build-up of German Aggression*, 373–540. New York: Oxford University Press, 1990.
Deist, Wilhelm. "Verdeckter Militärstreik im Kriegsjahr 1918?" In Wette, Wolfram (ed.), *Der Krieg des kleinen Mannes: Eine Militärgeschichte von Unten*, 146–167. München: Piper, 1992.
Deist, Wilhelm, and E. J. Feuchtwanger. "The Military Collapse of the German Empire: The Reality behind the Stab-in-the-Back Myth." *War in History* 3, no. 2 (1996): 186–207.
Diamond, Hanna. *Women and the Second World War in France, 1939–1948: Choices and Constraints*. London: Longman, 1999.
Dietrich, Barbara, Joachim Perels, and Wolfgang Abendroth. *Wolfgang Abendroth: ein Leben in der Arbeiterbewegung*. Frankfurt am Main: Suhrkamp, 1976.
Doehler, Edgar, and Horst Haufe. *Militärhistorische Traditionen der DDR und der NVA*. East Berlin: Militärverlag der DDR, 1989.
Doernberg, Stefan. *Im Bunde mit dem Feind. Deutsche auf alliierter Seite*. Berlin: Dietz, 1995.
Döring, Jörg, Felix Römer, and Rolf Seubert. *Alfred Andersch desertiert Fahnenflucht und Literatur (1944–1952)*. Berlin: Verbrecher Verlag, 2015.
Dörken, Georg, and Werner Scherer, eds. *Militärstrafgesetzbuch mit Erläuterungen. Neufassung von 10 Oktober 1940*. Berlin: Franz Dahlen, 1941.
Dräger, Marco. *Denkmäler für Deserteure ein Überblick über ihren Einzug in die Erinnerungskultur*. Wiesbaden: Springer Fachmedien, 2018.
Duda, Daniel. "Ideological Battles in Medicine Hat: The Deaths of August Plaszek and Karl Lehmann." In *For King and Country: Alberta in the Second World War*, edited by Kenneth W. Tingle, 304–310. Alberta: Provincial Museum of Alberta, 1995.
Dudink, Stefan, Karen Hagemann, and John Tosh. *Masculinities in Politics and War: Gendering Modern History*. New York: Palgrave, 2004.
Dülffer, Jost. *Weimar, Hitler und die Marine; Reichspolitik und Flottenbau, 1920–1939*. Düsseldorf: Droste, 1973.
Dülffer, Jost, and Hans Gotthard Ehlert, eds. *Deutsche Militärhistoriker von Hans Delbrück bis Andreas Hillgruber*. Potsdam: Militärgeschichtliches Forschungsamt, 2010.
Dupuy, Trevor N. *A Genius for War: The German Army and General Staff, 1807–1945*. Englewood Cliffs, NJ: Prentice-Hall, 1977.
Echternkamp, Jörg. *German Wartime Society 1939–1945: Politicization, Disintegration and the Struggle for Survival*. Oxford: Clarendon Press, 2008.
Ehm, Wilhelm. "Die revolutionären Traditionen der Volksmarine für die klassenmässige Erziehung nutzen." *Marinewesen* 6, no. 5 (1967): 515–532.
Eichmüller, Andreas. *Keine Generalamnestie: die strafrechtliche Verfolgung von NS-Verbrechen in der frühen Bundesrepublik*. München: Oldenbourg Verlag, 2012.
Elinor Florence et al., "The Defection of Oblt. Herbert Schmid with Ju 88 to the United Kingdom." n.d., available at https://aircrewremembered.com/schmid-herbert-defection.html [accessed August 8, 2024].
Emendörfer, Max, Horst Grünberg, and Hannelore Grünberg. *Rückkehr an die Front. Erlebnisse eines deutschen Antifaschisten*. East Berlin: Militärverlag der DDR, 1972.
Evans, Richard J. *The Coming of the Third Reich*. New York: Penguin, 2004.

Evans, Richard J. *Rituals of Retribution: Capital Punishment in Germany 1600–1987*. Oxford: Oxford University Press, 1996.

Evans, Richard J. *The Third Reich in History and Memory*. London: Little & Brown, 2015.

Evans, Richard J. *The Third Reich in Power, 1933–1939*. New York: Penguin Press, 2005.

Evans, Richard J. *The Third Reich at War*. New York: Penguin Press, 2009.

Fahle, Günter. *Verweigern, Weglaufen, Zersetzen: deutsche Militärjustiz und ungehorsame Soldaten 1939–1945*. Bremen: Edition Temmen, 1990.

Fay, Sidney B. "German Prisoners of War: A Suggestion for the Proper Treatment of War Prisoners." *Current History* 8, no. 43 (1945): 193–200.

Ferguson, Niall. "Prisoner Taking and Prisoner Killing in the Age of Total War: Towards a Political Economy of Military Defeat." *War in History* 11, no. 2 (2004): 148–192.

Fest, Joachim. *Plotting Hitler's Death: The Story of the German Resistance*. New York: Weidenfeld & Nicolson, 1996.

Filbinger, Hans. *Die geschmähte Generation*. München: Universitas, 1987.

Förster, Jürgen. "Ideological Warfare in Germany, 1919 to 1945." In *German Wartime Society 1939–1945: Politicization, Disintegration and the Struggle for Survival*, edited by Ralf Blank and Jörg Echternkamp, 485–669. Oxford: Clarendon Press, 2008.

Förster, Jürgen. "Motivation and Indoctrination in the Wehrmacht, 1933–45." In *Time to Kill: The Soldier's Experience of War in the West 1939–1945*, edited by Paul Addison and Angus Calder, 263–273. London: Pimlico, 1997.

Förster, Jürgen. "Wehrmacht, Krieg und Holocaust." In *Die Wehrmacht. Mythos und Realität*, edited by Rolf-Dieter Mueller and Hans-Erich Volkmann, 948–963. München: R. Oldenbourg, 1999.

Fraenkel, Ernst, Edward Shils, Edith Lowenstein, and Klaus Knorr. *The Dual State*. New York: Oxford University Press, 1941.

Fraenkel, Ernst, Edward Shils, Edith Lowenstein, Klaus Knorr, and Jens Meierhenrich. *The Dual State: A Contribution to the Theory of Dictatorship*. Oxford: Oxford University Press, 2017.

Frese, Hans, and Fietje Ausländer. *Bremsklötze am Siegeswagen der Nation: Erinnerungen eines Deserteurs an Militärgefängnisse, Zuchthäuser und Moorlager in den Jahren 1941–1945*. Bremen: Ed. Temmen, 1989.

Fritz, Stephen G. *The First Soldier: Hitler as Military Leader*. New Haven, CT: Yale University Press, 2018.

Fritz, Stephen G. *Frontsoldaten: The German Soldier in World War II*. Lexington: University Press of Kentucky, 1995.

Fritz, Stephen G. *Ostkrieg: Hitler's War of Extermination in the East*. Lexington: University Press of Kentucky, 2011.

Garbe, Detlef. "Abschrekungsjustiz im Dienst der Kriegsführung." In *Wehrmachtsjustiz: Kontext, Praxis, Nachwirkungen*, edited by Peter Pirker and Florian Wenninger, 29–46. Wien: Braumüller, 2011.

Garbe, Detlef, and United States Holocaust Memorial Museum. *Between Resistance and Martyrdom: Jehovah's Witnesses in the Third Reich*. Madison: University of Wisconsin Press, 2008.

Gellately, Robert. *Backing Hitler: Consent and Coercion in Nazi Germany*. Oxford: Oxford University Press, 2001.

Gellately, Robert. *Hitler's True Believers: How Ordinary People Became Nazis*. New York: Oxford University Press, 2020.

Geyer, Michael, and John Boyer. *Resistance against the Third Reich*. Chicago: University of Chicago Press, 1994.

Gilmour, John, and Jill Stephenson. *Hitler's Scandinavian Legacy: The Consequences of the German Invasion for the Scandinavian Countries, Then and Now*. London: Bloomsbury, 2013.

Goda, Norman J. W. "Black Marks: Hitler's Bribery of His Senior Officers during World War II." *Journal of Modern History* 72, no. 2 (2000): 413–452.

Goldhagen, Daniel Jonah. *Hitler's Willing Executioners: Ordinary Germans and the Holocaust.* New York: Knopf, 1996.

Greenfield, Nathan. *Hanged in Medicine Hat.* Toronto: Sutherland House, 2022.

Gruchmann, Lothar. "Ausgewählte Dokumente zur Deutschen Marinejustiz im Zweiten Weltkrieg." *Vierteljahrshefte für Zeitgeschichte* 26, no. 3 (1978): 433–498.

Haase, Norbert. "Desertion und Kriegsdienstverweigerung." In *Aufstand des Gewissens: militärischer Widerstand gegen Hitler und das NS-Regime 1933–1945*, edited by Heinrich Walle, 519–539. Berlin: Mittler, 1994.

Haase, Norbert. "Die Wehrmachtdeserteure und die deutsche Nachkriegsliteratur." In *Deserteure der Wehrmacht: Feiglinge—Opfer—Hoffnungstraeger? Dokumentation eines Meinungswandels*, edited by Wolfram Wette, 95–106. Essen: Klartext Verlag, 1995.

Haase, Norbert. "Die Zeit der Kirschblüten...Zur aktuellen Denkmalsdebatte und zur Geschichte der Desertion im Zweiten Weltkrieg." In *Verräter oder Vorbilder? Deserteure und ungehorsame Soldaten im Nationalsozialismus*, edited by Fietje Ausländer, 130–157. Bremen: Ed. Temmen, 1990.

Haase, Norbert. *"Gefahr für die Manneszucht." Verweigerung und Widerstand im Spiegel der Spruchtätigkeit von Marinegerichten in Wilhelmshaven (1939–1945).* Hannover: Hahnsche, 1996.

Haase, Norbert. "Von 'Ons Jongen,' 'Malgré-nous' und anderen. Das Schicksal der ausländischen Zwangsrekruierten im Zweiten Weltkrieg." In *Die anderen Soldaten: Wehrkraftzersetzung, Gehorsamsverweigerung und Fahnenflucht im Zweiten Weltkrieg*, edited by Fietje Ausländer, Norbert Haase, and Gerhard Paul, 157–173. Frankfurt am Main: Fischer Taschenbuch Verlag, 1995.

Haase, Norbert. "Wehrmachtangehörige vor dem Kriegsgericht." In *Die Wehrmacht: Mythos und Realität*, edited by Rolf-Dieter Müller, Hans-Erich Volkmann and Militärgeschichtliches Forschungsamt. Germany, 474–485. München: Oldenbourg, 1999.

Haase, Norbert, and Otl Aicher. *Deutsche Deserteure.* Berlin: Rotbuch Verlag, 1987.

Haase, Norbert, and Fietje Ausländer. *Die anderen Soldaten: Wehrkraftzersetzung, Gehorsamsverweigerung und Fahnenflucht im Zweiten Weltkrieg.* Frankfurt am Main: Fischer, 1995.

Hagemann, Karen, and Stefanie Schüler-Springorum. *Heimat-Front: Militär und Geschlechterverhältnisse im Zeitalter der Weltkriege.* Frankfurt am Main: Campus, 2002.

Hamacher, Gottfried, and André Lohmar. *Gegen Hitler: Deutsche in der Résistance, in den Streitkräften der Antihitlerkoalition und in der Bewegung "Freies Deutschland."* Berlin: Karl Dietz, 2005.

Hamerow, Theodore S. *On the Road to the Wolf's Lair: German Resistance to Hitler.* Cambridge, MA: Belknap Press of Harvard University Press, 1997.

Hamilton, Richard F. *Who Voted for Hitler.* Princeton, NJ: Princeton University Press, 1982.

Hancock, Eleanor. *Ernst Röhm: Hitler's SA Chief of Staff.* New York: Palgrave Macmillan, 2008.

Hannemann, Ludwig. *Die Justiz der Kriegsmarine 1939–1945.* Regensburg: S. Roderer, 1993.

Hase, Friedrich-Wilhelm von. *Hitlers Rache: das Stauffenberg-Attentat und seine Folgen für die Familien der Verschwörer.* Holzgerlingen: SCM Hänssler, 2014.

Hass, Gerhart. "Zum Bild der Wehrmacht in der Geschichtsschreibung der DDR." In *Die Wehrmacht: Mythos und Realität*, edited by Rolf-Dieter Müller and Hans-Erich Volkmann, 1100–1112. München: Oldenbourg, 1999.

Heer, Hannes, and Klaus Naumann, eds. *Vernichtungskrieg: Verbrechen der Wehrmacth 1941–1944.* Hamburg, 1995.

Heer, Hannes, and Klaus Naumann. *War of Extermination: The German Military in World War II, 1941–1944.* New York: Berghahn Books, 2000.

Heide, Eivind. *Deserteringer fra den tyske okkupasjonshæren i Norge 1940–1945.* Atnbrua: Sollia forlag, 1994.

Heider, Paul. "Die Arbeitsgemeinschaft ehemaliger Offiziere (AeO)—Propaganda- und Diversionsinstrument der SED." *Militaergeschichtliche Zeitschrift* 61, no. 2 (2002): 461–488.

Heider, Paul. *Offiziere der Wehrmacht beim Aufbau der bewaffneten Organe der DDR und die Rolle der Arbeitsgemeinschaft ehemaliger Offiziere (AeO)*. Potsdam, 2000.

Heider, Paul. "Reaktionen in der Wehrmacht auf Gründung und Tätigkeit des Nationalkomitees 'Freies Deutschland' und des Bundes Deutscher Offiziere." In *Die Wehrmacht: Mythos und Realität*, edited by Rolf-Dieter Müller and Hans-Erich Volkmann, 614–634. München: Oldenbourg, 1999.

Heinicke, Otto. "Auszüge aus der Wehrmachtkriminalstatistik." *Zeitschrift für Militärgeschichte* 5 (1966): 438–456.

Herwig, Holger H. "Clio Deceived. Patriotic Self-Censorship in Germany after the Great War." In *Forging the Collective Memory*, edited by Keith Wilson, 87–127. New York: Berghahn Books, 1996.

Herwig, Holger H. *The German Naval Officer Corps: A Social and Political History, 1890–1918*. Oxford: Clarendon Press, 1973.

Herwig, Holger H. *"Luxury" Fleet: The Imperial German Navy, 1888–1918*. London: Allen & Unwin, 1980.

Herwig, Holger H. "Of Men and Myths. The Use and Abuse of History and the Great War." In *The Great War and the Twentieth Century*, edited by Jay Winter, Geoffrey Parker and Mary R. Habeck, 299–330. New Haven, CT: Yale University Press, 2000.

Herzog, Dagmar. *Brutality and Desire: War and Sexuality in Europe's Twentieth Century*. New York: Palgrave Macmillan, 2009.

Herzog, Dagmar. *Sexuality and German Fascism*. New York: Berghahn Books, 2005.

Hilberg, Raul. *The Destruction of the European Jews*. New York: Holmes & Meier, 1985.

Hill, Leonidas E. "Signal zur Konterrevolution? Der Plan zum letzten Vertstoß der deutschen Hochseeflotte am 30. Oktober 1918." *Vierteljahrshefte für Zeitgeschichte* 38, no. 1 (1988): 113–130.

Hitler, Adolf, Alvin Saunders Johnson, and John Chamberlain. *Mein Kampf*. New York: Reynal & Hitchcock, 1940.

Hitler, Adolf, and Henry Picker. *Hitlers Tischgespräche im Führerhauptquartier*. 3rd ed. Stuttgart: Seewald, 1976.

Hitler, Adolf, Gerhard L. Weinberg, Krista Smith, and Adolf Hitler. *Hitler's Second Book*. 1st English language ed. New York: Enigma, 2003.

Hoffman, Peter. *German Resistance to Hitler*. Cambridge, MA: MIT Press, 1988.

Hoffmann, Peter. *The History of the German resistance, 1933–1945*. Montreal: McGill-Queen's University Press, 1996.

Hoffmann, Peter. *Stauffenberg: A Family History, 1905–1944*. Montreal: McGill-Queen's University Press, 2003.

Horn, Daniel. *The German Naval Mutinies of World War I*. New Brunswick, NJ: Rutgers University Press, 1969.

Horn, Daniel. *War, Mutiny and Revolution in the German Navy: The World War I Diary of Seaman Richard Stumpf*. New Brunswick, NJ: Rutgers University Press, 1967.

Hornung, Ela. "Denunziation als soziale Praxis. Eine Fallgeschichte aus der NS-Militärjustiz." In *Wehrmachtsjustiz: Kontext, Praxis, Nachwirkungen*, edited by Peter Pirker and Florian Wenninger, 100–117. Wien: Braumüller, 2011.

Horton, Aaron D. *German POWs, der Ruf, and the Genesis of Group 47*. Lanham, MD: Fairleigh Dickinson University Press, 2014.

Housden, Martyn. *Resistance and Conformity in the Third Reich*. London: Routledge, 1997.

Howe, Ellic. *The Black Game: British Subversive Operations against the Germans during the Second World War*. London: M. Joseph, 1982.

Hull, Isabel V. *Absolute Destruction: Military Culture and the Practices of War in Imperial Germany*. Ithaca, NY: Cornell University Press, 2005.

Hürten, Heinz. *Das Krisenjahr 1923: Militär und Innenpolitik 1922–1924*. Düsseldorf: Droste, 1980.

Hürten, Heinz. *Der Kapp-Putsch als Wende: über Rahmenbedingungen der Weimarer Republik seit dem Frühjahr 1920.* Opladen: Westdeutscher Verlag, 1989.

Hürten, Heinz. "Die Tätigkeit Hans Filbinger als Marinerichter." In *Hans Filbinger. Der "Fall" und die Fakten*, edited by Bruno Heck, 47–102. Mainz: Hase & Koehler, 1980.

Hürten, Heinz. "Im Umbruch der Normen. Dokumente über die deutsche Militärjustiz nach der Kapitulation der Wehrmacht." *Militärgeschichtliche Mitteilungen* 28 (1980): 137–156.

Hürten, Heinz. *Zwischen Revolution und Kapp-Putsch: Militär und Innenpolitik 1918–1920.* Düsseldorf: Droste, 1977.

Jägerstätter, Franz, Erna Putz, and Robert Krieg. *Letters and Writings from Prison.* Maryknoll, NY: Orbis Books, 2009.

Jahr, Christoph. *Gewöhnliche Soldaten: Desertion und Deserteure im deutschen und britischen Heer 1914–1918.* Göttingen: Vandenhoeck & Ruprecht, 1998.

Jünger, Ernst, and Elliot Yale Neaman. *A German Officer in Occupied Paris. The War Journals, 1941–1945.* Translated by Thomas S. Hansen and Abby J. Hansen. New York: Columbia University Press, 2018.

Kammler, Jörg. *Ich habe die Metzelei satt und laufe über…Kasseler Soldaten zwischen Verweigerung und Widerstand (1939–1945). Eine Dokumentation.* Fuldabrück: Hesse, 1985.

Kammler, Jörg, and Marc Poulain. *Ich habe die Metzelei satt und laüfe über: Kasseler Soldaten zwischen Verweigerung und Widerstand (1939–1945). Eine Dokumentation.* 3rd expanded ed. Fuldabrück: Hesse, 1997.

Karner, Stefan. "Deutsche Kriegsgefangene und Internierte in der Sowjetunion 1941–1956." In *Die Wehrmacht: Mythos und Realität*, edited by Rolf-Dieter Müller and Hans-Erich Volkmann. Germany, 1012–1036. München: Oldenbourg, 1999.

Kater, Michael H. *Hitler Youth.* Cambridge, MA: Harvard University Press, 2004.

Kehoe, Thomas J. "The Reich Military Court and Its Values: Wehrmacht Treatment of Jehovah's Witness Conscientious Objectors." *Holocaust and Genocide Studies* 33, no. 3 (Winter) (2019): 351–372.

Kershaw, Ian. *The End: The Defiance and Destruction of Hitler's Germany, 1944–1945.* New York: Penguin Press, 2011.

Kershaw, Ian. *Hitler.* 2 vols. New York: W.W. Norton, 1999.

Kershaw, Ian. *The Nazi Dictatorship: Problems and Perspectives of Interpretation.* 4th ed. New York: Oxford University Press, 2000.

Kersting, Franz-Werner. "Wehrmacht und Schule im 'Dritten Reich'." In *Die Wehrmacht: Mythos und Realität*, edited by Rolf-Dieter Müller and Hans-Erich Volkmann, 436–455. München: Oldenbourg, 1999.

Kersting, Rudolf, and Paul Meyer. *Der Hauptmann von Muffrika—Eine mörderische Köpenickade* (documentary). 73 minutes. Germany: Filmförderung Hamburg, Filmförderung Niedersachsen, Paul Meyer Filmproduktion, 1996.

Kirschner, Albrecht. *Deserteure, Wehrkraftzersetzer und ihre Richter: Marburger Zwischenbilanz zur NS-Militärjustiz vor und nach 1945.* Marburg: Historische Kommission für Hessen, 2010.

Kitterman, David H. "The Justice of the Wehrmacht Legal System: Servant or Opponent of National Socialism." *Central European History* 24, no. 4 (1991): 450–462.

Kitterman, David H. "Those Who Said 'No!': Germans Who Refused to Execute Civilians during World War II." *German Studies Review* 11, no. 2 (1988): 241–254.

Klausch, Hans-Peter. *Die Bewährungstruppe 500. Stellung und Funktion der Bewährungstruppe 500 im System von NS-Wehrrecht, NS-Militärjustiz und Wehrmachtstrafvollzug.* Bremen: Temmen, 1995.

Knippschild, Dieter. "Deserteure im Zweiten Weltkrieg: Der Stand der Debatte." In *Armeen und ihre Deserteure: vernachlässigte Kapitel einer Militärgeschichte der Neuzeit*, edited by Ulrich Bröckling and Michael Sikora, 222–251. Göttingen: Vandenhoeck & Ruprecht, 1998.

Koch, Magnus. "Das Stigma Fahnenflucht. Überlegungen zur Bedeutung männlicher Selbstbilder von Wehrmachtsdeserteurnen." In *Wehrmachtsjustiz: Kontext, Praxis, Nachwirkungen*, edited by Peter Pirker and Florian Wenninger, 118–213. Wien: Braumüller, 2011.

Koch, Magnus. *Fahnenfluchten: Deserteure der Wehrmacht im Zweiten Weltkrieg—Lebenswege und Entscheidungen*. Paderborn: Schöningh, 2008.

Korte, Jan, and Dominic Heilig, eds. *Kriegsverrat: Vergangenheitspolitik in Deutschland*. Berlin: Karl Dietz, 2011.

Kosthorst, Erich, and Bernd Walter. *Konzentrations- und Strafgefangenenlager im Dritten Reich*. 3 vols. Düsseldorf: Droste, 1983.

Kosthorst, Erich, and Bernd Walter. *Konzentrations- und Strafgefangenenlager im Emsland 1933–1945: Zum Verhältnis von NS-Regime und Justiz*. Düsseldorf: Droste, 1985.

Koszuszeck, Paul A. *Militärische Traditionspflege in der Nationalen Volksarmee der DDR*. Frankfurt am Main: Haag & Herchen, 1991.

Krammer, Arnold. *Nazi Prisoners of War in America*. Chelsea, MI: Scarborough House, 1991.

Krause, Dietrich. "Marinerichter in der NS-Zeit." *Marine Forum*, no. 3 (1998): 23–27.

Kühne, Thomas. "Gruppenkohäsion und Kameradschaftsmythos in der Wehrmacht." In *Die Wehrmacht: Mythos und Realität*, edited by Rolf-Dieter Müller and Hans-Erich Volkmann, 534–549. München: Oldenbourg, 1999.

Kühne, Thomas. *Kameradschaft: die Soldaten des nationalsozialistischen Krieges und das 20. Jahrhundert*. Göttingen: Vandenhoeck & Ruprecht, 2006.

Kühne, Thomas. *The Rise and Fall of Comradeship: Hitler's Soldiers, Male Bonding and Mass Violence in the Twentieth Century*. Cambridge: Cambridge University Press, 2017.

Lapp, Peter Joachim. *Arbeitsgemeinschaft ehemaliger Offiziere—DDR-Propaganda gegen die Bundeswehr*. Aachen: Helios, 2000.

Lapp, Peter Joachim. *Ulbrichts Helfer: Wehrmachtsoffiziere im Dienste der DDR*. Bonn: Bernard & Graefe, 2000.

Large, David Clay. "Uses of the Past: The Anti-Nazi Resistance Legacy in the Federal Republic of Germany." In *Contending with Hitler. Varieties of German Resistance in the Third Reich*, edited by David C. Large, 163–182. Cambridge: Cambridge University Press, 1991.

Laurie, Clayton D. *The Propaganda Warriors: America's Crusade against Nazi Germany*. Lawrence: University Press of Kansas, 1996.

Lockenour, Jay. *Dragonslayer: The Legend of Erich Ludendorff in the Weimar Republic and Third Reich*. Ithaca, NY: Cornell University Press, 2021.

Lormier, Dominique. *Bordeaux brûle-t-il?, ou, La Libération de la Gironde, 1940–1945*. Bordeaux: Dossiers d'Aquitaine, 1998.

Ludendorff, Erich. *Der totale Krieg*. München: Ludendorff Verlag, 1935.

Ludendorff, Erich. *My War Memories, 1914–1918*. 2 vols. London: Hutchinson, 1919.

Lüerßen, Dirk. "Wir sind die Moorsoldaten." PhD diss., Universität Osnabrück, 2001.

Mader, Ernst, and Jakob Knab. *Das Lächeln des Esels. Das Leben und die Hinrichtung des Allgäuer Bauernsohnes Michael Lerpscher*. Friesenried: Verlag an der Säge, 1987.

Madsen, Chris. "Victims of Circumstance: The Execution of German Deserters by Surrendered German Troops under Canadian Control in Amsterdam, May 1945." *Canadian Military History* 2, no. 3 (1993): 93–112.

Malick, Terrence. *A Hidden Life*. 174 minutes. Fox Searchlight Pictures, 2019.

Mallmann, Klaus-Michael, Jochen Böhler, Jürgen Matthäus, Deutsches Historisches Institut Warschau. *Einsatzgruppen in Polen Darstellung und Dokumentation*. Darmstadt: WBG, 2008.

Manoschek, Walter. *Opfer der NS-Militärjustiz: Urteilspraxis, Strafvollzug, Entschädigungspolitik in Österreich*. Wien: Mandelbaum, 2003.

McElligott, Anthony, Tim Kirk, and Ian Kershaw. *Working towards the Führer: Essays in Honour of Sir Ian Kershaw*. Manchester: Manchester University Press, 2003.

Megargee, Geoffrey P. *Inside Hitler's High Command*. Lawrence: University Press of Kansas, 2000.

Megargee, Geoffrey P., ed. *The United States Holocaust Memorial Museum Encyclopedia of Camps and Ghettos, 1933–1945*. Bloomington: Indiana University Press, 2009.

Megargee, Geoffrey P. *War of Annihilation: Combat and Genocide on the Eastern Front, 1941.* Lanham, MD: Rowman & Littlefield, 2006.

Megargee, Geoffrey P., Rüdiger Overmans, and Wolfgang Vogt, eds. *Camps and Other Detention Facilities under the German Armed Forces.* Bloomington: Indiana University Press, 2022.

Meier-Welcker, Hans, and Manfred Messerschmidt. *Offiziere im Bild von Dokumenten aus drei Jahrhunderten.* Stuttgart: Deutsche Verlags-Anstalt, 1964.

Messerschmidt, Manfred. "Das System Wehrmachtjustiz. Aufgaben und Wirken der deutschen Kriegsgerichte." In *"Was damals Recht war…" Soldaten und Zivilisten vor Gerichten der Wehrmacht,* edited by Ulrich Baumann and Magnus Koch, 27–43. Berlin-Brandenburg: Bebra, 2008.

Messerschmidt, Manfred. "Deserteure im Zweiten Weltkrieg." In *Deserteure der Wehrmacht: Feiglinge—Opfer—Hoffnungstraeger? Dokumentation eines Meinungswandels,* edited by Wolfram Wette, 58–73. Essen: Klartext Verlag, 1995.

Messerschmidt, Manfred. *Die Wehrmacht im NS-Staat. Zeit der Indoktrination.* Hamburg: R. v. Decker, 1969.

Messerschmidt, Manfred. *Die Wehrmachtjustiz, 1933–1945.* Paderborn: Schöningh, 2008.

Messerschmidt, Manfred, Hans Gotthard Ehlert, Arnim Lang, and Bernd Wegner. *Militarismus, Vernichtungskrieg, Geschichtspolitik: zur deutschen Militär- und Rechtsgeschichte.* Paderborn: Schöningh, 2006.

Messerschmidt, Manfred, and Fritz Wüllner. *Die Wehrmachtjustiz im Dienste des Nationalsozialismus: Zerstörung einer Legende.* Baden-Baden: Nomos, 1987.

Metzler, Hannes. *Ehrlos für immer? Die Rehabilitierung der Deserteure der Wehrmacht.* Wien: Mandelbaum, 2007.

Moeller, Robert G. "War Stories: The Search for a Usable Past in the Federal Republic of Germany." *American Historical Review* 101, no. 4 (1996): 1008–1048.

Mosse, George L. *The Image of Man: The Creation of Modern Masculinity.* New York: Oxford University Press, 1996.

Mosse, George L. *Nationalism and Sexuality: Respectability and Abnormal Sexuality in Modern Europe.* New York: H. Fertig, 1985.

Mueller, Michael. *Nazi Spymaster: The Life and Death of Admiral Wilhelm Canaris.* New York: Skyhorse, 2017.

Mueller, Rolf-Dieter, and Hans-Erich Volkmann. *Die Wehrmacht. Mythos und Realität.* München: R. Oldenbourg, 1999.

Mühlhäuser, Regina. *Eroberungen: Sexuelle Gewalttaten und intime Beziehungen deutscher Soldaten in der Sowjetunion 1941–1945.* Hamburg: Hamburger Edition, 2012.

Müller, Ingo. *Furchtbare Juristen: die unbewältigte Vergangenheit unserer Justiz.* München: Kindler, 1987.

Muller, Klaus-Jurgen. *Generaloberst Ludwig Becks Entwicklung vom regimebejahenden General zur Zentralfigur des Widerstandes.* Hamburg: Fuhrungsakademie der Bundeswehr, 1998.

Müller, Klaus-Jürgen. *The Army, Politics, and Society in Germany, 1933–45.* New York: St. Martin's Press, 1987.

Müller, Klaus Jürgen. *Der deutsche Widerstand 1933–1945.* Paderborn: F. Schöningh, 1986.

Müller, Klaus Jürgent. *Generaloberst Ludwig Beck: eine Biographie.* Paderborn: F. Schöningh, 2008.

Müller, Klaus Jürgen, and Ernst Willi Hansen. *Armee und Drittes Reich, 1933–1939: Darstellung und Dokumentation.* Paderborn: F. Schöningh, 1987.

Müller, Rolf-Dieter, and Janice W. Ancker. *Hitler's Wehrmacht, 1935–1945.* Lexington: University Press of Kentucky, 2016.

Müller, Rolf-Dieter, and Hans-Erich Volkmann, eds. *Die Wehrmacht: Mythos und Realität.* München: Oldenbourg, 1999.

Nolzen, Armin. "The NSDAP, the War, and German Society." In *German Wartime Society 1939–1945: Politicization, Disintegration and the Struggle for Survival*, edited by Jörg Echternkamp, 111–206. Oxford: Clarendon Press, 2008.

Oleschinski, Wolfgang. "Ein Augenzeuge des Judenmords desertiert. Der Füsilier Stefan Hampel." In *Zivilcourage: Empörte, Helfer und Retter aus Wehrmacht, Polizei und SS*, edited by Wolfram Wette, 51–59. Frankfurt am Main: Fischer Taschenbuch, 2006.

Oleschinski, Wolfgang. "Empörung über den weltanschaulichen Vernichtungskrieg im Osten." In *Zivilcourage: Empörte, Helfer und Retter aus Wehrmacht, Polizei und SS*, edited by Wolfram Wette, 35–59. Frankfurt am Main: Fischer Taschenbuch, 2006.

Oram, Gerard. "Armee, Staat, Bürger und Wehrpflicht. Die britische Militärjustiz bis nach dem Zweiten Weltkrieg." In *Wehrmachtsjustiz: Kontext, Praxis, Nachwirkungen*, edited by Peter Pirker and Florian Wenninger, 186–203. Wien: Braumüller, 2011.

Oram, Gerard. *Death Sentences in the British Army*. London: Francis Boutle, 1998.

Overmans, Rüdiger. *Deutsche militärische Verluste im Zweiten Weltkrieg*. München: R. Oldenbourg, 1999.

Overmans, Rüdiger, and Ulrike Goeken-Haidl. *Soldaten hinter Stacheldraht: deutsche Kriegsgefangene des Zweiten Weltkriegs*. München: Propyläen, 2000.

Pantcheff, T. X. H. *Der Henker von Emsland. Dokumentation einer Barbarei am Ende des Krieges 1945*. 2nd ed. Schuster: Leer, 1995.

Paul, Gerhard. "Die Erschießungen in der Geltinger Bucht." *Demokratische Geschichte: Jahrbuch für Schleswig-Holstein* 9 (1995): 163–179.

Paul, Gerhard. "'Die verschwanden einfach nachts.' Überlaufer zu den Allierten und den europäischen Befreiungsbewegungen." In *Die anderen Soldaten: Wehrkraftzersetzung, Gehorsamsverweigerung und Fahnenflucht im Zweiten Weltkrieg*, edited by Norbert Haase and Fietje Ausländer, 163–179. Frankfurt am Main: Fischer, 1995.

Paul, Gerhard. *Ungehorsame Soldaten: Dissens, Verweigerung und Widerstand deutscher Soldaten (1939–1945)*. St. Ingbert: Röhrig, 1994.

Peifer, Douglas Carl. "From Enemy to Ally: Reconciliation Made Real in the Postwar German Maritime Sphere." *War in History* 12, no. 2 (2005): 208–224.

Peifer, Douglas Carl. "The Past in the Present: Passion, Politics, and the Historical Profession in the German and British Pardon Campaigns." *Journal of Military History* 71, no. 4 (2007): 1107–1132.

Peifer, Douglas Carl. "Selfless Saviors or Diehard Fanatics? West and East German Memories of the Kriegsmarine and the Baltic Evacuation." *War & Society* 26, no. 2 (10/2007): 99–120.

Peifer, Douglas Carl. *The Three German Navies: Dissolution, Transition, and New Beginnings, 1945–1960*. Gainesville: University Press of Florida, 2002.

Peters, Heinrich, and Inge Peters. *Pattjackenblut: Antreten zum Sterben-in Linie zu 5 Gliedern. Das Herold—Massaker im Emslandlager II Aschendorfermoor im April 1945*. McFarland, WI: Books on Demand, 2014.

Petersson, Lars G. *Hitler's Deserters: When Law Merged with Terror*. Stroud: Fonthill Media, 2013.

Pirker, Peter, and Florian Wenninger. *Wehrmachtsjustiz: Kontext, Praxis, Nachwirkungen*. Wien: Braumüller, 2011.

Plowman, Andrew. "Deserters from the Bundeswehr on Page and Screen: Shifting Cultural Meanings of an Act between Desertion from the Wehrmacht and Conscientious Objection." *German Studies Review* 32, no. 2 (2009): 377–395.

Pomerantsev, Peter. *How to Win an Information War. The Propagandist who Outwitted Hitler*. New York: PublicAffairs, 2024.

Powers, James H. "What to Do with German Prisoners: The American Muddle." *The Atlantic Monthly*, November 1944, 46–50.

Rass, Christoph. "The Social Profile of the German Army's Combat Units, 1939–1945." In *German Wartime Society 1939–1945: Politicization, Disintegration and the Struggle for Survival*, edited by Jörg Echternkamp, 671–770. Oxford: Clarendon Press, 2008.

Reichel, Peter. *Politik mit der Erinnerung: Gedächtnisorte im Streit um die Nationalsozialistische Vergangenheit.* München: Carl Hanser Verlag, 1995.

Reichelt, Stefanie. *"Für mich ist der Krieg aus!" Deserteure und Kriegsverweigerer des Zweiten Weltkriegs in München.* München: Buchendorfer, 1995.

Rettl, Lisa. "Fahnenflucht in den Widerstand. Kärntner Slowenen als Deserteure und Partisanen." In *Wehrmachtsjustiz: Kontext, Praxis, Nachwirkungen*, edited by Peter Pirker and Florian Wenninger, 152–166. Wien: Braumüller, 2011.

Richter, Hans Werner. *Beyond Defeat.* New York: Putnam, 1950.

Richter, Hans Werner. *Die Geschlagenen.* München: K. Desch, 1949.

Rigg, Bryan Mark. *Hitler's Jewish Soldiers: The Untold Story of Nazi Racial Laws and Men of Jewish Descent in the German Military.* Lawrence: University Press of Kansas, 2002.

Röhm, Eberhard. *Sterben für den Frieden, Spurensicherung Hermann Stöhr.* Stuttgart: Calwer, 1985.

Rust, Eric C. *Naval Officers under Hitler: The Story of Crew 34.* New York: Praeger, 1991.

Rust, Eric C. *U-boat Commander Oskar Kusch.* Annapolis, MD: Naval Institute Press, 2020.

Salm, Karl. *Fahnenflucht als politische Weltanschauung? Eine zeitgeschichtlich-politische Studie zum Fall Richard Freiherr von Weizsäcker.* Tübingen: Hohenrain, 1989.

Scheurig, Bodo. *Freies Deutschland: das Nationalkomitee und der Bund Deutscher Offiziere in der Sowjetunion 1943–45.* Cologne: Kiepenheuer & Witsch, 1984.

Schmaedeke, Juergen, and Peter Steinbach, eds. *Der Widerstand gegen den Nationalsozialismus. Die deutsche Gesellschaft und der Widerstand gegen Hitler.* München: Piper, 1994.

Schnackenberg, Martin. *"Ich wollte keine Heldentaten mehr vollbringen" Wehrmachtdeserteure im II. Weltkrieg Motive und Folgen untersucht anhand von Selbstzeugnissen.* Oldenburg: BIS, 1997.

Scholtis, August, and Frans Haaken. *Die Fahnenflucht: Novelle.* Berlin: Chronos, 1948.

Schörken, Rolf. "'Schülersoldaten'—Prägung einer Generation." In *Die Wehrmacht: Mythos und Realität*, edited by Rolf-Dieter Müller and Hans-Erich Volkmann, 456–473. München: Oldenbourg, 1999.

Schröter, Heinz. *Stalingrad "... bis zur letzten Patrone."* Osnabrück: Neuer Kaiser Verlag, 1991.

Schulte, Theo J. "The German Soldier in Occupied Russia." In *Time to Kill: The Soldier's Experience of War in the West 1939–1945*, edited by Paul Addison and Angus Calder, 274–283. London: Pimlico, 1997.

Schweling, Otto Peter, and Erich Schwinge. *Die deutsche Militärjustiz in der Zeit des Nationalsozialismus.* Marburg: Elwert, 1977.

Schwentke, Robert. *Der Hauptmann.* 119 minutes. Germany, France, Poland: Filmgalerie 451, Alfama Films, Opus Filma, 2017.

Seidler, Franz W. "Die Fahnenflucht in der deutschen Wehrmacht während des Zweiten Weltkrieges." *Militärgeschichtliche Zeitschrift* 22, no. 2 (1977): 23–42.

Seidler, Franz W. *Fahnenflucht: der Soldat zwischen Eid und Gewissen.* München: Herbig, 1993.

Seydlitz, Walther von. *Stalingrad, Konflikt und Konsequenz: Erinnerungen.* Oldenburg: Stalling, 1977.

Shepherd, Ben. *Hitler's Soldiers: The German Army in the Third Reich.* New Haven, CT: Yale University Press, 2016.

Shils, Edward A., and Morris Janowitz. "Cohesion and Disintegration in the Wehrmacht in World War II." *The Public Opinion Quarterly* 12, no. 2 (1948): 280–315.

Sikora, Michael. *Disziplin und Desertion.* Berlin: Duncker, 1996.

Stadelmann, Jürg. *Umgang mit Fremden in bedrängter Zeit: schweizerische Flüchtlingspolitik 1940–1945 und ihre Beurteilung bis heute.* Zürich: Orell Füssli, 1998.

Steinbach, Peter. *Deserteure aus politischer Gegnerschaft.* Berlin: Gedenkstätte Deutscher Widerstand, 1998.

Steinbach, Peter. *Hilfen für Kriegsgefangene, Zwangsarbeiter und Deserteure.* Berlin: Gedenkstätte Deutscher Widerstand, 1998.

Steinbach, Peter. *Kriegsdienstverweigerer Widerstandskämpfer in den "Bewährungseinheiten" 999*. Berlin: Gedenkstätte Deutscher Widerstand, 1992.

Steinbach, Peter. "Widerstand hinter Stacheldraht"? Zur Diskussion über das Nationalkomitee Freies Deutschland als Widerstandsorganisation seit 1943." In *Der 20. Juli. Das "andere Deutschland" in der Vergangenheitspolitik*, edited by Gerd R. Ueberschaer, 332–346. Berlin: Elefanten Press, 1998.

Streit, Christian. *Keine Kameraden. Die Wehrmacht und die sowjetischen Kriegsgefangenen 1941–1945*. Stuttgart: Deutsche Verlags-Anstalt, 1978.

Streit, Christian. *Keine Kameraden: die Wehrmacht und die sowjetischen Kriegsgefangenen 1941–1945*. Bonn: J.H.W. Dietz, 1991.

Suhr, Elke. *Die Emslandlager: die politische und wirtschaftliche Bedeutung der emsländischen Konzentrations- und Strafgefangenenlager 1933–1945*. Bremen: Donat & Temmen, 1985.

Swedish Parliamentary Investigation Commission. Parliamentary Investigation Commission on Refugees and Security Services (Sandler). *Report on Treatment of Refugees*. Swedish government (Stockholm, 1946).

Thamer, Hans-Ulrich. "Die Erosion einer Säule. Wehrmacht und NSDAP." In *Die Wehrmacht: Mythos und Realität*, edited by Rolf-Dieter Müller and Hans-Erich Volkmann, 420–435. München: Oldenbourg, 1999.

Theweleit, Klaus. *Male Fantasies*. 2 vols. Minneapolis: University of Minnesota Press, 1987.

Thiele, Hans-Günther, ed. *Die Wehrmachtsausstellung: Dokumentation einer Kontroverse*. Bremen: Edition Temmen, 1997.

Ueberschär, Gerd R., ed. *Das Nationalkomitee "Freies Deutschland" und der Bund Deutscher Offiziere*. Frankfurt am Main: Fischer Taschenbuch Verlag, 1995.

Ueberschaer, Gerd R., ed. *Der 20. Juli. Das "andere Deutschland" in der Vergangenheitspolitik*. Berlin: Elefanten Press, 1998.

Ueberschaer, Gerd R., ed. *Für ein anderes Deutschland: der deutsche Widerstand gegen den NS-Staat 1933–1945*. Frankfurt: Fischer, 2006.

Ueberschaer, Gerd R., ed. "Von der Einzeltat des 20. Juli 1944 zur 'Volksopposition'? Stationen und Wege der westdeutschen Historiographie nach 1945." In *Der 20. Juli. Das "andere Deutschland" in der Vergangenheitspolitik*, edited by Gerd R. Ueberschaer, 125–157. Berlin: Elefanten Press, 1998.

Ueberschär, Gerd R., Rolf-Dieter Müller, and Rolf-Dieter Müller. *1945: das Ende des Krieges*. Darmstadt: Primus, 2005.

Ueberschär, Gerd R., and Winfried Vogel. *Dienen und Verdienen: Hitlers Geschenke an seine Eliten*. Frankfurt: S. Fischer, 1999.

Ullrich, Volker. "'Ich habe mich ausgestossen...' Das Los von Zehntausenden deutscher Deserteure im Zweiten Weltkrieg." In *Deserteure der Wehrmacht: Feiglinge—Opfer—Hoffnungsträger? Dokumentation eines Meinungswandels*, edited by Wolfram Wette, 107–122. Essen: Klartext Verlag, 1995.

United States Army. Judge Advocate General's Corps. *The Army Lawyer: A History of the Judge Advocate General's Corps, 1775–1975*. Washington, DC: Government Printing Office, 1975.

Van Creveld, Martin. *Fighting Power: German and US Army Performance, 1939–1945*. Westport, CT: Greenwood Press, 1982.

Volkmann, Hans-Erich. "Vom Blomberg zu Keitel." In *Die Wehrmacht: Mythos und Realität*, edited by Rolf-Dieter Müller and Hans-Erich Volkmann, 47–65. München: Oldenbourg, 1999.

Walle, Heinrich. *Aufstand des Gewissens: militärischer Widerstand gegen Hitler und das NS-Regime 1933–1945*. Berlin: Mittler, 1994.

Walle, Heinrich. *Die Tragödie des Oberleutnants zur See Oskar Kusch*. Stuttgart: Steiner, 1995.

Watson, Alexander. *Enduring the Great War: Combat, Morale and Collapse in the German and British Armies, 1914–1918*. Cambridge: Cambridge University Press, 2008.

Wegner, Bernd. *The Waffen-SS: Organization, Ideology, and Function.* Oxford: Basil Blackwell, 1990.

Weinberg, Gerhard. "Rollen- und Selbstverständnis des Offizierskorps im NS-Staat." In *Die Wehrmacht. Mythos und Realität*, edited by Rolf-Dieter Mueller and Hans-Erich Volkmann, 66–73. München: R. Oldenbourg, 1999.

Weinert, Erich. *Stalingrad Diary.* Translated by Egon Larsen. London: I.N.G. Publication, 1944.

Welch, Steven R. "Commemorating 'Heroes of a Special Kind': Deserter Monuments in Germany." *Journal of Contemporary History* 47, no. 2 (2012): 370–401.

Welch, Steven R. "'Harsh but Just'? German Military Justice in the Second World War: A Comparative Study of the Court-Martialing of German and US Deserters." *German History* 17, no. 3 (1999): 369.

Wenzke, Rüdiger. "Das unliebsame Erbe der Wehrmacht und der Aufbau der DDR-Volksarmee." In *Die Wehrmacht: Mythos und Realität*, edited by Rolf-Dieter Müller and Hans-Erich Volkmann, 1113–1138. München: Oldenbourg, 1999.

Westermann, Edward B. "'Ordinary Men' or 'Ideological Soldiers'? Police Battalion 310 in Russia, 1942." *German Studies Review* 21, no. 1 (1998): 41–68.

Wette, Wolfram. *Der Krieg des kleinen Mannes: eine Militärgeschichte von Unten.* München: Piper, 1992.

Wette, Wolfram. *Deserteure der Wehrmacht: Feiglinge—Opfer—Hoffnungsträger? Dokumentation eines Meinungswandels.* Essen: Klartext, 1995.

Wette, Wolfram. "Deserteure der Wehrmacht rehabilitiert. Ein exemplarischer Meinungswandel in Deutschland (1980–2002)." *Zeitschrift für Geschichtswissenschaft* 52, no. 6 (2004): 505–513.

Wette, Wolfram. *Ehre, wem Ehre gebührt! Täter, Widerständler und Retter 1939–1945.* Bremen: Donat Verlag, 2015.

Wette, Wolfram. *Feldwebel Anton Schmid: ein Held der Humanität.* Frankfurt am Main: Fischer, 2013.

Wette, Wolfram. *Filbinger, eine deutsche Karriere.* Springe: Klampen, 2006.

Wette, Wolfram. "Ideology, Propaganda, and Internal Politics as Preconditions of the War Policy of the Third Reich." In *The Build-up of German Aggression*, edited by Wilhelm Deist, 9–156. Oxford: Oxford University Press, 1990.

Wette, Wolfram. "Verweigerung und Desertion im Wandel der öffentlichen Meinung (1980–1995)." In *Die anderen Soldaten*, edited by Norbert Haase and Gerhard Paul, 189–204. Frankfurt am Main: Fischer, 1995.

Wette, Wolfram. *The Wehrmacht: History, Myth, Reality.* Cambridge, MA: Harvard University Press, 2006.

Wette, Wolfram. *Zivilcourage: Empörte, Helfer und Retter aus Wehrmacht, Polizei und SS.* Frankfurt am Main: Fischer Taschenbuch, 2006.

Wette, Wolfram, and Helmut Donat. *Pazifistische Offiziere in Deutschland 1871–1933.* Bremen: Donat, 1999.

Wette, Wolfram, Detlef Vogel, Ricarda Berthold, Helmut Kramer, and Manfred Messerschmidt. *Das letzte Tabu: NS-Militärjustiz und "Kriegsverrat."* Berlin: Aufbau, 2007.

Wheeler-Bennett, John Wheeler, and R. J. Overy. *The Nemesis of Power: The German Army in Politics, 1918–1945.* 2nd ed. New York: Palgrave Macmillan, 2005.

Whittingham, Richard. *Martial Justice: The Last Mass Execution in the United States.* Annapolis, MD: Naval Institute Press, 1997.

Wüllner, Fritz. *Die NS-Militärjustiz und das Elend der Geschichtsschreibung.* Baden-Baden: Nomos, 1991.

Wüllner, Fritz, and Otto Hennicke. "Über die barbarischen Vollstreckungsmethoden von Wehrmacht und Justiz im Zweiten Weltkrieg." In *Deserteure der Wehrmacht: Feiglinge—Opfer—Hoffnungsträger? Dokumentation eines Meinungswandels*, edited by Wolfram Wette, 74–94. Essen: Klartext, 1995.

Wüllner, Hermine. "...*kann nur der Tod die gerechte Sühne sein" Todesurteile deutscher Wehrmachtsgerichte eine Dokumentation*. Baden-Baden: Nomos-Verlag, 1997.
Zahn, Gordon C. *In Solitary Witness: The Life and Death of Franz Jägerstätter*. London: Chapman, 1966.
Ziemann, Benjamin. "Fluchten aus dem Konsens zum Durchhalten." In *Die Wehrmacht: Mythos und Realität*, edited by Rolf-Dieter Müller and Hans-Erich Volkmann, 589–613. München: Oldenbourg, 1999.
Zwerenz, Gerhard. *Soldaten sind Mörder: die Deutschen und der Krieg*. München: Knesebeck & Schuler, 1988.

Index

For the benefit of digital users, indexed terms that span two pages (e.g., 52–53) may, on occasion, appear on only one of those pages.